New York. D. Appleton &

THE LIFE

OF

JAMES W. GRIMES,

GOVERNOR OF IOWA, 1854-1858;

A SENATOR OF THE UNITED STATES, 1859-1869.

BY

WILLIAM SALTER.

NEW YORK:
D. APPLETON AND COMPANY,
549 AND 551 BROADWAY.
1876.

PREFACE.

My acquaintance with Mr. Grimes commenced in 1846. Mrs. Grimes has honored me with her confidence, and placed his home letters in my hands. From this and his other correspondence, and from the public records, I have arranged as clearly and succinctly as possible these memoirs of his life. They are substantially autobiographical, and afford, in his own language, his views of the questions and events in the consideration and determination of which he bore his part.

Burlington, Iowa, *November* 17, 1875

CONTENTS.

CHAPTER I.

Early Life and Education, 1816–1836.

CHAPTER II.

Life at Burlington, 1836–1853.

CHAPTER III.

GOVERNOR OF IOWA, 1854–1858.

CHAPTER IV.

A SENATOR OF THE UNITED STATES, 1859–1869.

§ 1.—*In the Thirty-sixth Congress*, 1859–1861.

PAGE

§ 2.—*In the Thirty-seventh Congress*, 1861–1863.

ILLUSTRATIONS.

THE LIFE OF JAMES W. GRIMES.

CHAPTER I.

EARLY LIFE AND EDUCATION.

1816–1836.

IN the early part of the seventeenth century a colony of people from Argyleshire, Scotland, emigrated to the north of Ireland, and settled in the Province of Ulster, encouraged by grants of land from James I., made for the purpose of strengthening his throne and the Protestant interest in Ireland. From being the most wild and disorderly province of Ireland, Ulster soon became the best cultivated and most civilized. In process of time the appellation "Scotch-Irish" was fixed upon the descendants of this people, though they always insisted upon their pure Scotch blood. Emigrants from this body of people came to America, and commenced the settlement of Londonderry, New Hampshire, in 1719, and others of them, about the same time, settled in and near Boston, Massachusetts.

Of this sturdy and vigorous stock, JAMES WILSON GRIMES was born in the town of Deering, Hillsborough County, New Hampshire, on the 20th of October, 1816. His parents—John Grimes, born August 11, 1772, and Elizabeth Wilson, born March 19, 1773—were natives of the same town. He was named for a brother of his mother. Her parents, Captain David Wilson and Sarah Cochran, were born in Londonderry in 1743. On his father's side, his grandfather, Francis Grimes, was born, in 1747, upon Noddle's Island, now East Boston; and his grandmother, Elizabeth Wilson, a sister of his mother's father, in Londonderry, in 1736. The first permanent settlement of the town of Deering was made in 1765, and these persons were among the early settlers. The town was incorporated in 1774, and named, with Francestown, which adjoins it on the south, for Frances Deering, wife of John Wentworth, the last royal governor of the Province of New Hampshire. In response to a resolution of the Continental Congress of March 14, 1776, the male inhabitants of Deering Colony over twenty-one years of age, with two exceptions, signed the following declaration, April 12, 1776:

"To show our determination in joining our American brethren in defending the lives, liberties, and properties of the inhabitants of the United Colonists, we, the subscribers, do hereby solemnly engage and promise that we will to the utmost of our power, at the risk of our lives and fortunes, with arms, oppose the hostile proceedings of the British fleets and armies against the United American Colonies."

Among the thirty-three subscribers to this declaration were Francis Grimes and David Wilson.

Born of such an ancestry, among a people inheriting these traditions, he breathed the free air of the hills in a community of intelligent, self-reliant, and independent farmers. He was the youngest of eight children, of whom one died in infancy; the others survived him, except a sister, Susan, who became the wife of Mr. Alden Walker, and died October 31, 1846. She was the mother of Captain John G. Walker, United States Navy. Being thirteen years older than her brother, she assisted very much in the care of his childhood. Through life he cherished a grateful recollection of her kindness, and regarded her children with peculiar tenderness and affection. His father, whom he resembled in temperament and appearance, was a substantial farmer, a man of unpretending goodness, warmly attached to his family, hospitable and kind to all, of thrifty habits, and highly esteemed among his neighbors and in the surrounding region for sterling integrity and worth. His mother was a woman of energy and determination, and gave herself to the duties of home with careful industry and devotion. The happy parents lived together more than half a century, the mother dying in 1850, and the father the next year. His father's farm was situated in the northern part of Deering, about two and a half miles from the village of Hillsborough Bridge, upon the broad expanse of a hill-top that affords an extensive outlook over the valley of the Contoocook, and far away to distant hills that ennoble the landscape on every side. In 1806, the house which his grandfather built in the early settlement of the town gave place to a large, two-story double house, erected by his father. Here was his birthplace. A short distance down the road was a district schoolhouse, where the child mingled with his mates in study and play. The town of Deering had ten school-districts, each with a schoolhouse, and possessed a social library.

From early childhood he was fond of reading, and eagerly devoured books. He commenced the study of Latin and Greek with Rev. Eber Child, pastor of the church in Deering, and boarded in his family a few months. Mr. Child was highly esteemed in the region as a scholar. He was a graduate of Dartmouth College in 1821, and of the Theological Seminary at Andover in 1826. His widow gives the following reminiscences of her husband's pupil:

Mr. Grimes was but a lad when I knew him over forty years ago, but I can think of no young man out of my own family of whom I have such vivid recollections. I remember the tones of his voice and his smiling countenance. He always laughed with his eyes. He had a happy disposition and an uncommon flow of spirits. I have no recollection of ever seeing him angry or put out at anything. If for nothing else, I should love his memory because he was so kind to my children. He would often undress our youngest child, and put him in his cradle to hear him sing his lullaby. After the child's death, he went to his scrap-book, and cut out some beautiful lines written over the grave of a child. I think he did not like his studies, still he always got his lessons. My husband thought a great deal of James, and was proud to hear of his success in life. When my husband died (December, 1847), I was left in a land of strangers, with my family of little ones, to get through the world as best I could. My husband left a small farm of unimproved land in Rock Prairie, Wisconsin, but mortgaged for all it was worth at the time of his death. I managed to clear the incumbrance, and went on it to make a home. I needed money, and wrote Mr. Grimes, asking the loan of a hundred dollars, to which he readily responded. In his letters to me he never alluded to self in any shape, only the state of his health and his family, but always remembered his old friends and relations with unabated interest and affection. In one he said, "Could you see my gray hair and wrinkled face, you would not recall the gay, rollicking boy I used to be." In the dark hours of the nation's peril, when I read in a description of the Senate, "There is Senator Grimes—he is always found in the right place," I thought, "James has not altered any—the boy is father to the man." When the disappointment of "Impeachment" flashed over the land, I told a neighbor I was confident there was one who decided according to the evidence; that I knew Mr. Grimes and his father before him, and he had not swerved from what he thought was right and duty.

The lad completed his preparation for college at Hampton Academy, under the instruction of Rev. Roswell Harris. In one of his compositions, while a member of the academy, he describes the beauty of Hampton Beach, and the picturesque and sublime scenery of Boar's Head. At this period many portions of the country were visited with seasons of special religious awakening. The year 1831 was memorable in this respect. Several eminent clergymen of the vicinity visited Hampton, and preached to the students. The following letter, the earliest that has been preserved, gives an account of the interest that prevailed, and records the impressions and convictions of ingenuous youth:

1.—*To his Parents, and Sister, Mrs. Susan G. Walker.*

HAMPTON, *October*, 1831.

It is certainly with feelings of quite a different nature I address you now, from those with which I have hitherto addressed you. On Monday Dr. Dana addressed the students, and it was an affecting time; my sins were exposed to me. It seemed as if I was the greatest sinner under heaven. I immediately retired to my room, and before that night found joy, and peace, and comfort to my soul. Yesterday, in the morning, there was a prayer-meeting. Mr. Harris proposed that all who were determined to have religion and to seek the Lord should rise. Ten in our department arose. It is a very interesting time among us. It seems as if the Holy Spirit was in our midst. And may the Divine Spirit be with you!

My dear sister, it seems as if I wanted to write to some one of our family continually, but I sometimes forbear for fear I shall not do the subject justice. You have professed an interest in Christ. You have taken upon you the solemn covenant of the Church. You have said you would devote yourself to the cause of the Redeemer, who has died and done so much that you, and I, and every one of the human family, might be saved. Now, will you live up to this affirmation, and do everything in your power to bring precious and immortal souls to taste of the waters of life? Do you administer help to the sick and needy? If you do, you are doing your duty. If not, it is the sad reverse. Let me entreat you to take impenitent sinners by the hand, and tell them, "Now is the accepted time. To-day, if you will hear his voice, harden not your heart. The Spirit and the bride say, come; and let him that heareth say, come; and let him that is athirst come; and whosoever will, let him take the water of life freely."

During the last week, eighteen belonging to the academy have obtained hopes. Oh, imagine, if it is possible, the happiness I now feel! Supposing there was no hereafter, I would be constrained to have religion for the sole purpose of having temporal happiness.

Mr. Harris is very much engaged, and I am afraid will wear himself out. Indeed, who would not be engaged in such a time as this? I suppose you are enjoying all that domestic happiness which this world can give. But do not fail, while you are enjoying this happiness, to give the praise to Almighty God. He alone can make you happy or miserable.

He entered Dartmouth College, August, 1832, in the sixteenth year of his age. Here his tastes led him into general and miscellaneous reading, rather than close application to the prescribed course of study. His favorite books were of history and light literature. His journal of reading and reflections at this period shows a free range of mind over a wide circle of subjects. One of his essays is a criticism on the college course of study, as prescribing too much Latin, Greek, and metaphysics, and not enough deep and laborious reading of the British classics. He handled the following, among other topics:

"Independence of Spirit."

"Gibbon's 'Decline and Fall of the Roman Empire,' with an Abstract of the Fortieth Chapter."

"Hume and Robertson as Historians."

"The English Constitution, and the Superior Advantages of the Constitution of the United States."

"British Jealousy of America."

"Cooper's Novels."

"Paulding's Novels."

"Sketches of Public Characters: Webster, Calhoun, Livingston, Chancellor Kent."

"A Republican Government for France."

"Dissensions among Christians."

"The Error of Students in depending too much upon their Talents, and not enough upon Application."

"The Mistake of depending upon Riches."

"Intellectual Improvement conducive to True Happiness."

An esteemed classmate, for whom he predicted, in their Freshman year, the distinction he has attained as a scholar—Rev. Samuel C. Bartlett, D. D., professor in the Chicago Theological Seminary—says:

He was a man of general intelligence, and had acquired an easy, fluent style, both of writing and talking, but was entirely modest, and free from arrogance or assumption. He was a very genial person, with a steady vein of humor and good-nature. I always liked and respected him. I think he had no enmities or jealousies. He took little active part in class or college excitements and office-seeking. He gave no offense and took none. He was liked by his classmates, who all knew he could have made more of himself in college. When he left, he was beginning to wake up to greater earnestness of purpose, thought, and application.

Another classmate, subsequently a member of Congress for twelve years, two of which were during the period of Mr. Grimes's senatorial career—Hon. John Wentworth, of Chicago —says:

I never saw or heard of Grimes until we met at Hanover, Freshman year, 1832. He left at the close of the first term of the Junior year, 1835. James F. Joy was our tutor that year, and I have often heard him say that Grimes and myself recited in Tacitus to him. After that, I did not meet him until he came to Washington while I was Congressman. Grimes was a Whig and I was a Democrat, but was then quarreling with our Democratic President (Pierce) about the Douglas Kansas-Nebraska bill. General Pierce knew Grimes's people well, and he knew their Whig affinities, and I thought it would be a good joke to take Grimes to him, and introduce him as the next Governor of Iowa, as he was. Pierce thought he would have to change his politics first. After I got into Congress, I called upon President Lord to send him his degree, the same as if he had graduated, and I noticed that his name appeared in the next triennial catalogue as a graduate. Our classmate, Rev. E. E. Adams, now deceased, preached at Washington in the winter of 1866–'67, and Grimes, Daniel F. Merrill, and myself, went together to hear him.

2.—*To his Father.*

DARTMOUTH COLLEGE, *October* 20, 1834.

My birthday! I am eighteen years old. How I have spent these eighteen years, and to what advantage, time will show. But one thing I know, I have spent the happiest part of my life. It is melancholy to think I have lived so long, and where we shall be at the end of another eighteen years. That length of time will undoubtedly make a great alteration in our family. What change there will be, I know not. I do not wish to know. The whitened hair and furrowed brow of yourself and dear mother seem to foretell a change which no human foresight can prevent. But a truce with this for the present. I have written in a mournful strain; but when is a better time to feel mournful? It is indeed a serious occasion.

I was extremely sorry to hear Mr. B. accused me of neglect in not calling oftener to see him. I called there oftener than upon any of my brothers and sisters. You know I heartily hate to visit, not because I do not wish to see my friends, but I like to be at home all the time. Besides, to go and talk about nothing seems strange, and I appear perfectly ridiculous.

Immediately on leaving college, February, 1835, young Grimes entered the law-office of James Walker, Esq., in Peterborough, N. H. In Mr. Walker's absence from home, he was frequently intrusted with important matters of business. He became a member of his family, and won a place in the affectionate regards and care of his wife, a gifted and amiable lady, whose superior intelligence and enlightened counsels were so helpful to his studies, that he sometimes said that he read law with Mrs. Walker. A few extracts from her letters show her appreciation of the young student. When he was planning to go West, she wrote to his parents:

I wish to see and converse with you respecting his project. Allow me to say that I am much interested in his welfare, and I should be ungrateful were it otherwise. His whole conduct since he entered our family has been that of a kind and dutiful son, and his society has added much to my happiness.

Soon afterward she writes to her young friend:

Do you still look to the West as your future home? If so, I pray God it may be a happy one. The world is open before you, a world full of blessings to the wise and the good. Let me hope that you will be both. I can hardly account for the interest I feel in your welfare. I have known those a great deal better than you, that I did not like half so well. Now you must turn out well, that I may have some excuse for this predilection. What pride I shall take in my old age, when I shall see your name among the great ones, in saying, "I aye thought he would be something!"

The following summer, after hearing from him of his settlement in the West, she wrote to him in a letter full of affectionate counsel:

Let me caution you against expecting uninterrupted good

fortune, and do not make haste to be rich. Every day's experience confirms me in the belief that our happiness does not depend on the abundance of the things which we possess. Be honest and honorable in your dealings, and leave the event to Him who orders all things for our good. Excuse the motherly counsels of one who feels it her privilege to address you in that character.

A few years later, she wrote:

Can you really think that I have forgotten you, or that time and distance have made me indifferent to your welfare? Do you not know that, in spite of all your faults, I loved you almost as well as if you had been my own son? I hardly know why, but so it was. Most sincerely do I rejoice in your brilliant success, and most earnestly pray that you may be a good and happy man. Do not let prosperity make you unmindful of the bountiful Giver. There is much in your situation unfavorable to serious thought; but you have a mind capable of judging whether something more than fame and riches be not necessary to your happiness. I cannot bear to think of your being devoted wholly to politics and money-making. I have always hoped you would marry a sensible woman, who would influence you to all that was good. What is the prospect? Remember, I shall never give my consent to your marrying any woman, however rich and pretty, that does not possess firm, religious principles. This world is not always bright to the most favored; and there are times when our hopes and wishes go forward to another.

CHAPTER II.

LIFE AT BURLINGTON.

1836–1853.

In the spring of 1836, the young adventurer left the paternal roof to seek his fortunes in the far West. He came first to Alton, Illinois, and after visiting Pittsfield, Peoria, and Monmouth, in that State, his attention was directed to Burlington, a new town on the west bank of the Mississippi River, in what was known as the "Black Hawk Purchase." Thither he turned his steps, and landed in the town on the 15th of May, and at once embarked in business as an attorney-at-law, though not yet twenty years of age.

The Black Hawk Purchase was a strip of land lying along the west bank of the Mississippi River, from the north line of the State of Missouri to opposite Prairie du Chien, and extending back forty or fifty miles, which was ceded to the United States upon the close of the Black Hawk War, by treaty, September 21, 1832. It contained about six million acres of fair and fertile land, and by the terms of the treaty the Indian possession ceased on the 1st day of June, 1833. From that day explorers and settlers flocked rapidly into the country. A census, taken a few months after his arrival, showed a population of more than ten thousand, viz.: 6,257 in the county of Des Moines, 4,274 in the county of Dubuque. These counties had been organized by an act (September, 1834) of the Legislative Assembly of the Territory of Michigan, to which Congress had attached (June 28, 1834) the territory north of the State of Missouri. The division line between these counties was a line drawn due west from the foot of Rock Island. Burlington was the seat of justice of Des Moines County. The town was laid out in 1834, and named after Burlington in Vermont. The business and trade of the region found a natural centre at this point, and assured the growth of a flourishing town. The first court was held here in April, 1835.

By an act of Congress, approved April 20, 1836, the country north of the States of Illinois and Missouri to the boundary-line of the United States, lying between Lake Michigan and the upper peninsula of the State of Michigan on the east, and the Missouri and White Earth Rivers on the west, was constituted on the 4th of July, 1836, a separate Territory by the name of Wisconsin. The second session of the first Legislative Assembly of this Territory was held at Burlington, November 6, 1837, and a special session June 11, 1838. By an act of Congress, approved June 12, 1838, the Territory of Wisconsin was divided, and the portion west of the Mississippi River was constituted a separate territorial government, by the name of Iowa. This act took effect on the 4th of July, 1838. The Legislative Assembly of the Territory was convened at Burlington for three successive years, 1838, 1839, and 1840.

Thus, in a little more than two years, Mr. Grimes lived under three different territorial governments; under that of Iowa, during the whole period of its existence, eight years and a half.

In September, 1836, he went up the Mississippi River to attend a council of the chiefs, braves, and principal men of the Sac and Fox Indians, at Rock Island. By appointment of Henry Dodge, Governor of Wisconsin Territory, and commissioner on the part of the United States, he served as secretary of the commission. Two treaties were made. One relinquished to the United States the lands lying between the then boundary-line of the State of Missouri and the Missouri River, which were soon after added to that State, and contained six counties, with a population of 102,441, and the flourishing city of St. Joseph, with a population of 19,565 (census of 1870). The other ceded to the United States four hundred sections of land lying along both sides of the Iowa River, in what is now Louisa County, and which Keokuk, Wapello, and their bands, had occupied as a reservation, under the treaty of September 21, 1832.

In the mutation of affairs, it came to pass that from the territory ceded to the United States under the first treaty, there went forth, in less than twenty years, a violent effort to carry slavery into Kansas, in resistance to which Mr. Grimes bore a conspicuous part, and rendered efficient service.

The young lawyer took the attorney's oath, "to demean himself honestly," before Judge Irvin, one of the Associate Judges of the Territory of Wisconsin, February 24, 1837. In the practice of law he early secured business, and established a reputation for ability and integrity in the management of cases. In April, 1837, he was appointed city solicitor by the trustees of the town of Burlington. He pleaded nonage, but the board insisted upon the appointment, and he entered upon the duties of the office, and assisted in drawing up the first police laws of the town. He again held the same office in 1840. During the second session of the first Legislative Assembly of Wisconsin Territory, held at Burlington in the winter of 1837–'38, he was employed as assistant librarian of the Territorial Library. At this session, a member of the House from Dubuque County was charged with having taken a bribe of three hundred dollars from John Wilson, for the purpose of obtaining a charter for a ferry over the Mississippi River at Davenport. The matter excited a stormy discussion. A committee of investigation was appointed, who recommended the expulsion of the offending member, and that Wilson should be brought before the bar of the House and be reprimanded by the Speaker. Mr. Grimes, who had been employed, with Henry W. Starr, Esq., as counsel for John Wilson, promptly sent a communication to the Speaker, protesting against the right to reprimand him, and asked to be heard in his defense. On the 16th of January, 1838, the House heard Messrs. Grimes and Starr, and rejected the proposition to reprimand Wilson by a vote of seventeen to seven; the whole number of members of the House was twenty-six.

During the same winter he was appointed a justice of the peace by Hon. Henry Dodge, Governor of Wisconsin Territory, and formed a law-partnership with William W. Chapman, United States District Attorney for Wisconsin Territory, and subsequently the first Delegate to Congress from Iowa Territory. In the threatened disturbances between Missouri and Iowa on the "boundary question," in 1839–'40, he was commissioned by Governor Lucas as first-lieutenant, and afterward captain of the Iowa Guards, and shared in the humor of the period.

In January, 1841, he entered into a partnership with Henry W. Starr, Esq., which continued twelve years. Their practice was large and lucrative, and the firm stood at the head of the legal profession in Iowa. Mr. Grimes gained wide repute as a prudent and sagacious counselor, attentive to the interests of his clients, and as having a superior faculty for detecting sophistry, for lucid statement, and for disentangling things confused and mixed. Courts, and juries, and opposing counsel, listened to him with respect and confidence, assured of his knowledge of the law, and of his clear sense of truth and justice. Thoroughly independent and self-reliant, and shunning irrelevant and verbose speech, his mind grasped the strong points of a case, and his efforts were confined to the law and the evidence.

He said to a young student:

> Stick to your law until you can make a lawyer of yourself, and get a practice, and save money; then it will do to play with politics. You do not need much money. I commenced with fifty dollars worth of law-books, and accumulated by degrees, until I had the best library in town. A determined, persistent industry will secure your success anywhere, and without it no one can succeed. Learn to read and speak deliberately; you can do neither too slowly.

His home-letters of this period afford some information of the course of his life, and occasionally give his views of passing events.

3.—*To Miss Sarah C. Grimes, Deering, N. H.*

BURLINGTON, DES MOINES COUNTY,
WISCONSIN TERRITORY, *July* 3, 1836.

I intended to have written you when I first arrived in Alton, but not concluding to stay (and glad I am I did not, for it is very sickly there), and rambling about over Illinois, I did not find time for a convenient opportunity to write much. I am now permanently located, I hope, at this place. I am building an office,[1] and shall move into it next week. I shall then be on my own footing, and in my own possession.

It is natural to suppose that you want to know something about the people of this country. Imagine yourself just where you are, but fifty years ago. The countries are very different. Here we have not so much wood as there is in New England at the present day, and the soil is not half nor one-sixteenth part so fertile there as here, but the people here now, and there then, are very much alike. The country is rather more thickly settled here, but the character of the people, their manners, customs, and dress, are similar. There are no more schools here now than there then. Imagine your grandmothers dressed in their old garments, whalebone stomachers, etc., and you will have a very correct idea of the dress of Illinois females. The morals of the people are as good as they were then in New England. You have heard father tell of the wild doings of the young men of those days, and it is just so here. Every one goes in for sport and social enjoyment, more so on this side the river than on the other.

Burlington is on the bank of the Mississippi, and is about as large as Nashua village. The houses are not as large and splendid, for a good many are built of logs. But there are as many inhabitants, taking out the factory-girls there. One street runs exactly up the bank, facing the water. There is but one row of buildings on this street; the other side is a steamboat-landing. There are twelve stores on this street, not more than fifty feet from the water. My office is on Second Street, right back of Water Street, and parallel with it. There are three stores on Second Street, offices, etc. There are six doctors, five lawyers with myself, sixteen stores, five or six groceries, or, in New England, called grog-shops. No minister in town. We had one, but he died a few days ago.

I found Mark M. Aiken in Peoria. I should not have known him, if he had not come up to me and called me Mr. Grimes. I had not seen him for ten years. He did not know I was in the country, but he said he knew it was one of our family from the re-

[1] On Main Street, west side, between Columbia and Court Streets. It stood until destroyed by fire, June 19, 1873.

semblance to father; but he thought it was David, for he had forgotten me, that I ever was. The resemblance between me and father must be very great to cause one to know me by him, among strangers, two thousand miles from home. He is pious, a great temperance man, is getting rich, and looks very much like the Aikens, or like the Aiken boys.

4.—*To Miss Sarah C. Grimes.*

BURLINGTON, W. T., *December* 29, 1836.

I was very sick in the summer, for some time was not expected to live by my physician or myself. Do you ask whether I thought of home and my mother, etc., at that time? I did, but was so stupid, I did not care whether I got well or not; but, when I got up, I was determined to leave the country; and, had it not been for the urgent solicitation of my friends, I should not now be in Wisconsin Territory. A young lawyer, by the name of Stockton,[1] and myself had determined to go to Cincinnati, and attend the law-school there. My health is now excellent. When I left home I weighed a hundred and thirty pounds; I now weigh a hundred and seventy-five.

The hundred dollars I received from you I invested in town property in Bloomington, in Muscatine County. I was this very day offered two hundred and fifty dollars for the lot and refused it. I will sell when I can get enough for it, and purchase you a farm. I should have been independently rich if I had had any money when I came to this place. It is now the seat of government for the Territory, and property is worth ten times as much as it was when I came. Here is a fine field for any one who has industry, prudence, and economy, or a speculating turn. —— is better fitted for the Eastern country than the Western. He is, if I mistake not, wanting in an essential requisite, energy of character. One must be a driving, bustling person to take well in this country, and must look out for himself, putting not much dependence on any one. I wish a host of my old friends would come out and make fortunes here. A good blacksmith can make fifty dollars per month; carpenters, masons, joiners, etc., three dollars per day; a man for common work the

[1] Lacon D. Stockton, appointed a Judge of the Supreme Court of Iowa by Governor Grimes, May 17, 1856, afterward elected by the General Assembly, and again by the people. Died June 9, 1860.

year round twenty-five or thirty dollars per month. I will give H—— twenty-five dollars per month to work on my farm, at splitting rails, breaking prairie, and putting up fence. I own a claim of four hundred acres, in company with a Boston firm of merchants, Dickinson, Hedge & Sears. I own one-half, and we must get work done on it, in order to make it more valuable, and bring more in the spring. F—— is to be married! I give up all hope of seeing him out here. He will probably settle down on his farm, and never go off it but to mill and to meeting. It is strange how people can content themselves—young people, I mean—to live in that cold country, when they know from representations that there are preferable climes and more fertile lands.

5.—*To Miss Sarah C. Grimes, Hillsborough Bridge, N. H.*

BURLINGTON, *October* 9, 1837.

How can I spend the hour that remains between this and daylight otherwise than in writing to you? It is now three o'clock in the morning, and since "yesternight's sun" I have closed the eyes of one of the best friends I had upon earth. You have heard me speak of Sears, formerly of Boston. He is no more; one of the most amiable, accomplished, and beloved young men in our place. I told you that I wrote to you generally when I felt mournful, and seldom have I felt more so than at present. To me belonged the painful duty of closing his eyes, robing him in the habiliments of death, and preparing him for the grave; but the most painful duty is yet to come, of acquainting his parents and friends of his decease. Readily can I imagine the sorrow that my letter will produce in his father's family, easily can I picture the anguish of a bereaved mother, the uncurbed sorrow of brothers and sisters, and the heartfelt sympathy of neighbors and kindred. He died of congestive fever, suffered excruciating agony for the last six days, was sick only ten.

Never did I feel more sensibly than at this moment the folly of abandoning one's home and all its endearments for passing fame or fleeting wealth. To have the last rites that man pays to man performed by strangers, no relatives to soothe the last pangs of the departing spirit, how mournful the thought! Yet such was poor Sears's case, and such would be mine, too, if in the inscrutable wisdom of Providence I should be thrown on a bed of sickness and death.

But let me turn from this mournful subject. I have now been in Burlington since my return about two weeks. There are a great many sick in town, some whole families, one close by me, in which the father, mother, and four children are down with the fever. I am very pleasantly situated, more so than when I was here before. My health is excellent, never better. I have written this letter under the effect of strong excitement. Pray excuse it; I dare not read it, for I know I should tear it up, and you would not hear from me at present.

6.—*To Miss Sarah C. Grimes.*

Burlington, *March* 10, 1838.

Since I have begun to recover—

"My thoughts are in my native land,
My heart is in my native place,"

and I think of hardly anything but home. I sit in a little room, no one with me, hardly able to rise or turn my chair round, with eyes so poor that I cannot read. I suppose I never was so near eternity as during my last sickness. The people were once called in to see me die. My pulse had stopped, my extremities were cold, and my eyes fast setting in my head; fortunately, the doctor came in just then. He commenced the work of resuscitation, and I revived. I was in this situation five days, not expected to live from hour to hour. Oh, if I had died in this far-distant land, among strangers, what would be the feelings of our dear mother! I have cried when I thought of it. I ought to congratulate myself on my recovery. I owe a great deal to the good nursing I had. I have no recollection of anything that occurred during about three weeks of my sickness.

We have hard times here, such as were never conceived of in the East. There is no money in the country. I saw a man to-day, who has been keeping a shop. He was obliged to sell out on credit, and he had, besides, small notes due to the amount of twenty-five hundred dollars; yet he could not raise money enough to buy a bushel of corn-meal for his family. I expect I shall be one of the first to go by the board, for my sickness will cost me at least one hundred and twenty-five dollars, which I shall be obliged to pay, as board bills and sickness bills are considered cash articles. As for collecting, it is impossible; for the Legislature passed a stay law of twelve months; that is, a stay of execution on judgment. They thought they would relieve the people; but it serves to oppress them. If I could only be at home, and have your living, I should regain my strength in a week. You who never tried it cannot imagine the difference between New England and Western living. I would give a hundred dollars for three good meals at home; they would do me so much good, and I should gain strength so fast from them. But it is of no use to wish for them, and I had perhaps better, like the fox, call the grapes sour, because I cannot get them.

—— is not a minister who will be popular a great while. He is not a man of much mind, and a very ordinary preacher. He has a fine voice, which helps him; but, come to digest what he says, it does not amount to much.

Mr. Grimes was chosen one of the Representatives of Des Moines County in the first Legislative Assembly of the Territory of Iowa, which convened at Burlington, November 12, 1838; and in the sixth, which convened at Iowa City, December 4, 1843; and in the fourth General Assembly of the State, which convened at Iowa City, December 6, 1852. Though generally in a political minority in the county, such was his established character for ability and fairness, and so general the confidence awarded him, that he received the suffrages of many who were not of his own party. Reared in the traditions of the Whig party, he adhered to that organization from preference and conviction, but not as an unscrupulous partisan. In the halls of legislation he bore an active and leading part, and from the first took front rank among the most enlightened and sagacious public men of Iowa. He was chairman of the Judiciary Committee in the House of Representatives of the first Legislative Assembly of the Territory of Iowa, and all the laws for the new Territory passed through his hands. In this Assembly he introduced a memorial to Congress, asking an appropriation of lands for the construction of a railroad from Burlington to Mount Pleasant, and to the Missouri State line, and secured its adoption, December, 1838.

A conflict of authority early arose between the Assembly and the Governor of the Territory, Hon. Robert Lucas; the latter claimed a power of veto upon all acts of the former, and exercised it in a number of matters regarded as important. A bitter controversy ensued. The House appointed a Standing Committee on Vetoes, of which Mr. Grimes was made chairman. On the 7th of January, 1839, the committee presented an elaborate report, reviewing the grounds upon which the Executive vetoes were based, and concluding thus:

We have attempted to ascertain where the Governor derives the power of unconditionally vetoing bills; but in vain. We find no such authority delegated in the Organic Law, and we believe no such power can be obtained by implication. It is a power of too much importance to the people, and too liable to abuse, to be executed but by positive grant. It is a power now obsolete even in the monarchical government of Great Britain. Notwithstanding the peremptory manner in which it can be exercised in that government, it has not been used since the reign of William III., in 1692; and then that sovereign was obliged to sanction the same bill at the commencement of the next Parliament which he had before disapproved of.

The Congress of the United States has a restraining and annulling power over the acts of this Legislature, and it certainly could not have been intended that there should be more than one "vetoing" power suspended over our heads. As representatives of the people, we should be recreant to their rights and interests, if we should acquiesce in the "veto-power," as used by the Executive, when there was the least doubt whether that *despotic* privilege belonged to his office or not. We believe the people should be heard through those who represent them, and are responsible to them, that their wishes should be regarded, and not those of the Federal Government, or a Federal officer. We believe the principle claimed by the Governor dangerous and pernicious, contrary to the spirit of republican institutions, degrading to the Legislative Assembly, and subversive of independent legislation; and as the representatives of freemen we cannot acquiesce in it.

The House concurred in the report by a vote of sixteen to six, and a memorial to the President of the United States was adopted by both Houses, asking for the removal of Governor Lucas.

Congress intervened by an act, providing that two-thirds of each House could enact a law over the Governor's objections.

In the sixth Legislative Assembly of the Territory (1843–'44) Mr. Grimes was a member of the Judiciary Committee, and chairman of the Committee on Corporations. To the former were referred ten petitions for divorces, upon which he presented an elaborate report. In that report the power of the Legislature to grant divorces was fully discussed, and the conclusion reached that the Legislative Assembly was not invested with it. A resolution to this effect was adopted by the House, and thus an end put to a reprehensible practice of several earlier Territorial Legislatures.

7.—*To Miss Sarah C. Grimes.*

BURLINGTON, IOWA, *January* 29, 1839.

Our Legislature has adjourned, and our little city is comparatively deserted. We are now drawn into two great parties in this Territory: one in favor of the Governor and his course; the other opposed. I come in for a tolerably large share of executive maledictions, as I took a somewhat decided and conspicuous stand against him. I was called the leader of the opposition. We were divided in the House of Representatives, eighteen in opposition, and eight in favor of the Governor. I hardly know or anticipate the result. Politics are very uncertain, but I believe the Legislature was right, and will be sustained by the people. The members from this county will be, at all events.

I presume I shall be very lonesome, and perhaps homesick, the remaining part of the winter. The excitement has been so great for the last three months, that my office will seem uncommonly dull, and the hours very heavy. I wish I could be instantaneously placed by the family fireside.

8.—*To his Father, Hillsborough Bridge, N. H.*

BURLINGTON, I. T., *September* 20, 1840.

I am under infinite obligations for the books and money, and particularly to mother for the shirts and socks. I am now almost twenty-four years old, and it seems but a short time since I was fourteen, and entered college. There was a very great mistake on my part, or on yours. I entered college too young. I am now old enough to reason correctly upon such subjects, and believe a boy should not enter until he is at least eighteen or nineteen years old. His habits will then be formed somewhat, and his mind disciplined. Do not let any of my nephews be sent to college until they are at least of that age. I hope some of them will be sent there, or to West Point. They ought to be prepared well.

My health has generally been good this summer. I have been all over the Territory, making political speeches, and shall make one to-morrow at Fort Madison, about twenty miles distant. My professional business is very good, but I receive no money. I am so well established here that I have some credit; else I should starve to death assuredly.

Our town is improving rapidly, between sixty and seventy buildings erected this season, many of them three-story bricks. We shall some day have a very large town here. I hope New Hampshire will not vote for General Harrison. We do not want her. We can elect him without, by the largest majority by which a President was ever elected. Did you know that I came near being nominated for Congress? I could have had a unanimous nomination, if I had seen fit to accept it. Indeed, it was pressed upon me, and I was obliged to come out and tell them that I lacked a year of being eligible. I shall give them a turn for it after a while.

9.—*To Miss Sarah C. Grimes.*

BURLINGTON, IOWA, *April* 27, 1843.

I returned a day ago from attending courts in distant counties. You will have learned, from a newspaper I sent, that young Ross has been acquitted for killing Bradstreet. The trial lasted five full days, and five laborious and tedious days they were to me, but I was amply compensated for my labor by the result. For you must know that a lawyer acquires a deep interest in and solicitude for his client, however guilty he may suppose him in reality to be. In this case Ross was not so much to blame as many supposed; yet he acted very imprudently, foolishly, if not wickedly. In New England he would have been hung; but here, under no circumstances, could it be made more than manslaughter. This is the fourth person I have defended for murder, and all have been acquitted. This is a source of self-felicitation, for I hardly know what my feelings would be if I defended a man who was condemned. I should fear I had made some misstep, had left unexerted some energy I possess, or some influence I ought to have brought to bear on the case, and that, through my unskillfulness or neglect, a fellow-creature had been sent into eternity.[1]

I doubt not that the melancholy news of Chase's death caused the hearts of his parents to bleed, and tore open afresh the wounds created by the death of their other son. We are so constituted that we can hardly refrain from mourning the loss of those we love, and I am one of the few who believe that there is nothing effeminate or unmanly in tears. Yet, why should we sorrow? Death is the lot of all, and what matters it, whether it takes us in the tender years of infancy, the bloom of youth, the strength of manhood, or when we are in the sere and yellow leaf? We and our friends must obey a law universal in the animal, vegetable, and organic worlds, and we could not expect nor even wish that the law should be changed as to us. We might as well expect or desire the law of gravitation to be changed so far as we are concerned.

I can hardly realize that it is more than seven years since I left home for the West. It is indeed a large space in a man's life, and not unfrequently spent to but poor advantage. For and to what purpose I have lived, time alone will develop. May we all act upon the saying of an ancient philosopher, that it is sweet to live after one's death in the remembrance of friends!

10.—*To Miss Sarah C. Grimes.*

House of Representatives, Iowa City,
January 24, 1844.

Your favor of December 30th, announcing among other things the death of Elvira Forsaith, has just been received. It came at a time when it would be well calculated to make the deepest impression upon my mind. I am myself unwell, and was to-day compelled to go to the House, to give my vote upon an exciting question, and while there, amid the noise and bustle of business and of conflicting interests, your letter was handed to me. It seemed as

[1] "Sometimes, years after a case had been tried, he would feel a pang of reproach that he had not urged some argument which at that moment flashed across his mind. He always fought his *lost* causes over again, to see if he could find any argument whereby he might have gained them."—"Life of Rufus Choate," by S. G. Brown, p. 30.

though I heard her funeral knell, and saw her coffin-lid closed. When I say that I esteemed her, I express but half of my affection for her. I always loved her almost like a sister. In fact, it could hardly be otherwise, for I have known her ever since I have known any one, and have spent with her many of my youthful and happiest days. I have been taught by her as an instructress, and associated with her as a relative and friend. Many of the scenes around which my recollection most tenderly clings are connected with her. But she is gone where we must all soon go. She is probably but a few months, or years at most, in advance of us; and it is not the part of wisdom or religion to mourn over the blest early dead. I hope we shall be prepared to meet her in that world of uninterrupted blessedness where I doubt not she now is.

11.—*To his Father.*

BURLINGTON, *September* 13, 1845.

I reached this place after a pleasant and prosperous journey of some eighteen days (from New Hampshire).

It has been and is yet very sickly. Throughout the entire Western country it is probably more sickly than in any year since 1838, which was emphatically the sickly season. The weather is still extremely warm—warmer than it was at Hillsborough during any part of the past summer. The crops are excellent. So abundant are they, that wheat is worth only forty cents, and spring wheat will bring little or nothing. All other kinds of produce bring correspondingly low prices. I found that our town had increased astonishingly during the summer. Several fine brick edifices have gone up, and several others are in progress. The value of property is slowly advancing, though we labor under some difficulties in that respect. We have no currency except what is furnished from other States. If we had banks, where our citizens could obtain accommodations, our business would be greatly increased, and the prices of property improved.

Our people have again rejected the constitution, and the result will probably be that we shall remain a Territory for two or three years. It is fortunate for the people that the question has been decided as it has, for they will now be free from a heavy debt that must inevitably be saddled upon them in the event of becoming a State.

The business of our firm is steadily increasing all the time. In truth, we have as much as we ought to do, if not more. Money, however, although nominally made fast, yet comes in very slow. In Albany, on my way West, I made a large purchase of land, over eleven thousand acres. I do not know how I shall come out, but hope to make money out of it; cannot believe I shall lose; shall give a good deal of attention to sales for a few months, so as to pay what I still owe speedily as possible.

12.—*To his Parents.*

BURLINGTON, IOWA, *March* 12, 1846.

I intended to have written to you on the 5th of the present month, which you will recollect as the anniversary of my first leaving home for the West. It was ten years ago the 5th day of March that I started from the paternal mansion with a heavy heart, but with buoyant hopes, to seek a home in this strange and far-off land. These ten years have produced wonderful changes in us all. I feel that a great, an incomprehensible change has been wrought in me. Instead of a boy of nineteen, without experience, or judgment, or business habits, I am now in the meridian of life, and, if either way, past its culminating point. From the sudden and premature deaths of my companions and friends around me, I am reminded that in all probability the better and larger portion of my life is past. But such is the fate of all. This is a world of change, and it is foolish to wish it otherwise. My health has been excellent since I returned, though there has been much sickness here, and many deaths. Our Congregational clergyman [1] was buried yesterday. He was a talented and quite promising young man from Massachusetts, and has left a young widow to whom he had been married only twelve months. She too came from Massachusetts, and is now left entirely destitute among strangers.

Our winter has been remarkably mild and pleasant. We have had no sleighing, and only two snow-storms. The snow at neither time remained upon the ground more than forty-eight hours. The weather is now so mild that we have for the last week or ten days dispensed with stoves and fires. Our town has been very active this winter, and our merchants have done a good business. I am

[1] Rev. Horace Hutchinson (Amherst College, 1839, Andover Theological Seminary, 1843).

MR. GRIMES'S RESIDENCE.

p. 25.

told by some of them that there are ten thousand barrels of flour, one hundred thousand bushels of wheat, fifteen thousand barrels of pork, and one hundred thousand bushels of corn, and other articles of produce in proportion, ready to be shipped from this place. Winter wheat is now worth fifty cents, spring wheat thirty-five cents, corn ten cents, oats twelve and a half cents per bushel.

I know not whether I told you about a speculation that I was trying to make while I was East, in the purchase of lands. I do not like to talk about myself so much, nor to brag, but I know you want to hear all about me, and I will therefore say that I was fortunate in the operation and succeeded, beyond my hopes even, in making money by it. Our law business is still good, much the best of any lawyers in the Territory.

Mr. Grimes was married to Miss Elizabeth Sarah Nealley at Burlington, November 9, 1846. For a few years he kept house on Main Street, between Elm and Maple Streets, and in 1850–'51 built a comfortable residence upon a commanding elevation on the South Hill, which he occupied the rest of his life. At both places he gave personal attention to his garden, which he stocked with choice fruits. He was one of the original members of the Southern Iowa Horticultural Society, organized May, 1849, and for several years exhibited at its public meetings fruits and flowers from his garden. In September, 1853, at the annual exhibition, which was peculiarly rich and brilliant, he delivered an address replete with enlightened views upon the utility, value, and methods of fruit-culture. Specimens of fruit from his garden were taken to Chicago, and exhibited at a fruit-growers' convention held in that city.[1] One specimen was sent to the Cincinnati Horticultural Society. In 1853–'54 he served for a year and a half as one of the editors of the *Iowa Farmer and Horticulturist*, a monthly journal, published at Burlington. His services were rendered with no other compensation

[1] "Conspicuous among the notable collection of fruit shown here at the Fruit Convention by Mr. Avery, were some of Coe's golden-drop plums, the largest we ever saw. They were from the garden of James W. Grimes, editor of the *Iowa Farmer*. Some Northern Spy apples, raised by the same person, were also of unusual size."—*Prairie Farmer*, Chicago, November, 1853.

than results from a conscientious effort to incite inquiry, to stimulate manly and generous rivalry, to disseminate correct and important information, and do good. He took especial care to select the best essays and practical suggestions of the leading agriculturists of the country, and made a paper of permanent value, still interesting and instructive to read. At one period he gave some attention to the oversight of a farm, especially to the raising of stock, and improving the breed of horses. He put himself among the farmers, in a list of occupations of the members of the fourth General Assembly.

He was appointed, January, 1847, one of the school-inspectors of Burlington, with his friends, Hon. Charles Mason and Mr. George Partridge, and was twice chosen to the same office by the people. He presided at an educational convention, held in Burlington, June 7, 1847, in which the duty of the State to provide for the education of all children by equitable taxation was earnestly advocated, and the profound regret expressed that the first General Assembly of Iowa had made no provision for building school-houses by law, but had left the whole matter to voluntary subscription. He was one of the school-directors of Burlington in 1850, and president of the board in 1851.

He coöperated with the temperance reformation, under the auspices of the "Sons of Temperance," and gave an oration at their anniversary, April 13, 1848.

He attended the Whig National Convention, which met at Philadelphia, June, 1848, as a delegate from the State at large, and was appointed one of the vice-presidents of the convention. At the first ballot he voted for John McLean for President, subsequently for Zachary Taylor. He disapproved of the course of President Fillmore on slavery, and was indignant at the passage of the fugitive-slave law.

He took an active part in awakening public attention to the importance of plank-roads and railroads, and in efforts to build them. Upon the completion of a plank-road from Burlington to Mount Pleasant, at a celebration held at the latter place, December 18, 1851, he spoke of ardently looking for the time when a railroad should connect the Mississippi with the Missouri, and be part of one to the Pacific Ocean through Southern Iowa, by a nearer route than any other then proposed or contemplated; and he advocated memorializing Congress for a grant of public lands to aid in its construction. He was one of the original directors of the Peoria & Oquawka Railroad, organized in 1851, of which the western terminus was on the bank of the Mississippi, opposite Burlington. The same year he was chosen an alderman from the Fourth Ward.

In the deliberations of the fourth General Assembly of the State (1852–'53), he was a leading member. He was on the Committee of Ways and Means, and chairman of that on charitable institutions. He introduced a memorial to Congress, asking for a grant of land to aid in building a railroad from Burlington to the Missouri River, and secured its adoption against a powerful influence that was interested to obtain legislative action in favor of a north and south road. As chairman of a special committee, he reported a general law granting the right of way to railroads, under which in twenty years, to December 31, 1872, three thousand six hundred and forty-two miles of railroad have been built. His sympathies were particularly awakened in behalf of the insane, many of whom at this period were confined in county poor-houses and jails, and he made their condition and relief a special study. He was an earnest advocate for submitting the question of amending the constitution of the State to a vote of the people, but Governor Hempstead interposed his veto twice against any legislation for that object.

13.—*To Miss Sarah C. Grimes.*

BURLINGTON, *November* 17, 1846.

The news of Susan's death came upon me unexpectedly, and has thrown a chill upon my heart, and a gloom around my otherwise cheerful fireside. She was to me almost a mother, as well as a sister. Her age being so much greater than mine, she had in my youth something of the control of me, and I can conscientiously and thankfully say that her government was always exercised for my good. She first taught me to lisp the prayer of our Saviour, and endeavored to direct my steps in the paths of truth and virtue, and always had a word of sweet encouragement to bestow, when I had acted a manly and praiseworthy part, nor failed to discharge her duty by proper remonstrances when I had done wrong. It was her aim to make us happy, amiable, and good. My only regret is, that I have not sought to make myself more like her.

She is gone, and why should we repine? She is freed from pain and suffering, and I entertain no fears for her future condition. She has exchanged a corruptible for an incorruptible world, and we should rather sigh and mourn for ourselves who are left behind, than for her who has preceded us in that happy world, "where the wicked cease from troubling, and the weary are at rest." That we should mourn is natural, but it should not be a selfish sorrow for the loss we sustain. It should be, though it seldom is, a heartfelt sorrow for our own errors and imperfections.

You have now a heavy responsibility to be a mother to the motherless, and train and guide our deceased sister's children in the most important period, and teach them to act their parts in life. I know she would prefer that charge should be yours, and that you will fulfill the office with your best ability. But always remember that, as there is nothing so sweet as a sense of duty discharged, so there is nothing so bitter as a sense of duty violated.

14.—*To his Father.*

BURLINGTON, *May* 26, 1850.

Two days ago I received the melancholy announcement of the death of my mother. I would have written you sooner, but I have not felt in a proper frame of mind to do so until now. The news of her death was wholly unexpected; yet I had no reason to suppose she would live long. I could see the hand of disease upon her when I parted from her, and then feared that I was taking my last look of her. But now, when I know that such is the fact—that she is dead—I can hardly realize it or reconcile myself with the idea that I am never to meet her again. When I was with you, her tottering step and emaciated form told me too well that death had marked her for his own; but her mind was so unclouded and strong, and her energy and determination so great, that I thought she might perhaps almost conquer disease, and live some years to come. It has been otherwise ordained, and it becomes us to bow with meek resignation to the will of Him who orders all things for the best.

We have all sustained a great loss, but the loss of her children is as nothing compared with yours. You have lost her who has been your bosom companion for more than fifty years, who has shared all your griefs and partaken of all your joys, who has borne and reared your children, and sympathized in all your desires and efforts for their welfare. That mysterious bond of union which connects the father with the mother of his offspring has been sundered in your old age, and you must totter on to the close of life without the aid or comfort of her from whom you hoped never to part. I know how solitary you must feel. I sympathize in your afflictions, and would mingle my sorrows with yours. And yet, why should we sorrow? Our mother has gone down to the grave full of years. She has lived far past the allotted age of man. While here, she acted well her part. Her children have cause to rise up and call her blessed, for she did everything in her power to make them prosperous, respectable, and happy. She discharged all her obligations to the community. What more could we expect or desire?

I have only one regret in relation to mother. My folly used to be the source of a great deal of anxiety and pain to her, and she may have continued to think that I would make shipwreck of myself. But I hope she did not think so. It would certainly pain me much if I thought she did.

15.—*To Mrs. Grimes.*

IOWA CITY, *December* 16, 1850.

I wrote a few lines night before last in great haste and in the midst of a crowd. I have now more leisure, as it is Sunday morning, when people are quiet here. Not very quiet either, for there is all sorts of electioneering going on at all hours of the day and night. The business I came up to attend to will be arranged pretty comfortably, I think, though I have been compelled to manage tolerably shrewdly. There is some opposition in the House of Representatives, but I think I shall succeed in quelling it before any final action is had. I shall return as soon as it will be safe for me to leave. I think I am doing a great deal of good for Burlington by being here, but others may be of a different opinion. At any rate I am trying.

16.—*To his Father.*

BURLINGTON, *February* 15, 1851.

We have a great railroad and plank-road fever here now. We have nearly completed a plank-road thirty miles west of this place. I am the president of the company, have had the entire responsibility and management of the work, and I think it will pay well. I have four thousand dollars of stock in it. We are now about to build a railroad from this place east about one hundred miles. In three years there will be continuous lines of railroad from Burlington to Hillsborough Bridge, and the trip will be made in three or not exceeding four days. This is a great change from what was the case when I came to this country fifteen years ago.

I am building a new house for my own occupation. It will be a tolerably good one. You will no doubt think I am rather extravagant, and perhaps I am, but I believe I can afford it. I shall have much the finest place in town, though by no means the most costly house. There are houses here that cost twice as much as mine, but there are no pleasure-grounds around them.

17.—*To Miss Sarah C. Grimes.*

BURLINGTON, *October* 27, 1851.

The melancholy intelligence of the death of our dear father came upon me suddenly; still I was not wholly unprepared for the news. His advanced age and full habit have led me to anticipate his dying in an apoplexy or something of the kind. It should be a consolation to his children that he has been permitted to be with them so long—that he has placed before us so good an example—that he has lived a life so blameless. I do not believe he ever intentionally wronged any man. Without making any pretensions to goodness, he was a good man. He was hospitable and kind to all, and he loved his children. I pray that we may all imitate his example, and that his memory may ever be kept green in our hearts. We are now without parents. Let the love we felt toward them be turned toward each other.

18.—*To Mrs. Grimes.*

WASHINGTON, D. C., *February* 15, 1852.

I am at the largest house in the town, where most of the members congregate, and where it is the fashion to sit up all night, and sleep nearly all day. Out of five hundred persons staying here, there were but five of us at breakfast this morning at half-past seven o'clock. This Washington is a fashionable, false-hearted, uncomfortable place, where all kinds of immorality and vice are rampant. I could not be induced to live here as a home, upon any consideration whatever.

February 20th.—I cannot endure the practice of turning night into day, eating dinner from four to six o'clock in the afternoon, and going to bed at three or four in the morning ; yet I am compelled to fall in, in some degree, with this method of living. As I have strolled about the city, you cannot imagine how often I have thanked God that I was not cursed with a fashionable wife. I do not believe I have seen a woman since I came here who was not painted, and the affectation and foreign airs of both ladies and their whiskered attendants are exceedingly disgusting to me. I have often wondered whether it was possible for such artificial, made-up persons to have any hearts, and whether they were capable of feeling any real love for either their own or the opposite sex.

I called upon Mr. Webster two nights ago, and spent an evening with him, and was invited to breakfast the next morning, but declined. He was exceedingly affable and polite, and made my call quite agreeable.

I have just heard Mr. Bellows again, and he delivered by far the best sermon I ever listened to in my life. It would be a great treat indeed, to have him within reach, so that we could attend upon his ministrations. I would be willing to pay liberally for such intellectual feasts as he would spread before us.

19.—*To Mrs. Grimes.*

IOWA CITY, *December* 6, 1852.

I reached this town yesterday after two days and a half of tedious and hard driving. There is a large crowd of people here ; the taverns full, and all the private boarding-houses. Everybody is busy electioneering, some for one office, and some for another, but the all-engrossing subject is the election of United States Senator. It has already been the subject of one bloody fight, and many more are anticipated. Of course, being a Whig, I take no part in the controversy.

December 10th.—I am kept as busy as a bee. There is a great excitement all the time about senatorial elections, railroads, etc.

I am pretty well mixed up in them, it being understood that I have more votes at my back than any five members of the House combined. I have succeeded in all my efforts thus far; hope I shall deserve and win success in future.

December 18th.—I have succeeded in the principal object for which I came here, viz., upon the subject of railroads, and, I am told, have elevated the character of your husband as a tactician and parliamentary leader. We had a fierce struggle for four days, but won the battle triumphantly. Our opponents now beg of us for quarter, and I am magnanimous and give it to them. If I can get all my cherished projects out of the way handsomely, so that they cannot be interfered with, I may come home before the close of the session. You may be sure that I wish I was there now. I love the excitement of a legislative assembly, but I love the quiet of a happy home more. There are no laurels to be gathered in the position I am in, but some one must discharge the duty assigned to me, and it may perhaps as well be done by me as by others.

20.—*To Mrs. Grimes.*

House of Representatives, Iowa City, *January* 9, 1853.

This is Sunday. I have just returned from church. The House may adjourn on the 24th inst. As an individual, I want to adjourn; but as a legislator, I vote against it. It is utterly impossible for us to mature and pass all the laws we ought to pass in the short period indicated.

This week we are to have up the question of whiskey. I have been expecting numerous petitions upon the subject from home, but thus far have received only a little over two hundred, including men, women, and children. Unless there is a stronger demonstration than this from a county containing fourteen thousand, I shall be compelled, under instructions, to let the present law stand, so far as my vote will go toward that result.

January 14th.—We sit immediately after breakfast, and, with a recess for dinner and supper, until nine or ten o'clock at night. I have to work hard, doing not only my own business, but the business of a great many old fellows, who are not able to write bills and reports, and in the evening I am the presiding officer.

CHAPTER III.

GOVERNOR OF IOWA.

1854–1858.

In February, 1854, Mr. Grimes was nominated by a Convention of the Whig party for Governor of the State. It was the largest State Convention of that party ever held in Iowa, and the last. The following month, March 28th, a Free-Soil Convention, held at Crawfordsville, of which Isaac Field, of Denmark, was president, recommended the Free Democracy to cast their votes for him; and a candidate who had previously been nominated by that party withdrew. The country was violently agitated by a proposition in Congress to declare inoperative and void the prohibition of slavery in those vast regions which have since been constituted into the States of Kansas and Nebraska. Mr. Grimes perceived that the proposition involved a crisis in the nation's history, and at once threw himself against it with determined resolution and energy. Entering upon the campaign with vigor, he rallied to his support the great body of the Whigs, the original abolitionists and Free-Soilers, as they were variously called, who had polled more than a thousand votes in the presidential elections of 1848 and 1852, and not a few Democrats, who were opposed to the repeal of the Missouri compromise. Visiting nearly every portion of the State, he addressed the people in speeches that won him high reputation for ability and candor. He drove from county to county in his own conveyance, and was often weary with exposure and fatigue. Meeting a friend near the close of his travels, he spoke of being worn and tired, and remarked, pointing to his attenuated and jaded horses:

> "What shadows we are,
> And what shadows we pursue!"

The issues of the period were clearly set forth in the following paper:

To the People of Iowa.

The Whig State Convention assembled at Iowa City, on the 22d day of February last, did me the honor to present my name before the people of the State as a candidate for the office of Governor. I accept the nomination.

As I am compelled to be absent from the State during a portion of the summer, and shall, in consequence of such absence, be deprived of the pleasure of addressing the people in many places where I have desired to address them, I take this method of stating my views in relation to such subjects as are likely to enter into the canvass, and about which the public mind is now agitated. The limits of this paper will necessarily compel me to be brief.

1. For the constitution of our State I do not entertain the highest reverence. I believe that the best interests of the State require its speedy amendment. In favor of such amendment numerous substantial reasons might be assigned, but one or two will be sufficient to be stated here.

The experience of the past eight years has demonstrated that the power to elect judges is more wisely and satisfactorily exercised by the people than by the Legislative Assembly. The people have shown that they will not be *dragooned* into voting for incompetent and faithless partisan judges. Everybody admits that the character of the inferior tribunals of the State is superior to that of the Supreme bench. If, therefore, it is important to elevate the character of the Supreme Court, as I believe it is, the Judges of that Court should be elected by the people, as are now the Judges of the District Courts. If learning, firmness, and impartiality, are superior, as qualifications for judges, to party fealty and partisan services, the selection of those important officers should be left with the people, instead of being made the subject for corrupt legislative bargainings.

That part of the constitution which prohibits banks and banking institutions should be changed so as to allow them to be established in the State under proper restrictions. On this subject I am sorry to differ, as far as I believe I do, from my respected competitor, Mr. Bates. He was a member of the Constitutional Convention, and was chairman of the Committee on Incorporations, by whom the prohibitory article was framed and reported. He at that time thought that it was the highest reach of human wisdom on that subject. I never thought so. But it is a question about which our respective political parties differ as widely as their candidates. The Whig State Convention, on the 22d of February, unanimously adopted a resolution in favor of amending the constitution so as to allow the introduction of banks. The Democratic Convention, on the 8th of January last, refused to adopt such a resolution. On this question, therefore, the two parties are at issue in this State—the Whigs believing that banking should be permitted, and a domestic currency furnished to the people of the State, and the Democrats negativing these propositions.

When the constitution was adopted eight years ago, its advocates predicted that, long before this time, Iowa would be blessed with an exclusive metallic currency. They will hardly pretend that their prediction has been verified. So far from it, the entire business of the State during these eight years has been conducted upon the issues of foreign banks, and the profits derived therefrom have gone into the pockets of foreign stockholders, instead of enriching our own citizens. In place of having a domestic currency, the value of which *might* be known to every one, the country has been furnished with the worst conceivable currency from every State in the Union, and of the value of which nothing *could* be known. It has been estimated that from a quarter to half a million dollars has been annually realized by foreign banks upon this kind of circulation furnished to Iowa, all of which might be saved to the State, but for the constitutional prohibition.

If every other State in the Union would abolish banks, and the value of the supply and products of the whole country were reduced to a specie standard, there would be but few advocates for the creation of banks here. But so long as they are allowed and encouraged elsewhere, their circulation cannot be driven from the State, except by a currency of our own, without greatly depreciating the value of our agricultural, mechanical, and mineral products, and producing a general derangement and paralysis in the business of the community. Other States have tried the experiment. I need not refer to the recent experience of the neighboring States of Illinois, Indiana, Michigan, and Wisconsin. Why shall not Iowa profit by their experience? Why shall she not secure to her citizens the same facilities for transacting business as are enjoyed by the citizens of other States? Are not our people as competent to manage the affairs of banking institutions discreetly and safely as those of any other State? Is there not the same necessity for banks here as elsewhere?

The argument urged by some that banks are not in accordance with the principles of the Democratic party, is unworthy of consideration. How can it be democratic to charter banks in New Hampshire, Virginia, South Carolina, Illinois, Pennsylvania, and Indiana, and be *un*democratic to do the same thing in Iowa? There is not a State east of the Mississippi River in which there are not banks incorporated by Democratic Legislatures, and yet, in the view of some *wise* men, it is a gross violation of democratic principles to create them west of that river.

I do not propose to discuss the mode of banking that should be adopted in this State, nor have I space to point out the benefits that would result to the community by the establishment of banks in furnishing facilities for business—in diminishing the rate of interest, etc. The people are capable of determining the system that should be adopted satisfactorily to themselves, through their delegates to a constitutional convention, or by their representatives in the General Assembly. All I contend for is that they shall have the privilege of doing so.

A submission to the people of the question of amending the constitution of the State can be attended with no expense, and there is not a valid argument to be urged against it. If the principle of a government by a majority is correct—if the people *are* really capable of self-government, why should they not be permitted to decide for themselves a question of so vital importance? Why should Legislative quibbling and Executive vetoes be interposed to prevent an expression of the popular will on this subject?

A majority of the members of the last General Assembly were professedly in favor of a change in the constitution. They had been elected by constituencies who required them to commit themselves in favor of the proposition before their election. But many of them were at heart opposed to any change, and, after interposing frivolous objections, amendments, and delays, finally refused to pass a bill submitting the question to the people, over the Executive veto. Thus, by the exercise of two vetoes, and the timidity and faithlessness of some representatives, the principle of self-government was virtually denied, and the people refused the privilege of determining for themselves whether or not their constitution should be amended.

Let the voters of Iowa understand that, if they desire a change in their constitution, they must elect public servants who are in favor of that change from principle and honest conviction. Let them remember that the best criterion of a man's future conduct are his past opinions and conduct. Let them elect men who will not be driven from their positions by the frowns of party leaders, nor be seduced from them by Executive fawning or the bestowment of Federal offices. Then, and not till then, will the desired and much-needed change be effected.

2. It is no doubt expected that I shall state my views of the temperance question.

I have been repeatedly inquired of, by letters and otherwise, whether I would (if elected) veto a prohibitory liquor law.

It is a cardinal principle of the Whig party that all questions of expediency belong legitimately to the people, and should be settled by the legislative department of the government. The veto should be exercised only for the gravest constitutional reasons. Should, therefore, an act be passed either prohibiting the sale of intoxicating liquors, or licensing their sale, I would (if elected) approve the law, unless, in my judgment, palpably unconstitutional. It would be a violation of my own principles, as well as of the party to which I belong, to endeavor to thwart in any degree the wishes of the people of the State as expressed through their representatives. The friends of both the prohibitory and the license systems must bear in mind that the Executive of the State has nothing whatever to do with the preparation of the laws. To the members to be elected to the General Assembly, therefore, they must look for the consummation of their wishes in this behalf.

3. It has ever been the Whig doctrine that to the General Government belong the power and duty of increasing and protecting

the commerce of the country by works of internal improvement that are general and national in their character. Hundreds of millions of dollars have been expended by the General Government in the improvement of the rivers and harbors on the Atlantic seaboard, and now, when they are completed, and the commerce of the Western rivers and lakes has increased to $560,000,000 annually, we are told that the system of internal improvements is improper and unconstitutional, and that, if we wish to improve our rivers, we must assent to *tonnage duties on our own commerce.* After draining the West to perfect the improvement of Eastern harbors, and while voting annually millions of dollars to build lighthouses and breakwaters, and to support a navy, all for the protection of Eastern commerce, the West is told that *her* commerce must languish unless she commits a *felo-de-se* by voluntary taxation.

Mr. Douglas has introduced a bill into the United States Senate, by which the nine States bordering on the Mississippi River are authorized to bind themselves into a confederated commercial community, for the purpose of levying these duties and making the necessary improvements. How he disposes of the first clause of Article I., Section 10, of the Constitution, which declares that "no State shall enter into any treaty, alliance, or confederation," is not known; or, how the section of the celebrated Ordinance of 1787, which declares that "the navigable waters leading into the Mississippi and St. Lawrence, and the carrying-places between the same, shall be common highways, and *forever free*, as well to the inhabitants of the said Territory as to the citizens of the United States, and those of any other States that may be admitted into the Confederacy, *without any tax, impost, or duty therefor*," is to be evaded, I have not learned.

But, in whatever way these and many other very serious objections are overcome, it is enough for us to know that the proposed plan is both impracticable and unjust. It is a system that is calculated to injure the West by depreciating the value of her agricultural productions and mineral wealth to the extent of the tax imposed. It is hardly possible to suppose that any one believes that the system is at all practicable. Who believes that these nine States can act in harmony on a single question? How is their business to be conducted? Is there to be a Constitution to bind them together, and a new Congress to legislate for them? Is there to be a new

Supreme Court to decide disputes arising between them, and a new army raised and supported to enforce its decrees? It seems to me that a more absurd and preposterous project was never presented to Congress, and a more suicidal policy could not be adopted by the West.

4. I regard the homestead bill as beneficent in its character, and as calculated to greatly advance the material interests of Iowa. But I cannot give my assent to all the provisions of the bill recently passed by the House of Representatives, and now pending in the Senate. I cannot assent to the principle of discriminating against foreigners who come to the country with a *bona-fide* intention to become citizens. I do not concur in the recent promulgations of Southern politicians, that our institutions are in danger from foreign immigration, and I abhor the sentiment announced by Senator Butler,[1] that Iowa would be more prosperous with the institution of slavery than with her industrious and patriotic German population.

I believe that the homestead bill, now under consideration in the Senate, should be so amended as to allow foreigners coming to our shores with the intention to remain, and who declare their intention to become citizens, to enjoy the same advantages under the law as though they were born on American soil.

5. But the most important of all the questions now engrossing the public attention is the attempt to introduce slavery into the Territories of Nebraska and Kansas, by the repeal of the Missouri Compromise act.

Let us briefly review the history of the Missouri Compromise, and the reasons given for its violation.

When the Constitution of the United States was adopted, acquisitions of new territory were never contemplated. Slave-labor was then unprofitable, and it was thought to be alike the interest and the duty of the slave States to gradually abolish slavery, but in such way and at such time as might be most convenient to themselves. Upon the supposition that successful efforts would be made to accomplish this result, the North consented to the slave representation in Congress, as provided in that instrument.

By the treaty with France, in 1803, the United States acquired a vast domain, then known as Louisiana, embracing the whole coun-

[1] In the Senate of the United States, February 24.

try between the Mississippi River and the Rocky Mountains, and bounded on the north by the British possessions, and on the south by the Gulf of Mexico. That the Constitution never contemplated such a purchase is sufficiently shown by its contemporaneous history and exposition, and by the solicitude of President Jefferson that it should be amended solely to confirm this acquisition. The commercial advantages derived from the purchase, however, were so great that the *people* of the country at once confirmed it, and the Constitution was never amended. From this Territory of Louisiana, which was bought with the common treasure of the country, the slave States of Louisiana, Arkansas, and Missouri, have been created, and the free State of Iowa.

When Missouri applied for admission into the Union, in 1820, her application was resisted by the North on the ground that the expectation of the gradual abolition of slavery, entertained by the whole country at the time of the adoption of the Constitution, had not been realized—that slavery was about to swallow up the entire country acquired from France, and thus, by virtue of the slave representation allowed by the Constitution, an undue preponderance would be obtained in Congress and in the electoral colleges by the slave-owners of the South over the freemen of the North. She was finally, however, admitted into the sisterhood of States, but not until after the adoption of the Missouri Compromise act, the eighth section of which declares:

"That in all that territory ceded by France to the United States, under the name of Louisiana which lies north of thirty-six degrees and thirty minutes of north latitude, not included within the limits of the State contemplated by this act, slavery and involuntary servitude, otherwise than as the punishment of crimes, shall be and is hereby FOREVER PROHIBITED."

This act was passed *thirty-four years ago*, at the instance of the South, and almost exclusively by Southern votes. By that act the admission into the Union of the slave State of Missouri was secured, and all of the country purchased from France north of 36° 30′ was FOREVER dedicated to freedom. The question of the constitutionality of the eighth section was submitted by President Monroe to his cabinet, then composed of John Quincy Adams, John C. Calhoun, William H. Crawford, Smith Thompson, and William Wirt, each of whom gave a written opinion in its favor, and, from that time until the present, it has been regarded as inviolable as the Constitution itself.

It is now pretended that this prohibition of slavery north of the line indicated is unconstitutional and void. That Mr. Douglas and his friends did not so consider it in 1845 is shown by the amendment he proposed to the joint resolution admitting Texas into the Union, which reads, "and in such States as shall be formed out of said territory, north of said Missouri Compromise line, slavery or involuntary servitude, except for crime, shall be prohibited." That he did not regard it as unconstitutional in 1848 is shown by his attempt to extend the Missouri Compromise line to the Pacific Ocean, and apply it to the country acquired from Mexico by the Treaty of Guadalupe Hidalgo. On the 10th of August, 1848, he offered in the Senate the following proposition:

"That the line of 36° 30′ of north latitude, known as the Missouri Compromise line, as defined by the eighth section of an act entitled 'An act to authorize the people of the Missouri Territory to form a constitution and State government, and for the admission of such State into the Union on an equal footing with the original States, and to prohibit slavery in certain Territories,' approved March 6, 1820, be and the same is hereby declared to extend to the Pacific Ocean; and the said eighth section, together with the compromise therein effected, is hereby revived and declared to be in full force and binding for the future organization of the Territories of the United States, in the same sense and with the same understanding with which it was originally adopted."

In favor of this proposition voted every Southern Senator who voted for the repeal of the compromise, now in Congress. How could the principle contained in the eighth section of the Missouri Compromise be constitutional in 1845 and in 1848, and be unconstitutional now? And if it *has* no constitutional validity, wherefore the necessity or propriety of repealing it?—Why not suffer the courts to decide the question without any legislative interference on construction?

The unconstitutionality of this prohibition is a new discovery. The committee of the Senate, that reported the Nebraska bill on the 4th of January last, did not think of basing the repealing attempt upon any such argument. It is an after-thought, designed to cover up a discomfiture on other arguments. Until the present time, the acts of Territorial Legislatures have been subject to revision by Congress, and nobody ever doubted the power or the propriety of that revision. Congress no power to prohibit slavery in the Territories! The Constitution expressly declares that "Congress SHALL have power to dispose of and make all needful rules and regulations respecting the territory of the United States." The great expounder of the Constitution, Mr. Webster, whose opinions were regarded by his enemies even as of more than ordinary value, says:

"The power, then, of Congress over its own territories, by the very terms of the Constitution, is unlimited. It may make all 'needful rules and regulations,' which of course include all such regulations as its own views of policy or expediency shall from time to time dictate. If, therefore, in its judgment it be needful for the benefit of a Territory to enact a prohibition of slavery, it would seem to be as much within its power of legislation as any other act of local policy. Its sovereignty being complete and universal as to the Territory, it may exercise over it the most ample jurisdiction in every respect. It possesses in this view all the authority which any State Legislature possesses over its own territory; and if any State Legislature may, in its discretion, abolish or prohibit slavery within its own limits, in virtue of its general legislative authority, for the same reason Congress also may exercise the like authority over its own Territories. And that a State Legislature, unless restrained by some constitutional provision, may do so, is unquestionable, and has been established by general practice."

Such has been the uniform opinion of the statesmen and jurists of the country, until it was discovered that the interests of certain presidential aspirants required the introduction of slavery into Nebraska and Kansas. Such, too, has been the legislation of the country.

It is also said that the Compromise acts of 1850 were inconsistent with, and hence repealed, the Compromise of 1820. If so, the question is again pertinent, Why then attempt to repeal it a second time? Why not allow the question to rest until an opportunity is afforded the proper tribunals to settle it conclusively?

If the Compromise of 1820 was repealed by that of 1850, then it was a fraud. It was not so understood by the people of the country, nor by Congress. It is well known that not a man voted for the measures of 1850, who entertained the most remote idea that those measures interfered with or affected in any degree the Compromise of 1820. In no one of the thousand speeches made on the Compromise of 1850, in Congress and out of Congress—in none of the comments of the press—was such an idea expressed or even remotely insinuated. On the contrary, until the introduction of the Nebraska bill into the Senate, on the 4th of January last, the Missouri Compromise was everywhere, and by everybody, regarded as irrepealable and inviolable as the Constitution. Mr. Webster, in his celebrated compromise speech on the 7th of March, 1850, declared:

"I now say, sir, as the proposition on which I stand this day, and upon the truth and firmness of which I intend to act until it is overthrown, that there is not at this moment in the United States, or any Territory of the United States, one single foot of land, the character of which, in regard to its being free Territory or slave Territory, is not fixed by some law, and some irrepealable law beyond the power of the action of this Government."

The irrepealable law that settled the character of Nebraska as a free Territory, was the Missouri Compromise act. To the maintenance of that law the public faith was pledged, and that great man little thought that so soon after his death an open and wanton attempt would be made to violate it.

An attempt has also been made to raise a popular clamor against any restraints upon what is called *squatter sovereignty*. It is said that if Congress *has* the power to legislate on the subject of slavery in the Territories, yet in justice to the people of the Territories it should not be exercised. It is somewhat singular that the same men who used this argument were all found voting against a proposition to allow the people of the Territories to elect their own officers. According to the doctrine of Mr. Douglas and his obedient followers, the people of the Territories are fully competent to do their own legislation, but are wholly incompetent to elect their Governor, judges, and other public servants. The President has the power to appoint Governors for the Territories, who by virtue of the veto power can control the legislation of the people. He has the power to appoint judges, who are in no degree responsible to the people, and who may be required to obey the Federal authorities at the risk of being evicted from office. All the officers of the Territories are to be foreign officers—appointed by a foreign authority—in no way amenable to the people, and have the power to set at defiance the popular will of the Territories, and will be required to do it, when it comes in conflict with the slavery propagandists at Washington. What a commentary is here presented of the doctrine of "squatter sovereignty!"

On the 2d of March last, an amendment was offered in the Senate to the Nebraska and Kansas bill, adding a distinct declaration of the right of the people to exclude slavery if they chose, and it was rejected by a vote of thirty-six to ten. Against this proposition were arrayed the following believers in "squatter sovereignty:"

Messrs. Adams, Atchison, Badger, Bell, Benjamin, Brodhead, Brown, Butler, Clay, Clayton, Dawson, Dixon, Dodge of Iowa, Douglas, Evans, Fitzpatrick, Gwin, Houston, Hunter, Johnson, Jones of Iowa, Jones of Tennessee, Mason, Morton, Morris, Pettit, Rusk, Sebastian, Slidell, Shields, Yancey, Walker, and Williams.

All the peculiar friends of non-intervention were found voting against the amendment. How sincere were their professions of non-intervention, the country can decide. They have certainly furnished some beautiful *illustrations* of their belief in "squatter sovereignty." It must be a singular sovereignty over the subject of slavery which cannot be declared capable of excluding it!

One would suppose that the new principles of "squatter sovereignty" would be comprehensive enough to allow aliens the same rights of citizenship that they enjoy in other Territories. But the man who imagines so would be egregiously mistaken. The bill that passed the Senate, and for which Mr. Douglas and all his willing followers voted, denies to the "squatters" who happen to have been born on the banks of the Rhine or the Shannon, and who reside in these Territories, the privilege of voting for or against the constitution of the new States, even after making declarations of their intention to become citizens. And this, too, when the uniform practice has been to grant the elective franchise to foreigners under such circumstances. Five hundred slaveholders from Virginia or South Carolina may carry slaves into the Territory and legislate for the protection of slave property, while five thousand German settlers—free laborers—who become landholders in the Territory, and have made oath of their intention to become citizens, shall have no control in its government and no opportunity to protect themselves against the degrading competition with slave-labor. Another evidence of the meaning of this doctrine of "squatter sovereignty!"

And to what does this doctrine of "squatter sovereignty" tend if carried to its legitimate conclusions? What is to prevent the Legislature of Utah from declaring that no man shall enjoy the rights of citizenship in that Territory unless he becomes a member of, and pays tithes to, the Mormon Church? What is to hinder the Catholics from taking possession of New Mexico, the Methodists of Nebraska, and the Presbyterians of Kansas? Why cannot the first thousand settlers create a state religion in each Territory, and exclude people of all other creeds from the rights of citizenship? Where will be the remedy against such religious and political tyrranny? Not in Congress; for, according to the theory of "squatter sovereignty," it has no legislative jurisdiction over the Territories. Not at the ballot-box; for none but the state religionists will be entitled to the elective franchise. Revolution, revolution by the sword, will be the only remedy.

It has been asserted by some of the advocates of this infamous attempt to nationalize slavery, that the first violation of the Missouri Compromise was by the North, and that that violation now justifies the South in entirely repudiating it. How, when, and where was it violated by the North? Why, forsooth, because Northern Senators and Representatives refused to extend the compromise line of 36° and 30′ through to the Pacific Ocean! Is there a man in the State who does not know that the Missouri Compromise line only applied to the country purchased from France? Does it not by its very terms apply only to the Territory of Louisiana? What right, then, had the South to demand or expect that it should be extended and applied to country afterward acquired? Upon this slender foundation is built this whole argument against the compromise, and in favor of its violation by the South.

It is urged by some that if the Missouri Compromise *is* repealed, slavery will not become a permanent institution in Nebraska and Kansas. So it was said of Missouri thirty-four years ago. It was then confidently predicted, in Congress and elsewhere, that slaves would be excluded from that State by the action of the State government. Instead of this being the case, they have increased from that time to the present, at the rate of three thousand a year, and

Missouri now contains more than one hundred thousand slaves! Those who are most familiar with the institution, and with the Territories of Nebraska and Kansas, entertain no doubt but that they will become slave States. Senator Atchison, who lives near the line of Nebraska, and is a large slaveholder, expressed the opinion a year ago, that but for the Missouri Compromise they would become extensive slaveholding States. He is said to have expressed the same opinion at the time of the passage of the bill by the Senate, provided his amendment disfranchising the Germans and Irish should be adopted, and it was adopted accordingly. And why would they not become slave States? They embrace a rich agricultural country. The soil and climate are well adapted to the production of corn, hemp, tobacco, and all the cereals. They are in close proximity to the slave States of Arkansas and Missouri. They are in the same parallel of latitude with Missouri, Kentucky, Maryland, and Virginia.

What does the history of the West teach us of the insidious and aggressive character of slavery? The sixth article of the Northwestern Ordinance, the provisions of which, until the past winter, have been regarded as imperative as the Constitution, declares that—

"There shall be neither slavery nor involuntary servitude in said Territory otherwise than in the punishment of crimes, whereof the party shall have been duly convicted."

When the first Constitutional Convention of Ohio assembled in 1802, a committee of nine members was appointed to prepare and report a bill of rights. A proposition was made to incorporate a clause that "no person shall be held in slavery, if a male, after he is thirty-five years of age, and if a female, after twenty-five years of age," and was voted down by a vote of *five* to *four*. This in a Territory where slavery had been for fifteen years excluded. In the same year the Legislature of Indiana Territory petitioned Congress to suspend the operation of the sixth article of the same Ordinance for the space of ten years. The petition was refused. These propositions were evidently designed to prepare the way for the permanent establishment of slavery in Ohio and Indiana, and, had the authority been vested in the Legislature of Indiana, that State would now be a slave State.

Every one familiar with the early history of this State knows that, but for the prohibitions of the Missouri Compromise act, and of the Northwestern Ordinance, the provisions of which were extended over Iowa by the organic law of the Territory, this would to-day be a slave State. Prior to 1838, when the Territory of Iowa was organized, numerous slaves had been introduced in all the principal towns and villages. They had been purchased and brought here for the alleged reason that servants were scarce, or could not be procured at all. The very first decision made by the Supreme Court of the Territory was in the case of the negro Ralph, who had been retained by his master in slavery, in the County of Dubuque. Other suits of the same character followed, and the slaves were either run by their owners from the State, or allowed their freedom here. Had the question remained open, or had the Supreme Court decided that it was a matter for determination by the Territorial Legislature, there would have been found men enough about the villages and towns to mould the legislation of the Territory in favor of slavery. And if there is no expectation that slavery will take possession of Nebraska, why the strenuous effort to repeal the Missouri Compromise?

If there is one State in the Union more interested than another, in the maintenance of the Missouri Compromise, it is the State of Iowa. With a free, enterprising population on the west, our State will be vastly benefited by an early organization of Nebraska. With a slave State on our western border, I see nothing but trouble and darkness in the future. Bounded on two sides by slave States, we shall be intersected with underground railroads, and continually distracted by slave-hunts. Instead of having a population at the west who will sympathize with us, we shall find their sympathies and interests constantly antagonistic to ours. The energies of our people will be paralyzed, our works of internal improvement will languish, and the bright anticipations of the future greatness of Iowa forever blasted. In the boastfulness of anticipated triumph, the citizens of Iowa have been told by a Southern Senator[1] how much better would be the condition of our State with negro slaves than with our foreign population. A distinguished Representative from Georgia[2] has announced that in fifteen years Iowa will be a slave State. I sincerely believe that, should the Missouri Compro-

[1] Hon. A. P. Butler, of South Carolina.

[2] Hon. Alexander H. Stephens.

mise be repealed, there will soon be a contest for the mastery between freedom and slavery on the soil of Iowa. The principle of non-intervention so strenuously contended for by the South will soon be extended to the free States of the Northwest. It is already contended in some quarters that slaves are mere appendages and attachments to the person, and that the owner has the same right to remove them to a free State that he has to remove his cattle and horses. Let the Missouri Compromise act be repealed, and this will be the next question to be met. Citizens of Iowa, are you ready to meet this issue? Are you prepared for the conflict that must assuredly come? Whatever may be your opinions of the abstract question of slavery, or whatever might be your opinions of the Missouri Compromise, were it a new question, are you ready and willing to disturb it? Do you believe it right to open this question which was settled thirty-four years ago by Southern votes, and as the South desired? Are you willing to sanction a palpable violation of the public faith, merely for the sake of nationalizing slavery, and having another slave State adjoining our own? Shall populous, thriving villages and cities spring up all over the face of Nebraska, or shall unthrift and sparseness, stand-still and decay, ever characterize that State? Shall unpaid, unwilling toil, inspired by no hope and impelled by no affection, drag its weary, indolent limbs over that State, hurrying the soil to barrenness and leaving the wilderness a wilderness still, or shall it be thrown open to the hardy and adventurous freemen of our own country, and to the constantly-increasing tide of foreign exiles?

So far as the Senate of the United States is concerned, this fraud has been consummated. The Nebraska and Kansas bill, with its attendant wrongs, has passed that body by a large majority. It is now pending before the House of Representatives. Its advocates predict that it will be triumphantly passed into a law. They claim that the people desire and will sanction its enactment. To obtain an evidence of the approbation of the people, they have attempted to rally the Democratic party to its support. The *Burlington Gazette*, the recognized organ of the Iowa Senators, has sounded the tocsin of party. In its issue of the 30th of March last, in speaking of this measure, it declares:

"It is in vain to say the bill is not a party question; the national Democrats of the North are for it, almost to a man; and these constitute nine-tenths, or more, of the Democratic party there; the Whigs and Free-Soilers alone are opposed to it. It is true that in the South both parties are united on the subject. . . .

"It is an eminently popular measure, and must ultimately prevail. It is founded on truth and justice, and the longer it is before the people, the more popular it must become. The sober, second thought will rally all reflecting, honest men to its side, and it is bound to be triumphantly sustained. On this we are willing to stake our existence."

A majority of the Democratic press in the State have followed the example of the *Gazette.*

Fellow-citizens, shall this attempt to induce you to support this measure by the force of party ties and affinities succeed? Is there no moral and high political responsibility resting upon you in this matter? Are you not bound by the highest considerations of duty to assist in building up the institutions of the empire on our western border on a substantial and free basis? The Constitution has given you the power through your Senators and Representatives to "make all needful rules and regulations" respecting the Territories of the United States, and will you shrink from the discharge of that duty? Are you willing to jeopardize the interests of Iowa by surrounding her by slave States? Will you exclude your own children, and the free laborers of Iowa, from those fertile Territories, or force them to compete with slave-labor? What object can be gained for Iowa by the repeal of the Missouri Compromise? On the other hand, what interest of the State will not be jeopardized or destroyed?

I am aware that, for entertaining these opinions of the Nebraska question, and for fearlessly expressing them, I am denounced in some quarters as an abolitionist. I heed not the senseless charge. It is too late in the day for any man to be deterred from expressing his opinions by the mad-dog cry of abolitionism. No imputations or false charges shall force me to be false to my convictions of duty and right. I will not surrender the right of private judgment on this or any other subject, to avoid a false clamor, or a willful perversion of my sentiments. I do not attempt or desire to interfere with slavery in the slaveholding States. I do not seek to violate any of the compromises of the Constitution. I am content that the slaveholders of the South may possess their slaves, and be responsible for their control over them to their own laws and to their consciences. I will not even presume to judge them. But, with the blessing of God, I will *war and war continually* against the abandonment to slavery of a single foot of soil now consecrated to freedom. Whether elected or defeated—whether in office or out of office—the Nebraska outrage shall receive no "aid or comfort" from me. And I here declare that, while I am as anxious as any man for the speedy organization of the new Territories, yet I will not only everywhere and at all times oppose their organization under a bill allowing the introduction of slavery, but, should the present bill pass, I will advocate its repeal and oppose the admission of Nebraska and Kansas into the Union as slave States.

I have thus briefly and frankly given my views of the issues presented by the Whig Convention on the 22d of February last, and that are involved in the approaching canvass. They have not been hastily adopted. They will not be hastily abandoned. Knowing them, the electors of the State can determine whether they are such as they will be willing to sanction at the ballot-box. The result is with them.

JAMES W. GRIMES.

BURLINGTON, *April* 8, 1854.

21.—*To Rev. Henry Clay Dean, West Point, Lee County.*

BURLINGTON, *March* 2, 1854.

I have received your letter of the 28th of February, in which you addressed to me the following question: "Should you be elected, will you veto, or approve, such a law, consistent with the constitution of the State, as may be enacted by the State Legislature, for the prohibition of the sale of ardent spirits as a beverage?" And I hasten to reply, most unequivocally, that I should certainly approve such an act.

It has ever been a principle of the Whig party that the Executive veto should be exercised only for the greatest constitutional reasons. All reasons of expediency should be determined by the legislative department of the Government. And should I be so fortunate as to be elected, I should endeavor to avoid encroachment in the remotest degree upon the prerogative of that department.

22.—*To Mrs. Grimes.*

OSKALOOSA, *June* 4, 1854.

I have now been absent one week, have made six speeches, none less than one hour and a half long, and, what is singular, I am entirely well, except that my throat is a little out of order. I have had very good audiences in point of numbers and respectability, and at three of my meetings have had the ladies to hear me. Yesterday I was honored with the presence of Mrs. Frances D. Gage, and took tea with her at Mr. Dart's. I found her more agreeable in conversation, and less manly in her intercourse, than I had expected. She is evidently a well-informed, talented woman, and I presume is doing much good. I have heard her lecture twice, last evening on temperance; both lectures were good.

I think the prospects for me in this region are very good, but there is no knowing how men's minds may change between this and the day of election. I shall start on in a few minutes, and speak at Pella to-morrow. It is monstrous hard work that I have undertaken, and I am fearful that I shall not be able to perform all that is allotted me to do.

23.—*To* ——.

COUNCIL BLUFFS, *June* 16, 1854.

Your favor in regard to traveling on Sunday is received. I started from Burlington between six and seven o'clock on Sunday evening, because I knew I would be too exhausted to speak at Mount Pleasant, if I rode all the way there on Monday morning. I therefore rode to New London Sunday night, mostly after dark. Since then, I rode from seven to ten o'clock one Sunday evening. The other Sundays I have laid up, and have pressed through on week-days, much to my inconvenience and fatigue. I endeavor to respect the opinions, prejudices, and inclinations of both my friends and enemies. I think I have done nothing wrong, and that there is no good occasion for fault-finding. There would not be, if I traveled all the day. I am proclaiming the great gospel of liberty wherever I go. I flatter myself that I have already done more good to the cause of humanity and liberal ideas than has ever been done by all the speeches made in the State, and by many sermons. I have had large audiences, and very attentive ones. I have no fears of the result.

24.—*To Mrs. Grimes.*

COUNCIL BLUFFS, *June 16th.*

I am well, though fatigued and worn down by traveling and speaking. I have undertaken too much hard labor, but am resolved to persevere unto the end. I speak here this afternoon. I have poorer prospects before me here than at any point I have been. The majority of the people here are Nebraskaites and whiskey-men. I write in the midst of a crowd, and am in trouble to find time to do anything.

GLENWOOD, MILLS COUNTY, *June 18th.*

I had just time, night before last, to merely acknowledge your letter. I have since read it two or three times, and each time with additional pleasure. It affords me words of encouragement and hope, from one by whom I desire to be encouraged more than by all others in the world—one whose approbation I seek more than the approval of all my other kind friends. The sentiments you utter make me strong. They have caused me to renew my resolution to continue to proclaim the gospel of liberty until the day of the election.

When I came here I found that the population is entirely Southern. My friends were tender-footed, and did not wish me to denounce the Nebraska infamy. I did not tell them what I would do, but when we met in the court-house I told them that the principles I maintained on the Mississippi River I should maintain and express just as boldly on the Missouri River. I then discussed the subject an hour, and pleased both my friends and enemies. They all saw that my principles did not change with a change of latitude, and they applauded me to the skies. Although this is a Democratic county, my friends assure me that I will receive fifty majority in the county.[1]

I am much better now than a week ago. I think I shall be able to stand the canvass until the election. It is a comfort to know that before three weeks elapse I shall be at home. But I shall be compelled to absent myself again for three weeks. Then, thank Heaven, the election takes place, and this business will be over.

At the election (August 3d), of 43,594 votes, Mr. Grimes received a majority of 2,486. His energetic canvass of the

[1] The vote of Mills County was 177 for Grimes, 155 for Bates.

State, and the result, were regarded with great interest throughout the country. Said the *Galena Gazette:*

The freemen of the North are indebted to Mr. Grimes, in a great measure, for one of the most brilliant victories ever achieved in the annals of politics. His recent contest, and its results, have given him a national reputation which he has nobly earned.

In his native State his election was welcomed as a fitting rebuke to another son of New Hampshire, who had said in his first message to Congress (December, 1853), in relation to the peaceful condition of the country, at that time, upon the question of slavery:

This repose is to suffer no shock during my official term, if I have power to avert it.

Mr. Grimes and President Pierce were natives of adjoining towns. Hon. S. P. Chase wrote (Cincinnati, September 24th):

Allow me to congratulate you on the result in Iowa. It surpasses my hopes, and is due in great measure to your indefatigable exertions. We all owe you a debt of gratitude. But now as much of wisdom will be needed to secure the fruits of victory and permanent ascendency, as there was of courage, energy, and tact, to gain it. Your message will be looked for with great interest.

Two years later, Mr. Chase wrote (August 23, 1856):

Your election was the morning star. The sun has risen now.

Soon after his election, it was proposed in some quarters that he should be sent to the Senate of the United States. He at once gave it to be understood that he should fill the term of office for which he had been chosen by the people. *The Hawkeye,* October 12th, said:

The papers need not trouble themselves about having Mr. Grimes presented to the Legislature for election to the United States Senate. He was elected to be simply Governor of the State, which position he is satisfied to occupy, at least for the term of his election; after that, we cannot speak for him. He will then be in the hands of his friends, for Governor, or the Senate, or something else; maybe for President, for aught we know.

5

25.—*To Hon. S. P. Chase, Cincinnati.*

BURLINGTON, *October* 3, 1854.

I regret that I am unable to meet you at Galena. Other engagements, and my ill health, will prevent. I wish much to have a few minutes' conversation with you. I shall take about the ground you suggest, in my message. I have not prepared it, but I have thought I would occupy about the positions taken by the recent Whig State Convention in Massachusetts.

I am astonished at my own success in this State. I fought the battle nearly alone. My colleagues on the congressional ticket were dead weights; one of my colleagues on the State ticket declined, because I was too much of a Free-Soiler; and I had the *Burlington Hawkeye*, a professedly Whig paper, and the whole *silver-gray* interest, openly against me. Thank Heaven! I triumphed over the combined powers of darkness, and carried a handsome majority (ten) of the Legislature with me. We lost two members by drawing lots, where there was a tie.

The southern half of our State is strongly pro-slavery, but I think we will be able to carry a majority with us for free principles, and for a disconnection with slavery. The Whigs are just now learning that it does not hurt them to be called "abolitionists, woolly-heads," etc., and, when the great contest of 1856 comes on, they will be prepared for and callous to all such epithets. The north third of our State will be to Iowa, politically, what the Western Reserve is to the State of Ohio. No man can obtain the electoral vote of Iowa, in 1856, who was in favor of the passage of the Nebraska bill, and who will not favor the repeal of the "Fugitive-Slave law." Such, at any rate, is my opinion at *this* time.

I would be much pleased to hear from you, and to receive any suggestions at any time when you have the leisure or inclination.

Mr. Chase wrote in reply (Cincinnati, October 31st):

The people are in advance of the politicians on the slavery question. Now is the time for that other wisdom, whose name is courage. Hence my solicitude for your message. You have the credit of fighting, under the most auspicious circumstances, the best battle for freedom yet fought. From your State, the extreme West, will most appropriately come the suggestions which shall shape this new movement. I feel thoroughly persuaded that if your message shall grapple directly and boldly with the question, and take the high but safe ground of consistent principle, you will do yourself the greatest honor, and your country the greatest good. Such a message cannot fail to have a most important and beneficial effect on the events of 1856, including the presidential election itself. He who speaks clearest will be best understood and most honored.

Mr. Chase wrote again (November 13th):

If I may judge of your forthcoming inaugural by the part you have sent me, it will be an excellent one. It does me good to think that a New Hampshire boy, and a Governor of a Western State, will have the honor of being the first to lay down the great principle on which the slavery question must be finally settled, if peacefully settled at all. As a New Hampshire boy, and Western man, I am proud of it.

The salary of the Governor was twelve hundred and fifty dollars a year. The term of office under the constitution was four years. Mr. Grimes was inducted into office on the 9th of December, 1854, the oath of office being administered by Hon. Maturin L. Fisher, president of the Joint Convention of both Houses, and delivered on the occasion the following

ADDRESS.

Gentlemen of the Senate and House of Representatives:

Having now, in your presence, assumed the duties of the office to which I have been elevated by the suffrages of my fellow-citizens, it becomes my duty, under the constitution, to call your attention to such subjects as I believe demand your consideration.

No one, however connected with legislation, can too highly estimate the responsibilities of his position. He cannot feel too deeply the delicacy of his labors, and his ignorance of the complicated structure and conflicting interests of society over which he is called to exercise control. To legislate is the noblest employment in which he can be engaged, and the most difficult of satisfactory execution.

It is so everywhere, but it is peculiarly so in a new and growing State, where the population is drawn from all parts of the civilized globe, where the public policy and public institutions are just being established, and where different portions of the State are in different conditions of progress and development. It is a difficult task to protect and advance the pioneer interests of our western settlements, and also encourage, and establish on a substantial basis, the commercial and manufacturing interests of the old counties, by general laws that shall operate equally and beneficently upon all. It is not an easy matter to lay strong and deep the foundations of the educational institutions of a new State, and to rear thereon superstructures that shall honor the State and bless mankind. The duty of restoring reason to those who are bereft of it, of giving sight to the blind and hearing to the deaf, by the establishment and proper endowment of charitable institutions; of repressing evil, of punishing crime, of stimulating industry, of protecting public virtue, and of maintaining the integrity of the State sovereignty, cannot be exercised without incurring grave responsibilities.

Government is established for the protection of the governed. But that protection does not consist merely in the enforcement of laws against injury to the person and property. Men do not make a voluntary abnegation of their natural rights, simply that those rights may be protected by the body politic. It reaches more vital interests than those of property. Its greatest object is to elevate and ennoble the citizen. It would fall far short of its design if it did not disseminate intelligence, and build up the moral energies of the people. It is organized "to establish justice, promote the public welfare, and secure the blessings of liberty." It is designed to foster the instincts of truth, justice, and philanthropy, that are implanted in our very natures, and from which constitutions and laws derive their validity and value. It should afford moral as well as physical protection, by educating the rising generation, by encouraging industry and sobriety, by steadfastly adhering to the right, and by being ever true to the instincts of freedom and humanity.

To accomplish these high aims of government, the first requisite is ample provision for the education of the youth of the State. The common-school fund of the State should be scrupulously preserved, and a more efficient system of common schools than we now have should be adopted. The State should see to it that the elements of education, like the elements of universal Nature, are above, around, and beneath all.

It is agreed that the safety and perpetuity of our republican institutions depend upon the diffusion of intelligence among the masses of the people. The statistics of the penitentiaries and alms-houses throughout the country, abundantly show that education is the best preventive of pauperism and crime. They show, also, that the prevention of those evils is much less expensive than the punishment of the one, and the relief of the other. Education, too, is the great equalizer of human conditions. It places the poor on an equality with the rich. It subjects the appetites and passions of the rich to the restraints of reason and conscience, and thus prepares each for a career of usefulness and honor. Every consideration, therefore, of duty and policy impels us to sustain the common schools of the State in the highest possible efficiency.

I am convinced that the public schools should be supported by taxation of property, and that the present *rate* system should be abolished. Under the present system of a *per capita* tax upon the scholars, the children of the poor are in a measure excluded from the benefit of the schools, while the children of the opulent are withdrawn from them to be educated in private institutions. Property is the only legitimate subject of taxation. It has its duties, as well as its rights. It needs the conservative influences of education, and should be made to pay for its own protection.

I suggest the propriety of establishing in each school district in the State a district-school library. I believe that an act appropriating to each district a small sum of money for this purpose, provided the district would appropriate an equal amount, would be received by the people with the highest satisfaction. It would establish in each district complying with the provisions of the act a *nucleus*, around which in a few years would be gathered respectable libraries that would be accessible to all. These libraries would be great aids in the diffusion of general intelligence.

I am not informed of the amount or condition of the university fund of the State. It is known, however, that a munificent grant of land was made by Congress for the establishment of a seminary of learning; that a large part of those lands has been sold, and that the proceeds have never been applied to any specific use, except the sum of five thousand dollars heretofore granted to the Medical School at Keokuk. I think the time has come when steps should be taken to carry out the design of Congress in making the grant. If the State can ever establish an institution of learning, it can be done under as favorable auspices now as at any future time. I do not believe it to be sound policy to establish a literary institution that shall come into rivalry with the various denominational colleges now struggling into existence. Those institutions should be encouraged, and not depressed. They can and will educate the young men who wish to enter the professions of law, physic, and divinity. But the State has a greater want than of lawyers and doctors. She wants educated farmers and mechanics, engineers, architects, chemists, metallurgists, and geologists. She needs men engaged in the practical duties of life, who have conquered their professions, and who are able to impart their knowledge to others. She wants farmers who shall be familiar with the principles of chemistry, as applied to agriculture ; architects and mechanics, who will adorn her with edifices worthy of so fair a land ; and engineers and geologists who will develop her resources, and thus augment the wealth and happiness of her citizens. This want can only be supplied by the establishment of a school of applied sciences. I have no hesitation, therefore, in recommending that the university fund be appropriated to establish a practical scientific or polytechnic school.

The State and county agricultural societies are doing much to improve agriculture and the industrial arts, and deserve encouragement from the government.

The General Assembly cannot be too urgently called on to take immediate steps to establish State charitable institutions. According to the most reliable information, there are now more than one hundred pauper insane persons in the State. One-half of these are confined in the common jails, and are thus placed beyond even a reasonable expectation of recovery; the other moiety are roaming at large, a terror to their friends and neighbors, and by exposure to exciting causes rendering their disease hopelessly incurable. Every dictate of humanity—every principle of sound public policy—demands that the State should make immediate provision for the care and treatment of this unfortunate class of our fellow-citizens.

There can be no question of a desire on the part of the people of the State that their constitution should be amended. It is needless at this time to allude to the arguments that may be urged in favor of a change in that instrument. The amendments can only be made by a constitutional convention. The only question now presented is, Shall the people have the privilege of determining for themselves, at the ballot-box, whether they want revision and amendment at all? Not a single valid argument can be urged against this proposition. A submission of the question of revision to the people can be attended with no expense, for, according to the constitution, it must be done at a general election. If the decision, therefore, is against revision, the State will sustain no injury; if in favor of it, the genuine doctrine of popular sovereignty will be vindicated.

There is a strong public sentiment in favor of a radical change of the present laws regulating the manufacture and sale of intoxicating liquors. Every friend of humanity earnestly desires that something may be done to dry up the streams of bitterness that this traffic now pours over the land. I have no doubt that a prohibitory law may be enacted that will avoid all constitutional objections, and meet the approval of a vast majority of the people of the State.

The public mind has been, and is now, greatly excited on the subject of slavery in the Territories of the United States. At the last session of Congress, that solemn compact, known as the Missouri Compromise, which had existed more than thirty years without any attempt to disturb it—which was passed at the instance of the South—and which the people of the whole country have been taught by the great expounders of the Constitution to regard as inviolable as the most sacred provisions of that instrument itself—was repealed. By that compromise, all that portion of the original Territory of Louisiana that lay north of the parallel of 36° 30′ was forever dedicated to freedom. By its repeal it is attempted to subject that vast domain to the withering influences of African slavery.

This only compromise that favored freedom was ruthlessly violated by the very men who were most clamorous for the maintenance of every compromise that favored slavery. It was done in defiance of the remonstrances of the people, and by a palpable violation of parliamentary rules. The motive with which it was done is apparent. While its few supporters in the North attempt to justify the act, and shield the perpetrators from reproach, by appealing to the doctrine of *popular sovereignty*, its principal supporters in the South utterly repudiate that doctrine, and openly avow that they will never submit to it. The primary motive was to extend the area of slave territory, and thus give a political supremacy to the slaveholding States, by virtue of representation of slave property.

The Federal Government was established "to secure the blessings of liberty," and not to perpetuate and extend human bondage. Its founders intended to confine slavery to its then existing limits. It was with this settled conviction of the policy of the government, and with the universal opinion, moreover, that new territory could not be acquired by purchase, that the several States consented to that provision of the Constitution which allows three-fifths of the slave population of the country to be enumerated as the basis of representation in the electoral colleges, and in the House of Representatives. But, without any change of the Constitution, the whole policy of the Government seems to be changed on this subject. Vast territories have been acquired. Five new slave States have been admitted into the Union from territory purchased with the common treasure of the country. The number of slaves has increased from 697,897 in 1790 to 3,204,313 in 1850, now represented by twenty-one votes in the electoral colleges and in Congress.

I trust that there is no citizen of Iowa who desires the General Government to interfere with slavery in the States of this Union. It is a local institution, and to the States that maintain it belong its responsibilities and its perils. But while the people of the North should scrupulously regard the rights of others, they should manfully maintain their own. They are recreant to their own interests; they betray the rights of their posterity; they give a fatal blow to the principles of free and equal government, when they consent to the creation of new slave States and a consequent further representation of slave property.

The removal of that great landmark of freedom—the Missouri Compromise line—when it had been sacredly observed until slavery had acquired every inch of soil south of it, has presented the aggressive character of that system broadly before the country. It has shown that all compromises with slavery, that are designed to favor freedom, are mere ropes of sand, to be broken by the first wave of passion or interest that may roll from the South. It has forced upon the country an issue between free labor, political equality, and manhood on the one hand; and on the other, slave-labor, political degradation and wrong. It becomes the people of the free

States to meet that issue resolutely, calmly, and with a sense of the momentous consequences that will flow from its decision. To every elector, in view of that issue, might appropriately be applied the injunction anciently addressed to the Jewish king, "Be strong, and show thyself a man."

It is both the interest and duty of the free States to prevent the increase and extension of the slave element of power, by every constitutional means. To do so successfully, they must adhere to the principles of the founders of the republic. In the view of those principles, slavery is a local institution, depending wholly on State laws for its existence and continuance. Freedom being the natural condition of all men, and no authority being delegated to the General Government to establish or protect slavery, Congress can pass no law establishing or protecting it in the Territories. If Congress can pass no such law, much less can it delegate such authority to the Territorial Legislatures, over whose acts it has ever exercised a supervisory and restraining power. By a wide departure from constitutional principles, slavery has been tolerated in some of the Territories. Let such toleration forever cease. Let the Government be brought back to its original purity. Let the principle be authoritatively announced and persistently adhered to, that there can be no slavery outside of State sovereignties. Let the Government, in all its relations, be divorced from the system, and the agitation of this subject will cease, the conscience of the North will be quieted, and the rights of the people of the South fully sustained. It is only by an entire disconnection of the General Government from the institution of slavery, that the people of the free States can find safety and honor. In no other way can they maintain their political equality, and stand acquitted before the bar of an enlightened public sentiment.

It becomes the State of Iowa—the only free child of the Missouri Compromise—to let the world know that she values the blessings that compromise has secured to her, and that she will never consent to become a party to the nationalization of slavery.

I desire to coöperate with the General Assembly in every measure that may tend to promote the prosperity of the State.

I trust that our mutual counsels will be characterized by calmness and prudence; and I devoutly pray that, in our respective spheres, we may be guided by "that wisdom which is from above."

26.—*To Mrs. Grimes.*

IOWA CITY, *December* 23, 1854.

I find my time entirely occupied with duties that properly pertain to my office, and others that are assigned me by the Legislature. They pretend that they have more confidence in my judgment than they had in my predecessors, and hence intrust to me various duties that have never been assigned to the Governors of the State. The Senate called on me a few days ago for a report and suggestions in relation to the insane, etc. I sent in a message yesterday in reply. They ordered two thousand copies to be published. It was prepared in a hurry, and does not amount to much.[1]

There has, as yet, been no senator elected. I understand that Warren went away with the impression that I was opposed to his election, and in favor of Harlan. He was never more mistaken. I preferred him to any one named, but I did not choose to mingle in the strife that was going on for the office. I did not believe that it became the position I occupy, and I still think so. I trust the result may be in favor of progress and freedom.

We have had a grand ball. There was a large crowd. I did not attend. I find that I shall have a great deal more to do than I

[1] I am an advocate for economy. But I conceive that it would be the poorest possible economy to erect any other than the most substantial buildings. Unlike the deaf, dumb, and blind, insane persons cannot be kept in ordinary buildings. Structures must be erected for their special use and treatment.

I think it would be wise to appoint commissioners of intelligence and character, with authority to visit asylums for the insane in other States, to obtain plans for proper buildings, and to lay these plans before the superintendents of those asylums for such suggestions as their experience may dictate. Improvements are being constantly made in the construction, ventilation, and heating, of such structures, and the State should avail herself of all such improvements.

It should be borne in mind that it will be but a few years before a second asylum for the insane will be required. This unfortunate class will increase with the population of the State. Massachusetts, with a population of 994,514, has 1,661 insane, or one in 604 of her population. She has three asylums filled to overflowing.

Vermont, with 314,120 souls, not as many as there are now in the State of Iowa, has 560 insane, or one in 569 of her population. Ohio is now erecting two new asylums, one in the northern and another in the southern part of the State. Our State asylum, therefore, should be located with a view to the future increase of the number.—*Extract from the Message.*

had expected, and that it will probably be necessary for me to visit Iowa City frequently. I shall endeavor to preserve my *honesty*, as you desire. The abuse of the *Gazette* does not disturb me in the smallest degree. Inclosed you will find a private letter from Mr. Giddings.[1] Do not show it to any one.

27.—*To* ——.

IOWA CITY, *January* 4, 1855.

I have been attempting to bring Davis forward, but ineffectually. There is no man in the State I prefer to him. To-day I had a talk, for the first time since last spring, with Browning, and endeavored to induce him to support Davis. He could not conscientiously do so, he replied, on account of Davis's Free-Soil proclivities. Mr. Harlan's friends think his chances are improving. I had my first conversation with him to-day, and talked to him frankly and freely. He avowed himself a Republican. Russell and the Washington and Henry County Free-Soilers nominated him. There are but ten Whigs in the Legislature. The other forty-five are known as anti-Nebraska men, Republicans, and Woolly-Heads. Harlan is too Free-Soil for the Whigs, and is regarded by the Free-Soilers as sufficiently antislavery for them. Father Turner says they will hold a meeting at Denmark, and wipe their hands of Whiggery. I say amen to that, if he means to get clear of such Whiggery as we have here.

There will be but very little done this winter by the Legisla-

[1] HALL OF REPRESENTATIVES, *December* 18, 1854.

MY DEAR GRIMES: Thanks for your message, for its doctrines. They are well and fearlessly expressed. One thing more, and Iowa will lead the great Republican party. Let your Legislature back up the Governor by resolutions, on your grounds, and your State, our youngest sister, will stand in a most admirable position. The point you make is the true issue, and I wonder that our State Legislatures have not taken it long since. It is now admitted by all that our issue must soon be fixed on the principle expressed in your message of a total separation of the Federal Government from all participation in the support of slavery, leaving the institution entirely with the States in which it exists, while we of the free States will stand lustrated from its contagion. This issue cannot be withstood in any free State; it will overwhelm all opponents in every free State.

"God bless and prosper you!" is the prayer of

Your obedient servant,

J. R. GIDDINGS.

His Excellency J. W. GRIMES.

ture. The Democrats have the Senate under their control, and seem to have adopted the do-nothing policy.

I find my office no sinecure. I have a hundred-fold more to do than I expected when I came here.

28.—*To* ——.

IOWA CITY, *January* 7, 1855.

The great national party of Iowa has exploded! The Democrats resolved in caucus to go for Browning. There were but two who stood out. He hoped to be elected on the first ballot, Friday morning, but, before the convention assembled, it was discovered that the Cook men would not vote for him. The Democrats did not, therefore, all rally on him, as had been agreed, because it was found that there would be no use in doing so. He received thirty-five Democratic votes, but not a Whig or anti-Nebraska man could be brought up to vote for him. After balloting a few times, our folks made a motion to reverse the order of things, and elect Judges of the Supreme Court first. This took our opponents by surprise, but we carried it. Wright and Woodward were elected judges. Isbell could only get forty-seven votes. He needed fifty. The convention adjourned to ten o'clock yesterday morning. The objection with four or five men was that Isbell was a Free-Soil elector in 1848 and in 1852. For the first time this winter I turned out to electioneer, and the Democrats discovered, in the morning, that Isbell would be elected on the first ballot. The Senate met at nine o'clock, and immediately adjourned to Monday morning. At ten o'clock, our-side Senators went into the House of Representatives, and a joint convention was declared. The recusant Senators filled the lobbies, and attempted to kick up a row, but were overawed by General Brown, the House Sergeant-at-Arms. After making speeches and wrangling two or three hours, all the Democratic representatives but three withdrew, and the convention proceeded to elect Isbell and Harlan, the Cook men voting for each of them. They received fifty-two and fifty-three votes respectively; fifty is a majority of a full convention. The proper officers have certified their election to me, and I will issue their commissions to-morrow.

There was not the least apology for this *revolutionary* proceeding. The parties engaged in it only attempt to excuse themselves on the ground that time enough had been expended in attempting to elect a Senator, and that they wanted to go on with the regular business of the session. Yet they adjourned over to Monday the moment that Parson Shearer got through his prayers. An unsophisticated man would imagine that they might as well spend the day in joint convention as in the drinking-houses about the city.

The Locofocos do not intend that anything shall be done this session, and imagine that they will hold the Whigs and anti-Nebraska men responsible for a failure to do the necessary legislation. We shall see. Harlan would not have been elected, if the Locos had not revolutionized. We would have elected Isbell. Let them hear from their acts in the papers.

29.—*To Mrs. Grimes.*

IOWA CITY, *January* 24, 1855.

I shall start home the last of this week. The Legislature has done an immense amount of business, more than has been done by any two Legislatures before. The Constitution bill; Maine law; Insane Asylum; Blind Asylum; Deaf and Dumb Asylum; Sunday law—that will prevent the dancing on the Sabbath that so much annoys us and our neighbors in the summer—Geological Survey bill—all have passed and become laws.

Very cold here; ball last night; thermometer 21° below zero; some of the members got drunk, and are ashamed of themselves today; capital of the State to be located at Fort Des Moines.

By an act of the General Assembly, approved January 24, 1855, the Governor, and Hon. Edward Johnstone, and Charles S. Clarke, M. D., were appointed commissioners to locate and superintend the erection of an asylum for the insane, at or near Mount Pleasant, in Henry County. In discharge of this duty, they purchased an eligible farm of one hundred and seventy-three acres, for twenty-five dollars per acre, one mile distant from Henry County Court-House; and visited the best institutions, and those recently erected, or in process of erection, in the Eastern States. After an examination of nine asylums, and consultation with architects, superintendents, and persons interested in institutions of the kind, they became satisfied that the General Assembly, in limiting the cost of the asylum to fifty thousand dollars, could have known as little what was required as the commissioners did before they began their investigations. They therefore determined to adopt such plans as they believed the wants and interests of the State demanded. Massachusetts was then commencing the erection of a third asylum, at Northampton, with all modern and desirable improvements. The commissioners procured transcripts of the plan, with a view to lay it before the General Assembly for approval. In the mean time, they proceeded with the excavation for the foundation, quarried rock, and made brick, but did nothing by which the State would be injured a thousand dollars, if the Legislature should disapprove their action. The General Assembly met in extra session, July, 1856, before the foundations of the building were laid, when the plans and specifications were submitted to committees of the Legislature, and after a thorough canvass of the whole matter an additional appropriation of fifty thousand dollars was made, not that the money would be needed before the next regular session, but as an indorsement of the recommendations of the commissioners.

The following is from Governor Grimes's message of January, 1858:

I am pleased to be able to say that the Hospital for the Insane at Mount Pleasant has advanced rapidly toward completion. The whole work is of the most substantial character; the plan of the structure meets the approbation of all who are familiar with the treatment of insane persons, and I think I hazard nothing in saying that when completed the hospital will be creditable to the State.

It may be thought by some that the size of this building is greater than the necessities of the State require, and more expensive than the finances of the State will justify.

In response to such suggestions, I beg leave to say that there are now insane people enough in the State to fill it to its utmost capacity, and that, while it has thus far been most substantially built, no money has been spent, nor does the plan contemplate the expenditure of any, for useless finish or adornment. When it is remembered that each patient requires a separate dormitory, inclosed by brick walls, thus requiring three hundred rooms for the inmates alone; that there are day-rooms and associated dormitories; dining-rooms, wash-rooms, bathing-rooms, and water-closets, in each of the sixteen wards; and that there must necessarily be large accommodations for baking, cooking, washing, ironing, etc., etc., for a household of nearly four hundred persons, the magnitude of the building and its cost will not be surprising.

No one who examines the census returns of this State f r 1856, and informs himself of the proportion of insane cases that ›ecome chronic and incurable when treated as they now are in this State, to the proportion that are cured when sent immediately to an asylum, will hesitate to believe that humanity, economy, and safety require that this institution should be immediately completed, and hereafter liberally supported.

In August, 1859, he made the following statement with reference to attacks of unscrupulous partisans upon the Republican party, and upon himself, in a foolish attempt to mingle politics with the asylum:

It was established, the commissioners appointed, and the plans for the building approved by a Legislature, of which one branch was Democratic, and the other anti-Democratic, and all appropriations for the work were voted for by members of all parties, without the slightest regard to their political predilections. No one of the commissioners was ever influenced in the slightest degree in his conduct as commissioner by political considerations. I am well satisfied that Judge Johnstone was not, and, as an evidence that the other commissioners were not, I will state that the man who was selected to supervise the whole work, Henry Winslow, Esq., ever was and is now an uncompromising Democrat, who never voted any other than the Democratic ticket, and was discharged from a similar position in the State of Maine, on account of his advocacy of Democratic principles, and his hostility to Know-Nothingism. He was employed by the commissioners on account of what were believed to be his merits, and they are happy to know that his conduct has justified the selection. He has employed, discharged, and paid every man employed about the work, purchased all the material, and superintended the construction of the entire building. Almost all the chiefs of the carpenter, brick-making, brick-laying, stone-cutting, stone-laying, etc., departments have been Democrats. I will say, however, that I have only learned this latter fact recently, for no one of the commissioners ever thought to inquire to what political party any employé belonged.

As a citizen, I protest against the precedent, now sought to be established, of making the humane institutions of the State shuttle-cocks, to be knocked back and forth between the two political parties. I have made this statement that the people may know the exact facts with regard to the asylum, and not by way of apology. I am proud of my connection with that institution, and the time is not remote when the Democratic party will be proud that their representatives stand so unanimously recorded in its favor. I read last year, in the speech of a candidate for a State office, that the asylum was established by the commissioners at Mount Pleasant especially for my benefit, as a large owner of real estate in that city and its vicinity. The laws of the State show that the location was made by the General Assembly, and the records of Henry County will show that I never owned but one lot in Mount Pleasant, which I sold long before the insane asylum was established there; and that I do not, and never did, own any property in the vicinity of that place. It must have required a very fertile imagination to conceive the idea that the proximity of a lunatic asylum would enhance the value of real estate!

Governor Grimes took a lively interest in providing for a geological survey of the State, and in securing the highest scientific ability for the work. Mr. James Hall, the State geologist, having named a new species of fossil shell, of large size, found in the Burlington limestone, *Spirifer Grimesii*, it afforded no small amusement to the Governor to find this represented by some jealous opponents as his act—done for the glorification of his name!

30.—*To Hon. Salmon P. Chase.*

Burlington, *April* 8, 1855.

What is going to be done in 1856? How are we to bring the antislavery forces into the field, and under whose standard? I believe a very large part of the friends of freedom in Iowa would be glad to see you a candidate for the presidency. I am one of the number. How do you feel on the subject, and are your aspirations that way inclined at present?

I think there is too much asperity of feeling throughout the country to justify us in placing Mr. Seward forward as the Republican candidate, and, to confess the truth, I must say that I have horror of New York politicians.

It seems to me that it is time to thoroughly organize the Republican party. The Know-Nothings have pretty well broken down the two old parties, and a new one, now organized, would draw largely from the foreign element that goes to make up those parties, while it will draw away one-half of the Know-Nothings, at least.

31.—*To Mrs. Grimes.*

BUFFALO, N. Y., *April* 15, 1855.

I have heard Mr. Hosmer preach twice to-day. In the forenoon his theme was the necessity and duty of obeying all the physical laws, as well as those that relate to the moral nature. He claimed that it was a sin to disobey the one as much as the other, inasmuch as we are taught the principles of the laws of Nature, by our instincts, experience, and observation, as conclusively as we are taught to believe any of the principles of the divine law. His afternoon discourse was on the duty of good citizens to sustain the prohibitory law, and was mostly a history of the rise and progress of the temperance movement during the last forty years. The Unitarian Society here is large and popular. Among its members are Mr. Fillmore, Judge Hall, of the United States Court, and, I presume, many other quite as good if not better men, though not so noted.

I have been through one or two insane asylums. There is one near Cleveland, Ohio, which I think we shall mostly copy. It is just completed, and is rather a model institution. When I went through the building, and saw how nearly the poor creatures are provided with every comfort, how tidy everything was, how the poor insane women had tastefully decorated their rooms with evergreens and flowers, and appeared for the most part happy, I rejoiced that I had so urgently called the attention of the Legislature to the necessity of providing an institution for our State, and that it will, in some measure, be built through my instrumentality.

I shall leave here for Utica, to examine the State asylum in that place.

NEW YORK CITY, *April* 21, 1855.

I spent one day in Utica, two in Albany. At Albany I saw Prof. Hall, and secured his services at the head of our geological survey. The State authorities of New York are unwilling to surrender his services entirely, and we cannot therefore have his entire time; but he will have the general direction and entire responsibility of the survey. He is one of the most modest, unobtrusive men I ever met, and all the various scientific cliques speak well of him. Prof. Whitney is to meet me here to-day, with Prof. Hall, when I expect to engage him, also, as State chemist. He seems to have a high reputation, also, in scientific circles, and I doubt not will prove to be an accession to our State.

32.—*To Hon. S. P. Chase.*

BURLINGTON, *May* 12, 1855.

I found yours of April 13th on my return from the East a couple of days ago.

I have more hope than you have. I am sanguine that we shall organize a party that will carry the elections in most of the Northern States in 1856, and in all of them in 1860. I abhor the principles of the Know-Nothings, so far as I understand them, yet I think they are accomplishing a great work in breaking down the old parties. When new parties are constructed, as they shortly will be, ours will be uppermost, in my opinion. I find encouragement in every movement that is made by our enemies. I think that they are resolved to ruin themselves, and that there is every prospect of success.

Names are of no consequence to me. There are objections in the minds of some to any name that can be used. I would be content with any designation, for I do not believe that a party name is of much consequence after all. People in New York seem to be as well satisfied with the titles of Hunker, Barnburner, Silver-Grays, and Woolly-Heads, as with the old distinctions of Whig and Democrat.

When in New York I saw Governor Medill. He told me that you would be the candidate against him, and that you would beat him. He seemed to think so in truth, and I hope he will not be disappointed.

During my trip I was attending to business of the State, and was not brought into connection with politicians, so that I could not learn what was going on. I was in New Hampshire forty-eight hours. It was conceded that Hale would be returned to the Senate. I learn that you are to deliver an oration in July, at Dartmouth. I hope you will arouse that pre-Adamite institution from its slumbers. It is from fifty to a hundred years behind the age, and the President is a real antediluvian. He is the strongest pro-slavery man in the North.

You see by the returns of our April election that Iowa "takes no step backward."

33.—*To Mrs. Grimes.*

BURLINGTON, *June* 17, 1855.

The Burlington people went on Wednesday on an excursion to Chicago.[1] They had a magnificent reception. I chose to remain at home. It is no pleasure to me to travel, or to make speeches, as I would have been compelled to do, had I been one of the company.

You ask why I did not attend the supper at Burlington, and speak, as desired. In the first place, I did not think it became me, occupying the position I do, as a temperance man, and a Governor, who recommended and approved a prohibitory liquor law, to attend a supper where it was known that champagne was to be drunk, and when I had reason to believe from past observation that some of the guests and hosts would be drunk. In the second place, no one of the company at my house wished to attend, and I thought it more becoming to remain with and entertain them, than to leave them to themselves; and in the third place, I abhor public dinners, and suppers, and especially do I detest dinner speeches. Another reason was this: unfortunately, some people think that I am a passable public speaker, and they try to dragoon me into speaking on all occasions. I wished them to know that if I have any gifts that way, they are not to be prostituted to their use at all times and everywhere. Do you need any more reasons assigned to convince you that I did right?

I have been rejoicing for two days over the result of the Know-Nothing National Convention at Philadelphia. I have been afraid of that organization. I knew it would break down in a year or two, but I was fearful that before dissolution it would give a pro-slavery

[1] To celebrate the opening of a railroad.

tinge to the sentiment of many of its members. It has gone overboard sooner than I expected, and I can see nothing now to obstruct a perfect anti-Nebraska and antislavery triumph. God speed the day! The right sentiment becomes firmer and more intense every day in this State. Strong ground was taken on the subject of slavery at the Congregational Association here. I am almost every day receiving letters, some from those who opposed my election a year ago, saying that, if I were now a candidate, it would not be necessary to canvass the State, and speak in every county, as I then did. And I do not believe it would be necessary. The outrages in Kansas have opened the eyes of the people to the *intent* with which the Missouri Compromise was repealed.

34.—*To Mrs. Grimes.*

BURLINGTON, *June* 20, 1855.

I would go East to you in July, were it not for the Insane Asylum. One hundred and fifty poor people in the jails and almshouses of the State are calling upon me to relieve them, as far as may be in my power, from their present wretched condition, and I would not be justified in turning a deaf ear to their petition. We may perhaps get it started during the month, so that I can be absent in August. Then, again, it is made my duty, in conjunction with the Secretary of State, to locate the Blind and Deaf and Dumb Institutions, and that ought to be done this summer, though there is no pressing necessity for it.

June 24th.—Exciting times here. Yesterday morning Dr. James[1] was captured on the Illinois side of the river, with a fugitive slave in his carriage. Bowie knives and revolvers were drawn on him by the Missourians in pursuit, and he and the negro were forced back to town. A process was afterward obtained, the negro thrown into jail, where he is to remain to await his trial on Tuesday. There was great excitement in town yesterday and to-day, and several personal collisions have grown out of it. How it will end no one knows. I shall certainly furnish no aid to the man-stealers, and it has been determined that the negro shall have able counsel, and a resort to all legal means for release, before any other is resorted to. I am sorry I am Governor of the State, for, although I can and shall

[1] Edwin James, M. D., botanist and historian of Long's Expedition to the Rocky Mountains, in 1820. Died October 28, 1861.

prevent the State authorities and officers from interfering in aid of the marshal, yet, if not in office, I am inclined to think I should be a law-breaker. It is a very nice question with me, whether I should act, being Governor, just as I would if I were a private individual. I intend to stand at my post, at all events, and act just as I shall think duty may require under the circumstances.

June 27th.—The negro is free, and is on his way to Canada. A great crowd yesterday in town. I sent on Monday to David's, *via* Yellow Spring and Huron, and told my friends and the friends of the slave to be present at the trial. They were here *en masse.* Marion Hall was filled, and guards were stationed at the door, to prevent any more people entering, and around the house. Rorer and Crocker appeared for the negro. When the decision was made, such a shout went up as was never heard in that hall before, and then it was caught up by the people outside the building, and the whole town reverberated. A thousand men followed Dr. James and the negro to the river, and rent the air with their cheers, as the boat was unlashed from her moorings, and started with the poor fellow on his road to freedom. Judge Lowe was brought from Keokuk Monday in the night, and a writ of *habeas corpus* was ready to be served, if the decision had been adverse to us. Writs were sued out against the negro-stealers for kidnapping, assault, etc., but, unfortunately, they escaped, before service could be made upon them. I am satisfied that the negro would never have been taken into slavery from Burlington.

Our friends, Colonel Warren and Rev. W. F. Cowles, showed that there was some marrow in their spinal columns.

Thus has ended the first case under the fugitive-slave law in Iowa. The State, the town, and the people, thank God, are saved from disgrace. How opinions change! Four years ago, Mr. —— and myself, and not to exceed three others in town, were the only men who dared express an opinion in opposition to the fugitive-slave law, and, because we did express such opinions, we were denounced like pickpockets. Now I am Governor of the State; three-fourths of the reading and reflecting people of the county agree with me in my sentiments on the law, and a slave could not be returned from Des Moines County into slavery. It is a blessed thing that there is no ebb to the principles and progress of freedom: it is always a flood-tide.

He attended a celebration of the Fourth of July, at Denmark. Among the sentiments of the day were the following:

The State of Iowa: Fortunate in geographical position on the Father of Waters, and midway between the two oceans, fortunate in natural resources, fortunate in an enterprising and rapidly-increasing population, and fortunate in the possession of a chief magistrate who knows how to employ all these advantages to make a model State.

Governor Grimes: As he has been fortunate enough to sign a Maine law in Iowa, may he remain Governor long enough to sign a personal-liberty law!

35.—*To Mrs. Grimes.*

BURLINGTON, *July* 5, 1855.

I received your letter from Bath. I am glad to learn that we have friends in the Fatherland, who feel an interest in us.

Yesterday, Mary and I spent the day at Denmark. There was a very agreeable celebration of the Fourth. The orator of the day was Mr. Dixon, of Keokuk. At the dinner-table Colonel Warren, Rev. E. Adams, and myself, made speeches. Everything passed off harmoniously, and very pleasantly. M—— enjoyed herself well with Vinnie and the other little girls. Vinnie has been attending singing-school, and sung with the other children in the church. Her term will be out next week, when I shall go after her. We are getting along very quietly and comfortably, though I must confess that we are a little lonely at times.

There is no news in town or country, except that everybody is coming to Iowa, and that has ceased to be news. There seems to be no check to the immigration. We shall before long be a *model* State, if we act right, and I hope we shall. As one of the signs of advancement, a lady has just become associated with her brother in the editorial management of a newspaper in Cedar County. I have, of course, become a subscriber.

Mr. Sumner, of Massachusetts, was at Davenport last Monday. I do not agree with the estimate of your friends of his intellectual calibre, as compared with Webster. They are not to be mentioned in the same day. They are as unlike as a beautiful silver brooklet meandering through a rich meadow, amid flowers and fragrance, is unlike the Niagara River, with the Falls thrown in for great occasions. I won't pretend to say that the brooklet, within its sphere, is not more useful than the river, and it is certainly more ornamental. Mr. Sumner is a fine scholar, a finished gentleman, and, what is wonderful in a politician, *has a heart;* but he has not half the *intellectual stamina* that Mr. Chase, of Ohio, has. Mr. C—— is generally right on small as well as great questions, and on these small matters Mr. S—— is frequently wrong. Mr. C—— has invariably voted against all the stealing bills that have been before Congress, and Mr. S—— has sometimes voted for them. By-the-way, I had a letter day before yesterday from Mr. C——, in which he says that he shall be nominated and elected Governor of Ohio. He says he does not wish the office, but thinks it his duty to consent to take it.

I cannot yet say when I can go East, if at all. Our plans for the asylum Dr. Bell cannot forward to us before the 15th of this month. It will require thirty days to advertise before the contracts can be let, which will be August 15th. From the 20th August to September 1st, Profs. Hall and Whitney will be here, to commence the geological survey, and I ought to be here to receive them, and concert measures to carry the work forward.

36.—*To Hon. S. P. Chase.*

BURLINGTON, *July* 16, 1855.

I duly received yours of the 27th of June, and have delayed answering it until I could hear from your Republican Convention of the 13th inst. I have just seen a telegraphic dispatch that you have been nominated, but I have not heard who are associated with you on the ticket, nor do I know the character of the platform upon which you go into the canvass. It is to be presumed, however, that the men who would nominate you would be sure that the resolutions should be orthodox upon the slavery question, and that is the only subject connected with politics about which I care a farthing.

I congratulate you upon your nomination, and, above all, I congratulate every lover of freedom and correct principles upon an event that shows such progress in the public sentiment of Ohio. The entire Northwest is guided in a great degree by the opinion and action of your State, and no one who is not in the habit of watching political occurrences pretty closely can appreciate the influence which your election by a large majority would have upon all the States west of you. You may be assured that the contest in Ohio will be watched with a great deal of anxiety by the friends of freedom everywhere, but nowhere more anxiously or more hopefully than by your friends in Iowa. Be sure that your majority shall not be less than fifty thousand. Cannot you in some way secure the German vote? We must in some way secure the German vote in the free States, and that class of citizens elsewhere will in a great measure follow the example of those in Ohio.

I am beginning to despair of carrying the presidential election next year. It appears to me that there is very little prospect of consolidating a party by 1856 that can accomplish much, as against the old-line Democracy. But you are a much better judge of this than I am. . . . I pray you, give me a good report of Ohio in October.

Mr. Seward (Auburn, September 8th) wrote to Mr. Grimes:

"I rejoice to see that you are preparing to meet the exactions of the slaveholders with firmness on the constitutional ground of State rights and State authority."

To a recently-arrived foreigner employed in his service, who asked the meaning of our day of Thanksgiving, he replied that it was in honor of Saint Jonathan; who, though a stranger in the calendar of Europe, was the patron saint of this free country, and worthy of respect by every one who wanted to be an American citizen. He issued the following

PROCLAMATION.

It is a venerated custom, in the older States of this Union, to dedicate one day toward the close of each year to public thanksgiving and praise to God for his continued blessings and protection. Such public recognitions of the government of a Divine ruler, and such manifestations of gratitude for benefits received at his hand, are worthy of imitation everywhere, and eminently become the people of Iowa. The past year has been crowded with blessings to our State. We have been exempt from pestilence. Abundant harvests have rewarded the toil of the husbandman. We have been preserved from intestine commotions and bloodshed. No distracting evils have occurred to impede our prosperity. Our population, wealth, and productive resources of every character, have increased in a wonderful degree. The facilities for educating the youth of the State have been greatly multiplied. Steps have been taken to establish charitable institutions corresponding to the progress and spirit of the age, and the demands of humanity. There are evidences all around that the State has made unexampled progress in everything that tends to promote her best physical and moral interests.

As citizens, we have enjoyed liberty without licentiousness. Civil and religious freedom, without distinction of party, sect or nationality, has been enjoyed by all.

Our nation has been prosperous. Peace has been preserved. While other nations have been plunged into bloody and desolating wars, we have been preserved from that great calamity.

For these, and for numberless other blessings, it has been deemed proper that a day should be set apart by the Executive of the State for praise and thanksgiving.

Therefore I, James W. Grimes, Governor of the State of Iowa, do designate Thursday, the 22d day of November next, as a day of public thanksgiving and praise to Almighty God for the innumerable blessings which, as a people and individuals, we have enjoyed.

I recommend that the people of the State assemble on that day in their respective houses of public worship, and devoutly raise their hearts and voices in gratitude to our heavenly Father for his past protection, and beseech its continuance. Let us give thanks that he reigns; that we are the product of his hand, and not of a blind, unreasoning chance. Let our hearts swell with gratitude for the blessings of civil and religious liberty; and pray for their extension to every human being. Let us be thankful that war, with its devastation, its slaughter, and its agonies, does not desolate our land; and pray that peace may be established among all mankind. Let us be thankful for the Government we have inherited from our fathers; and pray that it may ever be preserved worthy of the confidence and support of their descendants. Let us be thankful for comfort and plenty, for peace and order, for the means of education, for health, and for all other national and personal blessings. Let us ask to be preserved "alike from poverty and riches," from bigotry and intolerance, from pride and hatred, from anarchy and civil strife, from immorality and crime of every grade.

But above all, let us be thankful for the Christian religion, which has raised man from a state of barbarism, given him the means of intelligent happiness in this life, and the hope of glory in that which is to come.

In testimony whereof, I have hereunto set my hand and caused to be affixed the Great Seal of the State of Iowa.

Done at Iowa City, this 20th day of September, in the year of our Lord 1855, of the Independence of the United States the eightieth, and the State of Iowa the ninth.

By the Governor:

JAMES W. GRIMES.

GEORGE W. MCCLEARY, *Secretary of State.*

37.—*To Hon. S. P. Chase, Cincinnati, Ohio.*

BURLINGTON, *October* 14, 1855.

Allow me to congratulate you upon your glorious triumph. I had been all along fearful of the result of your election in Ohio, and the first returns received at Chicago (where I was, for the purpose principally of learning the result) indicated your defeat. But, happily, Know-Nothing and Nebraska news seems to travel very much as Whig election news used to, somewhat in advance of the mails and telegraphs. But Friday morning satisfied us how strong was the principle of free soil in the hearts of the people of Ohio. For surely that must be a strong and active principle that could cause such a glorious majority of the people of your State to forget all their past political proclivities and prejudices, and rally them around you. Your election has given to good men throughout the country new hope, and will inspire them to renewed and still more vigorous effort.

38.—*To Hon. S. P. Chase.*

BURLINGTON, *November* 2, 1855.

I am sorry that I am so poorly qualified to respond to your inquiries as to our future course and prospects. I am not properly informed of the condition of things in the States east of us, and cannot say what the prospects for the Republican organization may be; but I feel justified in saying that Iowa will be erect in any conflict that may come. I think that there can be no difficulty in combining all the opposition to the Nebraska swindle in this State, and arraying it under the Republican banner. I fear that this cannot be done in Illinois. I am satisfied that there is a large majority of the people of that State opposed to the Administration, and to Douglas, but there will be very great difficulty, if not an entire impossibility, to unite them so as to insure their defeat. From what I hear, such is the case, too, in Pennsylvania and Indiana. With these three States secured to us, the Republican cause would, I conceive, be certain of a triumph next year in the presidential canvass. Can they be secured?

I have heard (I have seen nothing of it) that one of the Cleveland papers has placed my name in its columns as a candidate for Vice-President, with yours for President. I am convinced that I can add nothing to your strength, nor to the strength of any man who may be a candidate—that I am not qualified for the position even if elected—that a political life is uncongenial with my habits of life and modes of thought; in a word, that the office is unfit for me, and I am unfit for the office. I am a Governor by accident. Nothing could have induced me to accept a nomination but a desire to expose to the people of the State the infamous exactions and encroachments of the slave-power. Being elected, I endeavored to play the Governor as well as possible; but I do not want another office, nor do I wish to be put in the attitude of a seeker for one. I beg you, therefore, if an opportunity presents, to dissuade our friend at Cleveland and all others, if there are any so foolish, or so blindly partial to me, from mentioning my name in connection with any office. I assure you that I would esteem it the highest honor of my life to have my name connected with yours in any way, but I conceive that the use of my name in connection with yours would only injure you in this instance. That I wish to avoid.

39.—*To Hon. S. P. Chase.*

BURLINGTON, *March* 28, 1856.

The difficulty with the Germans, if it can be called a difficulty, arose from the fact that the Republican Convention of the 22d February declined to say that they abided by the present naturalization laws. I was at Iowa City at the time, and favored the insertion of the clause, but the Know-Nothings opposed it, and then there were some, not of the order, who were opposed to saying anything on any subject save that of slavery. The latter policy prevailed, and our State platform looks to no other question.

I have never had any conversation with any of the delegates to the National Convention, except Mr. Seward's "administrator" in this State, and his preferences are for him. In a conversation a few days ago, I told him that I had not the remotest idea that Mr. Seward could be elected, that there were too many old chronic prejudices to be overcome to allow him to make a respectable poll; and he seemed to coincide in that opinion.

It is impossible to say how the Germans in this State will vote in November. They will be greatly influenced by Remelin, and the Germans in Cincinnati and New York. They will act with many of the Republican county parties, where the platforms and candidates suit them.

The Fillmore nomination will damage us considerably in this State, and I fear will render the result doubtful. I think it will affect us as much here as in any State in the Union, especially in the Southern part, where the people are mostly Southern by birth.

Mr. Grimes presided over a public meeting in Burlington, May 31st, called to consider the assault upon Senator Sumner in the Capitol, May 22d, and the outrages in Kansas. Upon taking the chair he remarked that "we had assembled together, as was our privilege, to express our feelings and opinions in reference to recent and most important occurrences. We had indeed fallen upon perilous times, when our legislators, for words spoken in debate, were attacked with murderous weapons in the Senate of the United States. It was not Senator Sumner and the State of Massachusetts alone that suffered by this violation of the Constitution. We were all interested. The State of Iowa might next be stricken down in the persons of her Senators or Representatives. It was a blow at the foundation of our liberties, the freedom of our legislators. Mr. Sumner was a ripe scholar, a statesman, and an orator—a credit to Massachusetts and to the deliberative body of which he was a member. What had he said to justify the cowardly and murderous assault that had been made upon him? His speech fell short in invective of the philippics of Randolph, Calhoun, McDuffie, Hayne, Prentiss, and Henry A. Wise. It was diluted when compared to Daniel Webster's onslaught upon Charles J. Ingersoll. But what Mr. Sumner may have said in debate was of no consequence—was no palliation or excuse for the outrage that had been committed."

Governor Grimes spoke also of affairs in Kansas, of the legalized robberies, burnings, and murders, in that unfortunate Territory; of its conquest by citizens of the adjoining State of Missouri and of distant States, with the complicity of the President of the United States, and said that any man or set of men who would palliate, excuse, or justify the assault upon Mr. Sumner, or the state of affairs in Kansas, were fit for slaves, and deserved to be enslaved.

More than seventeen years after Mr. Grimes had introduced a memorial to Congress, in the first Legislative Assembly of the Territory, asking an appropriation of lands for the construction of a railroad in Iowa, a grant of lands was made to the State, by act of Congress, approved May 15, 1856, for the purpose of aiding in the construction of four different lines of railroads, viz., from Burlington, from Davenport, from Lyons, and from Dubuque, across the State to the Missouri River. The grant was hailed with high satisfaction and hope by the people of Iowa. The Governor, deeming immediate legislative action demanded, issued his proclamation, June 3d, for a special session of the General Assembly, which met at Iowa City on the 2d of July. The following extracts are from his message to the Assembly:

THE RAILROAD GRANT.

I have convened you, gentlemen, in special session, that you may determine—

1. Whether or not the State shall accept the grant made under the act of the 15th of May last; and, if so—

2. Whether the lands granted shall be transferred to any specific railroad companies; and, if so, to what companies they shall be transferred; and—

3. Upon what terms shall the transfer be made.

My experience in matters of this kind has been so limited, that I am not prepared to submit to you any plan for the proper disposal of these lands. Your wisdom will doubtless mature a system which, while it promotes the present material interests of the State by developing its resources and advancing its settlement by the construction of lines of intercommunication, will protect the people against the sometimes oppressive monopolizing tendencies of powerful corporations.

THE RIGHTS, DUTIES, AND LIABILITIES, OF RAILWAY COMPANIES.

The introduction of railroads within the State has rendered necessary an act more clearly defining the rights, duties, and liabilities, of railway companies. The law should declare that, where *death* is caused through negligence or misconduct of the agents or servants of such companies, the same remedies shall be open in a suit at law, as for like injuries to the person resulting in disability and not in death. Among other things, the speed of trains passing through cities, and villages, and across highways, should be regulated by law; and the disasters that have occurred in a neighboring State have admonished us of the necessity for a law prohibiting a company from carrying passengers over a new road until it has first been examined and pronounced safe by a competent and disinterested Board of Engineers. It is evidently as much the duty of the State to protect the lives and safety of the citizens from accidents, resulting from carelessness, misconduct, or cupidity, as from open and premeditated violence.

THE PARDONING POWER.

The constitution confers upon the Governor of the State "the power to grant reprieves and pardons and commute punishments after convictions," for offenses against the laws. In a large proportion of cases, the friends of the persons convicted endeavor to procure the exercise of this power; and as few, if any, of the judges preserve minutes of the testimony taken on the trial of criminal causes, these efforts are, for the most part, based upon *ex-parte* statements, made without the sanction of an oath, and obtained without notice to the prosecuting attorney, or other person representing the government. It is frequently alleged that there was error in the trial; that the judge mistook the law; that there was a mistake of fact by the jury; that there is newly-discovered evidence, showing the sentence to be unjust; or that the case, although within the letter of the law, was not within the spirit of it.

The interests of society require that this great power should be exercised with humanity, but, at the same time, with the greatest discrimination and caution. Justice to the officer who is compelled to investigate each case presented to him, as well as to the parties more immediately interested, requires that every fact proved upon the trial should be accessible to him, to the condemned, and to the prosecutors. I therefore recommend that the judges of the several district courts be required to reduce the evidence given in all criminal cases to writing, to be preserved as a permanent record in the county where the trial was held; and that, before any application shall be made to the Governor for pardon, a notice of the time and place, when and where the application will be presented, shall be served upon the prosecuting attorney of the county where the offense was committed.

THE AFFAIRS OF KANSAS.

Concurring in the general desire that your session may be short, and that your time may be occupied solely by matters relating to the State, I do not deem it proper at present to call your attention at length to the deplorable condition of affairs in Kansas and at our national capital. It would be an error to suppose that my failure to do so is attributable to any want of sympathy with the patriotic and devoted men who are struggling to uphold the rights of free speech, free labor, free soil, and a free press in that Territory, and in the councils of the nation.

Having extended an invitation to Hon. Abraham Lincoln to address a public meeting in Iowa upon political questions, prior to the State election in August, Mr. Grimes received the following reply:

SPRINGFIELD, ILLINOIS, *July* 12, 1856.

Yours of the 29th of June was duly received. I did not answer it because it plagued me. This morning I received another from Judd and Peck, written by consultation with you. Now let me tell you why I am plagued:

1. I can hardly spare the time.

2. I am superstitious. I have scarcely known a party preceding an election to call in help from the neighboring States, but they lost the State. Last fall, our friends had Wade, of Ohio, and others,

in Maine; and they lost the State. Last spring our adversaries had New Hampshire full of South Carolinians, and they lost the State. And so, generally, it seems to stir up more enemies than friends.

Have the enemy called in any foreign help? If they have a foreign champion there, I should have no objection to drive a nail in his track. I shall reach Chicago on the night of the 15th, to attend to a little business in court. Consider the things I have suggested, and write me at Chicago. Especially write me whether Browning consents to visit you.

Your obedient servant,

A. LINCOLN.

40.—*To His Excellency Franklin Pierce, President of the United States.*

EXECUTIVE OFFICE, IOWA,
BURLINGTON, *August* 28, 1856.

During the last twelve months I have been constantly receiving letters, memorials, and affidavits, from former citizens of Iowa, now residents of the Territory of Kansas, alleging that they are not protected by the United States officers in that Territory in the enjoyment of their liberty and property. They charge, and the evidence fully supports the charge, that at the first, and at each subsequent Territorial election, armed bodies of men from an adjacent State invaded the Territory, took possession of the polls, deprived the actual settlers of the right of suffrage, and perpetrated gross outrages upon such citizens as professed political sentiments disagreeable to the invaders. By threats and lawless violence, they secured the election of a majority of the members of the Legislative Assembly —many of whom were then, and are now, citizens of another State. By this Assembly a code of laws was enacted, unparalleled in the history of legislation—laws palpably unconstitutional, and which no man with the spirit of a freeman could obey, without personal dishonor and a violation of his conscience.

In this condition of things, and without any attempt to repel violence by violence, the people of Kansas sought a peaceful remedy for the wrongs that had been perpetrated, by forming a State constitution, electing State officers, and asking admission into the Union as a sovereign State.

Although the Constitution of the United States declares that treason "shall consist ONLY in levying war," yet a man holding a commission under the seal of the United States, and exercising the office of Chief-Justice in that Territory, has decided that the persons who accepted office under the State constitution are guilty of treason. Under his instructions, the State officers have been indicted, arrested, and bail denied them. Under the pretense of judicial proceedings, but without a trial or hearing of any kind, an armed *posse* has invaded the town of Lawrence and destroyed printing-presses, private dwellings, and an hotel. Human lives have been sacrificed, property to a large amount has been destroyed, citizens have been driven from the Territory by violence, and anarchy and disorder everywhere prevail.

Among the sufferers have been former citizens of Iowa, who went to Kansas in no spirit of propagandism, but with the intention of becoming permanent residents of that Territory. Three of them have been slain by arms said to have been placed by a Federal officer in the hands of a band of outlaws from a remote State. Some have been compelled to flee from the Territory for no offense save that of having emigrated from a free State, while others remain there, stripped of their property, and appeal to their fellow-citizens of Iowa for sympathy and protection.

In my conviction their appeal should not be in vain. They went to Kansas relying upon and having a right to expect the protection of the General Government. In this expectation they have been disappointed. Citizenship has been virtually denied them. Their right to defend themselves and "to keep and bear arms" has been infringed by the act of the Territorial officers, who have wrested from them the means of defense, while putting weapons of offense into the hands of their enemies. They have been oppressed by a code of laws unequaled in atrocity in modern times. The character and conduct of the Territorial judges have shown that an appeal to the judicial tribunals is worse than useless.

The Central Government having failed to perform its duty by protecting the people of Kansas in the enjoyments of their rights, it is manifestly the right of each of the States to adopt measures to protect its former citizens. If the people of Iowa are not permitted to enjoy the right of citizenship in that Territory, they retain their former citizenship in this State, and are as much entitled to protection from the State while upon the public domain, as they would be if the General Government failed to protect them in a foreign country.

7

While I write, an army raised in the State of Missouri is marching into Kansas, with the avowed purpose of driving out all those citizens of the Territory who emigrated from the free States, and who express a preference for a free State constitution. Another armed body of men have placed themselves on the emigrant route from the State of Iowa, to prevent at the point of the bayonet any further emigration from this State.

The State of Iowa cannot be an indifferent spectator of these acts of lawless violence. She demands that her citizens shall be protected in Kansas, and stand upon an equality there with the citizens of other States. She will not submit to the closing of the emigrant route through her domain into that Territory.

As the Executive of Iowa I demand for her citizens in Kansas protection in the enjoyment of their property, their liberty, and their political rights. I ask that the military force on the line of immigration into the Territory be dispersed.

A compliance with these reasonable requests will tend to restore peace in Kansas and quiet the public mind of this State. In the event of a non-compliance, in my view, a case will have arisen clearly within the principle laid down by Mr. Madison in the Virginia Resolutions of 1798, when it will be the duty of the States "to interpose to arrest the progress of the evils" in that Territory.

41.—*To Hon. S. P. Chase.*

BURLINGTON, *August* 30, 1856.

Yours of the 23d instant, from New York City, has been duly received.

I am quite as powerless as you are, and must appeal to you for counsel and direction. All our information in relation to Kansas affairs comes from the East, and especially from Chicago.

I have written to the President a letter, a copy of which I inclose herewith. I do not expect it to do any good, but it will convince him how I feel on the subject.

I am ready and anxious to unite in any feasible scheme to rescue the free-State men in Kansas. Suppose the Governors of Ohio, Michigan, Wisconsin, and Iowa, meet at Chicago, say 7th September, to consider what can be done, and what ought to be done in the premises? I name that day because I have agreed to stump the State, and it will not conflict with any of my other appointments or business. I would have the meeting unheralded by notices in the newspapers.

I have not made my letter to the President public. Perhaps it had better not be done. If you think, however, that any good might come of it, you are at liberty to make such part of it public as you choose.

In the course of the summer and fall, Mr. Grimes addressed public meetings at many different places, in behalf of the Republican party, and spoke with the force and earnestness of deep conviction. He attributed the evils of the country to the wanton repeal of the Missouri Compromise, with the evident purpose of forcing slavery upon a people who detested it. Regarding old parties and old issues as dead, he said that the issue before the country was the extension or non-extension of slavery into the Territories; that by no act of his, either of omission or of commission, should slavery be extended over free territory, and that, when called to rest with his fathers, he did not wish the stain of having extended slavery, or of having fastened shackles upon a single human being, to rest upon his name; and he further declared that under all circumstances, whether the Republican party was defeated or victorious, the Union should be preserved.

The sixth General Assembly of the State convened at Iowa City, December 1, 1856. The following extracts are from the Governor's message:

GROWTH OF IOWA.

The progress of the State during the past two years has been extraordinary, and in many respects unexampled. In population, in wealth, in productive power, in educational facilities, the advance has been such as to astound the doubtful and to surprise the most sanguine. Iowa occupies a proud position, and with wise legislation a glorious destiny awaits her. You are called to assist in shaping that destiny, and to aid in laying the foundations of a future empire. It is impossible to be too deeply impressed with the responsibility and delicacy of the great trust confided to you.

STATE STATISTICS.

An enumeration of the inhabitants of the State, and of her productive resources, was taken in June last, as required by the constitution. It is somewhat defective; two counties and several townships in other counties not having been returned at all, while in almost all the counties there are very great omissions. Many townships and some counties are returned without any statistics, save those in relation to population. Such will always be the case, so long as the census shall be taken by township assessors, instead of being taken by marshals, to be appointed by the census board.

The following statement will show the increase of population since the settlement of what is now the State:

Population in 1836	10,531		Population in 1847	116,204
" 1838	22,859		" 1849	130,945
" 1840	43,116		" 1850	192,204
" 1844	71,650		" 1854	326,014
" 1846	78,988		" 1856	503,625

The population of the State is probably at this time not far from 600,000. The vote polled on the 4th day of November last reached 92,644, and indicates the truth of this supposition.

GEOLOGICAL SURVEY.

In pursuance of the act of the last General Assembly, authorizing a geological survey of the State, I appointed Prof. James Hall, of Albany, New York, State geologist, and, in conjunction with Mr. Hall, appointed Prof. J. D. Whitney, of Massachusetts, State chemist. These gentlemen prosecuted their survey during a portion of the years 1855 and 1856, and to their report, which will be shortly transmitted to you, I refer you for an account of their explorations and the results.

The high rank among scientific men enjoyed by each of these gentlemen gives ample assurance that the survey will be thorough, practical, and creditable to the State.

STATE PENITENTIARY.

I transmit herewith the report of the Inspectors of the State Penitentiary, and solicit your attention to the suggestions it contains. The penitentiary is established in one corner of the State, and the ground connected with it is limited in extent and not well adapted to the purpose for which it is used.

I am not prepared to say that sound policy does not dictate a removal of the institution to some more central and accessible part of the State. Should it be deemed expedient to maintain the present as a permanent penitentiary, very considerable appropriations will be required to build an additional number of cells, a hospital for the sick, and erect a substantial wall around the prison-yard. If, on the contrary, it is thought expedient to establish a penitentiary in a more central position in the State, then the manner in which it shall be constructed, and the system upon which it shall be conducted, become subjects for very grave consideration.

Notwithstanding the very general prejudice that exists against it, many wise and good men, after a thorough investigation of the subject, are convinced that the solitary system, as practised at Pentonville, in England, and in the Eastern Penitentiary, in Pennsylvania, would be most conducive to the interests of the State and to the reformation of convicts. Before any permanent system of prison discipline shall be established, it is to be hoped that the subject will receive a most thorough examination.

REGISTRY LAW.

Almost every person, residing in any of the large towns in the State, acknowledges the imperative necessity for some law to protect the purity of the ballot-box. That gross frauds are perpetrated at every exciting election, by the voting and double voting of unqualified persons, is not to be denied. To remedy this great and constantly-increasing evil, the passage of a registry law is respectfully recommended. Such laws have been in operation in several States from a period long anterior to the adoption of the Federal Constitution, and have fully answered their design.

SCHOOL FUNDS.

I again call your attention to the propriety of entirely disconnecting the office of Superintendent of Public Instruction from all control over the school money and school lands.

The five-per-cent. fund, arising from the sale of public lands within the State, has always, until the past year, been distributed by the Superintendent among the several County School Fund Commissioners, under what was supposed to be the requirements of the laws of this State. The amount of $226,800.56 received from the General Government as the five per cent. accruing on the 31st of

December, 1854, has, I learn, been partially distributed among the County School Fund Commissioners, and partially loaned out by the Superintendent of Public Instruction, but, as I conceive, wholly without authority of law. This is too important and too large an interest to suffer any doubt to exist as to the proper disposal of the fund, or as to the powers, rights, and liabilites, of any officer connected with it. I therefore commend the snbject to your immediate consideration.

REVISION OF SCHOOL LAWS.

In compliance with the provisions of the act of July 14, 1856, Hon. Horace Mann, of Ohio, Hon. Amos Dean, President of the State University, and F. E. Bissell, Esq., of Dubuque, were appointed commissioners to revise the school laws of the State. The commissioners are engaged in the discharge of their duties, and will be able to lay their report before you in a few days.

STATE UNIVERSITY.

It would seem that with a population in the State of half a million of souls, and a university fund of nearly two hundred thousand dollars, the time had arrived for a thorough and efficient organization of this institution. If it is the design of the General Assembly to surrender the Capitol buildings, at Iowa City, for university purposes, provision should be made to that effect at an early day.

STATE CAPITOL.

In compliance with the act of 25th of January, 1855, entitled "An act to relocate the seat of government," I appointed commissioners for that purpose, and they have discharged their duty. The site selected for the future Capitol is on a gentle swell of land about three-quarters of a mile east of Fort Des Moines, and on the east side of the river. It commands a good prospect, and seems to be well adapted to the purpose for which it has been selected.

COUNTY INDEBTEDNESS.

The constitution wisely provides that the State shall not in any manner create a debt exceeding one hundred thousand dollars. The framers of that instrument did not imagine that there was as great a necessity to prohibit the counties from creating large public debts, for the reason that the history of the country did not then present the case of a county becoming a large stockholder in private corporations.

Within the past few years, however, so great has been the anxiety to procure the construction of works of internal improvement, that many counties and cities in this State have adopted the very doubtful policy of creating large municipal debts, for the purpose of becoming stockholders in railroads and other private corporations. The amount of municipal indebtedness already voted by the different cities and counties exceeds seven million dollars.

Without stopping to inquire into the authority under which the loans have heretofore been voted, it seems to me that prudence and sound policy require that some check be imposed upon the future exercise of this power to create public indebtedness. It is true that many investments made by the counties and cities may result profitably to the stockholders; but, it is equally true that many will prove disastrous, as some have already done.

Municipal corporations are designed for local and limited purposes, and it is a perversion of their organization when they are embarked in internal improvement beyond their jurisdiction. Nor is that an equitable principle which allows the people of one portion of a county to fasten an indebtedness upon a remote portion of the county, for other than legitimate county purposes. Equally unjust is it to allow the property of one man to be heavily burdened by taxation, imposed by the vote of another man, who is without property, without a household, and who sustains none of the burdens of government. There is a manifest propriety in allowing every man the right of suffrage, under ordinary circumstances. It is proper that every man should have the privilege to join in the selection of his own law-makers, and his own executioners, but there is not the same propriety in allowing to every man the privilege of creating an indebtedness for others to pay.

It occurs to me that too many checks and safeguards cannot be thrown around this power, if such power exists at all, of creating municipal indebtedness for purposes of internal improvements. It is a dangerous power, and liable to the grossest abuse.

KANSAS.

During the past summer it was reported and generally believed that the President of the United States only failed to interpose his authority for the protection of the rights of the free-State people in Kansas, for the reason that no official intelligence had reached him that any outrages had been perpetrated in that unfortunate Territory. Having such information myself, I conceived it to be my duty to notify the President of the crimes that had been committed against the persons and property of former citizens of Iowa, and to demand for them that protection which the Federal Government was in part established to secure.

Accordingly, on the 28th day of August last, I addressed to him a letter on this subject, a copy of which I herewith transmit. Without desiring to forestall the opinion or action of the General Assembly in this regard, I beg leave to reiterate the opinion then expressed, that it is the right and duty of the State to protect the rights of her former citizens in Kansas when the Federal Government fails to perform that duty.

I desire to coöperate with the General Assembly in the adoption of any measures that may tend to uphold the sovereignty and promote the prosperity and honor of our noble State.

42.—*To Mrs. Grimes.*

IOWA CITY, *December* 5, 1856.

My message, much to my astonishment, is well received. I have been highly complimented on its conciseness and information. I send you a copy.

December 12th.—Night before last I heard your friend Wendell Phillips lecture on the "Lost Arts." It was, I think, the best lecture I ever listened to. Such seems to have been the experience of every one.

After the lecture, he was publicly requested to give to the audience an expression of his peculiar views. He gave us the length and breadth of Garrisonism, and, what was unexpected to me, the audience not only listened patiently to what he said, but received his utterances with unbounded applause. This is another evidence of the progress of antislavery sentiment. I know no place in this State where Mr. Phillips would have been permitted to give a free expression to his sentiments five years ago. Now, at the capital of the State, before an audience embracing almost all the members of the General Assembly, and very much of the conservatism and wealth of the State, his opinions are applauded to the echo. Let us thank God that the world moves.

Mr. Phillips spent an hour or more in my room after the lecture. Indeed, we did not go to bed until twelve o'clock. He is genial in his intercourse, has traveled all over Europe, apparently a man of great erudition, and is blessed with very fine sensibilities. I do not recollect when I have been so captivated by the manner and intellect and heart of a man with whom I have been brought in contact.

I shall spend Christmas at home. I rejoice to know that this is the last winter I shall spend away from that dear place.

43.—*To W. H. Buchanan, Sheriff of Clinton County.*

EXECUTIVE OFFICE, IOWA,
BURLINGTON, *July* 3, 1857.

Your letter of the 29th June, in which you state that you have warrants in your hands for the arrest of persons who seized and hanged Bennet Warren in your county on the 25th inst.; that you are "informed that a very large combination has been formed, banded together by agreement or oath to execute similar outrages upon other persons, and protect and defend any of their members who may be attempted to be dealt with according to law," and that this combination is supposed to number "about two thousand persons in Jackson and the adjoining counties," has been duly received.

You ask me "what course shall be pursued." I answer unhesitatingly, serve the warrants in your hands and enforce the laws of the State. You have authority to summon to your aid the entire force of your county. If you deem it to be necessary to do so, call for that force, and prosecute every man who refuses to obey your summons.

If the power of your county is not sufficient to execute the laws, a sufficient force from other counties shall be placed at your disposal.

If the persons arrested refuse to give bail, and you believe your county jail to be unsafe, you will have authority to establish a guard, or send the prisoners to some other county in the State, where they will be secure.

I am resolved that, so far as in me lies, this lawless violence, which, under the plea of administering justice to horse-thieves, sets at defiance the authorities of the State, and destroys all respect for the laws, both human and divine, shall be checked. I shall have no hesitation, therefore, when officially advised of the exigency, to call out the entire military power of the State, if necessary, to crush out this spirit of rebellion, which has shown itself in your county.

I shall direct all the military companies in the State to hold themselves in readiness for duty.

As I have been written to on this subject by your county judge, and by other citizens of Clinton, and as I desire that there should be no doubt as to my opinions on the subject, or as to what my action will be, I request you to give publicity to this communication.

Mr. Grimes participated in a Fourth of July celebration upon the grounds of the Burlington University, and made an address of great originality and force in behalf of the education of women.

A new constitution of the State of Iowa, with such provisions substantially as Mr. Grimes had long advocated, was approved by the people, August 3, 1857, and he issued a proclamation September 3d, declaring it to be adopted, and proclaiming it the supreme law of the State. The votes for the adoption of the constitution were 40,311, against 38,681. At the same election, there were 8,207 votes for striking out the word "white" from the article on the "right of suffrage." Suitable buildings having been prepared for the accommodation of the General Assembly and the officers of State at Des Moines, Governor Grimes issued his proclamation, October 19th, making known his opinion to that effect, and declaring the capital of Iowa to be established, under the constitution and laws, at Des Moines, in Polk County, and the University of the State to be established at Iowa City, in Johnson County.

Under the new constitution an election was held October 13th. In view of that election he invited Mr. Lincoln to make a speech in Iowa. He presented his own views of public affairs in a circular. From Mr. Lincoln he received the following reply:

SPRINGFIELD, ILLINOIS, *August*, 1857.

Yours of the 14th is received, and I am much obliged for the legal information you give.

You can scarcely be more anxious than I that the next election in Iowa should result in favor of the Republicans. I lost nearly all the working-part of last year, giving my time to the canvass; and I am altogether too poor to lose two years together. I am engaged in a suit in the United States Court at Chicago, in which the Rock Island Bridge Company is a party. The trial is to commence on the 8th of September, and probably will last two or three weeks. During the trial it is not improbable that all hands may come over and take a look at the bridge, and, if it were possible to make it hit right, I could then speak at Davenport. My courts go right on without cessation till late in November. Write me again, pointing out the more striking points of difference between your old and new constitutions, and also whether Democratic and Republican party lines were drawn in the adoption of it, and which were for and which were against it. If, by possibility, I could get over among you it might be of some advantage to know these things in advance.

Yours very truly,

A. LINCOLN.

44.—*A Circular Letter.*

BURLINGTON, *September* 3, 1857.

I am led by my anxiety in relation to the approaching State election, to briefly address you on that subject. I confess that I am anxious about the result. That anxiety is caused by the extraordinary efforts that are made, and will continue to be made, to defeat the Republican nominees, and the disastrous consequences that must inevitably ensue, should those efforts prove successful.

About to retire from office, but still in office, it may be thought by some that I should abstain from all interference with the present contest. If nothing were involved in it but the personal aggrandizement of the rival candidates, I should do so. But, when I reflect upon the influence the result of this contest is destined to exercise upon the interests of this State, upon the public sentiment of other States, and upon the future action of the Federal Government, I cannot reconcile silence or apparent indifference with my sense of duty.

The design of the adherents of Mr. Buchanan's Administration is very apparent. They are resolved to carry Iowa at the October election. To this end the services of the whole prætorian band of office-holders in the State — every postmaster, land-officer, mail, timber, and other agents—will be put in requisition. Committees are appointed in every county and township—the Democratic party will be thoroughly organized—money will be freely spent, and the entire pro-slavery vote of the State will be polled. Should their efforts be crowned with success, the result will be heralded to the world as a triumph of the principles of the Kansas-Nebraska act. With a view to paralyze their efforts, the struggling free-State men in Kansas will be told that the freemen of Iowa have decided the issue in which they are involved in favor of the Administration, and its representative, Governor Walker.

That proconsul of the Government will be stimulated to enforce the collection of taxes, imposed upon the people of that unfortunate Territory by fraud and violence, at the point of Federal bayonets. The whole State will resound with rejoicings over the triumph of the principles embodied in the extra-judicial opinion of Chief-Justice Taney in the case of Scott *vs.* Sandford.

It cannot be disguised that this great issue between freedom and slavery is a prominent question in this contest. It has been made so by both political parties. They could not do otherwise. Freedom and slavery are the antagonistic elements in this government. They cannot harmonize, and must overshadow every other question until settled upon the principle enunciated by the Republican party. The success of the Democratic party in October will be an indorsement by the people of the State of the Democratic platform, as the triumph of the Republican party will be an indorsement of the Republican platform.

It is my sincere and mature conviction that the success of the Democratic party in Iowa, at the October election, would irretrievably fix the character of Kansas as a slave State, and inflict a malignant, if not fatal, wound upon the free labor and Free-Soil party everywhere.

It would discourage our gallant friends in Missouri, who have just achieved a noble triumph. It would encourage the slavery propagandists to proceed with their scheme of reopening the African slave-trade, as foreshadowed in the recent Southern Convention at Knoxville, and tend to hasten forward that day, so anxiously desired by the South, when we shall become a great nation of slaves and slave-owners.

It would be a great error to suppose that the slave propagandists have abandoned hope or relaxed their efforts to secure the Territories to slavery. In Oregon they are fiercely contending for the ascendency, with every prospect of success. In Minnesota, when defeated at the polls, they refuse to abide by the judgment of the people, and now strive to prevent the admission of that Territory as a State. We are justified in believing that at this moment parties are organizing to again invade Kansas with the design to carry the fall election. The *real* author of the Kansas-Nebraska bill, ex-Senator Atchison, in his letter to Colonel Baker, of South Carolina, of the 12th of July last, declares that *he still has hopes from the border counties of Missouri.* The *Charleston Mercury*, speaking of this letter, says:

"In addition to the letter published recently from General Atchison, we beg to say to our readers that, from other letters received from Kansas, we are informed that the pro-slavery party in Kansas is resolute in its determination of making Kansas a slave State. In consenting to become a Democratic party, the pro-slavery men did not mean to abandon their policy, but to lift the minority it placed with them to their support. On the 21st day of last month they were confident of success, and would form a constitution with slavery acknowledged in it. If this constitution is referred to the people for ratification, it is intended to refer it only to the registered voters, who will doubtless ratify it. We have more hopes of Kansas than we have ever had. *We have great faith in the fighting capacity of Southern men.*"

It requires no prophet to foretell what is meant by "the fighting capacity of Southern men."

It is very evident that the friends of free Kansas and "self-government" cannot rely upon the support of Mr. Buchanan. So far from aiding them, he is now attempting to force slavery upon that Territory against the well-known wishes of three-fourths of the actual citizens. He declares that the bogus taxes shall be collected, and the bogus laws enforced. He has refused to remove the infamous Lecompte, which even Mr. Pierce attempted to do. He appointed Emory, Whitfield, Clark, Woodson, and others, the most active and unscrupulous agents in all the frauds and violence and murders committed in that Territory, to the most valuable and influential offices. He has not appointed one known free-State Democrat to office, but he has removed every free-State Democrat from office, who was appointed by his predecessor.

The truth is, there is no hope for Kansas since the decision of the Dred Scott case, soon to be followed by a decision in the Lemmon case, except in the earnest, manful, resistless, public sentiment of the free States as expressed through the ballot-boxes.

At the first session of the General Assembly of the Territory of Iowa, held at Burlington in 1838, an act was passed "to regulate the practice in the Supreme and District Courts," which was an exact transcript of the Illinois statute on the same subject. It was adopted in that State at an early day, when slaves were held under her local laws, and contained an exclusion of negro, mulatto, and Indian testimony. In 1850 the commissioners appointed to revise the laws of the State (Judges Mason and Woodward, and Governor Hempstead) reported section 2,388 of the Code as follows: "Every human being of sufficient capacity to understand the obligation of an oath is a competent witness in all cases both civil and criminal, except as herein otherwise declared." This section was amended by the General Assembly by adding, "but an Indian, a negro, a mulatto, or black person, shall not be allowed to give testimony in any cause wherein a white person is a party." Thus the law stood until last winter, when this exclusion was removed.

The recent Constitutional Convention added to the fourth section of the Bill of Rights, "and any party to any judicial proceeding shall have the right to use as a witness, or to take the testimony of, any other person not disqualified on account of interest, who may be cognizant of any fact material to the case." The Democratic Convention, assembled on the 26th of August at Iowa City, declared in favor of an amendment to the new constitution so as to exclude the testimony of colored persons, or, in other words, to strike off this amendment to the Bill of Rights.

I find upon examination that in every free State in this Union, save in Illinois and Indiana (and I cannot ascertain what the law is in these States), by some law, or constitutional provision, every human being endowed with reason and conscience is admissible as a witness before judicial tribunals, leaving the credibility of the witness to be passed upon by the jury. Governor Hempstead, Judge Mason, Judge Woodward, the last General Assembly, and the Constitutional Convention, thought that the same should be the law in this State.

The members of the Democratic Convention, however, think otherwise. They strangely overlook the fact that the admission of this testimony is for the benefit of the white race, and not for the peculiar benefit of the black. It is no benefit, no interest to me to give testimony in my neighbor's suit. I am called as a witness, because I know some fact important to his cause, and I am permitted to testify for the very reason that I have no interest in testifying. So may the testimony of a colored man be important to my neighbor. He may be the only witness cognizant of the facts. If he is ignorant, degraded, false, let his testimony be weighed by all the surrounding circumstances, as the evidence of ignorant, degraded, false, white men is weighed. If he is truthful and honest, is it just or proper that my neighbor should be deprived of his testimony? Is the Democratic party willing to be held to the legitimate conclusion from their position, viz., that the jurors of this State are competent to weigh testimony, and do justice between parties, only in cases where the witnesses are of one race? I have always supposed the object of all judicial investigations was to reach the truth—"It is the truth that makes us free"—no matter where it comes from, provided it stands the tests applied to falsehoods.

I hardly need say that the law of the last winter, as well as the constitutional provision, sprung from the fact that several criminals have "gone unwhipped of justice" on account of this disability of witnesses. The facts that would have insured conviction were known only to colored persons, but their testimony was inadmissible under the law, though they were as credible men as were in the community in which they resided. But, what matters it why or how it originated, if the provision is just in itself?

I am anxious as to the result in this State, on account of our local and State policy.

We have now a new constitution. We want a banking system established under it that shall furnish facilities for transacting the business of our citizens, and be safe for the community. Principally for this reason, I think it was, that the people adopted it as the supreme law. Yet the effort will be made to defeat the very object of the new constitution, by electing a Governor and a majority of the members of the General Assembly who are opposed to all banking.

A great many friends of the new constitution imagine that, because it has been ratified by the people, all the reforms it proposes will be consummated. This is a great mistake. The new provisions are self-executing only in relation to the time of holding the annual election. All other essential provisions must be acted upon by the General Assembly. The power, therefore, to thwart the wishes of the people in this regard will be in the hands of the General Assembly in the first instance, and afterward in the power of the Governor. It would surely be the height of folly to intrust the constitution at this time to its enemies, and expect them to carry it into successful operation.

Upon the next General Assembly will devolve the duty of electing a United States Senator from this State. Shall he be a representative of the free-labor sentiment of the State, or shall his every vote pander to the slavery-extension sentiment of the South, and only tend to stimulate to further demands? That question will be decided by the result of the election in October.

I have been, during nineteen years, acquainted with the Republican nominee for Governor, Ralph P. Lowe. During the past five years he has been judge of the judicial district in which I reside, and discharged the duties of that important office to the satisfaction of every one. I am warranted in saying that, had he consented to be a candidate for reëlection, there would have been no opposition to him. His sense of propriety forbade him mingling actively in politics during the term of his judgeship. He stands firmly upon the Republican platform and possesses every qualification for a good Governor.

Of the Democratic nominee I have nothing to say. I believe Mr. Samuels to be an honorable man. I have always understood him to be an ultra, hard-money, anti-bank Democrat, with strong Southern proclivities. I presume he will so declare himself during the campaign. But I do not choose to look to his individual opinions. I look to the platform on which he stands. I find that platform indorsing the principle of the Kansas-Nebraska bill. I find it indorsing the Administration of Mr. Buchanan, with all its pro-slavery tendencies, and without one word in condemnation of such immense robberies of the Government as were perpetrated by the sale of the Fort Snelling reservation, or such smaller robberies, according to Commissioner Manypenny, as the forty thousand dollars paid to R. W. Thompson, of Indiana. I find it thus approving the course of Governor Walker in Kansas, including the recent outrageous apportionment of members to the Territorial Assembly, and the quartering a United States Army upon Lawrence with a view to harass and overawe its citizens. I find it virtually approving the Dred Scott decision, which breaks down every barrier against slavery and makes the whole nation responsible for the crime. I find it appealing to the lowest passions of the human heart in order to excite still greater prejudice against a degraded race, and full of revilings against those who would humanely ameliorate their condition. Every vote for the Democratic nominees is an approval of this platform.

With such principles to contend against, is it not your duty to take an active part in this contest?

Will not every one who prefers free soil and free labor to slave soil and slave labor, every one who recognizes the principles of self-government, as now attempted by the freemen of Kansas and Minnesota, every one who would rebuke the lawlessness, and violence, and wrongs perpetrated in those Territories under the apparent sanction of the Federal Executive, every one who recognizes his duty to humanity, whether exalted or degraded, every one who would arrest the attempt to reopen the African slave-trade in its incipient stage, every one who desires the genuine free-labor sentiment of the State to be represented in the United States Senate, and every one who desires for this continent a civilization of law and justice, not only vote for but labor for the Republican nominees?

We cannot be indifferent to the contest. We have no right to be indifferent. The issue has been made up. No man can shrink from meeting it. He is no friend to freedom who absents himself from the polls. In a republican government, it is as much the duty of every citizen to take care of and participate in the government as it is to provide for his own household.

I have addressed you with confidence and freedom. If I have exhibited zeal, it is because I feel strongly on the subject. I know the efforts that will be made by the pro-slavery party in the State, and I appreciate the humiliating effect their success would have upon the party of progress and freedom everywhere.

Hon. Ralph P. Lowe was chosen Governor, under the new constitution, and, upon his installation, January 14, 1858, Mr. Grimes laid down his office.

The following is from his message to the seventh General Assembly, January 12, 1858:

Gentlemen of the Senate and House of Representatives:

I congratulate you upon the continued prosperity of our State. Since you were last assembled, its population has continued to increase, and its resources of every character to be each day more and more developed. The earth has yielded liberally of its abundance, and peace, good order, and happiness, everywhere prevail. It becomes us to be devoutly thankful to that benign Providence that has blessed our beloved State with another season of prosperity, and brought us to the commencement of another official year.

You are convened under the provisions of a new organic law. You are expected to provide the proper methods for carrying that law into full effect. Your labors will exercise a potent influence upon the future character and prosperity of the State. That influence will extend to a period long after the last of you shall cease to be interested in human affairs. It is not to be doubted that you appreciate the just responsibilities of your position. It is expected that the spirit of moderation and prudence will preside over all your deliberations. It is hoped that all your legislation will be stamped with the utmost simplicity and singleness of purpose, and that you will abstain from all measures which, from their doubtful tendency, may needlessly distract the public mind and throw it into agitation and controversy.

All the general laws of the State require some modifications to adapt them to the provisions of the new constitution. Several new acts of a general character will also be necessary. Special legislation is opposed to the true theory of a republican government, and is the source of great corruption. The new constitution inculcates most strongly the duty of general legislation, and declares that "in all cases where a general law can be made applicable, all laws shall be general, and of uniform operation throughout the State."

REGISTRY OF VOTERS.

The general election law will require very material changes, and I again submit to the General Assembly the propriety, when revising this law, of incorporating into it provision for a complete registration of all the legal voters in the State. In no other way can the ballot-boxes be protected against fraud, and the elective franchise preserved in its purity. The argument, that a registry law from its complexity would be too burdensome to be complied with, is entitled to no consideration. It is predicated upon the idea, either that the General Assembly is incapable of maturing a simple and judicious law on this subject, or that the people of the State are incapable of comprehending and enforcing one, neither of which suppositions can be admitted to be correct. Such laws have been in operation in several of the States ever since the foundation of the Government, and have met the approval of all classes of citizens. With such a law, and with the strict and honest enforcement of the naturalization laws, we shall cease to see parties arrayed against each other on account of the birthplace of those who compose them, and every *bona-fide* citizen will be secure in his just weight in the affairs of the State. Without such a law, judging from recent events, it is feared that popular elections will become a reproach.

TOWNSHIP ASSESSOR AND TOWNSHIP ORGANIZATION.

It is much doubted whether the law of last session, substituting county for township assessor, was any improvement upon the former method of assessment. Judging from my own observation, I do not hesitate to conclude, that many millions of dollars' worth of property was overlooked at the last assessment, and is this year untaxed. I recommend the old law in this particular to be restored. Sound policy requires that administration as well as legislation should be brought as directly home to the people as possible. There must ultimately be a thorough township organization throughout the State, and the sooner the people become accustomed to it the less difficult and burdensome it will become, and the more perfect and satisfactory will be the transaction of public affairs.

BANKS.

The people of this State have indicated their opinion that, so long as banks of issue are tolerated in other States, our interests require that similar institutions be established here. If we must have a paper currency, it is infinitely better that it should be issued and secured and redeemed at home, under our own laws, than that it should be issued under laws of which we are ignorant, and controlled by men with whom we have no community of interest.

The constitution authorizes the General Assembly to establish, with the subsequent approval of the people—

1. A State Bank with branches, to be founded upon an actual specie basis, and the branches to be mutually liable for each other's issues.

2. A general free banking law with the restrictions and limitations imposed by Article VIII., Section 8, of the constitution.

In acting upon this subject, it will doubtless be ever borne in mind by the General Assembly that banks are to be established to secure the *public welfare*, and not to promote the purposes of stockholders and capitalists ; and that it is far better that banks should realize small profits, than that the public should be liable to injury by their suspension or failure.

THE PUBLIC SCHOOLS AND THE STATE UNIVERSITY.

I cannot forbear repeating the opinion expressed to the General Assembly three years ago, that "the public schools should be supported by taxation of property, and that the present *rate* system, or *per capita* tax upon scholars, should be abolished." I have seen no reason to change my opinion on this subject, but, on the contrary, I have been every day more and more strengthened in the conviction that it is the only wise and politic method of educating the people. The *per capita* system is based upon the idea that education is a personal benefit for which those who receive it should pay, while the true theory of popular education is that it is a public benefit for which the public should pay.

The Capitol-building at Iowa City has been surrendered to the trustees of the State University. The building is out of repair, and requires considerable change in its internal arrangements to adapt it to the purposes for which it is to be used. I recommend the General Assembly to appropriate a sum sufficient to put it in complete order for the uses for which it is now designed.

The report of the trustees of the university will be laid before you. The time has come when this institution should be put in vigorous operation and be made a benefit and honor to the State.

THE GEOLOGICAL SURVEY OF THE STATE.

In compliance with the instructions of the General Assembly, I have caused the report of the Geological Survey of the State to be printed at Albany, New York, under the immediate supervision of Prof. Hall. The work has been issued from the press, and is now in transit to this place. I am pleased to be able to say that it is regarded by men of science, who have had access to the proof-sheets, as one of the noblest contributions that have ever been made to the scientific history of the country, and is spoken of by all as an honor to our State.

BREACH OF FAITH ON THE PART OF THE UNITED STATES IN THE MATTER OF THE FIVE PER CENT. OF THE NET PROCEEDS OF THE PUBLIC LANDS.

By the act of Congress admitting Iowa into the Union, approved March 3, 1845, it is declared "that five per cent. of the net proceeds of sales of all public lands lying within the said State, which have been or shall be sold by Congress from and after the admission of said State, after deducting all the expenses incident to the same, shall be appropriated for making public roads and canals within the said State, as the Legislature may direct." This act of admission was accepted by the State on the 15th of January, 1847, with the provision that "the General Assembly shall have the right, in accordance with the provisions of the second section of the tenth article of the constitution of Iowa, to appropriate the five per cent. of the net proceeds of sales of all public lands lying within the State which have been or shall be sold by Congress from and after the admission of said State, after deducting all expenses incident to the same, to the support of common schools."

At the time this contract was made between the State and the United States—for it can be regarded in no other light than a contract—the United States disposed of the public lands in no other way than by *bona-fide* sales for money. This obligation on the part of the Federal Government was based upon the obligation on the part of the State that lands belonging to the United States should not be taxed, and that the lands of non-residents should not be taxed higher than the lands of residents.

The State had reason to believe that the same policy would be continued. Since that time, however, the policy has been changed, and immense quantities of land have been entered by military land-warrants, issued to former soldiers in the United States Army. The law authorizing them to be issued provides that these warrants shall be received in payment for lands. The Government, therefore, receives a consideration for the land thus entered, in the discharge of its obligations upon the warrants. It is exceedingly unjust for the Government to destroy the fund which it holds in trust for the State, for the purpose of rewarding those who have rendered it service. Between private persons, the same state of facts would justify a recovery in a court of law. It seems to me that the same principle should prevail between the two governments. The military land-warrants located in this State up to the 30th June, 1856, covered 10,929,692.30 acres. The percentage due to the State thereon is $682,980.20. I have no means of knowing the number of acres located in the fiscal year ending 30th June, 1857, but I judge that the aggregate percentage now due the State approaches very near $1,000,000.

I recommend that Congress be again memorialized on this subject, and that suit be authorized to be instituted against the United States, for the recovery of the amount due, in the Court of Claims.[1]

HOSTILE INCURSION OF INK-PA-DU-TAH'S BAND OF SIOUX INDIANS.

During the past three years my attention has been frequently called to the probability of a collision between the Indians and the settlers in the west and northwestern counties of the State. I have repeatedly addressed the President of the United States, the Secretary of War, and the Commissioner of Indian Affairs, warning them of the apprehended danger, and urging that immediate steps be taken to remove the Indians beyond our limits.

Without any military organization in the State, and without any power to act, except in the event of an actual hostile invasion; residing remote from the scene of anticipated difficulty, and fearful that some exigency might arise that would require prompt and energetic action; in January, 1855, I requested Major William Williams, of Fort Dodge, to assume a general charge of this subject, and authorized him, as far as I had power to do so, to act in

[1] Mr. Grimes, when he became Senator, moved for the payment of this five per cent., but the motion was voted down—yeas, 15 nays, 35—June 7, 1860.

my behalf, in any contingency that might arise in connection with the Indians.

In February last, Ink-pa-du-tah's band of Sioux Indians made a hostile incursion into the State, and perpetrated most horrible atrocities in Dickinson County. When intelligence of this event reached Fort Dodge, Major Williams at once enrolled three companies of men under Captains Richards and Duncomb, of Webster County, and Captain Johnson, of Hamilton County, and proceeded to the scene of difficulty. These heroic men left their homes in the most inclement season of the year, and endured almost unheard-of sufferings and privations; crossing swollen streams flooded with ice, and traversing uninhabited prairies in the most tempestuous weather, that they might save their fellow-creatures from a savage butchery, or rescue them from a captivity worse than death.

Two of their number, Captain J. C. Johnson, of Hamilton County, and William Burkholder, of Webster County, perished on the march. Others returned frozen and maimed. The expedition did not overtake the Indians; but they reached the scene of their barbarities, gave to the dead a Christian burial, and brought back with them two children, the sole survivors of the slaughtered settlement.

The men who thus gallantly and humanely periled their lives have received no compensation for the time employed in the expedition, or for their outfit. The Federal Government is in equity bound for their compensation. The Indian tribes are under its protection and control. It has allotted to each tribe a scope of country for its exclusive occupation. It has sold lands to settlers in this State with the understanding that these tribes shall be confined to their respective limits, and that the possession of the land purchased shall never be disturbed by the Government, or those under its management. If the savages break over their bounds, and inflict injury upon others, the Government should respond to the parties injured for the damages sustained, and for the expenses incurred in protecting themselves against a repetition of the injury. To this end I recommend that a memorial be addressed to the Congress of the United States.

But many of the members of Major Williams's command are unable to await the tardy action of Congress, and I therefore advise that the State assume the payment, and reserve the same from any appropriation that may be made.

I submit to the General Assembly whether some public recognition of the noble gallantry and untimely death of Messrs. Johnson and Burkholder is not alike due to their memory and to the gratitude of the State.

I do not anticipate any further trouble from the Indians. The rumors put afloat in regard to future difficulty can generally be traced to interested persons who seek by their circulation to accomplish some ulterior purpose. To be prepared for any such emergency, however, I have established a depot for arms and ammunition at Fort Dodge, and have procured a cannon, muskets, and ammunition for another depot in Dickinson County.

THE OPINION OF THE SUPREME COURT THAT SLAVERY IS A NATIONAL INSTITUTION.

I cannot close this communication without briefly calling your attention to the extraordinary doctrine announced by some of the Judges of the Supreme Court of the United States in the recent case of Scott *vs.* Sandford, and which the people of this country are now called on to indorse as the true construction of our national Constitution.

The founders of this republic entertained no doubt that Congress had power to make all needful rules and regulations for the government of the Territories of the United States, and that a prohibition of the introduction of African slavery within these Territories was legitimately within the scope of this authority. Such was the universal sentiment of the country, and the principle was recognized in numerous instances by Congress, prior to 1854, when the Missouri Compromise line was obliterated, and the Territories of Kansas and Nebraska created. The new and specious theory of "popular sovereignty" was then promulgated. The people of Iowa were besought to acquiesce in the repeal of the Missouri Compromise, on the ground that, by the principle established by the Kansas-Nebraska act, the people of the Territories would have the power to determine for themselves whether freedom or slavery should prevail within their several jurisdictions. It was contended that the inevitable effect of giving the people the power to settle this question for themselves would be to establish freedom in every Territory—that such were the vitality, and vigor, and advantages of free institutions over slave institutions, that so apparent were the withering influences of slavery upon all the best interests of society, that no intelligent people would encourage or allow it to be established within any of the new Territories. . There was such a degree of plausibility and fairness about this argument that it received the support of a considerable portion of the American people.

But the theory of popular sovereignty, and the theory of the power of Congress over the subject of slavery in the Territories, have alike been overthrown by the decision of the Supreme Court. After overturning the law, as it had been settled more than seventy years, by deciding that Scott was not a citizen, because of his African descent; that he had no right to bring suit; that the court had no jurisdiction of the case, for the reason that there was no case legitimately before it, for the want of a proper party—a majority of the judges proceeded to pass upon what they were pleased to consider the merits of the case.

I am aware that, except upon the single question of the citizenship of Dred Scott, their opinions are entirely extra-judicial, and entitled to no more weight than the opinions of any other citizens. But they are worthy of your consideration, because they foreshadow the opinion that will be authoritatively announced, whenever the proper state of facts shall be presented that may seem to justify it.

It is first declared by a majority of the judges that Congress has no power over slavery in the Territories, and, as a natural corollary, cannot delegate to the people of the Territories a power it cannot itself exercise. It is declared that the Constitution plants slavery upon all the public domain, and there nurtures and protects it.

It is no longer held, under this decision, that freedom is national, and slavery local, confined to the limits of the States that see fit to uphold it. Slavery is in effect declared to be a national institution, belonging not to the States, but to the United States. It is fastened upon every foot of soil belonging to the Government, and there is no power in Congress, or in the Territorial governments, to expel it. Whatever territory may be hereafter acquired by the United States, will instantly become slave-soil. Wherever the flag of the country goes, there goes slavery with its chains and manacles!

The logical result of this decision goes still farther. It carries slavery into every State in this Union.

One of the justices of the Supreme Court even declares that "the only *private property* which the Constitution has *specifically recognized*, and has imposed it as a direct obligation both on the States and the Federal Government to protect and *enforce*, is the *property* of the master in the slave; no other right of *property* is placed by the Constitution upon the same high ground or shielded by a similar guarantee." If this be true, the whole Union is slave territory, and there is no power on earth to abolish it. If both the States and the Federal Government are bound to protect this right of property, there is nothing to prevent slavery from taking possession of Iowa to-day.

But it is not true. There is no such obligation imposed upon the States. The Constitution nowhere regards slaves as property. They are uniformly spoken of as "*persons.*" As "*persons*" they are enumerated and entitled to representation. As "*persons*" they are subject to rendition as fugitives from "service or labor," as are apprentices and minors. As "*persons*" their "immigration or importation" could not be prohibited prior to 1808.

It needs no argument to show that this decision is unwarranted by the facts presented to the courts; that it is revolutionary in its character; subversive of the policy of the founders of the republic, and violates the rights of the States. Being wholly extra-judicial, so far as relates to the power of Congress and the States over slavery, it cannot bind the conscience, or command the obedience of any man.

I trust that, as the representatives of the freedom-loving citizens of Iowa, you will explicitly declare that you will never consent that this State shall become an integral part of a great slave republic, by assenting to the abhorrent doctrines contained in the Dred Scott decision, let the consequences of dissent be what they may.

KANSAS, AND THE TENDENCY OF THE FEDERAL GOVERNMENT TO CONSOLIDATION.

The condition of affairs in Kansas certainly demands your consideration.

Notwithstanding the grossest frauds, and the most unequal legislative apportionment, the people of that unfortunate Territory have declared by an emphatic majority in favor of freedom. No candid mind can now doubt that at least four-fifths of the *bona-fide* citizens of the Territory desire to erect it into a free State.

But the more evident it is that the people do not desire slavery fastened upon them, the more desperate are the efforts of the slavery propagandists to thwart the popular will. We have seen, within a few weeks, a small number of persons, pretending to be the representatives of only a small minority of the people, proclaiming what they call the constitution of Kansas. That constitution recognizes slavery as already established, makes provision for its protection, and undertakes to bind posterity against its abolition. The attempt is made to subvert every principle of popular government by fastening this constitution upon the people without their consent. Conscious that it would be overwhelmingly defeated, if fairly submitted for their approval or disapproval, they are denied the privilege of determining for themselves the character of the institutions under which they are to live. They are not permitted to settle for themselves any of the important questions connected with their judiciary, representation, taxation, internal improvements, education, finance, State indebtedness, or personal rights. For the purpose of riveting slavery upon them, a blow is thus struck at the very foundation principle of popular government. Had a similar attempt been made by the recent Constitutional Convention in this State to force a constitution upon the people, regardless of the popular will, it would justly have resulted in a revolution.

This pretended Constitutional Convention, it is true, proposed a separate article which was submitted to the people, and which, if adopted, establishes slavery in Kansas upon a more barbarous system than is known to any of the slave States of this Union. But no one was permitted to vote either for or against this separate article until he first voted *for* the constitution. He was not allowed to vote against it. Thus, whether the separate article was adopted or rejected, if the constitution, *which could not be voted against*, is permitted to stand as the organic law of the State, Kansas must become a slave State.

We cannot be indifferent to the efforts of the people of Kansas to perpetuate freedom in that Territory. We ought not to be indifferent. No people are deserving of freedom who do not sympathize with those who are struggling to attain it. The people of

Kansas are the champions of popular government everywhere. They are bringing to the test the great principle enunciated by our Revolutionary fathers, that government derives its power from the consent of the governed.

If the recent Constitutional Convention of Kansas, defended as it was by Federal bayonets against the just indignation of the people, can succeed by trick and fraud in fastening an obnoxious constitution upon them, and take away from them the power to amend it until slavery shall become further strengthened, there is an end to free government and American liberty.

The people of Iowa look with alarm upon the constant aggressions of the slavery propagandists, but I confess that I look with equal alarm upon the manifest tendency of our Government to consolidation.

The events of the past few years would seem to indicate that the predictions of some of the men who achieved our liberties for us were being fulfilled. Our Government is fast becoming an elective monarchy. The States are gradually losing their consequence, and will soon be reduced to the condition of mere municipal appendages to the central power. The influence of the Federal Government is prostituted to interference in State affairs, even to that of municipal elections. The doctrine inherited from our ancestors, that standing armies are dangerous to the liberties of the people, is repudiated by constant and strenuous efforts to increase the national army. The Federal Government now asks to control all the banking institutions in the States by virtue of some law of Congress. Sinecure offices are created for the purpose of influencing public opinion. The army of office-holders scattered through the States, uttering the sentiments, disbursing the money, and obeying the commands of the central authority, govern in a great degree the sentiment of the country. Thus, the Federal Government, instead of being, as it was designed to be, the mere creature and under the control of the States, is fast becoming their master.

This centralizing influence of the Government, the immense increase of our national expenses, the history of slavery propagandism in Kansas, and the complicity of the Federal Government therewith, the attempt to overthrow the clearest right of self-government, for the purpose of extending the institution of slavery, and the efforts to destroy the rights of the States by political decisions of the Supreme Court, should remind the freemen of Iowa that their political rights are in danger.

The liberties of the people can only be preserved by maintaining the integrity of the State governments against the corrupting influences of Federal patronage and power.

Closing with this communication my official connection with the government, I may be permitted to avail myself of the occasion to return to my fellow-citizens my heartfelt thanks for the honor and confidence they have bestowed on me, and to assure them of my continued aspirations for the advancement of our beloved State in virtue, prosperity, and happiness.

45.—*To Mrs. Grimes.*

DES MOINES, *January* 23, 1858.

I am pleased to know that my message is satisfactory to my friends, and, saving that portion relating to national affairs, to my political opponents also. It will please you, I know, to be assured that I retire from my late office with the almost universal (and, so far as I know, the universal) opinion of all parties that I made a good officer, and that I discharged the duties of Governor to the acceptance of all parties.

The senatorship will be settled in a few days. It is admitted on all hands, by both friends and enemies, that I am the choice of the people. No one denies that nine-tenths of the Republican voters in the State desire my election. But, it is arrogantly claimed, that the people do not and ought not to control the election of Senators, and that they may be made to acquiesce in whatever the politicians may do in the matter. This is not my theory of "popular sovereignty."

January 25th.—I have just been nominated by the Republican caucus for United States Senator, for six years from March 4, 1859. I received the nomination on the first ballot, by five majority. My vote would have been much larger, and nearly unanimous, on the second ballot—as many voted for persons in their own counties on the first ballot, by way of compliment, who would have voted for me on the second ballot, and for me on the first had their votes been necessary.

January 30th.—Last evening I gave a supper to the members of the General Assembly, State officers, some citizens of the town, and some from abroad. There were one hundred and seventy-eight guests. All the rival candidates were present. The best feeling prevailed. The only drawback was the laudations of me by the speakers. They were Governor Lowe, Lieutenant-Governor Faville, Hon. Lincoln Clark, Finch, Grinnell, and others. I inclose a bill of fare. It was got up, as you see, on temperance principles. Every one says that he never attended a more harmonious, well-conducted, or sumptuous feast.

I shall leave for home in three or four days, but no one can predict how long I shall be on the road. The traveling is horrible, and I fear that it may take me a week to get home.

Mr. Grimes made a brief address at this festival, and, expressing his appreciation of the honor that the General Assembly had conferred upon him, avowed his determination to be the Senator of no clique, or party, but of the whole State. His election was everywhere hailed as a fitting tribute to one whom the people delighted to honor, for his brave and earnest devotion to the Republican cause, and for his ability and fidelity in the office of Governor.

He had been the faithful leader in the political regeneration of the State. At the time of his nomination for Governor, an Iowa Senator said in Congress:

Iowa is the only free State which never for a moment gave way to the Wilmot Proviso. My colleague voted for every one of the compromise measures, including the fugitive-slave law, the late Senator Sturgeon, of Pennsylvania, and ourselves, being the only three Senators from the entire non-slaveholding section of this Union who voted for it.

Now Iowa was redeemed and disenthralled. The change was largely due to the earnestness, and ardor, and force, with which Mr. Grimes had advocated throughout the State his cherished convictions upon the questions at issue.

He maintained the dignity and promoted the welfare of the Commonwealth. He introduced enlightened and liberal measures to develop the resources of the State, to promote public instruction, and guard the sacredness of humanity in prison discipline, and in a considerate treatment of the insane and other unfortunate persons. He consulted in these matters the most advanced and cultivated minds in the land, and secured their suggestions and services in the geological survey, and in the educational and humane establishments of the State. Much is due to his sagacity for the vast system of railways in Iowa, and, had his counsels been heeded, many cities and counties would have been preserved from a heavy indebtedness. Not a few of his recommendations were embodied in the laws. The impress of his mind and character will thus be perpetuated. His wisdom, fidelity, and devotion to public duty in the executive chair, will be for a memorial to his successors in office. One of them has said:

If, in the high duties to which we are called, we would measure ourselves up to a worthy pattern, no better standard can be found than was illustrated in the public life of James W. Grimes.[1]

Rev. Asa Turner, pastor at Denmark, 1838–'68, gives the following reminiscences:

I think that Mr. Grimes has done more for Iowa, politically, than any man that ever lived in it. From its first organization as a Territory, the Democracy reigned supreme up to 1854. Our Representatives in Congress were the allies of the slave-power, and carried out its wishes. The Whigs pretended to be antislavery, but were not willing to do anything that would compromise them with their Southern allies. We had a Free-Soil organization, embracing a few voters, and had nominated Simeon Waters as our candidate for Governor, not with any hope of electing him, but to show our strength. In this state of things, Mr. Grimes came over to Denmark and said that if the Free-Soilers would vote for him he would be a candidate for Governor, and assured us that he would be true to the principles we wished should triumph. I believed he would, and that he could make our principles triumph. The Free-Soilers, after free and full discussion, voted to intrust in his hands the interests of our organization, and the principles we had been laboring to establish. We should not have been willing to commit such interests to any ordinary man, to any one of whose integrity or ability we had a doubt. But it was done—with fear and trem-

[1] Hon. Cyrus C. Carpenter, in his second inaugural, January, 1874.

bling by some, by others with the confidence of faith. He took the stump. I doubt whether any man ever worked harder. He gave his whole soul to the work. Wherever he went he secured favor with the people, and he was elected.

From that day, Iowa has stood in the front rank of liberty-loving and progressive States. And for all we have become, civilly—for all we have done, as a State, to make the United States a blessing at home, and an honor abroad—I look to Mr. Grimes as one of the first and principal instruments. Nothing less than his heart and soul, his resolute will and far-seeing mind, with his powerful influence, could have turned the tide and brought Iowa by the side of Massachusetts and Vermont. There was not a moment to lose. It was only seven years before the rebellion; Iowa must be regenerated, and allied to the right, in order to save the Union. With Iowa neutral, or on the side of the enemy, who can tell what the result would have been? But God purposed otherwise, and raised up Mr. Grimes to marshal her among the loyal States. The influence on the State, and on the country and world, no finite mind can measure. Much as he did as Governor, especially in heading off the Missouri raiders on Kansas, and much as he did in Congress, this early work was preparatory for all that followed. It used to be said that Isaac Hill made New Hampshire Democratic, and allied it with Jackson and Van Buren. It is not a figure of speech that Governor Grimes made Iowa Republican, and allied it with the loyal States.

46.—*To Hon. S. P. Chase.*

BURLINGTON, *February* 20, 1858.

I desire to thank you for your kind note of the 4th inst. The great comfort that my election gives me is enhanced by the apparent satisfaction the result gives to my many friends beyond the State. I have always regarded myself and the cause greatly indebted to you for your influence in my gubernatorial campaign, now four years ago. I was nominated then wholly without my knowledge, and against my desire. I was persuaded to run, not with any very sanguine hope of being elected, but with the view to educate the people, as far as might be possible from the stump, on the slavery question. Had we not succeeded in securing the old Free-Soil vote, which was done mainly through your influence (although I might have been elected, would have been), the General Assembly would have been against us, Mr. Dodge returned to the Senate, the State would have probably remained Democratic, and the succession of anti-Nebraska triumphs that followed our election in the autumn of 1854 would probably have never occurred.

I am conscious of my unfitness for the position I am to occupy. I shall feel constrained to follow in a good degree the counsel of those who have shown themselves to be older and better soldiers than I am. I need not say to you that there is no one by whose advice I shall be more cheerfully guided, than by that of the present Governor of Ohio, in everything that relates to our cause and party.

CHAPTER IV.

A SENATOR OF THE UNITED STATES.

1859–1869.

§ 1.—*In the Thirty-sixth Congress.*—1859–1861.

Mr. Grimes took his seat in the Senate on the 4th of March, 1859, and served in the thirty-sixth Congress on the Committees on Pensions and on Private Land Claims, and was placed, January 24, 1861, upon the Committee on Naval Affairs, in which he remained during the rest of his senatorial career, serving as chairman from December, 1864.

47.—*To Mrs. Grimes*

Washington, *March* 5, 1859.

I write you my first letter from the Senate-Chamber. I was sworn into office yesterday, with seven other new Senators, three of whom are of my complexion in politics, and as substitutes for pro-slavery Democrats.

March 6th.—It is remarked here that a great change has taken place with Southern Senators. For the first time, they came over to the Republican side of the chamber, and sought introductions to the new Republican Senators. Heretofore they cut them socially. I do not include all from the South in this statement. But Hunter, Chesnut, Fitzpatrick, Kennedy, Mallory, Brown, and Benjamin, were quite generous to me, and desire, I think, to be on amicable terms.

Last night I dined at Governor Seward's. Our repast commenced at seven o'clock, and ended when the clock struck twelve. The party was composed of Governor Wilson,[1] of Massachusetts;

[1] Free-Soil candidate for Governor in 1853.

Governor Anthony, of Rhode Island; Governor Bingham, of Michigan; General Shields, of Minnesota; Smith O'Brien, John Mitchel; Preston King, of New York; and your unworthy husband. Governor Seward told me that he went to find O'Brien to invite him, and discovered him at the house of John Mitchel. He was therefore in a measure compelled to invite Mitchel also. This offended Mrs. Seward and her daughter so much, that they declared they would not go to the table, or see him; and they kept their word.

March 9th.—I have come to the conclusion that this is very stupid business. " 'Tis distance lends enchantment " to the Senate. I have by no means had any occasion to complain of my treatment since I came here. I have been given the most conspicuous and important position on the committees of any of the new members of the Senate. Still, the life I shall be compelled to lead is not at all adapted to my habits or inclinations. I have no day since I came here been to dinner earlier than half-past four o'clock. I rise at six, wander about the city like a ghost until nine, when I am permitted to get some breakfast; most people not eating until an hour or two after. Then I am compelled to spend three lazy hours in the best way I can until twelve o'clock, when the Senate assembles. We sit about four or four and a half hours, with closed doors, and then go to dinner. I go to bed at ten o'clock, but the rest of the world sits up nearly all night.

48.—*To Messrs. Hillguertner, Olshausen, and others.*

BURLINGTON, *April* 30, 1859.

I have just had placed in my hands a copy of your letter to the congressional delegation from Iowa, in which you propound to them the following inquiries, viz.:

"1. Are you in favor of the naturalization laws as they now stand, and particularly against all and every extension of the probation time?

"2. Do you regard it a duty of the Republican party, as the party of equal rights, to oppose and war upon each and every discrimination that may be attempted to be made between the native-born and adopted citizens, as to the right of suffrage?

"3. Do you condemn the late action of the Republicans in the Massachusetts Legislature, attempting to exclude the adopted citizens for two years from the ballot-box, as unwise, unjust, and uncalled for?"

To each of these interrogations, I respond unhesitatingly in the affirmative.

In regard to the recent action of the Massachusetts Legislature, I have this to say: that while I admit that the regulation sought to be adopted is purely of a local character, with which we of Iowa have nothing whatever *directly* to do, and while I would be one of the last men in the world to interfere in the local affairs of a sovereign State, or with the action of any party in that State upon local matters, yet I claim the right to approve or condemn as my judgment may dictate. I believe the action of the Massachusetts Legislature to be based upon a false and dangerous principle, and fraught with evil to the whole country, and not to Massachusetts alone. Hence I condemn and deplore it, without equivocation or reserve. Knowing how much the proposed constitutional provision will offend their brethren elsewhere, the Republicans of Massachusetts owe it to their party that this amendment shall be overwhelmingly voted down, and I think it will be.

49.—*To Mrs. Grimes.*

PHILADELPHIA, *November* 24, 1859.

I am safely in this beautiful city of brotherly love, and shall be compelled to remain here a week, to close up some old business that has been dangling on my hands for years.

From Galesburg to Wheaton I was in company with Dr. Blanchard. He wished to be kindly remembered to you, and expressed the hope that you would be led at no distant day to change your religious views, though, I believe, he seemed to entertain a faint hope that you was good enough to go to heaven with your present heterodox opinions. He uttered no word of reproach, remonstrance, or persuasion to me, for having no settled religious convictions; so you perceive that in the view of some of our orthodox friends it is a good deal more dangerous to believe too much than not to believe at all. But Dr. Blanchard is an able, honest, ultra, enthusiastic, and somewhat bigoted man—a great friend of ours, and I entertain great respect for him. We also had on board Mr. Lovejoy, member of Congress of Illinois, a talented and agreeable man. From Crestline, Ohio, to this place, I have been in company with Mr.

Crittenden and his wife, who are on their way to Washington. Perhaps I have told you that Mrs. Crittenden, though a rather elderly lady, is one of the leaders of the *ton* in Washington, as she is in Kentucky, and as she used to be in St. Louis, when she was the wife and widow of General Ashley. She is a very kind, amiable lady, but there is so much precision and mock dignity about everything she says and does, that intercourse with her is not so pleasant as it would be if one could only persuade himself that her heart would come gushing out of her mouth once in a while.

50.—*To Mrs. Grimes.*

WASHINGTON, *November* 30, 1859.

Everybody but me is busy about the organization of the House of Representatives. That, and the execution of John Brown day after to-morrow, are the only topics discussed.

I heard Wendell Phillips lecture on l'Ouverture at Philadelphia, to an immense and breathless audience.

Senate-Chamber, December 6th.—This body was organized yesterday; Mason, of Virginia, immediately introduced Harper's Ferry resolutions, which are to be taken up, and discussed this morning on the assembling of the Senate. So you see the excitement is to be kept up upon the irrepressible conflict question.

Mr. Sumner appeared in his seat yesterday, looking in vigorous health. We expect to hear from him in a great speech during the session. There is an immense crowd of people here for one purpose and another, but I keep out of it pretty much. I am as retired here as ordinarily at home.

51.—*To Mrs. Grimes.*

WASHINGTON, *December* 10, 1859.

One week of congressional life is over, and I think it to be the stupidest business I was ever engaged in. We have done nothing in the Senate but discuss "John Brown," "the irrepressible conflict," and "the impending crisis," and no one can imagine where the discussion will stop. The House of Representatives is still unorganized, and daily some members come near to blows. The members on both sides are mostly armed with deadly weapons, and it is said that the friends of each are armed in the galleries. The Capitol resounds with the cry of dissolution, and the cry is echoed throughout the city. And all this is simply to coerce, to frighten the Republicans and others into giving the Democrats the organization of the House. They will not succeed.

I called on Mrs. Trumbull to-day. She is the only woman I have spoken with since I came here. I called on another, to whose party I was invited the other day, and did not go; but she was not at home. You cannot imagine how I dislike this fashionable formality. It is terribly annoying, and I think I shall repudiate the whole thing.

Sunday, December 11th.—I have just been to church, and heard a long and not remarkably entertaining sermon.

I have about as much as I can do to restrain myself from plunging into the debate in the Senate on John Brown, but I exercise self-denial, and do not.

In the Senate Mr. Grimes gave close attention to public business, and to whatever matters were referred to committees upon which he had been placed, and was early known as a working member of the body. Mr. Hammond, of South Carolina, spoke of him, May 28th, as "an active and able, and rather a young man." Mr. Jefferson Davis, of Mississippi, said, June 13th:

I have been repeatedly struck with the accuracy of view taken by the Senator from Iowa upon military questions. I think in principles he is usually correct, but in detail requires yet to obtain a good deal of information.

He was a skillful parliamentarian and a ready debater, curt, and to the point, never prolix, nor caring for the last word. He spoke in a clear, diréct, and succinct manner, and was heard with attention for his candor and power of elucidation.

Extracts will be given from his remarks at different times upon various subjects. They show his opinions, and the vigilant scrutiny and enlightened consideration he gave to public affairs.

His first remarks in the Senate were in reply to Mr. Toombs, of Georgia, who, January 24th, had arraigned Iowa, with other States, for having passed laws in contravention of the Constitution of the United States, and violative of the rights of sister States. Mr. Toombs said:

Whenever the Republicans have had power, notwithstanding their oaths to maintain the Constitution, they have proved false to it.

DEFENCE OF THE STATE OF IOWA.

Mr. Grimes said, January 30th:

It is true that the Republican party have been in possession of the government of the State of Iowa during the last five years and upward. They have had the unlimited control of the government of that State in every one of its departments. They have had a succession of Governors of that political party. They have had all the judicial tribunals, with very few exceptions; and all the judges of the Supreme Court have belonged to that party. Their majorities in the House of Representatives and in the Senate of the State have been predominating, almost two to one, during four successive Legislative Assemblies. But it is not true that the General Assembly of that State has ever passed any law in violation of the Constitution of the United States, in regard to the fugitive-slave law, or in regard to any other act of Congress. No law has been passed by that State, either since it has been under the domination of the Republican party, or before it came under their control, that in the remotest degree contravenes the rights of any of the sister States, or interferes with the relation of master and slave, or master and servant.

I have not risen for the purpose of making this explanation, because I am disposed to censure or approve the acts of this kind that have been passed by other States. I have no judgment to pronounce upon that subject. I have no criticism to make on that species of legislation. It is no part of my business, as I understand it, to sit here and arraign the action of sovereign States of this Union in regard to their local laws, whether they may be as objectionable as are the laws of Louisiana and South Carolina to Senators, like the Senator from Massachusetts, or whether they are as objectionable as are the laws of Massachusetts and Connecticut to the Senator from Georgia, and others who act and feel with him. That is not my business. But I am not disposed to let the State of my adoption, where I have the happiness to reside, and which I have the honor here in part to represent, have either the glory or the discredit—whichever way they may be regarded by Senators—

of passing any law which she did not pass. Whenever she shall see fit to pass a law of this kind, or of any other kind, I, as a citizen of that State, will express my opinion in approbation or in disapprobation of it, as my judgment shall dictate.

Nor do I allude to this subject at this time for the purpose of relieving myself, my State, or the people whom I represent, from the epithets which were so abundantly poured out upon them by the Senator from Georgia. If there are any people in my State who will be disturbed by them it will not be the men with whom I act, but those who profess a sympathy and affinity for the political party with which the Senator from Georgia associates. So far as the Republicans are concerned, I can vouch for them that they will never be won or intimidated by adjectives, no matter how boisterously, or how numerously, or how harshly, they may be applied.

THE COURT OF CLAIMS.

He said, March 13th :

A few years ago (1855) you organized a Court of Claims. You designed that that court should be a merely examining court; that they should marshal the accounts; that they should investigate questions of law, and submit their conclusions to you for final decision; but, like all courts that have been established since the foundation of the world, it has been constantly attempting to draw to itself more and more power, until now it seeks to acquire the control of the Treasury. During the last Administration, when you had one of the best Secretaries of the Treasury that you ever had—Mr. Guthrie—a decision was made by this court in regard to some drawbacks growing out of your revenue laws, in favor of the claim. Mr. Guthrie objected to that decision, and brought the attention of the Committee on Claims to it, and the committee decided that Mr. Guthrie was right, and that the Court of Claims was wrong; but, if that decision had been confirmed by the Senate, it would have drawn millions of dollars out of the Treasury.

I am opposed to the whole bill. I consider myself standing here as one of the guardians of the Treasury, and am not willing to say that one hundred thousand dollars shall be voted as a gross amount, to meet the judgments that may be rendered by the Court of Claims, upon the supposition that that is the amount which will be required for an average number of years, for I apprehend that the Court of

Claims will be continually drawing to itself more and more power, encroaching more and more on other courts in its jurisdiction, until finally we shall find that we have erected a tribunal dangerous to the Treasury, if not to the liberties of our people.

HOMESTEAD BILL.

Mr. Grimes moved, May 9th, to grant the preëmption right to a single person over the age of twenty-one years, as well as to the head of a family, and remarked:

I cannot see any principle on which Congress should undertake to distinguish between persons, as to their domestic and social relations. Because a man happens not to be a married man, or the head of a family, I do not conceive that a substantial reason why he should be deprived of the benefits of a preëmption, under the laws of the United States. I do not apprehend that gentlemen whom I see around me should be deprived of the benefits of a preëmption, because they are so unfortunate as not to enjoy the domestic felicity which some other members of the Senate are permitted to enjoy. I cannot conceive why the venerable President of the United States, for instance, when he shall retire from the position he now occupies, and shall seek to forget the cares and anxieties of public life, if he chooses to go upon the public domain, should not be permitted to go there and enjoy like privileges with the humblest citizen. It would be unjust to him, and it would be equally unjust to my friends around me, and to any other citizen, and it is in contravention of the settled policy of this Government on this subject.

You have passed since the first preëmption law was adopted, in 1799, fifty-nine preëmption laws. With the exception of three of them, you have granted them without distinction of right, whether persons were citizens, or had filed their declarations to become citizens, or were heads of families, or not. I cannot comprehend why any Senator should propose that this benefit should be conferred upon one class of citizens, to the exclusion of another. Perhaps I may judge of this subject from interested motives. I am myself a settler upon the public lands. I went upon the public domain at the early age of nineteen years, unaided and alone, and established for myself whatever fortune I have been able to acquire; and I was not a solitary instance. I know of hundreds and thousands of young men who went under the same circumstances, to hew out for themselves a fortune and a reputation, if possible. I say it is unjust to them, for Congress to declare that they shall not be permitted to enjoy the same benefits on the public domain with other men, because their domestic or social institutions may be variant. I predicate my action entirely on principle; I ask for the young men of the country no more than for anybody else; but I say that when a young man reaches the age of maturity he should have precisely the same privileges that anybody else has and no more. If it be the sense of the Senate that this amendment be voted down, I shall acquiesce in that decision. I am honestly in favor of the bill. I shall support it. This is the only proposition to amend that I shall make; and I think it is but fair that this should be adopted. I think the Senator from Arkansas ought not to call upon me to withdraw the amendment, for, I wish to show to those with whom I started in the career of my life, that I am still standing by them and by their successors, and undertaking to defend here those rights which I claimed twenty-odd years ago, as one of their number.

The amendment was rejected—yeas 27, nays 28.

Mr. Grimes made a clear statement as to the conflicting decisions respecting lands given to Iowa, in 1846, for the improvement of the Des Moines River navigation, and presented the claims of settlers upon the lands in dispute (three hundred and seventy-one thousand acres) for the interposition of Congress in their behalf (May 26th).

He criticised the extravagance in the Post-Office Department, and on the subject of railroad transportation of the mails said, May 28th:

A great deal of the evil flows from the fact that the railroad companies have got control of your postal routes. I am not arraigning the Department, but the public generally, and Congress, for not interposing in this matter, and passing some law by which we can secure some control over these companies. They ought to be classified into two or three different classes. We ought to fix the amount that each class should be allowed.

UNITED STATES OFFICES IN IOWA.

There are many in my State that are utterly useless, and ought to be abolished. We have half a dozen—I speak without knowing the precise number—custom-houses in our State, fifteen, sixteen, or eighteen hundred miles above tide-water, where we have surveyors of ports, to whom this Government is paying annual salaries of six or eight hundred dollars. We have many other offices which are useless. I have been waiting very patiently during the entire session, in the hope that some of the gentlemen on the other side, who are so much outraged at the profligate expenditure of the Republican party, would introduce a bill abolishing these offices. We have in the town in which I have the honor to reside a marine hospital, built at considerable expense to the Government, which never had a patient, and in all probability never will have. It ought to be abolished. I am not anxious that these offices shall be retained in my State. I am not anxious that the Federal Government shall own property there. If I had my way, I would not have the Federal Government own a foot of ground in the State of Iowa. I do not wish the State to be dotted over with Government offices and buildings, and filled with Federal officers. I do not wish the General Government to be aggrandized at the expense of the States. (June 14th).

52.—*To Mrs. Grimes.*

WASHINGTON, *June* 4, 1860.

We have just had a four hours speech from Sumner on the "Barbarism of Slavery." In a literary point of view it was of course excellent. As a bitter, denunciatory oration, it could hardly be exceeded in point of style and finish. But, to me, many parts of it sounded harsh, vindictive, and slightly brutal. It is all true that slavery tends to barbarism, but Mr. Sumner furnishes no remedy for the evils he complains of. His speech has done the Republicans no good. Its effect has been to exasperate the Southern members, and render it utterly impossible for Mr. Sumner to exercise any influence here for the good of his State. Mr. C. F. Adams made a manly, statesmanly speech in the House of Representatives, four days ago, which was attentively listened to by everybody. He read it, as did Mr. Sumner his.

Mr. Seward is now here, and made a speech in Executive session the other day on the Mexican Treaty, that to my view showed more intellectual vigor than did his speech which you heard. His speech to which I refer was short, extemporaneous, and very able, converting almost the whole Senate to his views.

The nomination of Lincoln strikes the mass of the people with great favor. He is universally regarded as a scrupulously honest man, and a genuine man of the people.

Mr. Grimes took an active part in advocating the election of Mr. Lincoln, and made speeches in many places during the fall, in Iowa and in Illinois.

THE MILITARY ACADEMY AT WEST POINT.

I think the Government expects that the officers of the United States Army shall be something more than mere fighting-men. It expects, and has a right to expect, that they shall be thoroughly educated gentlemen. I, for one, have entertained none of the prejudice that is felt by some toward the Military Academy, and those who graduate from it. That academy, and the character and conduct of those who have graduated from it, have sufficiently vindicated the institution from all aspersions that have been cast upon it. I look upon the military and naval academies as conservative institutions. It is the duty of the Government to give the young men who graduate at each of these institutions the highest attainable education. That is our duty; that is the interest of the Government; and while education is being elevated in every other institution of the country, while your common schools, academies, colleges, and universities, are raising their standards of education, I cannot comprehend any reason why we should not also elevate the standard in our military and naval academies. Hence I am in favor of anything that will have a tendency to operate in that direction. (June 7th.)

ON FURNISHING A POLICE FORCE FOR THE CITY OF WASHINGTON.

I should like to know on what principle it is that the Government of the United States furnishes a police-force to the city of Washington. I understand that the services of these persons are not confined to the public grounds—to the custody of the property belonging to the United States—but that they are the regular police-force of the whole city, under control of the city authorities. If this Government has the authority to furnish such police-officers for this city, why has it not for every city where the Government owns property? The furnishing of this police-force seems to me violative of every principle; and it is another evidence of the fact that this Government is gradually drawing to itself more and more power, and in the end this police-force will swell up from one hundred men to its thousands, and become a guard to any man who may undertake to assume the control of this Government. (June 14th.)

THE NAVY.

Having a favorite nephew in the navy, Mr. Grimes had for years been familiar with naval affairs, and now gave careful and thorough consideration to everything connected with the service. Advocating an increase of pay to minor officers, he said, March 27th:

I have always thought, ever since I paid any attention to the navy, that there were only two things that this Government could honorably do in connection with it; either disband it, or increase the pay of officers to something commensurate with what their services require. It is just as necessary to increase the pay of the minor officers as of the superior officers. The rate of compensation to midshipmen and passed midshipmen was fixed many years ago, when the expenses of living were small. It will be many years before the young men now at your Naval Academy will become lieutenants. The young men who entered the navy in 1840 were between fifteen and sixteen years in the service before they became lieutenants. Then, the service was not dammed up as it is now; there was not such an accumulation of dead matter at the head of the register. The young men who enter your Naval Academy this year will be in the service twenty years, in my opinion, before they become lieutenants. They will be performing as important duties as if they were lieutenants—the duties of passed midshipmen, masters, or acting lieutenants. You should increase the pay of these officers from eight hundred dollars up to something corresponding with the amount their services demand. We do not want to pay the mass of the money that we are going to pay to our officers to the superior officers.

It was his opinion that the navy was too much under the charge of civilians, and that it should be more under the control of naval officers. Accordingly, he proposed, March 28th, the creation of a bureau of registry and detail, to have the assignment of all officers and men to duty. His proposition was rejected.

He early gave attention to the subject of iron-clad vessels, and introduced a resolution, January 19, 1861, directing the Secretary of the Navy to furnish a detailed estimate of the expense of building a steel or iron-clad gunboat.

Advocating, February 11th, the construction of screw sloops-of-war of the second class, that might be as efficient as larger vessels to protect our commerce, with a saving of several hundred thousand dollars, he said:

I vote for this proposition as an economical measure, not with a view to coerce anybody, or for the purpose of entering the ports of any of the Southern States, except for some peaceful purpose; certainly not for any warlike purpose. I believe it is essential for the interests of the country, without regard to the present uneasy and disturbed condition of the Southern States. We cannot be influenced in our action here, and we ought not to abandon the navy because there happens to be dissatisfaction growing out of the slavery question, or out of the tariff question, or out of any other local question. I think we ought to go on in our legislation exactly as though we were at peace with all the world; not with the view to coerce any portion of the country, but to maintain the honor of our flag in foreign seas.

The same day, Mr. Grimes proposed the appointment of an Assistant Secretary of the Navy, from the line of the navy, to be charged especially with the detailing of officers and the discipline and efficiency of the service; and also the establishment of the grade of assistant pay-masters, appointments to be made from graduates of the Naval Academy. The propositions were rejected. His reasons for the last were given as follows (February 11, 1861):

If you go to the line, or to the academy for these officers, it ceases to be a political office, and is not to be bestowed upon anybody because he happens to have been an active or influential partisan in a political campaign. Then, again, you get one who is conversant with the duties of the situation to which he is called, and also acquainted with sea-life. Besides, you give to a purser in the navy a rank as an officer ; and there will be some reason for giving this rank to him, if you take him from the line, or from among the graduates of your academy, and have a man who is competent to discharge sea-duty. There was another reason, and that was because these pursers may be called upon to work the ship—to command the men. In cases of conflict with a foreign power, it may be not only important, but very necessary, to order a purser to command a prize ; or, if the officers were mostly shot down, it might be very important that he should command the vessel on which he was. If you take an officer from the line, or from the academy, and put him in this position, you have a man who is competent to discharge that duty.

That is not all. If you take a man from the academy, or one who has passed through the academy, you get one of perfect *physique.* These young gentlemen, when they go there, are thoroughly examined upon that subject; and you take a man who is perfect in his development and in the prime of life, when he is capable of performing important service to the country. I knew a purser, recently appointed, a man a little past the meridian of life, appointed probably on account of his having been an active partisan; and upon the first cruise, before he had been twelve months in the service, he was stricken down, disabled, and always will remain disabled, and he remains upon your hands a pensioner; and if he lives to be seventy years of age, you will have to pay him a salary amounting to leave-pay. But if you had taken that man at twenty-one, or at twenty-five, or twenty-nine, you would have had probably fifteen, or twenty, or twenty-five years of good, efficient, active service out of him. This amendment, therefore, limits the age at which these young men shall have arrived, in order that we may have men who are not partisans, or broken-down merchants, past the meridian of life, but young, active, thorough-going, efficient men, who can perform efficient duty for the Government.

53.—*To Mrs. Grimes.*

WASHINGTON, *December* 5, 1860.

Secession of one or more States is inevitable. The members of both Houses are in remarkable good-humor, but everybody seems firmly resolved to adhere to his professed principles and course of action. We are getting into deep water, and it is doubtful what shore we shall reach. Mr. Fessenden urges me every day to send for you.

December 16*th*.—I have been writing letters the whole day, and now conclude. I suppose I can hardly add anything to what you have already heard of the condition of things here. Public affairs certainly wear a very bad aspect at present. South Carolina will leave the Union, so far as she has the power, this week, beyond question. Five or six States *may* follow her, and I think that some of them will be sure to. There will be an effort to go peacefully, but war of a most bitter and sanguinary character will be sure to follow in a short time. We can never divide the army, the navy, the public lands, the public buildings, the public debt, the Mississippi River, etc., in peace. All these questions must be submitted in the end to the arbitrament of the sword, and the strongest battalions will be victors. This is certainly deplorable, but there is no help for it. No reasonable concession will satisfy the rebels. It is not that Lincoln is elected, or that there are personal liberty laws in some of the States, or that their negroes occasionally run off, that troubles them. They want to debauch the moral sentiment of the people of the North, by making them agree to the proposition that slavery is a benign, constitutional system, and that it shall be extended in the end all over this continent.

There is, as you have heard, much talk about all sorts of compromises, but there is not the slightest probability that anything will be done. We have a rumor every few hours of bloodshed that is to be, but I do not imagine that anything of the kind is to be apprehended here. A great many men make a great many foolish remarks, and they are sure to increase in magnitude and nonsense as they pass from mouth to mouth.

General Cass has resigned, as well as Mr. Cobb. The whole cabinet is tumbling to pieces, and what remains is without influence. Mr. Buchanan, it is said, about equally divides his time between praying and crying. Such a perfect imbecile never held office before. When Cobb resigned, he sent him a letter, saying that he was going home to Georgia, to assist in dissolving the Union, and breaking up the Government; and Buchanan replied to the letter, and *complimented Mr. Cobb*, as you have seen.

54.—*To Hon. S. P. Chase, Columbus, Ohio.*

WASHINGTON, *January* 11, 1861.

I desire to say, in as few words as possible, that it is the almost universal desire of our true friends here that you should accept the position of Secretary of the Treasury, which it is understood that Mr. Lincoln has tendered to you. We would all like to see you in the Senate. We very well know that you would do great good in this body, but it is vastly important to our party, and, above all, to the country, that we should at the present crisis have the right man at the head of the Treasury. I think I can safely say without any flattery to you, that the general idea among our friends is, that the country will regard the right man in the right place, with you there. Of course, I do not expect or desire to influence you in this matter against your better judgment. I know that you will sacrifice much, by surrendering your place in the Senate for the head of the Treasury, but I beg to assure you that it is my sincere conviction that the safety of the party, and probably of the country, depends upon your being there. Pardon this intrusion.

55.—*To Hon. Samuel J. Kirkwood, Governor of Iowa.*

WASHINGTON, *January* 28, 1861.

Your esteemed favor of the 17th inst. has reached me.

There appears to be a very great misunderstanding in the public mind, as to the present condition of affairs at the capital of the nation, and especially in relation to the demands of the disunionists upon the Union men of the North. I find that the impression prevails quite extensively that the "Crittenden proposition," as it is called, is simply a reëstablishment of the Missouri Compromise line. This is very far from the truth.

Mr. Crittenden proposes to extend the line of 36° 30′ through to the Pacific Ocean, and to agree, by constitutional provision, to protect and defend slavery in all the territory of the United States south of that line. Nor is this all. *He now proposes that this protection to slavery shall be extended to all territory that may hereafter be acquired south of that line.* The sum and substance of the whole matter is, that we are asked, for the sake of peace, to surrender all our cherished ideas on the subject of slavery, and agree, in effect, to provide a slave code for the Territories south of 36° 30′ and for the Mexican provinces, as soon as they shall be brought

10

within our jurisdiction. It is demanded of us that we shall consent to change the Constitution into a genuine pro-slavery instrument, and to convert the Government into a great slave-breeding, slavery-extending empire.

Every man blessed with ordinary foresight must see what would be the inevitable and almost immediate consequence of the adoption of this provision as a part of the Constitution. It would disclose itself to be the very reverse of a measure of peace. Raids would at once begin upon the provinces of Mexico; war would ensue; the annexation of Sonora, Chihuahua, Cohahuila, Nuevo Leon, Tamaulipas, and other provinces, would follow; they would be converted, at the instant of their acquisition, from free into slave Territories, and ultimately be admitted into the Union as slave States. Much as I love peace and seek to pursue it, I am not prepared to pay this price for it. Let no man in Iowa imagine for a moment that the Crittenden proposition is for a mere restoration of the Compromise line of 1820. It is simply and truly the *application* of the Breckinridge platform to all territory now acquired, or *hereafter to be acquired* south of 36° 30′, and would result, if adopted, in the acquisition and admission of new slave States for the ostensible purpose of restoring what is called the equilibrium of the sections. The restoration of the Missouri Compromise line has been offered to the disunionists and contemptuously rejected. Their maxim is "rule or ruin."

I confess that I look with amazement upon the course of the Northern sympathizers with the disunionists. Six years ago they assisted to break down a compromise of thirty-four years' standing, and defended their action by what they claimed to be the right of the people to determine for themselves what should be the character of their own domestic institutions. There was much plausibility in their argument. They made a party creed of it. Now, after the lapse of six short years, they have become so pro-slavery in their opinions that they are willing to ignore the past, and recognize and protect slavery in the very country which they boasted that their own act had made free.

There are other provisions in the Crittenden resolutions which to my mind are wholly inadmissible, but let them pass. My objection is to any compromise. I will never consent to compromises, or the imposition of terms upon me or the people I represent, under threats of breaking up the Government. I will not "give reasons under compulsion." No surer or more effectual way could be devised for converting this into a revolutionary Government than the adoption of a compromise expedient at this time.

Eight months ago the four political parties of this country, in their several conventions, announced certain abstract propositions in their platforms which each believed to be true, and which, if acted upon, would in their opinion most conduce to the prosperity of the whole country. The issue upon these propositions was submitted to the people through the ballot-boxes. One party was successful, as either might have been, but for the lack of votes; and now one of the vanquished parties seeks to overthrow the Government, because they were not themselves the victors, and will only consent to stay their work of demolition upon the condition that we will agree to make their platform, which is abhorrent to us, a part of the Constitution of the country. After taking their chances for success, and being defeated in a fair and manly contest, they now seek to overthrow the Government under which they live, and to which they owe their allegiance. How rapidly are we following in the footsteps of the governments of Mexico and South America!

I do not believe that the public mind is now in a condition to calmly consider the great questions involved in the amendments proposed. But suppose the people were willing and anxious that such amendments to the Constitution should be submitted to them; suppose they were in a proper frame of mind to weigh them and decide upon their adoption; suppose their adoption was not attempted to be enforced by threats, can we have any assurance that this is the last demand to be made upon us? Can we be certain that success in this instance will not whet the appetite for new concessions and new demands, and that similar threats of secession and revolution will not succeed every future presidential election? Will the demand for new guarantees stop here? Shall we not be as liable to have our trade paralyzed, our finances deranged, our national flag insulted, the public property wrested from us and destroyed, and the Government itself overthrown, four years hence, if we amend the Constitution, as we should be if we now stand firmly by our principles and uphold the authority of the Government?

The question before the country, it seems to me, has assumed gigantic proportions. It has become something more than an issue on the slavery question growing out of the construction of the Constitution. The issue now before us is, whether we have a country, whether or not this is a nation. Is this a Government which Florida, with eighty thousand people, can destroy, by resolving herself out of the Union and seizing the forts and arsenals within her borders? That is the question presented us for our decision. Can a great and prosperous nation of thirty-three millions of people be destroyed by an act of secession of some of its members? Florida and her sister revolutionary States answer in the affirmative. We deny it. They undertake to act upon their professed belief, and secede, or, as I term it, rebel against the Government. While they are in this attitude of rebellion a compromise is presented to us for adoption, by which it is proposed, not to punish the rebellious States, but to entice them back into the Union. Who does not see that by adopting these compromise propositions we tacitly recognize the right of these States to secede? Their adoption at this time would completely demoralize the Government, and leave it in the power of any State to destroy. If Florida and South Carolina can secede because of the slavery question, what shall prevent Pennsylvania from seceding because the Government declines to adequately protect her iron and coal interests, or New England because her manufactures, or New York because her commerce is not sufficiently protected? I could agree to no compromise until the right to secede was fully renounced, because it would be a recognition of the right of one or more States to break up the Government at their will.

Iowa has a peculiar interest in this question. If this right of State revolution be conceded, her geographical position is such as to place her completely in the power of revolutionary States. Will she agree that one State can secede and take from her the mouth of the Mississippi River, that another can take from her the mouth of the Missouri, and that others shall be permitted to deprive her of the right of passage to the Atlantic Ocean? If she will not agree to this, it becomes her people to insist that the Constitution of the country shall be upheld, that the laws of the land shall be enforced, and that this pretended right of a State to destroy our national existence shall be sternly and emphatically rebuked. I know the people of Iowa well enough to believe that appeals to their magnanimity, if not successful, will be kindly received and considered, while appeals to their fears will pass by them as the idle wind, and that they will risk all things and endure all things in maintaining the honor of the national flag and in preserving the national Union.

One word more and I close this letter, already too long. At the commencement of the session, before revolution had assumed its present gigantic proportions, before any State had pretended to secede except South Carolina, before the forts and arsenals of the United States had been captured, the flag of the country fired upon, and the capital of the nation threatened, I assented, as a member of the Senatorial Committee of Thirteen, to three propositions, which were to the following effect, viz.:

1. That Congress should never be permitted to interfere with the domestic institutions of any State, or to abolish slavery therein.

2. That the several States should be advised to review their legislation in regard to persons of color, and repeal or modify all such laws as might conflict with the Constitution of the United States or with any of the laws of Congress made in pursuance thereof.

3. To admit Kansas into the Union under the Wyandotte constitution, and then to admit the remaining territory belonging to the United States as two States, one north and one south of the parallel of 36° 30′ with the provision that these States might be subdivided and new ones erected therefrom whenever there should be sufficient population for one Representative in Congress upon sixty thousand square miles.

Those propositions, if adopted, would have quieted the apprehensions of the Southern people as to the intention of the people of the free States to interfere with slavery in the States, and would have finally disposed of all the territory belonging to the Government. They would have made two very inconvenient States, but they would have settled a very inconvenient question. They could have been adopted without any surrender of principle by anybody or any section, and therefore without any party and personal humiliation. But they were spurned by the disunionists. They preferred to plunge the country into revolution, and they have done it. It only remains for us now to obey and enforce the laws, and show to the world that this Government is strong enough to protect itself from rebellion within as well as from assault without.

The issue now made up for the decision of the people of this country is between law, order, the Union, and the Constitution, on the one hand, and revolution, anarchy, dissolution, and bloodshed, on the other. I do not doubt as to the side you and the people of Iowa will occupy in this contest.

January 21st Mr. Grimes gave his vote for the admission of Kansas into the Union.

February 5th, at the request of the Governor of Iowa, he attended a Peace Conference, held in Washington at the call of the Legislature of Virginia, but did not take part in its discussions, confident that they would end in naught.

THE TARIFF.

He said, February 18th:

I wish to insert "sugar" with tea and coffee in the amendment, so that at the expiration of two years there shall be no duty either on tea or coffee or sugar. I object most decidedly to the idea that those of us who shall vote in favor of the reduction of the duty on sugar are going to vote it from revenge, or out of retaliation, or out of any unkindness toward Louisiana, or the sugar-producers of that State. This bill comes before us as an entirely new bill, and I propose to vote on this sugar-duty, and on all other duties, precisely as I should vote if we had no tariff on our statute-books. I will not now, I never saw the time when I would, and I never expect to see the time when I will, vote for a duty on tea and coffee and sugar. I will not consent to tax the farmers of my State upon the iron they use for the benefit of Pennsylvania, and upon their jack-knives for the benefit of Connecticut and Massachusetts, and upon their woolens and cottons for the benefit of New England, and then add to that a tax upon tea and coffee and sugar, the necessaries of every man's home. I have my views in regard to secession, in regard to the attitude of Louisiana, and of all the States that have gone out; but, as the representative of my State, I cast my vote as I believe the interests of my State require on that particular measure, without any regard to the attitude of those outgoing States.

During the stormy months at the close of this Congress, treason coming to a head, distrust pervading every part of the Government, many in confidential positions being of doubtful loyalty, or privy to evil designs, Mr. Grimes was associated with several gentlemen in an effort to have persons of traitorous intent, in the public service or elsewhere, sifted out and marked, with an eye to the national safety in the trouble that threatened. The Superintendent of Police of the City of New York and skilled detectives were employed and kept upon watch at Baltimore, Washington, and other places, who reported to Mr. Grimes the actual position of doubtful persons, and the plots and conspiracies they unearthed. Contrary to his principles as was a system of surveillance and espionage, but possessing a remarkable power of worming men's secrets out of them, with an air of calmness and unconcern such as Napoleon attributed to his minister of police, he was called at this juncture to act as a sort of Fouché for the Government, in the interest of the incoming Administration. Under his direction this delicate and responsible service was performed, without trenching upon propriety, without injustice to any one, with acknowledged advantage to public order, and with such skill and caution as commanded respect, and obviated suspicion or offense.

§ 2.—*In the Thirty-seventh Congress.*—1861–1863.

Mr. Grimes was in his place in the Senate at the Special Session, March 4th, and on the last day of the session, March 28th, expressed his full agreement with the sentiment of a resolution, offered by Mr. Trumbull, that the true way to preserve the Union was to enforce the laws, and that it was the duty of the President to protect the public property in all the States.

After the attack on Fort Sumter, April 12th, and the President's call for troops, April 14th, he was requested to go to Washington in behalf of the Iowa soldiers, by Governor Kirkwood. At Annapolis he found a military force occupying the grounds of the Naval Academy. He proceeded with a naval officer to Washington, visited the Secretary of War and the Secretary of the Navy, before either was out of bed in the morning, secured orders for a temporary transfer of the Academy to Fort Adams, Newport, and saw the students embark on the ship Constitution.

56.—*To Hon. William P. Fessenden, Portland, Maine.*

BURLINGTON, *May* 12, 1861.

I have just received your note of the 9th inst., inclosing one to your son, which I reinclose to you. I returned from Washington last Monday in the night, whither I went at the instance of our State authorities, and found that Frank had been here and left, remaining but one day, and that he spent at the tavern. Mrs. G. says she tried to induce him to remain, and to make our house his home, but he had his head full of the army, and was in a great hurry to get away. I am sorry that he did not remain a little longer, that we might have seen more of him.

It is quite evident to my mind that this great rebellion is to be suppressed; but, in the effort, it occurs to me that we are about to encourage precedents that will be very dangerous to the rights of the States, and to the liberties of the people. This attempt of Mr. Lincoln to add ten legions to the regular standing army, each legion to equal in size three regiments, without any authority of law, and against law, is the most extraordinary assumption of power that any President has attempted to exercise. Our ancestors were so jealous of executive power that they refused to allow the President to call even the militia into service for a period exceeding thirty days after the assembling of the next ensuing session of Congress. Mr. Lincoln is not content with violating that law, and calling for volunteers for three years, making them in effect a standing army subject to his will, but he goes away beyond that, and more than doubles the standing army, and *issues commissions* to officers which are not authorized by law. Where is this to stop? Will he be content with ten legions? If so, will the next President? What do you think of this thing? I do not wish to oppose the Administration, but I will not support such a measure.

57.—*To Hon. W. P. Fessenden, Portland, Maine.*

BURLINGTON, *June* 6, 1861.

The whole action of the President in regard to the volunteers the blockade, etc., has been unconstitutional, but I am willing to overlook that, dangerous as it may be. But I cannot and will not agree that he shall be permitted to remodel the army, more than double its size, and appoint nine hundred new officers, without any authority of law, and without the slightest justification in the condition of the country. I say, condition of the country ; by that I mean, that the country demanded *immediate* troops, if any at all, and they could only be secured by volunteering. Do you know that, while we are paying the officers of the new regiments their salaries, there are not so many men as there are officers? While four hundred thousand volunteers have rallied to our standard, there have not been fifteen hundred men recruited for the regular army. These new regiments cannot be got ready for the field for a year yet, and then they will be raw men, no better than volunteers. They say we shall want them when the war shall be over. Well, who is to judge of that, the President or Congress? Was it not possible to wait until the 4th of July, to let the *constitutional* authority speak on that subject? The precedent is the thing that troubles me. Will it not justify the next President in doing the same thing, and if so, how extensive must the insurrection be that will justify him? Where is this thing to stop? I see conscription and direct taxes in the future. I shall be the only man in the Senate who will vote against the increase of the standing army.

58.—*To Mrs. Grimes.*

HILLSBOROUGH, N. H., *June* 23, 1861.

You cannot, perhaps, comprehend the depression of my spirits while I am here. I feel as though I were spending my time among the tombs, and long to have the morning come that I may start away. All about me are memorials of the past, mementoes of friends lost, and very few cheerful faces known to me. People are as much excited about the war in this region as elsewhere. Every one asks me, when will a battle take place, and when will the war cease, as though I knew any more on the subject than others. I am just going to church ; I know that information will please you.

The following correspondence of a later date explains an incident of this period, and his practical action with reference to slavery in the District of Columbia.

To Hon. J. W. Grimes.

SENATE-CHAMBER, *February* 20, 1868.

In reflecting over some of the earlier incidents of the rebellion, I call to mind a circumstance in connection with yourself with great interest and satisfaction. By the law and the custom of the District of Columbia a large number of escaped slaves were incarcerated in the jails of the city of Washington. To these were added a large number of free men confined on suspicion of being fugitive slaves, through a superserviceable zeal for slavery on the part of the local authorities. In calling my attention to this fact you portrayed the hopeless condition of the slaves, and the helpless plight of the free men. The former could only look forward to the lash for daring to seek liberty, the latter were bound to serve a period after their freedom was legally established, in violation of every principle of justice, and in contempt of every instinct of generosity.

The result of our interview was, that we determined on a general jail-delivery by military authority. On the 3d of July, 1861, I think, this conversation took place. It ended by your undertaking the work, and my signing an order for the enlargement of all such prisoners on the day following, July 4, 1861. It gratifies me to remember that in the execution of this order you did no violence to the proverbial promptness of military law.

As the historical interest of fixing the date of the first act of practical emancipation increases and may yet become a subject of controversy, I would be obliged if you will give me such facts in connection with this incident as may yet retain a place in your memory. Your friend,

SIMON CAMERON.

The following draft of a reply was found among Mr. Grimes's papers:

59.—*To Hon. Simon Cameron.*

WASHINGTON, *February* 22, 1868.

I remember very distinctly the circumstance referred to in your letter of the 20th instant, now before me.

In March, 1861, I was appointed chairman of the Senate District of Columbia Committee, and felt it to be my duty to inform myself of the condition of the public institutions of the District by personal inspection, as well as by an examination of the official reports of those in immediate charge of them. Upon visiting the jail, I found a large number of colored persons detained there ; some for safe keeping at the instance of those who claimed to own them, some on the ground that they were supposed to have escaped from their masters, though there was no evidence of that fact ; and some because of alleged acts of insubordination to their masters or mistresses. In a word, I found that the jail, perverted from the uses for which it was erected, was being used for private purposes, and as a means of oppression.

Public sentiment was not at that time sufficiently advanced to justify an appeal to Congress with any prospect of success, and, as the District of Columbia was under martial law, I appealed to you. You at once, as Secretary of War, directed an officer of the Army to proceed with me to the jail, and set all captives of the above description free, and from that time forward the jail has been used only for legitimate purposes. I cannot recollect the precise date at which this was done, save that it occurred in 1861, and before the subject of the abolition of slavery in the District of Columbia had been taken into consideration by Congress.

Mr. Grimes was in his seat at the assembling of Congress, July 4th. Knowing how fiery and resolute were the master-spirits of the rebellion, he advocated a definite war policy and the prompt and vigorous prosecution of the war. Counseling the concentration of all the forcēs of the nation upon this object, and the discontinuance meanwhile of appropriations for other things, he said, for instance, with reference to the Coast Survey:

Many of the officers are receiving their salaries to keep them ready for prosecuting the work at some future time. I want those gentlemen to have an opportunity to leave their present business, and that they shall not be kept at our expense without employment. Let them go into the Army or the Navy, and render the services we have a right to expect under the circumstances. I want to show to the country, that while we are appropriating one hundred and seventy-nine million dollars in one bill (for the Army) there is a little evidence of a disposition to curtail expenses somewhere else. I have been told that in order to keep up the Coast Survey, for which we appropriated nearly half a million of money, the forces have been transferred to the lakes; but I do not think we have the means for it now, and therefore I wish that that money may be diverted to another channel, and used for the energetic prosecution of the war.

He was a close observer of every military and naval movement, and of the skill and prowess of different commanders. A fine judge of official capacity, and quick to detect incompetency, he wanted to see inefficient officers retired, and men of ability and skill placed in important commands, irrespective of rank or grade. His advice and counsel aided in putting forward a number of naval commanders, who became illustrious for their exploits. Speaking of the Navy, he said, July 31st:

It is confessedly the fact that the younger officers are better educated, are more scientific than the older ones. There are men in your lieutenants' rank who possess more information in regard to the science of gunnery than your older captains. Why not avail yourselves of the information and scientific skill they possess? There are lieutenants to-day in command of some of your largest steamships. Why not avail yourselves of their ability, integrity, and capacity? I do not believe in the Army or the Navy being controlled as a close corporation for the benefit of any particular rank. It is for the interest of the country that the best talent in each of these grades should be put into service.

Jealous from long conviction of an increase of the standing army, Mr. Grimes felt that the proper reliance for the defense of the country was upon volunteers. He said, July 15th:

There is not a man in this Senate who will go before me in a disposition and in an anxiety to furnish to the President every means in the power of this body to put down this very causeless and wicked rebellion; but I do not believe that by the creation of these eleven regiments we put any power in his hands. Men do not wish to enlist into the regular service. You lack several thousand of as many as you are authorized to have in your old regiments, and yet undertake to raise another regular service to the extent of twenty-four thousand men, and to fasten that upon the country as a permanent standing army. I see it stated that the week before last, in New York, where are the headquarters of the Eleventh Regiment, and where are between forty and fifty officers in recruiting stations, the whole number of men recruited for six days was twelve—two men to a day. If, instead of sending forty men, you had sent one man, and called for volunteers, in the name of the United States, instead of twelve men, you would have had twelve thousand.

An argument urged here is, that we need a larger standing army. I do not believe it. I cannot sympathize in that argument. I believe, with my ancestors, that standing armies are hostile in their tendency and effect on republican government; that they are provocative of wars; and I am not willing to say to the people of my section of the country that they are hereafter to support a larger standing army than that which is now authorized. I am willing to vote all the volunteers that may be necessary; I am willing to assist in making these regiments into volunteer regiments; but never into regiments of a standing army. It is said that a proper force last fall, in the hands of proper men, would have prevented all this trouble. Now, my conviction is that if we had had a standing army last winter to the extent of seventy thousand men in this country, under the command of the then Secretary of War, the present President of the United States would never have been inaugurated in the office which he now holds. I want the yeas and nays. I want to record my name against the permanent increase of the standing army.

The Navy was Mr. Grimes's favorite arm of service. He made himself familiar with its entire organization, and with all its operations, and knew the rank and rate of every officer and ship. Though representing an interior State, not directly interested in the commerce and manufactures of the seaboard, he believed the Navy the right arm of the public defense, that it would be as efficient as the Army in the present troubles, and that it was destined to become of much more consequence to the nation. He was the first member of the Senate to suggest the introduction of iron-clad vessels into the Navy, and to bring the attention of the country to the subject. He brought in a bill for the construction of armored ships, July 19th. The following remarks show his habits of observation and inquiry:

It so happens that for two or three years I have read everything I have seen or come across on the subject of iron-clad ships, and on my way hither sought all the information I could in New York and Brooklyn. The experiments in France, in England, and in this country, have demonstrated that, however valueless or valuable armored ships may be as cruisers, they certainly are destined to be valuable for the defense of harbors. This is the opinion of the scientific men in this country and in Europe. In case a conflict with some foreign power might grow out of our present complications, it would be very important that the Government should have the power to construct floating batteries for the defense of our harbors, that could take position anywhere to resist the fleet of an enemy.

In the Assistant Secretary of the Navy, Hon. G. V. Fox, he found a gentleman of signal ability, intent upon public duty, possessing, after nineteen and a half years' service in the Navy, thorough insight into naval affairs, and who had been long enough in civil life to be clear of the jealousies and entanglements from which the naval profession is not exempt. Between Mr. Grimes and Mr. Fox a mutual confidence was at once established. Through the war, during the sessions of Congress, they were in the habit of meeting for consultation in Mr. Grimes's parlor, at least three times a week, when all naval matters of every description were discussed and settled. Mr. Grimes had himself a large naval correspondence. All the diverse views gathered from all sides, naval and political, he would carry in his head, bring them forth, force the Secretary to an opinion, and after full discussion he would sum up in his clear, concise, common-sense way. The next day he would present the whole matter before the Senate, in a little more elaborate but in the same truth-convincing manner. No one could answer him, and finally both sides accepted his statements as the end of the whole matter. Every measure, great or small, connected with the Navy, from July, 1861, until Mr. Fox left for Russia, had this discussion. There was no disposition of important commands that was not a matter of consultation with him.

60.—*To Mrs. Grimes.*

WASHINGTON, *July* 22, 1861.

Yesterday I was on the field of battle. No one can have a proper conception of its horror. Our army was totally routed, with immense destruction of life on both sides. I was not much exposed, except to capture, which I escaped by less than a minute. I have witnessed the last battle-field, certainly the last I shall visit voluntarily. I cannot picture its horrible details, but will tell you of them, if I can.

July 29th.—The enemy's pickets are close upon us, but we have no fears of what the result is to be. Our new general is here, and inspires great confidence. Would that we had the same confidence in some of the members of the cabinet!

61.—*To Mrs. Grimes.*

WASHINGTON, *August* 4, 1861.

I am happy to say that we shall adjourn in two days. I am on a select committee to investigate the causes of the loss of the Norfolk and Pensacola Navy-Yards, and Harper's Ferry Arsenal, which will sit in the recess, and that possibly may detain me a day or two, but I hope not. It will compel me, however, to leave home again in October. The city is now under the most rigid military discipline, and perfect order prevails everywhere. All have unbounded confidence in General McClellan. There are about eighty thousand troops in the vicinity.

John Grimes is getting well. He was blistered and dosed to his heart's content. His trouble was the shock of a large Minié-ball, which struck him in the chest, and knocked him over. The concussion, and going two entire days without food or sleep, and the last one in a drenching rain, caused a sort of hæmorrhage of the lungs. His officers say he behaved very gallantly. He did not shrink from any part of his duty, was the last to come in, and brought with him, alone, the remnant of the battalion of marines.

I hope to see you soon, and I long to have the day come. This congressional life is poor business—taking one away from all he loves, and that can make him happy. I have a great many things to tell you about the battle.

62.—*To J. H. Gear, W. F. Coolbaugh, A. W. Carpenter, Joshua Copp, J. G. Foote, and other Citizens of Burlington.*

BURLINGTON, *August* 17, 1861.

I have received your favor of the 15th instant, in which you congratulate me upon my return to the State, and invite me to address the people of this city, at such time and place as I may designate, on the important questions now before the country, involving the existence of the Government.

I appreciate, as I ought, the kind feeling that prompted this invitation, and return you my sincere thanks for it. I would address you at any time and at any place, if I supposed I could communicate a particle of information not already in the possession or within the reach of every citizen of the State. I could only say in many words, what I now say in a few, that it seems to me that there is no safe alternative before us, but to give a firm and ardent support to the Government in its attempt to put down insurrection and rebellion. More than any State in this Confederacy, Iowa should resist the pretended right of a State to secede from it. Our position in the centre of the continent, without foreign commerce, dependent upon other States for our markets and for our means for transportation to reach them, would soon, if the right to destroy the Union by the secession of the States be conceded, place us in the character of a dependent and conquered province. We need, and must have, at whatever cost, a permanent government and unrestricted access to the Atlantic Ocean and to the Gulf of Mexico. There must be no foreign soil between us and our markets.

As one of the Representatives of Iowa in the Federal Congress, I have sought to give expression by my votes to what I believe to be the opinions of the people of the State, and have uniformly voted all the men, money, ships, and supplies, that were asked for. In doing so, I have not only expressed what I believed to be their wishes, but I have acted upon my own convictions of duty. I shall continue to do so until this unholy war shall be brought to a successful conclusion.

The public debt that this war will impose upon us will appall some and perhaps dampen the patriotism of some. Most erroneous impressions, however, seem to prevail as to the magnitude of our present indebtedness, and that which we are likely to create. The entire public indebtedness of this country on the 6th instant, the day Congress adjourned, was a hundred and eleven million dollars, most of which was inherited from the preceding Administration, and the estimated expenses of the next year, for military, naval, and civil purposes, were less than three hundred million dollars, less than the annual expenses of Great Britain in a time of profound peace. In connection with the aggregate of these two sums let us remember that England paid eight thousand five hundred million dollars to carry on her wars with the first Napoleon. She was contending for her commercial rights, and the result showed that her money was well expended: we are not only contending for our commercial rights, but we seek to uphold and perpetuate the best Government ever known among men.

Foreigners call us, with great truth, the most impatient people on the earth. This natural impatience is greatly increased by our present troubles. We all want peace restored and business revived, and most of us believe that a permanent peace can only be established by the victorious arms of our soldiers. Our anxieties in this regard are very liable to cause us to do great injustice to the Government and to ourselves also. We clamor for victories, forgetting that the most thorough preparation is necessary to achieve them. We forget the condition of the country four months ago, and ask that that shall be done in a week which requires months of arduous labor to perform. Very few fully appreciate the difficulties by which the President of the United States found himself surrounded, when he assumed power on the 4th of March last. Many of the Executive Departments had recently been under the control of traitors. The army had been dispersed and demoralized, and many of the most trusted and prominent officers were disloyal. Our vessels-of-war were scattered upon foreign and remote stations. The Departments were full of spies and traitors. The public armories had been plundered and their contents delivered to the rebels. The President was without an army, without a navy, without arms or munitions of war, and with enemies within and without. In this condition of things, and after an almost uninterrupted peace of fifty years, he was called upon to organize in a few weeks five armies, each of them larger than any that had ever been marshaled on this continent, and to improvise a navy with which to blockade a coast greater in extent than that which England was unable to blockade with more than four hundred vessels-of-war in 1812–'14. That there have been mistakes committed in the selection of agents and officers cannot be denied, but, that there has been any lack of energy or of devotion to the cause of the country, it seems to me that no fair man who examines the subject will assert. Few persons comprehend all the labor, the time, and the perplexities involved in furnishing clothing, arms, transportation, stores and pay for four hundred and fifty thousand men, and in purchasing or building, manning, arming, and equipping two hundred vessels-of-war by a Government whose credit was impaired, whose armories had been destroyed, and whose munitions of war had been stolen, and to do all this in the space of three months.

It becomes us to be hopeful and patient, bearing in mind that the authorities in Washington are resolved that their preparation for the conflict shall correspond with the magnitude of the conspiracy they are compelled to encounter.

You say, gentlemen, that you address me without distinction of party, and I find among the signatures appended to your letter the names of many to whom I have always been politically opposed. Permit me to say that the time has arrived when I am anxious to forget all party names, and party platforms, and party organizations, and to unite with anybody and everybody in an honest, ardent, and patriotic support of the Government—not as a party Government with a Republican at its head, but as the national Government, ordained by and for the benefit of the *whole* people of the country.

63.—*To A. C. Barnes, Albia, Monroe County, Iowa.*

BURLINGTON, *September* 16, 1861.

Your letter of the 13th instant, in which you say, "Ever since Breckinridge made his treasonable speeches in the United States Senate, it is being constantly reiterated that President Lincoln has violated the Constitution, and, as evidence of the fact, it is asserted that the Senate refused to ratify his acts;" and in which you ask me "to state whether the charge that Congress did refuse to sustain the acts of the President is true or not," has come duly to hand.

By referring to the "Acts and Resolutions passed at the First Session of the Thirty-seventh Congress," page 89, section 3 of Act LVIII., a copy of which I send you, you will observe that it is enacted "that all the acts, proclamations, and orders of the President of the United States, after the fourth of March, eighteen hundred and sixty-one, respecting the Army and Navy of the United States, and calling out or relating to the militia or volunteers from the States, are hereby approved, and in all respects legalized and made valid, to the same intent and with the same effect as if they had been issued and done under the previous express authority and direction of the Congress of the United States."

This section ratifies and confirms, to the fullest possible extent, all the acts of the President that needed or that were susceptible of ratification, and was adopted by the vote of every Republican and loyal Democratic member of the Senate present. So far as I am informed, I believe it was all the confirmation of the acts of the President that he either expected or desired.

I know it is urged by some, but mostly, if not entirely, by those who are opposed to the vigorous prosecution of the present war, that it was also necessary to confirm the acts of the President suspending, in some cases, the writ of *habeas corpus*. It must be apparent, I think, to every one who will reflect upon the subject, that to have attempted such confirmation would be to inferentially admit that, as commander-in-chief of the Army and Navy of the United States, the President had no power to suspend the operation of that writ without congressional authority. Very few, if any, loyal members of Congress were willing to admit that. They did not doubt but that he had complete power in the premises, and they chose to leave him to exercise his authority under the Constitution according to his own judgment and as the exigencies of the country might require. They did not believe that his acts in this regard needed confirmation, and therefore confined their ratification and approval to such acts as required legal enactments for their basis, and in the initiation of which they had been anticipated by him.

There may be some who honestly believe that the Senate refused to support the President because of their failure to pass certain resolutions presented by Mr. Wilson, of Massachusetts. The facts in regard to those resolutions were these: They were introduced at an early day in the session, and were put aside from day to day to make room for what was considered more important business, until just at the close of the session, when they had reached that stage in parliamentary proceedings when it was impossible to amend them without unanimous consent, and that could not be obtained. The objection urged by some gentlemen against them as they stood without amendment was, that they were improperly drawn, inasmuch as the phraseology was in the past tense, and declared that the acts of the President *were* legal and valid when performed, whereas, as they insisted, they ought to have declared that those acts *should be* legal and valid as though done under the sanction of law. It was a question of grammatical construction. This, if my memory serves me correctly, was the position of Mr. Sherman, of Ohio, whose action has been much criticised in this State, as well as elsewhere. He declared his willingness, nay his anxiety, to justify and approve the acts of the President, but he was unwilling to say that those acts were legal at the time they were performed. Although not agreeing with him in his construction of the phraseology of the resolutions, it is due to him to say that no man in America was more anxious than he to give to the Administration an honest, hearty, and patriotic support. And, when the legalization of its proceedings was put in what he believed to be proper language, he cordially sustained it.

It was simply on account of this objection in the minds of a few Senators that the resolutions which it was impossible to amend were dropped, and the substance of them incorporated into a law.

Be assured that all these charges of a refusal to support the Administration by Republican and loyal Democratic Senators are devices of the enemy, and should only serve to make the path of duty more plain before us. That duty, it seems to me, is obvious. We should enthusiastically rally to the support of the noble and true men who were nominated by the convention held at Des Moines on the 31st day of July last. They are the representatives of the Government in this crisis. A vote for them will be a vote in support of the Administration, in favor of the integrity of the Government, and for peace through victory. Let us give to Governor Kirkwood, who, in the last six months, has done more hard work, incurred greater responsibilities, and been more causelessly abused than all the Governors that Iowa ever had, that cheering, sweeping majority that his patriotism, his integrity of purpose, and his devotion to the true interests of the State, so justly merit.

64.—*To Hon. W. P. Fessenden, Portland, Maine.*

BURLINGTON, *September* 19, 1861.

Of course, you are so terribly oppressed with the great affairs of the finance department of this Government as to be wholly unable to write a letter to one of the outside barbarians in Iowa. I would not disturb your labors or your repose, if I did not deem it important to glorify myself a little over the result of the "circulation Treasury-notes" measures, about the success of which those learned financial pundits, Fessenden and Chase, expressed so many doubts. You learn, of course, as I do, that at least one hundred thousand dollars of them can be floated to the manifest advantage of the Government, and to the immense advantage of this poor and benighted region. If that pure patriot and model of a public officer, whom you feel called on to defend when aspersed, would call some Pennsylvanians into the field, instead of keeping them all at home to fill army contracts, and let some of the army contracts and supplies be furnished here, business would once more assume a hopeful condition in the West. But we ought not to complain. We ought to console ourselves with the reflection that Pennsylvania furnishes one-third of all the officers to the army, and of course this draw upon her resources must impair her ability to furnish privates.

When it was reported that Fremont was suspended, cold chills began to run up and down people's backs, they bit their lips, said nothing, *but refused to enlist.* I know nothing of the merits of the controversy, but it is as evident as the noonday sun that the *people* are all with Fremont, and will uphold him "through thick and thin." My wife says, and I regard her as a sort of moral thermometer for my guidance, that the only real noble and true thing done during this war has been his proclamation. Everybody of every sect, party, sex, and color, approves it in the Northwest, and it will not do for the Administration to causelessly tamper with the man who had the sublime moral courage to issue it.

I wish you to understand that I do not intend by this letter to impose upon you the labor of answering it. I had nothing to write about, but I had not heard from you, and the spirit said, "write," and I have written as the spirit moved. If my wife knew that I was writing, she would send her love; as it is, you must content yourself with mine.

65.—*To Mrs. Grimes.*

WASHINGTON, *November* 6, 1861.

I reached Washington last night, weary with the journey, and disgusted with what I heard from quite authentic sources of the course of the Administration. If the other Northwestern members feel as I do, there will be something more during the coming session than growling and showing our teeth. And, from what I hear, they do feel excited and incensed.

November 10*th.*—I have just returned from church. Dr. Channing preached a very able, extemporaneous, philosophical, abolition sermon to a crowded house—such a sermon as no one would have dared to preach in Iowa twelve months ago, and yet it was received here to-day with profound attention and approval. Dr. Channing, in personal appearance, voice, and manner of enunciation and delivery, reminded me very much of Jeff. Davis. His voice is not strong, he has Davis's manner of sinking the last two or three words of each sentence to a low key, his forehead is high, broad, and overhanging, and his face thin and expressive of severe mental labor mingled with physical pain. It is several years since I have heard any sermon that compared with it in length and depth of thought, and in literary finish. There is nothing ornate about his style, no figures or tropes, no husks, all solid meat.

The society is greatly enlarged, and I shall increase it by one, for I have rented part of a pew. Rev. John Pierpont, who is over eighty years of age, but who looks for all the world like a man of sixty, was present. He is now a clerk in one of the departments.

We hear to-day that Colonel Sumner has been badly wounded. Nobody can imagine why that battle was fought. It seems to have been one of those resultless sacrifices of life of which we have had so many this year. There will be no battle on the Potomac this year; I think that is settled.

66.—*To Mrs. Grimes.*

WASHINGTON, *November* 13, 1861.

I cannot enlighten you very much about Fremont. He has no doubt done some impolitic and some very foolish things; but I judge from all I can learn that most of the extravagances with which he is charged were prompted or perpetrated by or under the direction of General McKinstry, a regular army officer, who was placed by the Government in charge of his department as quartermaster. Whatever may have been his acts, or omissions to act, however, there is no question in my mind that the real cause of his removal was the proclamation he issued, and which he failed to modify in accordance with the President's wishes. That was the great sin for which he was punished. The Committee of the House of Representatives appointed to investigate Cameron's alleged frauds was composed of Fremont's enemies, and they were soon induced to abandon Cameron and fall upon Fremont. They have drawn out all the *ex parte* testimony they could that was calculated to implicate him and his friends, giving him no opportunity to deny or rebut it ; and yet one of the committee who is very virulent against Frémont told me yesterday that they were unable to trace the transactions which they deemed so exceedingly censurable to him or to his knowledge.

67.—*To Hon. W. P. Fessenden, Portland, Maine.*

WASHINGTON, *November* 13, 1861.

Your letter of the 10th inst. is at hand, and your imprudence in writing to me will now impose upon you the infliction of a long letter.

First, as to personal matters; I am domiciled with our good friend, who seems to love you as though you were her own son, Mrs. Chipman, at 470 Seventh Street. She fancies that she can satisfy you in the matter of a room or rooms, and unless you are exceedingly particular you will be pleased with the company.

You ask me, Who and what caused the removal of Fremont? I answer, the primary cause of the removal was his proclamation. I learn from a most authentic source, a member of the cabinet, that before the Administration would bestow the appointment of major-general upon him a promise was exacted from him that he would not be a candidate for the presidency. Under that pledge he was appointed, and everything went "merry as a marriage-bell" until the proclamation was issued. When it appeared, the embryo Presidents in the cabinet at once took the alarm, and required him to modify it. This he refused to do, but published the President's modification instead. Then the war began, and a regular conspiracy was entered into to destroy his influence in the country and with the army, and finally to depose him. Every other day the report was published that he was removed, gross charges were made against him that were wholly unfounded in fact ; his subordinate generals were stimulated to disobedience, officers were sent out to act in confidential positions who were spies upon his every act, and the select committee of the House of Representatives appointed to investigate the frauds in this department, almost all of whom were original enemies of Fremont, were easily and speedily *induced* to let Cameron go, and begin on him. Yet with all their sifting of testimony, taking it from the mouths of disappointed rival contractors in an *ex parte* manner, and with no opportunity to rebut it, a member of the committee tells me that they have been unable to bring home the perpetration or the cognizance of a single one of the alleged frauds to General Fremont.

Now you well know that I was not and am not a partisan of Fremont. I told you and others in July that I doubted his capacity for so extensive a military command as was assigned to him. I would never have made him a major-general of the regular army ; but, being one, I intend to insist most strenuously and persistently that he shall have complete justice done him, no matter what may be the effect upon me. General Fremont has doubtless done some very impolitic, unwise, and extravagant things ; but I assert and can prove that he has himself done or caused to be done no impolitic or unwise or extravagant thing that has not been vastly exceeded in these qualities by the generals of the Army of the Potomac, under the nose and with the sanction of the Administration. The truth is, all the frauds perpetrated at St. Louis, according to the testimony before the committee, were perpetrated by and under General Justin McKinstry, an old officer of the regular army, belonging to the Quartermaster's Department, who was sent out to St. Louis by the Administration. I do not question that Fremont made some unfortunate selections of agents : so has the Secretary of War, Mr. Seward, Governor Chase, and it is shrewdly suspected that the " father of the faithful " has sinned in this way. So much, and enough you will say, of the Fremont imbroglio.

The truth is, we are going to destruction as fast as imbecility, corruption, and the wheels of time, can carry us. The administration of the Treasury has thus far been a success, and Chase, though accused of having no heart, has certainly a good head. But, if he had in his person all of the elements of greatness, he would be utterly powerless before the flood of corruption that is sweeping over the land and perverting the moral sense of the people. The army is in most inextricable confusion, and is every day becoming worse and worse.

Now, my dear sir, it is no flattery to say that an awful responsibility must devolve upon you. If you determine to probe the sore spots to the bottom, and that right shall be done, we can inaugurate a new order of things, and the country can be saved. You have followers—you can control the Senate. The wicked fear you, and will flee before you. But, if you rest quietly in your seat, we shall go on from one enormity to another, the evil of to-day will be urged as an apology for greater evil to-morrow, and the devil will be sure to get us in the end, and that right speedily. As for myself and my household, I am determined to serve the Lord. I only regret that I have not the means to do the good for the country that is in your power.

I congratulate you upon the fact that we now have a preacher here with brains in his head, and a heart in his bosom, whom it is a delight to hear, Rev. William H. Channing. I shall expect you to be a constant attendant with me upon his ministrations.

We have been giving the old commodores an overhauling about the Gosport Navy-Yard. The result shows that they destroyed ten million dollars' worth of property in a mere fright. We take up the Harper's Ferry Armory matter to-morrow, and I presume the same result will be reached.

Everybody here is jubilant over the victories at Beaufort and in Kentucky, both of the navy; for you must know that a navy lieutenant commanded in the battle at Pikeville, and that it was an impromptu army that he was at the head of; the Department only yesterday declining to furnish Nelson troops, at the instance of Maynard of Tennessee, who so told me.

With peculiar pleasure Mr. Grimes received news of the success of the Port Royal Expedition. An officer wrote to him:

U. S. S. WABASH, PORT ROYAL, S. C., *November* 15, 1861.

I have never ceased to remember the faith you expressed in the letter you wrote to me concerning the Naval School, that our ships-of-war might be relied on to do good work against the fortifications of our enemies, and that the chief hope of the nation would centre in iron-clad ships-of-war for coast-defense. I therefore think that you, as one of the navy's best friends, may be glad to hear something from the squadron, which with only wooden walls has reduced the strongest earthworks in the South, and captured a stronghold for a loyal army to rest upon. The Government had the wisdom to put at our head the best man in the navy and to clothe him with unusual powers. He chose this place of attack, and brought his squadron and the transports under his protection into the roads of Port Royal, from which all the aids of navigation had been removed. The defenses of the place were carefully reconnoitred, and the attack made with a vigor and nerve worthy of the navy's best days. The gallant bearing and confidence of our chief inspired us all, and we engaged and silenced the batteries at a distance of less than six hundred yards. It would have done your heart good to see the rapid and precise fire of our heavy guns. The enemy expected to repulse us, their works were carefully and skillfully constructed, they had heavy rifled cannon, columbiads of the largest size, and all their cannon were very heavy. The engagement was altogether naval on our side. The troops, sorely to their regret, were unable to take any part in it, or strike any blow to aid us. We had been in possession of the forts for several hours before a soldier landed. I am hardly authorized by our brief acquaintance to write to you so freely, but I remember with so much pleasure our intercourse at Annapolis, and was so much gratified by the kind letter you wrote me, that I will not deny myself the pleasure of rendering to one of the navy's truest champions this greeting from the spot so recently reclaimed from secession.

68.—*To Commodore Samuel F. Du Pont.*

WASHINGTON, *November* 23, 1861.

I have waited to learn the particulars of your grand achievement at Port Royal, and could not, if I would, any longer refrain from congratulating you upon the splendor of your success. And yet I was well satisfied before you sailed that you would do precisely what you have done. I have never suffered myself to doubt for a moment the skill, the pluck, and the devotion of the navy, and have never hesitated to say always and everywhere that it would be the right arm of the public defense, and that this unholy rebellion was to be put down more by the navy than by the army.

I need not say to you, for you already know it, that your name is fast becoming a household word all over the country, and that everybody is striving to be foremost in doing you that honor your merit so justly deserves. I think that the only other officers in your fleet that I personally know are Captain Davis and the two Commanders Rodgers. I beg you, if convenient, to extend my congratulations to them. Indeed, if I could, I would bid "All hail!" to every man and boy in your fleet. Be assured that no man rejoices over your success more than I do, and no man will rejoice more than I shall over any future success, as well on your personal account as on account of the glory your deeds reflect upon the navy, and the peace and unity which I pray to God they may ultimately give to the country.

Commodore Du Pont wrote in reply:

WABASH, PORT ROYAL HARBOR, *December* 2, 1861.

Your kind and gratifying letter reached me yesterday. It was especially welcome from a slight circumstance occurring last summer. I was in the Navy Department when Mr. Fox received a letter from you from your Western home, and he kindly let me read it. It related to the Hatteras affair, and contained comments and suggestions in reference to any future naval expeditions, which so impressed me that I thought of you immediately after our success here; but, being too much pressed to write to you, I requested Captain Raymond Rodgers to do so, and I hope his letter reached you, that you may see our remembrance was mutual.

69.—*To Mrs. Grimes.*

WASHINGTON, *November* 24, 1861.

I am now indebted to you for two letters, one of yesterday and one to-day; I am greatly indebted to you for them, and hope you will not fail to "keep up the fire." I heard to-day the ablest discourse I think that I ever heard. I wish you could have heard it; it would have done your heart good. This evening I have been spending with Mr. Channing. He is a very pleasant man in private as well as in public. He has a full house of very intelligent auditors, and there is no flagging of interest among them.

I had a long letter from Captain Rodgers, of the United States steamer Wabash, giving an account of affairs at Port Royal. He is one of the most accomplished men I ever met, and is said to be the best executive officer in the navy. You remember what I always told you about Captain Du Pont. His success has answered my expectations. Captain Porter goes out shortly in command of an expedition against New Orleans.

Hale and Johnson are both gone, and I am "running the committee"[1] alone.

December 7th.—You will see by the proceedings of Congress

[1] Committee to inquire into the abandonment and destruction of the public property at Pensacola, Norfolk, and Harper's Ferry.

that I am likely to have more business to do than anybody else; for all the labor of the two committees, of the District of Columbia and of the Navy, falls upon me.

On the assembling of Congress, Mr. Grimes at once advocated a searching inquiry as to the disasters that had befallen the public arms, and moved the appointment of a joint committee of both Houses on the Conduct of the War, December 5th–9th. He said:

The best interests of the country, the reputation of the country, of the army and of the officers of the army, require that there should be some investigation. Let me tell Senators that this is no new proceeding. Investigations like this are coeval with the Government. In 1790, during the administration of Washington, a grand expedition was fitted out to penetrate the Northwest, under the command of General St. Clair. That campaign was disastrous, and a resolution was introduced into the House of Representatives to raise a committee for investigating the causes that led to that disaster. A committee was raised, and in 1792 a report was made in response to that resolution. On July 9, 1813, a resolution was introduced for a committee to inquire into the causes which led to the multiplied failures of the arms of the United States. At the next session this resolution was modified and adopted, and an investigation was had. Justice to the officers, to the soldiers, and to the country, demands that we should have some sort of investigation now, and know where the blame does rest for the disasters that have occurred.

The committee was appointed, Hon. Benjamin F. Wade, chairman, and rendered considerable service in exposing abuses and weeding out incompetent officers.

It was reported that a colonel of the regular army, who commanded the reserve at Bull Run, July 21st, was intoxicated on that occasion. A court of inquiry found that he was "drunk to a certain extent," but not enough to justify the calling of a court-martial for his trial. Asking for full information of the case, Mr. Grimes remarked, December 5th:

It will be interesting to learn how drunk a man may be to justify another in applying that opprobrious epithet to him, and yet not drunk enough to warrant his trial and removal from command. The country, I think, would like to know the names of the astute officers who composed this remarkable court. It may be desirable to know the quantity and frequency of the prescriptions of brandy that were administered to Colonel Miles that day, and which the court gravely tell us they consider as very slight extenuation of the guilt attached to his condition. Such was the finding of the court in relation to the condition of the man who, on the memorable 21st of July last, exercised the most important military command next to that of the commanding general in the field. Let the world know precisely how great his guilt was, and why, if guilty, he has neither been ordered before a court-martial nor dropped from the army list.

The time when intemperate officers can be safely appointed to, or retained in, either the army or navy, has gone by. The people of this country are now too much in earnest to quietly endure the one or the other. These are no times to indulge in that sickly sentiment, sometimes improperly called kindness of heart, which is unwilling to do, or dares not do, justice to the country by maintaining discipline and sobriety in the army and navy. The people are unwilling to intrust the great interests they have at stake in this conflict into the hands of those who rest even under the suspicion of intemperance. They require the entire consecration of the best energies of their servants, mental and physical, to their cause; and they will not send out their sons to battle under the leadership of officers whose faculties are benumbed by excessive indulgence. It is idle to suppose that an army commanded by officers who indulge in or wink at such habits can command the respect and confidence of the country, or that this great struggle can be brought to a successful issue under their guidance. For myself, I declare that in my feeble way I will hold up to the reprehension of a just public sentiment any man, be he high or low, the head of a bureau, of a department, a commander in the army, or the President himself, who shall appoint, or retain, or seek or connive at the appointment or retention of any man in office who is of intemperate habits.

Mr. Grimes introduced a bill, December 9th, to further promote the efficiency of the navy, and secured its passage on the 12th. In explaining its provisions, he said:

The necessity of a reform in the navy, by which young, active, enterprising officers shall be substituted for the old and unseaworthy, seems to be admitted by all. The experience of every naval service in the world shows that old officers, however valuable for counsel and shore-duty, are generally incompetent to perform the arduous duties of a captain or commander of a fleet in times of active hostilities. In times of peace, when the ships have the full complement of a captain, lieutenants, masters, passed-midshipmen, and midshipmen, and when their duty does not require them to appear upon deck except when the sun shines and the sea is smooth, these old gentlemen may fulfill all the purposes of their office; but in times like these, when the line of the service is so reduced that but one lieutenant can be allowed to a ship, instead of five or six, as formerly, it is not reasonable to expect that they can endure all the privations and hardships that their positions as commanders would demand of them. More is required of a naval than of a military commander. The naval officer must contend against the elements as well as against the public enemy. His command is always, to a great extent, independent of others; and he must rely in a great measure upon his own ship for his means of attack and defense. He must be a thorough sailor, a skillful navigator and gunner; he must have enterprise and courage; he must have the power to inspire his crew with confidence; and, in order to have these qualifications, he must have a clear head and a sound body. Some old officers possess all these qualities in an eminent degree, and such will be recalled to the service. But there are many who tread the deck with a feeble step, and the country requires that all such should give place to younger men.

The bill provides for the temporary restoration and employment of such old officers as may be deemed qualified for duty, with the full pay of their respective ranks; and that any one of them, who, upon the recommendation of the President, shall receive a vote of the thanks of Congress for gallantry in action, may be restored to the active list. This provision was intended as an incentive to deeds of noble daring, and as a reward for their performance.

Surely there ought to be no objection to that provision which authorizes the President to select a flag-officer from the two highest grades of officers. The highest public interests require that this be allowed, and allowed at once. The organization of the navy at present is analogous to that of a regiment in the army without field-officers, the oldest captain commanding. It would be quite absurd to organize a whole army upon such a plan, giving the command of it to that captain whose birth was nearest the flood; yet the navy is organized upon precisely that plan. The bill now under consideration, if passed into a law, will abolish this hoary-headed absurdity, and give to the President an opportunity to select as the commanders of our fleets men in the prime of life, with minds and bodies in full vigor.

Mr. Grimes was watchful and prompt to detect and expose abuses in every quarter. For the delay in prosecuting the war, he said, January 7th:

The Senate is in a great degree responsible, not only on account of the political sentiments inculcated by individual members in former sessions, but by the course adopted at the July session, when they allowed majors, captains, and lieutenants, to be elevated from the line of the army, and put into positions of brigadier and major generals of volunteers. It is not in human nature to suppose that they will be exceedingly anxious to prosecute this war to a conclusion, because when it is concluded they will revert to their old positions, and cease to enjoy the emoluments and rank of major and brigadier generals.

As to the way in which Mr. Davis had managed West Point and the army during the time he was Secretary of War, Mr. Grimes said, January 15, 1863:

We created two new cavalry regiments some five years ago. Mr. Davis selected his favorites for the important offices in those regiments. He indoctrinated the officers of the army with the idea that they must be impregnated with his peculiar notions, else they could not have a favored position in the army. The result was, that when this rebellion broke out the second cavalry regiment, which used to be called "Davis's Own," was almost bereft of officers; there was hardly a man left in it in the grades of colonel, lieutenant-colonel, major, or captain.

As chairman of the Committee on the District of Columbia, Mr. Grimes gave sedulous attention to the interests of the District, and secured appropriate legislation for the correction of abuses and the prosperity and order of the national capital. He said with reference to the jail of the District, January 10, 1862:

I am not very fresh in my reading of history; but, from recollection of the description of prisons I have read of, I think there never was a place of confinement that would compare with the Washington Jail as it was at the commencement of the present session, except the French Bastile and the dungeons of Venice. The jail was erected at the expense of the United States a great many years ago, and was designed to accommodate forty or fifty persons. When I first visited it a few days before the session of Congress, there were confined in it two hundred and eighteen persons, "black spirits and white, blue spirits and gray" intermingled, of all complexions, colors, ages, of different sexes, and without any particular classification as to offenses. A little boy, confined for a trivial offense, who had followed, from youthful indiscretion, a regiment from Connecticut to this city, was incarcerated in the same cell with three men who were committed on a charge of murder. The prison is in better condition than it was before the especial attention of Congress was called to it. Many persons have been removed; many soldiers who had been put in for trivial military offenses have been taken out by order of the provost-marshal; a good many fugitives from service, or persons claimed to be fugitives from service, owned by citizens of the adjacent States, have been removed; but there are at this time about one hundred and seventy persons in the jail, more than three times as many as it is designed to accommodate.

When I visited the jail the other day, I had hardly entered the threshold before a colored boy stepped up and tapped me on the shoulder. He happened to know who I was. He said he was confined as a runaway. I asked him if any one claimed him. "No." "Are you a free boy?" "Yes." Turning round to the jailer, I asked him if that was so. He said it was. I asked him, "How do you know it to be so?" "I know it to be so because two men from Maryland, who were born and reared where this boy was born and reared, stated that he was free of their knowledge, for they had known him from the time he was born."

Now, I want such cases to be released. I do not believe it is my duty to vote money, to impose taxes upon my constituents, to keep a slave-pen here in the capital of the Union for the purpose of confining a free boy, who may be thrown in by one of your District justices of the peace or constables.

I found another case. A white man who was committed nearly six months ago told me that he had written to the magistrate who committed him, to the prosecuting attorney, and to other parties in this city, imploring them to inform him for what offense he had been committed; that he was unable to ascertain why he was committed. There had been a session of the grand-jury, and still he was held, and was lying upon a bed of sickness. Upon going to the record, I found that an order had been entered, directing that the prisoner should be discharged, yet the order had not been carried into execution. That the man was sick was no apology for retaining him in jail. He should have been sent to the almshouse, which we have provided and are supporting for the purpose of receiving persons who may be in his condition.

There was another case. A young colored fellow, who came as the servant of an officer from the vicinity of Pittsburg, was thrown into this jail in August last. The regiment to which he was attached went forward toward the face of the enemy. There was nobody here to look after him. There is no doubt as to his being a free boy, and yet he was there on the first day of this month.

There are other cases. They have in this District and in Maryland what they call an apprehension fee. They have a law which declares that, if any slave wanders a certain distance from the residence of his master, he may be taken up as a fugitive. There are persons in this vicinity, I am credibly informed, who are lying in wait around your city and the surrounding country, in the hope that they can find some poor colored man or woman who is out picking berries or visiting a friend, and who will wander a little farther than the distance established by law. The moment they can find such a person beyond the limited distance, these harpies pounce upon him or her, and, when the master tries to find the servant, in the course of two or three weeks he will find him in the Washington Jail; from which it will be impossible to extricate him, without paying a large sum for jailer's fees, for justice's fees, and for constable's fees, in addition to this apprehension fee.

I do not desire, and I do not think that the Senate or the country desires, that the Washington Jail shall be used for any such purpose.

Four days after the above remarks, the Marshal of the District sent a communication to the Senate, upon which Mr. Grimes said:

The communication does not contain the truth as stated to me at the jail personally yesterday. I applied for admission to the jail. I was refused. Now, a communication has come here telling us that a different rule prevails—not the rule that existed yesterday at two o'clock. I want this matter to be brought to the attention of the Senate, and I want it publicly brought to the attention of the President of the United States.

Perhaps the Senate itself is somewhat to blame for the manner in which the jail has been kept; for I trace a great many of the evils existing there, and the failure to remove them, to the appointment of a person as Marshal of the District who was made such by the advice and consent of this body. The President of the United States saw fit, in the plenitude of his wisdom, to import to this District from the State of Illinois Mr. Ward H. Lamon, and to appoint him the Marshal. It is not for me to say why one of the seventy thousand people of this District was not selected for this responsible position; I simply know the fact that a man was brought here from abroad, who had no interest in the District; who had no community of feeling or sympathy with the people of the District; who was and is wholly unfamiliar with the duties of the position. Among other important duties intrusted by law to the marshal is the control of the jail. A humane and Christian man might make it a Bethesda. Mr. Lamon has paid no attention to it until of late, and now only to make an order prohibiting the admission of all persons for the purpose of inspection or otherwise, without a special permit from him.

Shortly after I reached the city on the 1st of November last, supposing that I might possibly be continued as a member of the Committee on the District of Columbia, I felt it to be my duty to inform myself, among other things, of the true condition and management of the jail. Accordingly, I have visited it often. I have conversed with its inmates, examined the records of commitments, and I think I may safely say that I have been instrumental in securing the discharge of several innocent persons. Last Friday I took occasion to state to the Senate some of my observations in that jail. On the day following, Mr. Lamon made a peremptory order that no person—not even members of Congress, or members of the Committee on the District of Columbia, who have the general charge of all matters relating to the District—should be admitted to the jail, without first supplicating and securing a written permission from him, or unless he should be personally present. When intelligence of this order was brought to me yesterday morning by a member of the House of Representatives, a large number of Senators around me proffered to go with me to the President and demand the instant dismissal of this marshal—not because he had been strutting through the streets of Illinois and Missouri with stars on his shoulders, representing himself as a brigadier-general, as detailed by a select committee of the House of Representatives—not because he had purloined a regiment of troops and brought it at great expense from St. Louis to the Potomac—not because he had been traveling in special railway-trains at the public expense—although for these reasons he ought to have been instantly dismissed—but because of his manifest and acknowledged dereliction of duty as Marshal of the District, and because of the insulting character of the order he had made in regard to our admission to the jail.

Upon reflection, I concluded to determine with positiveness for myself whether such an order had been made. Accordingly, yesterday I went to the jail and sought admission. Entering its portal, I told the jailer that I wished to examine it. He told me that I could not be permitted to do so. I demanded to know the reason why I was excluded. He answered that he had a peremptory order from his superior, Marshal Lamon, forbidding the admission of any one without a written permission from him, or without he was personally present. I asked him if this rule applied to members of the Senate and House of Representatives. He replied that it did. I then asked him if he knew me, and that I was chairman of the District Committee of this body. He said that he did, but that that fact made no difference; the rule was peremptory, and must be enforced against all alike.

Upon this repulse at the jail, I concluded to go at once to the President of the United States, to state to him the facts I have detailed, and to give him some idea of the expression of opinion of those around me. When, for the first time in six months, I attempted to approach the footstool of power enthroned at the other end of the avenue, I was told that the President was engaged, and his servants declined to convey my name to him. I allude to this subject, not because I suppose that the influence of this marshal extends so far as to exclude me from the Executive mansion, as well as from the jail, but as the reason why I state publicly here what I intended to state privately there.

In the discipline of the penitentiary of the District Mr. Grimes recommended a reform, so that prisoners, for good conduct while in prison, should receive a deduction of a month in each year from their term of sentence.

Such a system (he said, June 6th) prevails in a great many States, in Ohio, in Iowa, in Indiana, with the most beneficial results. It is an inducement to a prisoner to behave well and work well. It is no pardoning power, but a curtailment of the judgment of the court.

70.—*To Commodore S. F. Du Pont.*

WASHINGTON, *February* 9, 1862.

I was sorry to learn, a few days ago, that you felt some chagrin at the fact that the resolution tendering to you and to the officers under your command the thanks of Congress for your exploit at Port Royal had not been acted upon. As I am alone responsible for everything in relation to it, I will tell you exactly what the facts were.

The highest honor we can confer at present upon any naval officer is a vote of thanks. To make such honors worth anything they must not be too common or cheap. Knowing that several resolutions of similar import, but for small affairs, were to be offered, I determined to forestall the action of the Senate by setting the example of referring such resolutions to the Committee on Naval Affairs, and thus get the control of them. Accordingly, I introduced the resolutions of thanks to you, and suffered them to remain quietly in the committee, smothering similar resolutions to others, until the sentiment of the Senate on such subjects should become a little rectified. In the mean time, the bill for retirement of old officers became a law, and since then I have waited for the President's recommendation, which would also, if acted upon, place you permanently on the active list. That came to us day before yesterday, and yesterday we passed the resolutions of thanks by a unanimous vote. There will be no difficulty whatever about its passage through the House of Representatives. You will, I trust, perceive that so far from there being the slightest disposition to ignore or slumber over the merits of your case, I have acted solely with a view to subserve your individual interests, and at the same time to advance the good of the service.

We are now all rejoicing over Foote's success in Tennessee. We are much more hopeful than we have been, and I fancy that I can see the end to the rebellion. The army is sore and a little dispirited at the naval successes, while they achieve none. May God bless and prosper you in all your efforts!

Commodore Du Pont wrote in reply:

WABASH, PORT ROYAL, *February* 23, 1862.

Your great kindness has made a deep impression on me. It has been no trait of mine to "court honor," and I can truly say visions of distinction formed no part or lot in my motives of action. To serve my country, do my duty, and meet the expectations of those who had given me the opportunity, have been the incentives uppermost in my mind. Yet I believe this temperament and such impulses are in no way inconsistent with feelings of profound gratitude and pride at the high distinction which has been awarded me, and which I owe to your kind instrumentality.

I am off to-morrow with a large division of my squadron to complete my work on the lower coast, and, if God is with us, in some three weeks I hope to hold everything by an inside or outside blockade from Cape Canaveral to Georgetown, South Carolina. Our hearts have been gladdened by the news from the North. Porter came in to-day on his way to the Gulf, and gave us the account of the surrender of Fort Donelson. I have never permitted any invidious feelings of rivalry with our military brethren, but we are thrilled in our *esprit de corps* at the deeds of the Navy, and I am sure they must be agreeable to you, as offering some return to that disinterested sympathy, guidance, and support, which you have extended to that branch of the public service since you took your seat in the councils of the nation.

We hear fine accounts of the Northwestern army, and Captain Rodgers had a letter from some officer in the West, who spoke of the impression made by the Iowa regiments. I thought this item, traveling back to you from South Carolina, would not be unacceptable.

The following extract is from a letter of Commodore Du Pont, dated Wabash, off Fernandina, March 6th:

Captain Davis has in charge for you a rifle captured at Fernandina, which I desire you to do me the honor to accept. The victory was bloodless, but most complete in results. The defenses have astounded us by their capabilities, scientific location, and formidable character, with wonderful immunity from danger. Their cannon are heavy and fine; one 120-pounder rifle-gun, which they had slung in the trucks to get away with, but dropped on the beach, we have nothing to compare with. The most curious feature in the operations was the chase of a train of cars by a gunboat for one mile and a half; two soldiers being killed, the passengers rushed out into the woods, one of your late members among them, Mr. Yulee; he passed the night under a bush, and I hope had a blanket, for it was the coldest of the season.

Objecting to a change in the rules of the two Houses, Mr. Grimes said, January 29th:

I do not believe that it is proper for us to cripple the power of a minority. I have been in a minority all my life until the present time, and I am unwilling to say that when we get into executive session a two-thirds vote may prevent a minority from expressing their views, or confine them to only five minutes. I believe in publicity in our debates.

With reference to the construction of iron-clad steam-gunboats Mr. Grimes said, February 4, 1862:

I believe that the introduction of steam into naval warfare has revolutionized the whole system of coast defenses, and I do not want any better evidence of it than the success of the rebels in attacking our vessels as they pass up and down the Potomac. Nearly eight thousand shots have been fired at our vessels from their fortifications along the line of that river, and only one has been materially injured, and only three or four have been damaged at all. One of these gunboats, made sharp at the ends, and thoroughly encased in iron, with a powerful engine, would do more to defend the harbor of New York than the best fortification there that cost this Government a million or two millions of dollars. I am in favor of this measure, not solely because I am anxious that these vessels shall be used in the present war, but because I believe they will more successfully defend the commerce of our country, and the harbors on our Atlantic seaboard (in which I, although a representative of a remote State, am as much interested as are the people living immediately along the Atlantic), than will even stone fortifications; and I would much more cheerfully vote money out of the national Treasury to build vessels of this description, and to man them, and place them in your harbors for coast defense, than I would to build stone-walls, as proposed by the Committee on Military Affairs. In my opinion, it is the only kind of coast defense that gentlemen of the Atlantic States will ultimately be compelled to rely upon.

For the disaster to the Cumberland and the Congress in Hampton Roads (March 8th) Mr. Grimes held the military branch of the Government responsible, in that they had not early organized an expedition against Norfolk, and captured the navy-yard and machine-shop there. He said, March 11th:

In no degree is the navy responsible. Upon two different occasions the navy officers have offered to go down and open the blockade of the Potomac, and upon one occasion for thirty-six hours was the flotilla under steam, prepared to go down; but a superior military officer, who undertook to control all offensive operations, refused to let it go.

A part of the blame for this disaster is perhaps due to ourselves, because we have not at an earlier day passed some appropriations to construct iron-plated ships. I congratulate myself that one of the first acts I did when I came to Congress was to introduce a resolution (January 19, 1861) calling for information in regard to iron-plated ships, initiating the very measures which the experience of the past few days has shown that it is necessary to adopt, if we will protect our sea-coast from the ravages of a hostile foe.

He said, March 27th and 28th:

There is a perfect panic in our Northern commercial cities. New York seems to think that in a few days the Merrimac is going to be seen sailing up Broadway! They have had, perhaps, some reason for excitement, growing out of the egress of the Merrimac from Elizabeth River; but they ought to remember that the Government has done something, and is doing something, to protect the commerce of the country and these commercial cities against any danger that may arise from the Merrimac coming out again.

It is well enough to know exactly what the department has done. In the first place, we have the Monitor. She has been tested, and in such a manner as no English or French vessel has been tested. We know exactly her capacities in actual warfare, and her sea-going capacities. We have, therefore, some basis upon which to build a system. If we go on and improve upon that foundation which the Monitor and her success seem to have laid, then we can establish something that will be creditable and useful to the country. The Monitor was built by Mr. Ericsson at his own risk. He entered upon the contract, and the Government did not agree to receive the vessel from him until she had been tested. She was on the way round to be tested upon the batteries at Pig Point and on the Potomac, when the Merrimac came out from her retreat. Then we have the Mystic and the Ironsides. In addition, the Government have contracted for four steamers, iron-clad, to be built by Captain Ericsson, upon the general plan of the Monitor, but larger and with heavier armament, each to carry two fifteen-inch guns, to be delivered in four months, and two more to be delivered in five months, and another to be covered with four-inch iron; and, in addition, they have entered upon the armament of the Roanoke.

I have stated these facts in order to satisfy the public that there is not any very great danger to be apprehended from the Merrimac, and that we shall have plenty of iron-clad vessels built upon a plan which we know must be successful.

The aspersions cast on naval officers are unjust when it is said that they were opposed to the introduction of steam-vessels into the navy. It is equally unjust to say that they were opposed to the introduction of iron-clad vessels. I know something about that. I happened to be one of the first members of this body who suggested the subject, and I tried to bring the attention of the country to the necessity of having iron-clad vessels, and consulted with gentlemen of eminence in that profession, and I did not meet with one who was not enthusiastic in favor of the proposition; and it is due to that service to say that a board composed of Commodore Smith, Captain Davis, and Commodore Paulding, were the men to whom the plans for Ericsson's steam-battery and for the other iron-clads that the Government is now building were submitted, and that those plans met their full approbation. It has been said here, that if naval officers had had their way these vessels would never have been constructed. The appropriation bill of a million and a half dollars, that we passed at the extra session, was drawn by a naval officer, was sent to us with the solicitation of a naval officer that we should pass it, and as soon as we passed it the whole question was referred to some officers of the line, and they determined as to the character of the vessels we should construct, and are now imploring us to abandon wooden, and adopt iron-clad vessels. I say this in justice to the officers of the navy; and my observation and experience, I think, go as far as anybody's here.

ACHIEVEMENTS OF THE WESTERN NAVAL FLOTILLA.

Mr. Grimes said, March 13, 1862:

I conceive it to be my duty, and it certainly is a great pleasure to me, to call the special attention of the Senate to the achievements of the newly-created naval flotilla on our Western waters, and to the gallant part borne by its officers and men against armed rebels in Kentucky and Tennessee. Surely, no one could more properly be proud of the deeds of our army in that quarter than a Senator from Iowa. Yet, I know that whatever adds to the glory of our navy in the recent conflicts in the West adds also to the glory of the army, and that the two branches of the service are so conjoined that no rivalry ought to exist between them, except a virtuous emulation in the performance of patriotic duty. No examples can be found in the history of any country of more important results, attained in an equal time, in an untried field of naval enterprise, than those we have lately witnessed on the Ohio, Mississippi, Tennessee, and Cumberland Rivers; and I feel assured that the successes which have thus far been achieved will be surpassed by the same forces whenever they can find an enemy to cope with between Cairo and New Orleans.

On the 16th of May last, Commander John Rodgers was ordered by the Secretary of the Navy to proceed to Cincinnati and purchase, or commence the construction of, several gunboats for service on the Western rivers. Under his auspices the three boats, Taylor, Lexington, and Conestoga, were purchased and fitted up for war purposes. They were put in commission, and reached Cairo after some delay, arising from the low stage of water in the Ohio River, on the 12th of August. The Taylor carried seven guns, of large calibre, the Lexington six, and the Conestoga four. Here was the beginning of the Western flotilla. We all remember the unfavorable criticisms indulged in when these three stern-wheel steamers, with oak casings, arrived at that military post. Some said they would be shaken to pieces by the recoil of their own guns; others that they would be speedily sunk by the shore-guns of the rebels; while not a few were alarmed by visions of Hollins's ram butting them to pieces with impunity. From the day they reached their destination to the present no rebel craft has shown itself ten miles above Columbus, and no rebel force of any description has harbored in a proximity which could be deemed threatening to navigation, or to the cities of St. Louis and Cairo. A few experimental trips dispelled all doubts of their efficiency, and all fears of a rebel incursion into any of the Northwestern States, other than Missouri. A band of Jefferson Thompson's robbers did, indeed, make a demonstration of crossing the Mississippi, in August last, from the town of Commerce, Missouri; but, at the first intimation that the gunboats were coming, they fled with what booty they could lay their hands on, pillaged impartially from friends and foes on the Missouri shore. The boon of security to the people of the Northwestern States is due in no small degree to these wooden gunboats; for, however numerous and brave our armies, it would have been impossible with them alone to guard all points on our river-line. Thus our people were not only protected from danger of invasion, but were enabled to give all their time and energies to preparation for those offensive movements which have reclaimed so much important territory from the domination of the enemy.

On the 23d of September Commodore Rodgers was detached from service in the West, and Captain A. H. Foote was ordered to take command as flag-officer. Since that time the following boats, with iron-clad bows, have been built or prepared for service: St. Louis, thirteen guns; Carondelet, thirteen guns; Pittsburg, thirteen guns; Louisville, thirteen guns; Cincinnati, thirteen guns; Essex, five guns; Mound City, thirteen guns.

The first engagement of the gunboats with the enemy took place on the 9th of September, at Lucas's Bend, in the Mississippi River, a short distance above the rebel stronghold at Columbus. In that engagement the Lexington and the Conestoga silenced two shore-batteries, dispersed a large body of rebel cavalry, and so disabled the rebel gunboat Yankee that she has not been heard of since. On the 29th of October the Conestoga proceeded, with three companies of Illinois volunteers, sixty-two miles up the Tennessee River, to Eddyville, Kentucky, where they jointly attacked and routed a rebel encampment, bringing away their horses, arms, camp-equipage, and negro slaves.

There could hardly have been an occasion where the presence of an efficient naval support was more necessary than at the battle of Belmont, fought on the 7th of November last; and there has been no conflict during the war where this support, when finally called into requisition, was more effectively and opportunely rendered. Nothing but the well-directed fire of grape and canister from the guns of the Taylor and Lexington saved our land-forces from being utterly cut to pieces, while retiring on board their transports. Every effort of the enemy to bring his artillery to bear on our columns was defeated by the storm of iron which assailed him from the boats. His pieces were dismounted, and his horses and men swept down as fast as they were placed in position.

A great deal has been said about the origin of the proposition to take possession of the Tennessee River. The credit of originating the idea of a campaign in that direction has been claimed first for one and then for another military commander. I desire that impartial justice may be done to every man; and, acting upon the intention to do justice, I must be permitted to say that, so far as I can learn, the project of turning the enemy's flanks by penetrating the Tennessee and Cumberland Rivers originated with Commodore Foote.[1] The great rise of water in those rivers was providential, and with the quick eye of military genius he saw at once the advantage that it might secure to our arms.

The fleet, consisting of four iron-clad and three wooden boats,

[1] He telegraphed General Halleck, January 28th, proposing an attack on Fort Henry with the gunboats and several regiments.

proceeded to Fort Henry and reduced it in one hour and twenty minutes, Commodore Foote being, as is his wont, in the fore-front of the battle. It appears that he knew before leaving Paducah that he should take Fort Henry, no matter what might be the force or the resistance he should meet there. He was thoroughly inspired with the great idea of victory. The contingency of failure did not enter into his calculations. He therefore addressed himself to plans for reaping the fruits of victory, rather than to plans for repairing the consequences of defeat. Of the gallant attack on Fort Donelson no one need be reminded. Subjected as our vessels were to a long-continued and hot fire from three rebel batteries, at four hundred yards' distance, they continued the fight for one hour and thirty minutes, and not until the wheel of one and the tiller-ropes of another of his boats were shot away did the well-managed guns of the commodore cease to scatter death and consternation among the foes of his country. Although wounded himself, and his gunboats crippled, yet, with the glory of the gallant combat on his brow, he indulged in no repinings for his personal misfortunes, or laudation of his successes, but like a true Christian hero thought only of his men.

The next movement of Commodore Foote with his flotilla was to take possession of Clarksville, three days before the arrival of the land-forces, though that fact, for some unexplained cause, nowhere appears in the official reports of the military commander of the department.

On the 21st of February, 1862, Commodore Foote telegraphed to General Cullum, the chief of General Halleck's staff, then at Cairo, as follows: "General Grant and myself were about moving on Nashville, when General Grant to my astonishment received a telegram from General Halleck, 'not to let the gunboats go higher than Clarksville.' No telegram sent to me. General Grant and I believe that we can take Nashville. Please ask General Halleck if we shall do it." It may be that there was some great military reason why General Grant was directed "not to let the gunboats go higher than Clarksville," but up to this time it is wholly unappreciable by the public. Had they been permitted to go, as proposed by Commodore Foote, Nashville would undoubtedly have capitulated some days earlier than it did, and an immense amount of rebel stores been captured, and he would probably have intercepted a part of the rebel General Johnston's army.

I ought not to omit to mention the gallant attack by a part of the flotilla upon the enemy at Pittsburg, on the Tennessee River, where fifteen hundred rebel infantry and cavalry were completely routed, with a loss of twenty killed and one hundred wounded.

The next fact of importance in the campaign at the West, and the most important of all, was the evacuation of Columbus. Why was this stronghold, which cost so much labor and money, abandoned without firing a shot? It is not for me to underrate the advantages of position secured by the valor of our troops at Fort Donelson; yet I undertake to say, from the knowledge I have been able to obtain of the defenses at Columbus, that there was nothing in the mere fact of the capture of Donelson and Nashville, and exclusive of our command of the river, which need have caused the evacuation, except after a long and bloody siege. The forts at Columbus were so located and constructed as to be almost impregnable to an assault by storm. It is well understood that Commodore Foote was opposed to giving the rebels an opportunity to leave Columbus. He felt sure of his ability, with his gun and mortar boats, to shell them into a speedy surrender, but was compelled to give way to the counsels of military commanders. When we couple the strategic position acquired by our occupation of the Tennessee and Cumberland Rivers with the completion of the mortar-boats, and the absolute command of the river given us by the armored gunboats, there remains no mystery about the evacuation of Columbus. The two arms of the public service are equally entitled to the credit of frightening the rebels from their strongest position on the Mississippi River, if not the strongest in their whole military jurisdiction.

Yesterday, the intelligence reached us that the Western flotilla, composed of ten gunboats and ten mortar-boats, had started for new scenes of conflict, to achieve, I doubt not, new and yet greater triumphs. The country is assured that whatever can be accomplished by gallantry and nautical experience will be performed by Commodore Foote and the brave officers and men under his command. We await the announcement of new victories.

I have thought it proper, as a Western Senator, in some degree charged with the examination of naval affairs by this body, to bear this testimony to the worth of that branch of the public service in the Western campaign, and to the noble deeds of the flag-officer in that command. No one can over-estimate their services to the country, and to the Northwest in particular; and in the name of that great section, and of the whole country, I thank them one and all, officers and men.

But I would avail myself of this occasion to accomplish another purpose. I am anxious that the people of this entire country may feel that the exploits of the Navy, wherever performed, are their exploits, that its glory is their glory, and that, while they are taxing themselves to support it, they are supporting the right arm of the national defense. I desire the citizen of the most remote frontier to feel that he is equally protected and equally honored by the brave deeds of our naval officers with the citizen of the Atlantic coast. I wish the men of Iowa and Minnesota to know that they are as effectually defended in their liberties at home and in their honor abroad, by the achievements of Du Pont, and Goldsborough, and Stringham, and Foote, on the water, as they can be by any victories won by our armies on the land.

Mr. President, ours must be a great maritime nation. Heaven has ordained that it should be such, and we could not make it otherwise if we would. We have a coast, both on the Atlantic and Pacific Oceans, which, with its numerous indentations, is many thousand miles in extent, occupied by a hardy, nautical population, and flanked on either side by soils and climates that furnish the most valuable productions of the globe, and which must be supplied to other nations. On the north we have a succession of great lakes, already bearing upon their bosoms a registered commercial tonnage of nearly half a million, and navigated by a race of daring, industrious, northern seamen. Unlike any other maritime nation, ours is traversed by navigable rivers, thousands of miles in length, floating an inland commerce unequaled by that of any country in the world, except, possibly, that of China, and capable of navigation by armed vessels of great capacity. With a country of such extent, a soil and climate furnishing such productions, and a population along our ocean, gulf, bay, lake, and river coasts, accustomed to navigation, who does not see that ours must, from the very necessities of our geographical position, and the conformation of our continent, become a great commercial people? Our products must be borne to remote nations in our own ships, navigated by our own seamen, and protected wherever they go by our own vessels-of-war.

I know not with whom originated the phrase "The Navy is the right arm of the public defense;" but I know that a truer sentiment was never uttered. In my opinion it will always be in this country the most efficient and far the least dangerous arm of the public service by which to maintain the national integrity and defend the national honor. History teaches us that every nation that has depended upon a navy for protection has been comparatively free by the side of those which placed their reliance upon armies. I need not go back to antiquity to prove this. I point to Holland and England in modern times. The former, while she continued to be the greatest naval power on earth, was the freest government on earth, and only began to be shorn of her liberties and of her territory when she neglected to maintain her fleets. England, the most liberal of all governments save our own, is in no small degree indebted for her present position to the fact that she maintains only a small military force in the British Islands, and relies upon her wooden walls as a means of attack and defense. She puts no faith in large standing armies, and will not until her people shall be prepared to surrender their freedom. With her garrisoned possessions encircling the globe, her entire military establishment does not exceed one hundred and twenty thousand men. France, Austria, Russia, and Prussia, maintain large standing armies on their soil; and in those countries the liberty of the people is measured by the will of the sovereign. The freedom they enjoy is the gratuity of emperors and kings; the servitude they endure is enforced by the presence of standing armies.

I do not believe that anybody but the public enemy has had anything to fear from the numerous and well-appointed armies we have raised; yet no one of us is prepared to say that, with an army much longer isolated from home-scenes and home-ideas, concentrated in large bodies, and taught the duty of implicit obedience to their superiors, danger to our free institutions might not arise. No such danger can arise from the existence of a navy, however large, or however commanded. Seamen are cosmopolitan. Always employed, and generally afloat, they never become, as armies sometimes do, as dangerous to friends in time of peace as to enemies in time of war.

I might go on and show that, situated as all our large cities are upon arms of the sea or upon navigable rivers, the Navy might be made more efficient in suppressing domestic insurrections, as well as in repelling foreign invasion, than the Army. I might show, too, that, notwithstanding much that has been said by professed statisticians, the support of a navy is less expensive, in comparison with the service it renders to a maritime nation, than that of an army. But I shall not detain the Senate by attempting to enter upon such an exposition at this time.

As I said at the outset, my purpose in rising to address the Senate at this time was to call the attention of the country to the successful operations of the Western flotilla ; but I cannot refrain from alluding, for one moment, before I close, to the successes of our Navy elsewhere in this war. The whole southeastern Atlantic coast has been swept by the fleet of the gallant Du Pont, and is now effectually held by both an inside and outside blockade. The enemy have been driven from the waters of North Carolina by Goldsborough, their whole navy in that quarter destroyed, and their coast towns occupied. Such progress has been made in the Gulf of Mexico, that I venture to predict that, in a few days at farthest, intelligence will reach us that the forts at the mouth of the Mississippi River have been captured, and that Farragut and Porter are now, or soon will be, in possession of New Orleans. But the startling events that have recently occurred in Hampton Roads attract, as they ought, the attention of all. It would be well for us to reflect upon what those events have clearly demonstrated. They are—

1. That in modern naval warfare wooden sailing-vessels are perfectly harmless and helpless.

2. That the strongest stone fortifications can be no obstruction to the entrance of iron-clad vessels-of-war into our harbors; and that one or two such vessels, unopposed by vessels of a similar character, can hold any commercial city on the continent at their mercy.

3. That we can now commence the creation of a proper navy, upon a footing of comparative equality with all the naval powers of the world.

No man sympathizes with the relatives and friends of the gallant dead who perished on the Congress and Cumberland more than I do. Perhaps, however, their loss was necessary to teach us our true path of duty to the country. Let us not suffer more valuable lives to be periled upon such worthless vessels; and, while we deplore the loss of so many brave men, let us rejoice that so many more are left to the service who are willing to do and die for their country. Especially let us give thanks for the brilliant example of courage, seamanship, and patriotism, furnished to the country and to the world by that matchless officer, Lieutenant John L. Worden, and the officers and men under his command on board the Monitor. In that unexampled engagement of Sunday last, after a terribly suffocating and dangerous passage from New York, without having slept, with an undrilled crew, and handling an untried experiment, Lieutenant Worden and his crew performed prodigies of skill and valor that will render all on board the Monitor immortal. They will be immortal not for their valor alone. Who shall undertake to estimate the influence that battle will exert upon all the maritime powers of the earth? Who shall undertake to tell the number of homes to which the news of its successful result carried quiet on that eventful evening, which had been for hours disturbed by the most distracting fears? Is it too much to say that it rescued our commerce and our commercial cities from ravage, and in one hour revolutionized all systems of naval architecture and naval warfare? Captain Ericsson, too, may well be proud of the place his name will occupy in the history of nautical science, and we may well be proud that the country of our birth is the country of his adoption.

But while I would honor the gallant living, I would bear my tribute of affectionate respect for the memory of the heroic dead who fell in the engagement at Hampton Roads. Let the remembrance of that brave young officer, whose obsequies are now being performed in another part of this city, who, when his vessel was sinking beneath his feet, replied to a summons to surrender that he would never give up the flag intrusted to his keeping, and the next moment met death with composure, be cherished by his countrymen. The name of Smith, already illustrious in the annals of the American Navy, will be added to the bright galaxy of those who have freely laid down their lives at the call of their country.

The speech was received in the country as a worthy tribute to valiant achievements, and gave especial satisfaction to the Navy. Captain Foote wrote:

I have been for some time on the point of writing to you to express my appreciation of the ability and discrimination with which you have managed the interests of the Navy, and for your views of the importance to the country of this arm of defense; but I can refrain no longer. For this manifestation of interest in me, and for our navy officers, together with the Western officers and men constituting almost the entire *personnel* of the flotilla, coming from the Senator of that glorious banner State of dashing, gallant officers and men who have been foremost in the field, I most gratefully in their behalf and my own make my acknowledgments.

Captain Ericsson wrote:

It would, indeed, prove a great stimulus for exertion, if all who labor for the public good could have their deeds placed before the country in such striking and eloquent language as characterizes your speech.

The wife of an accomplished naval officer wrote:

I received a few days since the remarks made by you in regard to our Western naval flotilla. I have taken great pleasure in reading them, and lending them to a good many friends, who have been equally delighted with them. Our gallant little navy has covered itself with glory in this war. I am so glad that it has had an opportunity of making itself known and appreciated in the West, where it will henceforth, I trust, be as much cherished and admired as it used to be in the East. The action of the Cumberland and the Monitor seems to me to be as sublime as anything that we read of in history, and I can never think of the going down of that beautiful vessel, with her guns firing and her colors flying, without the tears coming to my eyes. Please accept my thanks for your beautiful tribute to the Navy, and for giving me an opportunity to read it.

71.—*To Captain Samuel F. Du Pont, Flag-Officer.*

WASHINGTON, *March* 15, 1862.

I beg you to receive my thanks for your kind remembrance of me as shown by the valuable rifle sent me by Captain Davis. The gun of itself is valuable, but the fact that it comes from you renders it doubly so. You may be assured that your services on the South Atlantic coast are fully appreciated by the country.

I send you the *Globe* newspaper, containing some remarks of mine in the Senate on the operations of the Western flotilla under Captain Foote. There was to my mind a manifest intention on the part of the military commanders to do Captain Foote injustice; and, although I have no acquaintance with him, I was resolved to see "the record made right," as not only an act of justice to him, but also to the service. I flatter myself that the sentiment here is now with Foote; I know that it is wholly so in the Senate. He intended to attack the rebel forts at New Madrid, on the Mississippi River, to-day.

Upon hearing of the victory of the national arms at Fort Donelson, Tennessee, February 15th, Mr. Grimes addressed a congratulatory letter to General Charles F. Smith, and received the following reply:

SAVANNAH, TENN., *March* 13, 1862.

Your kind and complimentary note of the 24th ult., addressed to me at Paducah, was not received by me until this morning. I fear that yourself and others overrate the value of my services recently; I did not suppose I was doing anything remarkable; however, I am not the less sensible of the kindness and manliness you have exhibited toward one so entirely a stranger to you as myself. I am deeply grateful to you, believe me. As I know it will gratify your State pride, it affords me great pleasure to say that, although all of the Iowa regiments acted creditably, the behavior of the Second was, during the assault of the 15th, as fine an exhibition of soldierly conduct as it has ever been my fortune to witness.

I am here with a large force on a rather delicate mission, which will be developed in a few days. Again thanking you for your manliness and kindness, I remain

Very truly your friend and servant,

C. F. SMITH.

The Hon. JAMES W. GRIMES, *Washington.*

A few weeks afterward General Smith died at his post. In advocating a pension to his widow, Mr. Grimes paid the following tribute to his memory:

I should do injustice to my own feelings, and to the gallant men of my State who composed a part of General Smith's division, and who were led so valiantly by him in action, if I did not say a single word in advocacy of this bill. General Smith was nearly forty years in the service of the United States. He was recognized everywhere by everybody and at all times as one of the most skillful, one of the bravest and most gallant men we ever had. I have heard officers say that it seemed to them, who had seen him in action in Mexico and in this country, that when the action came, and he saw powder burning, he had a divine inspiration upon him. At Donelson he was wounded by a ball, and inflammation proceeding from that wound was the cause of his death. Yet so anxious was he that his officers and men should not know that he had been wounded, that he carefully concealed it, and it was not known except to a few until after his death, and even his widow was not made conscious of it until weeks after he had died. It is to the widow of that man who has led your soldiers for forty years, who has exhibited such bravery upon every field, who was brevetted three times in Mexico for his gallantry, who was everywhere considered one of the most accomplished officers the public service had, that I desired to give this pension, even if it may be considered a little more liberal than we can afford to give to the widows of all our brigadier and major generals hereafter; for I apprehend there will be very few cases so meritorious.

Mr. Grimes moved an inquiry, April 14th, as to what reorganization of the army in its *personnel*, or otherwise, may be necessary to promote the public welfare and bring the rebellion to a speedy and triumphant end; and made a speech against the surrender of slaves by the army, exposing the abuses of several commanders in that matter, and advising the employment of slaves in the military service of the United States. Mr. Sumner called it a persuasive speech, and said that he was grateful to the Senator from Iowa for the frankness with which he exposed and condemned the recent orders of several of the generals.

SPEECH ON THE SURRENDER OF SLAVES BY THE ARMY, *April* 14, 1862.

It is, of course, to be expected that there will be great differences of opinion among the friends of the Government as to the manner in which the present war should be conducted. Such differences are the natural results of our various domestic institutions, systems of education, modes of thought, degrees of civilization, and of individual opinions of the necessities of our situation. But there are certain great fundamental principles upon which, one would think, all ought to agree. We certainly ought to do nothing and suffer nothing to be done calculated in any degree to repel or paralyze the efforts of our friends at home, who are doing everything in their power to encourage and sustain the soldiers in the field. While inculcating the necessity of the strictest obedience to military duty, it should be constantly borne in mind that ours are a citizen soldiery, soon to return to the bosom of civil society, and that the performance of no unsoldierly duty should be required of them that would be calculated to impair their self-respect, diminish their regard for their officers, incite them to rebel against discipline, or taint their reputations at home. It must not be expected that the natural instincts of humanity will be stifled by military orders, and surely our soldiers should not be required to assist in the perpetration of acts against which every enlightened sentiment of their hearts revolts. One would think that all men would agree in pronouncing that a cruel and despotic order, which repeals the divine precept, "Inasmuch as ye did it not to one of the least of these ye did it not to me," and arbitrarily forbids the soldier to bestow a crust of bread or a cup of water upon a wretched, famishing fugitive escaping from our own as well as from his enemy. Yet, I grieve to say there are those high in rank in the service of the United States who have sought to break down the spirit of manhood, which is the crowning glory of true soldiers, by requiring them to do acts outside of their profession which they abhor, and to smother all impulses to those deeds of charity which they have been taught to believe are the characteristics of Christian gentlemen.

It was known to the country at an early day after the commencement of the war, that some military commanders were abusing the great power intrusted to them, and were employing the Army to assist in the capture and rendition of fugitive slaves, not in aid of any judicial process, but in obedience to their own unbridled will. The effect of this assumption of unauthorized power was to incite the soldiery to disobedience, and to arouse the people to the necessity of proper legislative restraints. It was in compliance with the popular sentiment on this subject that Congress enacted the additional article of war, which was approved on the 13th of March last, and which declared that "all officers or persons in the military or naval service of the United States are prohibited from employing any of the forces under their respective commands for the purpose of returning fugitives from service or labor, who may have escaped from any persons to whom such service or labor is claimed to be due, and any officer who shall be found guilty by court-martial of violating this article shall be dismissed from the service."

It was intended by this article to prevent the military service from becoming odious to the people who support the war, and degrading to those who have volunteered to fight under our banners. It simply declares that the Army of the United States shall not be perverted from the legitimate use for which it was raised, while it interferes in no degree with the claim of any man to a person alleged to be a slave; it leaves questions of that character to be settled, and rights of that description to be enforced, by other than the military authority. The intention of those who voted for this article was not to abridge any man's rights, but to leave every one to his legal remedies as though no war existed.

How is this new article of war enforced? It has been promulgated to the army it is true. It may not be openly and avowedly violated. Soldiers may not hereafter be required to actually perform the humiliating office of fastening manacles upon the limbs of persons said to be slaves, nor to escort them to the residences of their masters; but the experience of the last few days has taught us that, notwithstanding the new article of war, our military officers suffer their camps to be invaded by armed detachments of slave-hunters, without the support of any process of law, who there attempt to shoot, maim, and kill with impunity those whom they claim to be slaves, while our soldiers are required to stand indifferently by and witness the inhuman work.

How long, think you, will this method of dealing with the rebels be endured by the freemen of this country? Are our brothers and sons to be confined within the walls of the tobacco-warehouses and jails of Richmond and Charleston, obliged to perform the most menial offices, subsisted upon the most stinted diet, their lives endangered if they attempt to obtain a breath of fresh air, or a beam of God's sunlight at a window, while the rebels, captured by these very men, are permitted to go at large upon parol, to be pampered with luxuries, to be attended by slaves, and the slaves guarded from escape by our own soldiers?

In the month of February last, an officer of the Third Regiment of Iowa Infantry, stationed at a small town in Missouri, succeeded in capturing several rebel bridge-burners, and some recruiting-officers belonging to Price's army. The information that led to their capture was furnished by two or three remarkably shrewd and intelligent slaves, claimed by a lieutenant-colonel in the rebel army. Shortly afterward the master dispatched an agent with instructions to seize the slaves and convey them within the rebel lines, whereupon the Iowa officer seized them and reported the circumstances to headquarters. The slaves soon understanding the full import of General Halleck's celebrated Order No. 3, two of them attempted an escape. This was regarded as an unpardonable sin. The Iowa officer was immediately placed under arrest, and a detachment of the Missouri State militiamen, in the pay of the Government and under the command of General Halleck, were sent in pursuit of the fugitives. The hunt was successful. The slaves were caught and returned to their traitor master, but not until one of them had been shot by order of the soldier in command of the pursuing party.

Mr. President, how long shall we permit such conduct as this to go unrebuked? Does any one suppose that the people will quietly submit to the imposition of taxes to support a State militia in the field that is to be employed in the capture of slaves for the benefit of officers in the rebel army? Is it supposed that the Senators from Iowa will silently, patiently permit the gallant officers from that State to be outraged in the manner I have described?

It is quite time that some definite policy should be established for the treatment of escaped slaves; and I am of the opinion that Congress has been grossly derelict in permitting the evil to go so long unregulated and unchecked. We have almost as many diverse systems of dealing with this class of persons as we have military departments. In one, fugitive slaves have been pursued, flogged, and returned to their masters by our army; in another, they have been simply pursued and returned without flogging; in another, they have been pursued and shot in the attempt to return them; in another, they have been termed "contraband," and received within our lines in the mixed character of persons and property. In the absence of any authoritative declaration of Congress, none of these modes may be held to be in conflict with law, other than the law of common-sense and common decency.[1]

It is obvious that the article of war which I have quoted does not meet the case presented by Major-General Halleck in his Order No. 3. That celebrated manifesto declares in substance that all persons from the enemy's country shall be excluded from our lines. The plain purpose of the order is to prohibit fugitive slaves escaping from the rebellious district, and thereby securing freedom. It was doubtless competent for General Halleck to issue such an order, and it is equally competent for Congress, which has made and continues to make articles of war for the government of the army and navy, to countermand it. And it ought to be countermanded. I will not pause to discuss the humanitarian features of the question. Public policy, no less than popular feeling, demands that Order No. 3 be forever erased. There never was a war waged in the history of the world where the means of acquiring information of the enemy's position and numbers were more ample than here, and there never was one where the commanding officers have suffered more from lack of such information. Order No. 3 proposes to incorporate the fatuity and blindness which remained unwritten in other military departments into an historical record and a public advertisement. It proposes to warn all persons against bringing information of the enemy's movements to our camps, under penalty of being turned back to receive such punishment as the enemy may choose to inflict for betraying them, or for running away and betraying combined. No organization of secret service can meet all the requirements of an army operating in an enemy's country, unless aided by some portion of the inhabitants of the country. What folly, then, to wall out and repel the very inhabitants who might bring us the information we most need, and who have everywhere shown an eagerness to do so!

It is the undoubted right and the duty of every nation, when engaged in a righteous war—and no other than a righteous war is justifiable at all—to avail itself of every legitimate means known

[1] "Up to that date (July, 1862), neither Congress nor the President had made any clear, well-defined rules touching the negro slaves, and the different generals had issued orders according to their own political sentiments."—*Memoirs of General W. T. Sherman, written by Himself*, vol. i., p. 265.

to civilized warfare to overcome its enemies. What will be thought by posterity of this nation, if, in the present emergency, we not only fail to employ the agencies which Providence seems to have placed at our disposal, but actually seek every opportunity to exasperate and drive from our support those who are anxious to serve us? Were the Russian nobles now engaged in a rebellion against their Government, would we not regard their emperor as guilty of the greatest folly, if he not only declined to enlist the serfs of his empire to aid in suppressing the insurrection, but repelled them from his service and allowed his generals to return them to his rebellious nobles, to be used by them in overthrowing his authority? And can any one tell me the difference between the case I have put and our own?

The whole history of the world does not exhibit a nation guilty of such extreme fatuity as has marked the conduct of our Government in its treatment of the colored population since the present war began. It seems to be impossible to convince ourselves that *war*, with all of its attendant responsibilities and calamities, really exists, and that future generations will not hold those guiltless who refuse to use any of the means which God has placed in their hands to bring it to a speedy and successful termination. History will pronounce those men criminal who, in this crisis of the nation's fate, consult the prejudices of caste or color, and regard the interests of property of paramount importance to the unity of the nation.

It is useless to attempt to blink out of sight the great issues before us—issues that *must* be settled, and settled *by us*. It were wiser and more manly to meet them squarely and at once. We are in the midst of the greatest revolution that ever occurred in ancient or modern times. Such armies as are now marshaled in hostile array on this continent, in point of numbers, equipment, and expense, have been hitherto unknown in the annals of mankind. We are imposing burdens in the form of taxes that will be felt by unborn generations. We are suffering much now; we expect and are willing to suffer more. And why? Because we desire to preserve the integrity of our nation; because we believe that Heaven designed us to be one people with one destiny; the freest and happiest on earth. It was to preserve that unity of our national existence that our sons and brothers have gone forth to do battle. For this it was that the gallant men of Iowa have freely, triumphantly, laid down their lives at Wilson's Creek, Blue Mills, Belmont, Fort Donelson, Pea Ridge, and Pittsburg. And shall we, after these great sacrifices of life and treasure, hesitate about employing any of the instrumentalities in aid of the country that are known to civilized warfare? Shall we not be recreant to our high trust if we doubt or delay in this particular?

This war will go on until rebellion is subdued. Upon this point there need be no controversy. Rely upon it, the Northwestern States will submit to no temporizing or compromising policy. They are too much in earnest; they have suffered too much already; they know too well what they would be compelled to suffer in the future to allow treason to go unpunished. It is because they desire to prevent the recurrence of the rebellion that they demand that it shall now be thoroughly crushed out. Among things necessary to be done to fully accomplish this purpose, we must conquer and hold all the forts and strong positions on the South Atlantic and Gulf coasts. How shall they be garrisoned when captured? This is a question we shall soon be compelled to answer; and I am prepared for its solution. I answer it unhesitatingly that we should garrison them, in whole or in part, by soldiers of African descent; that instead of returning slaves to their rebel masters to fight against us, we should employ them in our own military service.

I know very well that this proposition encounters at once all the prejudices that have been engendered by differences of race, education, and social position; but let us look at it a moment soberly and practically. It is assumed as admitted by all that the Southern forts must be captured and strongly garrisoned for some years to come. They are situated in a warm and enervating climate, and the particular location of nearly all of them renders them more than usually unhealthy, even for that section of the country. In addition to the forts already established, we shall be compelled to build new ones. The rebels rely upon the diseases of their climate to decimate our Northern army in the summer and autumnal months; and their confidence is well placed. Our troops will wither before the fevers of the Gulf coast as vegetation does before the blast of the sirocco. Now, we have in our midst thousands of hardy, athletic colored men, fitted by nature to endure the heat and miasma of the tropics, and some of them accustomed to it, who are panting to be employed in the capacity of soldiers. Many of them having been in a state of bondage, have been abandoned by their masters, and are now thrown upon us for support. Some of them were forced by our enemies into their military service, and have deserted from it. They implore our protection, and we must give it, if we would not become a "scorn and derision" among the nations of the earth. They have shown on divers occasions, both on sea and land, that they belong to a warlike race. They are obedient and teachable. They can be subsisted much cheaper than white soldiers, can perform more labor, and are subject to fewer diseases in a warm climate.

Now, with these facts before us, shall we refuse to employ them? What substantial reason can be given for not doing so? Is it because they have not the proper capacity for command? Then give them white officers, as is done by the British Government to the same race, by the French Government to the Arabs, and by the Russian Government to the Tartars and other semi-barbarous soldiers within that empire. Is it because they do not possess the average courage of soldiers? In addition to the testimony in disproof of this, furnished a few days ago by the Senator from Massachusetts (Mr. Wilson), I refer you to your vessels-of-war, where you have hundreds of these men employed, and none more valiant. Is it because they are not obedient to command? The whole history of the race shows the contrary, for, if there is any one thing for which they are remarkable more than another, it is their confiding submission to the will of their superiors. Is it said that we have white soldiers enough for all of our purposes? True, we have a large army, composed of men of unsurpassed valor and patriotism, who, if we require it, will sacrifice their lives for their country, whether by the sword or by disease; but I would, if I could, recall a portion of them to their homes and to the industrial pursuits of life. Am I told that the enrollment of a few colored soldiers will be regarded by the Army as humiliating to them? Mr. President, those public men fail to comprehend the character of American soldiers who suppose that they are fighting for mere military glory, or that in this critical hour they are controlled by ignoble prejudice against color or race. They are citizens and taxpayers as well as soldiers. They want the rebellion speedily crushed and the supreme authority of the law established, leaving social and political questions to be settled afterward. They feel that the desertion of every colored soldier, artificer, or laborer, from the rebellious States, withdraws aid and support from the rebellion, and brings it so much nearer to an end. They cannot understand, nor can I, that refined casuistry that justifies us in converting the enemy's horse or ox to our use, and in turning their inanimate engines of destruction against themselves, but denies to us the right to turn their slaves, their animate hostile engines in human form, to the same purpose. They cannot imagine why it is that some gentlemen are so willing that men of the African race should labor for them, and so unwilling that they should fight for them.

What a wonderful difference of action and sentiment there is on this subject between the officers of the Army and Navy! While officers of the Army have disgraced themselves, annoyed and incensed their subordinates, dishonored the country, and injured the public service, by the promulgation of their ridiculous orders about slaves, no officer of the Navy, thank God, has ever descended to follow their example. Their noble, manly, generous hearts would revolt at the idea of having imposed upon them the humiliating duty of capturing and returning fugitive slaves. They serve their country, not rebel slave-owners. They think that duty to the country requires them to avail themselves of the services of these people, instead of driving them back to their masters, or suffering them to starve; and they act upon this conviction. At the taking of Hatteras, one of the large guns of the Minnesota was wholly manned and worked by persons called "contrabands," and no gun on the ship was better served. These people are, it is well known, remarkable for the proficiency they soon acquire as cannoneers. On the same ship is a boat's crew, every one of whom, including the cockswain, is a colored man, and there are none more skillful, or render more satisfactory service to the officers of the vessel. The whole country knows the services rendered by them to Commodore Du Pont and to the vessels under his command. They have acted as pilots, and in the most important positions, and I have the authority of the two superior officers of that fleet for saying that they have never been deceived or misled by any one of them. I am convinced that our expedition to the South Atlantic coast would not have been so perfect a success as it has been but for the slaves found there, and who were employed by our naval officers. There are more or less of them on all our vessels-of-war. They are efficient men, and their presence produces no discord among the crews.

Mr. President, I wish to be distinctly understood. I advocate no indiscriminate arming of the colored race, although I frankly confess that I would do so were it necessary to put down the rebellion. I do not favor this proposition merely because of its anti-slavery tendency. I approve it because it will result in a saving of human life, and in bringing the rebellion to a speedier termination. It is my business to aid in bringing this war to a close by conquering an unconditional peace in the least expensive and speediest manner possible. Acting upon this idea of my duty, and believing that humanity and the best interests of the country require the enrollment of a few colored regiments for garrisoning the Southern forts, I shall vote, whenever an opportunity shall be afforded me, for converting a portion of the colored refugees into soldiers, instead of forcing them back into servitude to their rebel masters and their rebel government. We may hesitate to do this. Our hesitation will cost us the valuable lives of many of our own race who are near and dear to us. Our hesitation to use the means which Providence seems to have placed in our hands for crushing the rebellion may carry desolation to many a loyal hearthstone. But we must adopt this policy sooner or later, and, in my opinion, the sooner we do it the better. The rebels have this day thousands of slaves throwing up intrenchments and redoubts at Yorktown, and thousands of them performing military duty elsewhere; and yet we hesitate and doubt the propriety of employing the same race of people to defend ourselves and our institutions against them. Mr. President, how long shall we hesitate?

Parker Pillsbury wrote to Mr. Grimes from Concord, N. H., April 26th:

Your whole speech breathes a spirit of humanity and love of justice, honorable to your heart. Almost forty years ago, I used to walk barefooted, and before daylight, by your father's house on my way to see the musters. I recollect you as a smaller boy than myself, in more comfortable conditions. I only desire to give you the good-speed of an humble, but, I trust, honest, earnest lover of liberty and of man, of *every man.* I have not forgotten your brave letter to Franklin Pierce, when he undertook to *play* President over the country, and *work* the tyrant in and over Kansas. My mission is (as for twenty years past) to demand freedom for every slave, not as a "military necessity," but in the name of humanity, and according to the laws of the living God.

Dissatisfied with vacillating counsels in carrying on the war, and advocating a definite policy, Mr. Grimes said, May 20th:

I am not so anxious to tax the people until I have some distinct line of policy laid down by the President, and by those in authority in this Government. The time has arrived when we, as the Senators of the States, when the members of the House, as the representatives of the people, and when the people themselves, have a right to expect and demand that there should be some definite line of policy established. How is it now? In one military district we have one sort of order enforced; in another military district, because it does not suit the views of particular men who have the ear of the Executive, it is countermanded, and another order submitted; and nobody knows what is the true policy of the Government in any district. Is it not due to us, is it not due to our constituents, whom we propose to tax heavily, that there should be something submitted to the people as to what that line of policy shall be? If the President reserves to himself, and possesses, as he seems to intimate, the prerogative, I want to know, for one, and as the representative of a sovereign State Idemand to know, how that prerogative is to be exercised.

Other matters demand our attention quite as much as the tax bill; and in behalf of the people that I represent I want to know what is to be the policy of the Government. Less than eight months ago five regiments of as gallant and true men as ever shouldered a musket went into the Army of the United States from my State with the full complement of men. Within the last ten days they have been brigaded into one brigade, and the total number of efficient men now is less than one thousand. Is not that a striking fact worthy of our contemplation? Are we to content ourselves with merely imposing additional burdens upon the people in the way of taxation, and take no steps to supply those ranks?

Mr. Grimes said, May 21st, with reference to numerous bills to confiscate the property and free the slaves of rebels:

I am in favor of a confiscation bill. I am in favor of a stringent one. I am willing to vote for the most stringent one that I can constitutionally vote for. I want the best one I can get. And, the sooner we pass it, the sooner the public mind will be satisfied upon the subject.

Weary of the hesitancy of the Administration to employ colored persons in the military service, Mr. Grimes submitted the following resolution June 18th:

Resolved (as the opinion of the Senate), That it is the right and duty of the Government to call all loyal persons within the rebellious States to its armed defense against the traitors who are seeking its overthrow.

On the 9th of July he offered an amendment to the militia bill, that there should be no exemption from military duty on account of color or lineage, and said:

I am now more anxious to vote than to speak.

Rev. George B. Cheever, D. D., of New York, wrote to him, May 22d, that he was encouraged by the firmness and severity with which he had denounced the pro-slavery policy of the Government.

Moving to abolish the grog-ration in the naval service, which was two dips a day, and to give in lieu of it a commutation of five cents, Mr. Grimes said, June 13th:

I am informed that hardly any difficulty has grown up during this war on board of a single one of our vessels, that has not been traced directly to the fact that spirituous liquors were allowed on board the ship. A great many difficulties have occurred both with the regular officers and with the volunteer officers, but in almost every instance it has been traced to that source, and I believe that the men are satisfied that it should be abolished. From what I can learn, I think that is the universal sentiment; but so long as we allow liquor to be taken on board, and allow a few to have the privilege, a great many others will be induced by the example to take it too. By abolishing the whiskey-ration we shall take away one of the strongest reasons why parents are unwilling that their minor sons should enlist in the naval service. I desire that this law shall apply to the officers as well as to the men, that no distilled spirituous liquors shall be allowed on board; for, so long as it is known to the men that the officers are allowed by the Government to indulge in this practice, it will promote insubordination and trouble on shipboard.

72.—*To Mrs. Grimes.*

WASHINGTON, *May* 4, 1862.

I have just returned from church; heard a good sermon from Dr. Channing, better than I ever heard from him, I think. The congregation is enlarging, and I am inclined to think that he will finally succeed in building up a good society here.

I met Miss Donelson yesterday. She returned from Port Royal three days ago. She speaks very favorably of the docility, obedience, and faithfulness, of the blacks at that place.

You observe that Mr. Wells has issued a circular, directing "contrabands," as he calls them, to be enlisted in the naval service. This *must* be finally followed up by an army order, sooner or later, and then comes the end of slavery. I regard the employment of colored persons in the Army and Navy as of vastly more importance in putting an end to slavery than all of the confiscation acts that could be devised by the ingenuity of man.

I wish I were at home with you, wandering about the garden, as I should be at this hour.

May 10*th.*—This letter (of Commodore Du Pont) will convince you of what I always told you, that Du Pont is a remarkably discreet, judicious, practical man, with generous, noble impulses, and withal a Christian gentleman.

This morning I drew up and passed through the Senate a bill for the benefit of Robert Small, giving him and his associates one-half of the value of the steamer Planter, and also one-half of the value of all the arms, munitions, etc., on board at the time she was captured. The amount to be distributed among him and his associates will be about fifteen thousand dollars.

The President has to-day rescinded Hunter's proclamation. The result will be a general row in the country. All the radical Republicans are indignant but me, and I am not, because I have expected it, and was ready for it. They did not anticipate it, though I have told them all along that it was sure to come. But the end must come, protracted by the obstinacy and stupidity of rulers it may be, but come it will nevertheless.

May 22d.—I have a long letter from Captain Porter at New Orleans, and one from Commodore Foote, and one from his wife, also. Confiscation got the "go-by" to-day, not by my vote, however.

Stanton has been on the "rampage" again, and called out the militia. There has never been any danger here.

June.—I was never so busy before. I have an immense amount of *real* business thrust upon me, and I doubt if there is any one in the Senate who does more.

I waked up the other day, and found myself quite unexpectedly famous, for having abolished the grog-ration in the Navy, and forbidding any spirituous liquors to be taken on board of ships-of-war. I inclose a letter from Commodore Foote to Lieutenant Wise (son-in-law of Mr. Everett), which I thought you might like to preserve, both on account of the compliment and the autograph.[1] I have been making another speech on naval matters, and am complimented on it. I have also engineered a bill through the Senate for the better government of the Navy upon modern and humanitarian principles.

Rev. John Marsh, D. D., Secretary of the American Temperance Union, New York, wrote to Mr. Grimes, June 28th:

A thousand thanks to you for getting the spirit-ration removed from the Navy!

[1] *Commodore Foote to Lieutenant Wise.*

CLEVELAND, *June* 19, 1862.

MY DEAR WISE: I have written six letters in my bed this morning, and am exhausted; but you have been so kind to me, and so accommodating to our flotilla in its darkest days, that I must say a word in acknowledgment.

Mr. Everett called on me, and I told him how much the country owed you for invaluable services in the Ordnance Bureau, etc., which elicited the remark that he was happy to hear such testimony from me. Your brother is a noble fellow, and stood up to his arduous duties in a way that should insure him any berth he wants in case the flotilla, as it should be, is turned over to the Navy Department.

Do thank Mr. Grimes from me for his resolution to stop the grog-ration, and keep the ardents out of our ships. It will even add to his reputation as the true friend to the Navy. I am proud that he who advocated my vote of thanks should also have introduced the resolution to banish liquor from our ships.

Your faithful friend, A. H. FOOTE.

Admiral Du Pont wrote, September 12, 1862:

You will be pleased to hear that the doing away with the spirit-ration has met with perfect acquiescence

The establishment of a national armory and arsenal on Rock Island, which Mr. Grimes regarded as the place of all others on the continent for it, was largely due to his exertions. He introduced a bill, July 12, 1861, and after the lapse of a year secured an appropriation for the object. In the course of debate, other points being proposed for the location of the arsenal, namely, Alton, Quincy, Springfield, and Keokuk, he said:

In 1816 the Government located a fort on Rock Island, in the Mississippi River. In 1836 the fort was abandoned, and from that time seven hundred and two acres of land on that island have been reserved by the Government for military purposes, and intended by the Ordnance men and those familiar with the military administration for this object, and for no other. There is a water-power there unequaled by any on this continent, unless it be that of Niagara Falls. The whole volume of the current of the Mississippi River can be used for mechanical purposes, if the Government sees fit; and that was one of the reasons why it was originally reserved for the specific purposes of an arsenal and armory. We do not ask for an armory in Iowa. We expect to be sufficiently benefited by the establishment of an arsenal on Rock Island, in the State of Illinois. It will be more accessible to the people of the western half of Wisconsin, and to the people of Minnesota, than it would be at Quincy, or at any other point below; and to the people of Iowa, and two-thirds or one-half of the people of Illinois. The bill I have introduced (February 20, 1862) authorizes the President to expend one hundred thousand dollars in clearing the way, and preparing for the erection of a proper armory at this point.

Mr. Grimes was jealous for the honor and credit of the Navy; claimed that it was doing as much for the country, and was entitled to as much consideration, as the Army, that greater advances had been made in the manufacture of arms in the Navy Department than in the War Department, and that there should be some equality in the relative rank and pay of officers in each service. He advocated establishing the grade of rear-admiral, and said, July 2, 1862:

If ever a great exigency may arise when the Government may need an officer of the higher grade, or when any of these rear-admirals may act so as justly to entitle them to the compliment of a higher grade, we shall have it in our power to give them a higher grade.

Referring to this measure as justified by events, he said, March 3, 1863:

We have had six rear-admirals appointed (nine was the limit allowed by law). We established at that time a ladder by which they might climb up to that distinguished rank. We said to them: If you will distinguish yourselves in this particular service, if you will achieve some great conquest in this part of the country or in that part of the country, you shall be made a rear-admiral, you shall have the highest honor belonging to your profession which the country can bestow. And what is the result? Why, we have admirals who command the admiration and respect of the whole country. Reference has been made to some naval officers of very considerable merit who are now serving in the capacity of acting admirals. It was a matter of favor that they were permitted to be acting admirals. They were given fine commands. They were told: Go, and take this place; go, and open the Mississippi River, distinguish yourselves, win your laurels and you shall receive them. These places have been kept open as incentives to emulous deeds, to noble daring, to the performance of high duties on the part of your officers.

Mr. Grimes advocated appointments to the Marine Corps from graduates of the Naval Academy, for the purpose of securing men fully competent for the duties of that service, and also to give every part of the country a fair representation in it. In the course of debate upon this subject, May 12, 1862, allusion being made to the Federal patronage in New York and Iowa, he said:

The Senator from New York mentioned Iowa as one of the States that had got its full share. In the Navy Department I think it has during this Administration got everything we have asked for and that it was entitled to, and I think we have asked for nothing more. But it is refreshing, for a gentleman from New York, where they have a navy-yard that employs three thousand men, and a custom-house that employs three thousand more, and an arsenal at Watervliet that employs twenty-three hundred men, and a navy-yard again at Oswego that employs I do not know how many more, and the West Point Academy, for which we appropriate several hundred thousand dollars a year, to bring that State in contrast with the State of Iowa, where we have three land-offices with six land-officers, each with a salary of five hundred dollars a year, one marshal, one United States judge with a salary of eighteen hundred dollars a year, and one clerk. These are all the Federal officers we have in Iowa, and I thank God for it. We do not want any more Federal officers in my State.

He repeated what he had said in the Thirty-sixth Congress with reference to a United States marine hospital at Burlington, Iowa, and remarked, February 7th:

It would be supposed that I would have some interest, perhaps, in keeping up the establishment, as the persons appointed to office there are my friends, and have been appointed, perhaps, slightly under my influence. But it is of no earthly benefit to the Government, and ought to be abolished, and I want to avail myself of this occasion to set an example of self-sacrifice, of disinterested patriotism, to gentlemen.

73.—*To Captain S. F. Du Pont.*

WASHINGTON, *June* 14, 1862.

Your letter in behalf of two officers in your squadron is at hand . . . . The difficulty arises from the displacement of those who have been continuously in the service, and the apparent impossibility of stopping restorations with a few of the most worthy ones. About a score of them have been before us, and the Senate has finally disposed of the matter. The officer who in my opinion has the least merit, was the only one who was strongly urged and insisted upon; all the others were made to hang upon the decision in his case. This would not have been fair (though I told the Senate what my opinion was on the subject), had not the question been decided squarely upon its real merits, viz., whether *any* one ought to be restored, who had resigned and gone into civil life, if the restoration would injure those who had remained all of the time in the service. It is doubtless true that the result was influenced by the fact that we have been besieged during the session by persons in the interest of those who seek to be restored, and whose names would probably have been sent to us, had we acted favorably upon those who *were* sent in. The number in favor of confirmation was very small indeed, not half a dozen; but you will understand that this decision was not predicated at all upon the merits of the officers themselves.

You are misinformed as to the action of the Senate on the vote of thanks to Farragut's fleet-officers. The President sent two recommendations, one embracing Farragut and his officers and men, which the committee advised the Senate to adopt, and it was adopted; and the other, recommending a vote of thanks to the commander of each vessel, specifying each officer by name. This last the committee has not acted upon, and will probably take no notice of.

We have just had the naval bill under consideration. I had put on amendments:

1. Abolishing spirit-ration after 1st September, and allowing no spirituous liquors to be carried on board, save for medical stores, and giving each man five cents per day in lieu of it.

2. Making board of visitors at Naval Academy a mixed commission from civil and naval life, and making an appropriation for mileage, as in the case of the Military Academy.

3. Authorizing ten naval cadets to be appointed each year, to be selected from the sons of officers and men in the military and naval profession, who have distinguished themselves.

4. Giving commodore's secretary fifteen hundred dollars per annum and one ration. And sundry other amendments in which you probably take no particular interest.

We hope to leave here soon. I shall hope to hear from you often at my Western home.

74.—*To Commodore Samuel F. Du Pont.*

WASHINGTON, *June* 29, 1862.

Your very kind letter inviting me to visit you at Port Royal was received yesterday, for which I am greatly indebted to you. At first, my friend Mr. Fessenden, of Maine, and myself about determined to accept your invitation, but my anxiety to see my home, where I have not been since last October, has constrained me to forego the pleasure which I am sure a visit to your fleet would afford me. Should you be in that vicinity in the autumn, I hope I may be able to make the trip.

We hope to adjourn next week. I shall return to Iowa thoroughly armed by your kind aid, prepared to kill all the deer, grouse, and other game that I may be able to *hit*.

I have sent you the bill for the government of the Navy, as it passed the Senate; also the grade bill as reported to the Senate. I am sorry to say that I am the only member of the Naval Committee who really desires to pass the bill to establish new grades, etc. By agreeing to two or three absurd amendments, I finally succeeded in "badgering" it through the committee, and got it reported to the Senate, with the understanding that every member of the committee might vote as he pleased; hoping and believing that I can carry it by dint of *impudence* and *will*.

The following extract from a letter of Admiral Du Pont shows what naval gentlemen thought of Mr. Grimes's labors in behalf of the Navy:

WABASH, PORT ROYAL, *September* 12, 1862.

Since Congress adjourned I have frequently desired to write you, waiting for a quiet hour to do so. That hour has not come, and I will no longer delay expressing my warm appreciation of your labors in behalf of the Navy during the last session. I believe this to be emphatically the opinion of the whole service. These labors have had their reward in one sense: never before has so much and such important legislation been carried through—I do not mean in one session—in a period of twenty years. In reference to the great change of all—the creation of the grade of admiral—there seems but one opinion. I never heard an officer, while fancying something might have been better here or there for his grade, who did not always wind up by saying: "But we have admirals; thank God for that!" I feel deeply grateful to you personally, though still more on public grounds, for carrying this great measure through.

In view of the excessive multiplication of generals, Mr. Grimes introduced a resolution, March 10th, that in the opinion of the

Senate no persons should be commissioned as generals of divisions or brigades, except such as exhibited superior competency in the command of men, or gallantry in action against the enemy. He said, March 28th, and in the course of debate subsequently:

I wish the Senate and the country to know that at this time there have been appointed one hundred and eighty brigadier-generals. The expenses of the appointment to the United States are one million dollars a year. The necessities of the Army and the country do not require one-half of this number. We went through the Mexican War with only three generals in the field. Brigades and divisions were then commanded by colonels; regiments by captains, in some instances by first-lieutenants. The comparative expense of conducting that war was nothing at all by the side of the expense we are now incurring. In addition to this number of brigadiers—and I think the number ought to appall every lover of his country—we have twenty major-generals; and all the staffs are upon a corresponding magnitude, and attended with a corresponding expense. Brigadier and major generals in our service have more aides and a larger staff than the generals of any other government in the world. I have taken the trouble to investigate the matter a little, and to look at the practice of other armies. I have the official "Army Register" of Great Britain and that of France here under my desk. Of course every general officer wants to have a brilliant staff; he wants to surround himself with as many aides as possible. It gives *éclat* to the officer; it is very convenient under many circumstances; but it will be exceedingly inconvenient for the people of this country to pay the salaries which are to be allowed to those officers. From the fact that they are not regarded as useful in other armies, I think it is a proper inference that they are not needed in this.

We have to-day the largest army, the best-fed army, the best-clothed army, the best-paid army on the globe. I am not going to say how it is commanded. In a few months this question and some other questions of economy will come home to us, when our constituents shall be called upon to pay the direct taxes to support these brigadier and major generals, and their adjuncts and assistants.

He afterward introduced a bill to limit the number of brigadiers to two hundred, and said:

I have made several ineffectual attempts to do something toward curtailing the number of general officers in the Army, or at least preventing the continued increase of them. We are told every day that this is going to be a financial war more than a war to be fought upon the battle-field. If so, we should attempt to curtail some of the expenses of the Government. We have now between two hundred and three hundred brigadier-generals, while the French Army, with a force of about seven hundred thousand men, has only one hundred and sixty on the active list. And yet we are constantly increasing them, and by the appointment not of men who have distinguished themselves upon the battle-field, not of men who have shown gallantry in action, not of men who have had military educations, not of men who have shown skill in the handling of troops, but mere political appointments, men who, so far as we know, have not the slightest military capacity. Why continue to increase them, while the line of service is being decreased? Each regiment, when it went into the field, embraced somewhere from eight hundred to a thousand men; but they have been greatly depleted. Take, for instance, some of the regiments from my State. The Seventh Iowa lost nearly three hundred at the battle of Belmont, upward of one hundred at Donelson, at Pittsburg Landing nearly two hundred more, and from disease another hundred or two, so that it is actually reduced to somewhere in the neighborhood of two hundred men. The Second is reduced in the same way; so are the Eighth, Twelfth, and Fourteenth, from the same causes. You can embrace a dozen such fragments of regiments in one brigade, and, instead of increasing the number of brigadier-generals, it is our interest and our duty to decrease them. I have been told by two generals of the Army, who have no interest either in the increase or in the decrease of the number, who are skillful officers, whose opinion I rely upon, that there is not the slightest necessity for more than one hundred brigadier-generals.

Now, there are some thirty appointments yet unconfirmed. The moment you fix a limit, we shall not have the appointments taken up at the heel of a day's session, when everybody is tired out, when everybody wants to go to dinner, when there is a very thin Senate, and when appointments are rushed through, against which there might be objections. Some of the appointments, we know, are not going to be confirmed; a good many of them probably ought not to be confirmed. Such places will be filled by the gallant men who deserve promotion. Another effect will be to influence the President to strike from the list of brigadier-generals such men as have been found by experience to be incompetent for command. The Senator from New York (Mr. Harris) objected to this, because he regarded it as a sort of strait-jacket to be put upon the President. He might just as well regard every law that we pass upon the subject in that light. So far from this being a strait-jacket, and any impeachment of the President, I, as a friend of his, insist that the Senate should pass the bill, in order to take away from him the importunities with which he is now beset, to have this man and that man appointed a brigadier. Every one of these brigadier-generals costs the Government about twelve thousand dollars a year. That is something. I confess that it is a very small consideration. I am in favor of this proposition on that account, it is true; but principally, that it will exercise a restraining influence upon executive power; it will cause the performance of the duty which I think the commander-in-chief ought to exercise; and it will cause the Senate to inquire more thoroughly into the conduct of these men. So far as the appointment of gallant men is concerned, fixing the number at two hundred will afford ample opportunity to give all the gentlemen who distinguish themselves the stars.

Mr. Grimes had the utmost confidence in President Lincoln as a discreet, prudent, kind-hearted, and benevolent man, but looked with distrust upon all increase of executive power, even in his hands. In the exigencies of the country he held the authority of Congress and of the law inviolate, and never lost his jealousy of unlimited power or official assumption. He said, July 1, 1862:

I am willing to vote for more men. I am willing to stay here until December and vote for them as needed. I am willing to be called back, upon five or ten days' notice from the President, to give all the additional men or money that may be needed; but, in my opinion, it is the duty of Congress to keep the control of the number of men, and of the amount of money, that shall be voted for war-purposes, as well as for other purposes. Various circumstances are occurring which show that it is the imperative duty of Congress to exercise a watchful care and supervision over the management of the Executive Departments of this country. I am not disposed to ignore my rights or my duties. I want to give to the Government all the support that it needs, but I want to vote that support. I am disposed to give it in a constitutional, legitimate, and legal way, and in no other.

The multiplication of army officers, of a high grade, before they had won distinction in the field, or even seen service, was obnoxious to his judgment. He called attention to a very great abuse in the appointment of aides-de-camp, upon the recommendation of generals in the regular Army, without the advice and consent of the Senate, and said:

I wish to stop it where it is.

When the President sent in a certain bill to the Senate, however much Mr. Grimes may have approved its provisions, he promptly said, July 14, 1862:

I do not recognize the right of the President to send a bill in here.

Mr. Grimes spent a day, December 12th, in the soldiers' hospitals about Washington, and acquainted himself with the details of their management. Prompt and watchful to observe and expose abuses, he said, December 18th:

Some of the medical officers are humane gentlemen. On the other hand, some are mere brutes, and will not answer you a question civilly, unless you tell them that you are in influential position, and then fear alone prompts them to give you the information they ought to be willing to give to any gentleman. If you have a man at the head of your medical department who will put the hand of power on such a man, turn him out, and substitute a good man for him, then you will have your Medical Bureau conducted properly; you cannot do it by legislation."

Disapproving the course of some of the members of the cabinet, and regarding their influence as adverse to the policy of emancipation and to the vigorous prosecution of the war, Mr. Grimes was one of a committee of nine, with Mr. Collamer and other Senators, who presented a paper to the President, December 18th, recommending such selections and changes in his cabinet as would secure to the country unity of purpose and action.

Complaint being made of the presence of United States troops at the polls in some of the election precincts at the November election in Delaware, Mr. Grimes favored an inquiry into the matter, and said, December 23d:

I have offered the resolution without consultation with any human being, upon my own volition. The Senators from Delaware have stated that a portion of the Army has been employed in attending the polls in that State, and have perpetrated violence upon certain of the citizens. Now, if sent for the purpose of preserving quiet, I think they were sent for a laudable purpose. If they have perpetrated violence, I want to know it, and I want the Secretary of War and the military authorities to apply the correction. I do not wish, as one of the representatives of a sovereign State, to shrink from any investigation in connection with that subject.

A proposal was introduced in both Houses of Congress, in December, 1862, to grant aid to the State of Missouri to emancipate the slaves in that State. Mr. Grimes said, January 30, 1863:

I feel that the purpose that is sought to be attained is a very laudable one—a very patriotic one. I am the representative, in part, of a State that is as much interested in having emancipation decreed in Missouri as any other State in this Union. I am personally very much interested, for I live near the border of the State of Missouri; and I am willing to do as much as I believe I can constitutionally and properly do, and as much as I think the people of my State will justify me in doing, in order to accomplish this purpose. In ordinary times, when war did not exist, I could not justify a vote in favor of an appropriation of one million dollars out of the Treasury to emancipate slaves in Missouri, nor one dollar. I can only justify my vote now, upon the idea that slavery is the cause of the war, and that by its removal we shall, in some measure, shorten the continuance of the war. I am willing to go before the people of my State, and undertake to justify an appropriation of ten million dollars, to create freedom and only freedom in Missouri, from and after 1865. I am willing to take the responsibility of giving that vote, and stand the test before the freemen of Iowa. But I am unwilling to vote more. It may be that the slaves are worth more. I have a great many doubts on that subject. It may be that we may be benefited by abolition in Missouri more than ten million dollars. I have a great many doubts on that subject. It may be that the Legislature of Missouri will be unwilling to accept a less sum. I have very many doubts on that subject. They are anxious to get as many millions as possible; but I think, when they discover that we are willing to give them immediately ten millions, and that that is the whole amount we are disposed to give, they will be perfectly willing to accept it.

A bill appropriating twenty millions passed the Senate, February 12th, but failed in the House. Mr. Grimes voted against it.

In relation to President Lincoln's Emancipation Proclamation, Mr. Grimes remarked, February 28th:

A great deal has been said about the effect of the President's proclamation of September last. We have been told that it is having a most disastrous effect upon the people of the country, and especially upon the armies of the country; that its tendency has been to demoralize the soldiers. I am not authorized to speak for any other State than that of which I am one of the representatives in this chamber; nor am I authorized to speak for any other portion of the Army than that gallant portion that my State furnishes. I desire to say, and I say it knowing, as well as any man can know, the sentiment of the people he represents, that, instead of the proclamation having had the effect attributed to it, it had precisely the contrary effect. It came to us while I was canvassing the State of Iowa preceding the last October election, and it was hailed by the loyal men of all parties, who were anxious to put down this rebellion, as one of the most efficient means of bringing it to a successful conclusion. The soldiers of Iowa have hailed it with acclamation. They have accepted it, as the citizens of the State have; and they are willing to use that or any other means, in order to preserve the Union in its glory and consistency. The motto of my State at home, in the field, everywhere, is "Onward and upward!"

THE UNITED STATES MILITARY ACADEMY.

Mr. Grimes was a friend to this institution. He said, July 12, 1861:

I believe it is the universal testimony of this country, and of citizens of foreign countries who have been brought in contact with officers educated there, that some of the most accomplished officers the world has ever seen have been produced in that institution. I do not believe that there is any army in the world that has more accomplished officers than we have in the American Army, who have been educated at West Point. That institution has been under the charge of the Engineer Corps. You know how that corps is constituted. It is the *élite* of the service. Those who graduate at the head of their classes are assigned to that particular department. They are men selected on account of their intellectual qualifications, their application, and the ability by which they have distinguished themselves while at the Academy.

It is proposed to change this, and open the Academy to the superintendency of anybody who may, for the time being, be connected with our Army. I am opposed to it. I would not object so much to open the superintendency to the three scientific corps of the Army, the two Engineer Corps, and the Ordnance Corps; but I do insist that we shall confine it to those three.

He said, January 7, 1862:

There never was a greater mistake than that under which gentlemen seem to labor when they suppose that West Point is the nursery of treason. The facts show the reverse. The proportion of persons appointed from civil life who turned out to be disloyal was much greater than of those educated at the Military Academy. Nearly one-half of those appointed from civil life were disloyal, while not quite one-third of those educated at the Academy.

In a debate upon the bill making appropriations for the support of the Academy, January 15, 1863, he said:

I have received many letters from my constituents urging me to vote against this bill. I do not propose to do so, and I desire to state in one word why I shall not.

The great want of an educated soldiery in this country was first discovered during our Revolutionary War; and he who will read the letters of General Washington will discover that in almost every letter to the Continental Congress he urged the necessity of securing engineer officers. It was in accordance with his desire that they secured through their representatives in France and the other Continental governments in Europe engineer officers to come here, who acted as engineers during the Revolutionary War. During his administration and that of his successor, efforts were made to establish a military academy upon the plan of the military academies then in existence in France, but I believe none was established until 1803, during the administration of Mr. Jefferson, when our present school at West Point was established.

True, you cannot make a good commander out of every one sent to West Point; but while we condemn and pass judgment upon West Point, or the character exhibited by one particular man of its graduates, who happens to be in the command of a large army, we forget the other six hundred men from that Academy in subordinate positions, who are looking after your artillery corps, fabricating and looking after your ordnance and missiles of war, attending to your quartermaster and your commissary departments, who are skilled in all the details of those different departments, and are keeping regularity and order throughout.

It may be that the time will come—and I should like to see it come—when military schools shall be established in the different States. Whenever the States shall establish these schools, and they turn out scholars fit to occupy the positions now given to graduates of the Military Academy, I would at once say, Let these young students go before a board of military officers, and, when they have passed an examination, let them be received into the Army, and let West Point be dispensed with. But are we prepared to do it now? Is there a single school of that description in any of the States? I know of none. There are some private schools where scholars are taught in the manual of arms; but no such foundation for a military education is laid as is necessary for an officer who goes into your Artillery, Engineer, or Ordnance Corps.

Mr. Grimes advised the early return of the Naval Academy to Annapolis, and said with reference to proposals for locating it elsewhere, June 16, 1862:

Let me warn my friends from New England that the worst

policy for them is this constant attempt to draw all the institutions of the country up into the Northeastern States. There is a feeling now in the public mind, in some sections, in the Northwest particularly, that they are being made in too great a degree tributary to the New England States; that you have all the arsenals, the armories, the navy-yards, custom-houses, officers, everything almost, up in that section. I do not entertain any of this feeling; I want to guard against it; and I want to crush out that sentiment as far as possible; but the attempt to draw these institutions there tends to increase this sentiment in other sections. It is not the true policy of any portion of this country to try to monopolize, or to have the idea go out that they are trying to monopolize the power and wealth of the country in a particular locality, or in a particular cluster of States; and it is not for the interest of those States that that idea should be propagated, because we all desire to preserve this Union just as long as possible. The very way to break it up is, to get the opinion entertained in other States that some of the States are using the patronage and wealth of the country for their particular advancement and emolument, and not for the common good. We all know that, from the fact that the New England and Atlantic States were settled much before the others, there has been an accumulation of these offices. We have our arsenals, armories, navy-yards, and military school, all clustered within a radius of two hundred miles. There are three navy-yards within a radius of two hundred miles, perhaps four; for I think that will include Philadelphia. Now, what I want to impress on the minds of Senators is this: that, everything else being equal, it would be for the interest of the Government to place your Naval Academy and some of your other institutions beyond those States. Everything else being equal, it would be for the interest of the Government, and for the interest of the New England States, and New Jersey, and New York, to keep your Academy at Annapolis, rather than to take it to Newport or Perth Amboy.

Favoring the appointment of boys to the Naval Academy, who were sons of officers, seamen, marines, or soldiers, Mr. Grimes said, July 2d:

The purpose is principally on account of the effect that it is calculated to have upon the men. I know many likely young boys, sons of boatswains, carpenters, forward officers, about your navy-yards. It would be a consolation to those officers to know, when they go into battle, to uphold the flag of the country, that there is a provision by which these sons of theirs may secure an appointment, and finally become officers, and that the bestowment of these places is not to be restricted entirely to the sons of politicians. The purpose was to encourage the men in both services, the military and the naval, by holding out this inducement, saying to them, We will not only take care of your widow, but we will educate your boy. And we have provided that the President shall have three appointments to the Naval Academy from the boys who have enlisted as boys in the naval service, to be conferred on such as the one who distinguished himself on board the Varuna at the mouth of the Mississippi, and another little boy who distinguished himself on the Cumberland, when she went down in Hampton Roads. It is a very small boon. We have now in the service of the United States thirty thousand seamen, and I do not know how many soldiers—five hundred thousand perhaps—and we merely authorize the President by this bill to select ten from the sons of these men, and agree that they shall have an education at the Naval Academy. The department wanted the limit of age fixed at sixteen. It was extended to seventeen in opposition to their wishes. In the English service they allow no boy to enter over fifteen, and it is stated to be the fact that no man makes a good officer or a good sailor who enters after he is sixteen years of age.

Mr. Grimes advocated the removal of the navy-yard at Philadelphia a mile and a half down the Delaware River to League Island, especially with reference to the necessities of an iron navy. He considered it the place of all others for that purpose. The island is made by the disemboguement of the Schuylkill into the Delaware. He made a speech in favor of the measure, June 24th, in which, after contrasting the navy-yards of Great Britain and France with those of this country, he showed that for capacity of site, insular position, fresh water, depth of water, susceptibility of defense, proximity to the coal and iron fields of Pennsylvania, and proximity to a manufacturing city with a large mechanical population, no place on the continent could fairly compete with League Island for a great iron-navy yard. In subsequent debates he vigorously supported its advantages over other locations, and his influence powerfully contributed to its acquisition by the Government. In the language of Hon. G. V. Fox, "his name is fixed to League Island as a perpetual record." Mr. Grimes said, January 24, 1863:

I am not here as the representative of any State that can be directly or indirectly interested in a navy-yard, except as to the general interests which my constituents may feel in our maritime defenses. I believe that I can approach this subject without any prepossessions in favor of any place, or any prejudices against one. If I had prepossessions in favor of any one, I think they would be in favor of my native New England; but there are considerations connected with this question of great importance to the welfare of the country, and we ought not to regard it as a simple question between League Island and New London, or Pennsylvania and Connecticut, but look at it in a statesmanlike view, and see what will probably be the consequences of the vote we may give on this subject to the country at large. The best interests of the country and of the Navy require that we should accept some place remote from the seashore, where an iron vessel can be cleaned, as it passes from the sea, and that shall be unapproachable by a hostile force. If we reject League Island, we shall regret it, and the country will forever regret it. Could Great Britain secure to herself such a fresh-water river as the Delaware, and such a site on its banks for a naval station as League Island, she would willingly give one of her most-valued possessions.

Mr. Grimes gave his influence, January 24, 1862, to constitute the States of Missouri, Iowa, Kansas, and Minnesota, the ninth circuit of the Supreme Court of the United States, on the ground that, though embracing a smaller population than any other circuit in the United States, these four States were increasing very rapidly in population, and that they had simplified their code, had dispensed with the old systems of practice, and adopted a nearly uniform system different from other States with which it had been proposed to unite them. The measure failed at the time, but subsequently became a law, approved July 15, 1862.

Mr. Grimes voted in favor of issuing the United States Treasury notes, commonly called greenbacks; but upon the direct question of making them a legal tender did not vote (February 13, 1862).

Disapproving the establishment of banks without a specie basis for their circulation, and not regarding the bill providing for national banks as expedient or wise, he voted against it. He supported an amendment, which failed, requiring the banks to keep in coin an amount equal to one-fourth of their notes (February 10, 12, 1863). In the next Congress, he supported, May 10, 1864, also ineffectually, an amendment requiring each bank to keep on hand one-fourth of the coin received for interest on its bonds, until specie payments should be resumed.

Upon the subject of the national debt, he said, May 31, 1862:

I want to say, for fear the constant repetition of the remark by various Senators may be regarded as an acquiescence in the doctrine by all the members of the Senate, that I am utterly opposed to the theory of those gentlemen who say they do not desire that any sinking-fund should be established, or any method devised by which the ultimate payment of the public debt that is now created shall be projected. I think I can see very distinctly what is going to be one of the effects of this war, especially if the theories announced on this floor are to prevail: that we are to have a Government that is to be controlled by the moneyed men and stock-jobbers of the country. That is what I am afraid of. We have to-day given a very significant vote, in my opinion, on that subject. We have declared that all the bonds that are issued by the United States shall be forever exempt from State taxation. And we shall create, before the end of another year, fifteen hundred million dollars of indebtedness.

The people that I represent decided about six years ago, when they established a new constitution, that no debt should be created unless there was a provision coupled with the act creating it by which steps should be taken for its speedy repayment; and it is their expression of opinion on this subject that I desire to represent, as well as my own. I feel exactly in regard to the creating of public indebtedness, as the gentleman who is now President said a few years ago the people of this country felt in regard to slavery. He said they were perfectly satisfied when they believed it was in the process of utter extinction; and so will I feel, and so will the people that I represent feel. They will be satisfied in paying taxes if they believe they are not only carrying on this war, but gradually getting out of the debt; because the agricultural people that I represent are not interested in the continuance of a large public debt. On the contrary, they want to have us recur to the first principles of the founders of this Government, and be entirely exempt from debt.

75 —*To Hon. S. P. Chase, Secretary of the Treasury.*

BURLINGTON, *July* 29, 1862.

I have now been at home ten days. Permit me to tell you what conclusions I have reached from my intercourse with the people of Iowa.

The people are far in advance of the Administration and of Congress in their desire for a vigorous prosecution of the war. They are unanimous for the confiscation bill, and execrate every man who opposed its passage, or who now opposes its stringent execution. There is but little disposition to enlist until it is known what the course of the Administration is to be on this subject.

I need not tell you that the expressions of confidence in the management of the President, his prudence, sagacity, etc., are in a measure enforced, and proceed from the confessed necessity of supporting him as the only tangible head of the loyal Government, and not from any real confidence in his wisdom. Rely upon it, if things drift along as at present, no volunteers will take the field, and the tax law will become so odious that it will require a larger army to enforce it than to put down the rebellion. Sixty days will determine whether we are longer to have a Government, and the Administration must decide it. It is folly to disregard the sentiment of the country in such a time as this—it is worse; it is wickedness. Either Mr. Lincoln disregards it, or else he willfully keeps himself in ignorance of it. Good men, the best we have, are beginning to utter expressions of despair; and they are not cowed by fear of the strength of the enemy, but by apparent weakness of our friends. I beg you not to be misled by the proceedings of war-meetings in our large towns. Volunteers will come when a "war policy" is declared and acted upon, and not to any considerable extent before. Speeches and resolutions will not bring them.

I thought I comprehended somewhat the popular sentiment before I left Washington. In this I was mistaken. It is far more ardent and extreme than even *I* ever supposed. It is nonsense to attempt to frighten the masses by the story that rigorous measures will "nail up the door against reconciliation of contending sections." We have too much at stake, the Government is of too much value, too much of the best blood of the nation is calling to us for vindication, to justify us in neglecting any methods to put the rebellion down known to civilized warfare. Would to God every man connected with the Administration could travel *incognito* through the country, and get the true expression of the people on these subjects! Instead of getting a knowledge of that sentiment from impartial sources, it now comes to the President and his cabinet from newspapers edited by men in office, from applicants for place, from sycophants, and from cowards who dare not tell a man in power what he knows to be the truth, if he supposes it will be unpleasant to him.

I pray and hope, but I confess that my hope is becoming daily fainter and fainter. I know you will pardon this intrusion upon you. I felt that it was a necessity that I should let out my soul on this subject, and I know no one else to write to but you. I have written very frankly, but very honestly. I hope the country is not in so bad a condition as I fear it to be in. In my opinion, if wisdom rules the hour at Washington, a rigorous confiscation war policy will first be declared, and then a *conscription* of one hundred thousand men made at once. *Men will not volunteer into the old regiments. One volunteer in an old regiment is worth three fresh men in a new regiment.* A conscription of one hundred thousand men would be of more value to the country than three hundred thousand volunteers, and, of course, cost only one-third as much. But why should I advise?

76.—*To Mrs. Grimes.*

INDIANOLA, IOWA, *October* 6, 1862.

I have received your various letters, and I believe they have done me great good by moving me to renewed exertions in behalf of the good cause. I am enthusiastically received wherever I have been, and have everywhere addressed large crowds. This is a Quaker county. A large number have said that they would not vote at the coming election. I had a very large number of them at my meeting yesterday in the public square in this town, and I am told that after the meeting, with one solitary exception, they avowed their resolution to vote.

The President's proclamation is everywhere well received. We shall easily carry the State, and elect all our Congressmen—and a very able delegation it will be. No State will be better represented in the next Congress than Iowa.

77.—*To Hon. W. P. Fessenden.*

BURLINGTON, *October* 12, 1862.

I have been absent nearly four weeks canvassing the State, and only returned last evening. I knew of the death of your son[1] before I left home. I attempted on two occasions to write to you, but failed to send or even complete either letter. I know the anguish that you must feel, and I feared that I would but open your wounds afresh. I think that the last conversation I had with you in Washington was in your room, and about Samuel. You know very well what I thought of him. I always thought that there were the elements of great success in him, and that he would one day be a credit to himself, his family, and to the country. If I knew how to do it I would condole with you. You know that you have my deepest sympathy in your affliction.

I have ceased to write or talk about the generals and the Administration. The men of brains are still overslaughed and ignored, and it would seem that they are to continue to be.

Our election takes place day after to-morrow. I have traveled nearly four weeks, speaking every day. I think we shall elect all six of our Congressmen, and they will all be capital men. My wife sends love. When I came home she was full of praises of your tax-bill speech,[2] pronouncing it the best she had seen from you. I tried to laugh her out of it, but, woman-like, she adheres to that opinion. Did you ever hear any one else say that?

78.—*To Hon. S. P. Chase.*

BURLINGTON, *October* 20, 1862.

We have carried the State triumphantly. We elect all of our six Congressmen. Without the aid of the army vote, our majority will be

[1] Mortally wounded at Bull Run, Virginia, August 30, 1862. [2] June 6, 1862.

greater than ever before; with that added, it will be overwhelming. We took the bull by the horns and made the proclamation an issue. I traversed the State for four weeks, speaking every day, and the more radical I was the more acceptable I was. The fact is, we carried the State by bringing up the radical element to the polls. The politicians are a vast distance behind the people in sentiment.

79.—*To Admiral Du Pont.*

BURLINGTON, *October* 20, 1862.

I found your very interesting letter of the 12th September awaiting my return to my home last week, after a month's absence in the interior of the State.

I judge, from what I see in the newspapers, that before this reaches you, you will be making preparations to attack Charleston. May God speed and protect you! I doubt not that an attack will be attended with great risk to our vessels and men; still, with the complete and thorough preparation that I know you will make, and the enterprise that I know you and your officers will exhibit, I am prepared to prophesy success. And what a glorious triumph it will be! It will thrill every loyal heart with delight. I wish it were possible for the Navy to take it unaided by the Army; but that cannot be expected.

I am in no wise deserving of the kind compliments you lavish upon me. I get credit for a geat deal of knowledge upon naval subjects, from the simple fact that I am surrounded by the most profound ignorance. A very small light in such utter darkness attracts attention, and seems to excite surprise, especially when the little ray proceeds from the region that this does. For you know that up to my time it was supposed that all information in relation to your branch of the public service was confined to a select "guild" about the Atlantic cities, no man from the interior having presumed to know anything about it. If I have been of any real service, it has been in breaking down and eradicating that idea, and in assisting to nationalize the Navy, in making the frontiersman as well as the longshoreman feel that he was interested in it, and partook of its glory.

Washington, November 21st.—I have seen photographs of you about the book-stores, no one of which satisfies me. I saw one in Mr. Fox's room to-day, that comes up to my idea of your present appearance, and if you are in possession of extra copies, and have no indisposition to confer such a favor upon me, I would be exceedingly pleased to receive one. Will you be kind enough to say to Captain Rodgers, that if he will permit me I will ask the same of him? In two or three years I shall retire to my home in the far West, to spend the remainder of my days. It will be pleasant to me and to my wife, who takes quite as much interest in the Navy as I do, to carry with us to our retreat the "*counterfeit presentments*" of the gentlemen I have known belonging to your service who have illustrated the history of our country.

80.—*To a Midshipman at the Naval Academy.*

BURLINGTON, *October* 28, 1862.

I have received your letter, and by the same mail one from H——. In the pressure of my business I must make this letter answer as the acknowledgment of both. I watch with a great deal of solicitude the progress that the Iowa boys are making at the Naval School. I am as anxious as your parents are that you should each and every one of you succeed and be ornaments of your profession. I shall hail your success with delight. But you all use one expression that I do not like. You speak of your anxiety and your desire to "*keep up*" with your class. You ought to set your mark higher than that. You should aim not only to "keep up," but to keep *ahead* of your class, you should *lead* and not *follow*. Be satisfied with no rank in your class below the first. You should strive for that position—not merely for the honor of it, that should be a secondary consideration—but because the habits, methods, and discipline, that will be necessary to enable you to take that high rank will prepare you for future successes through life, and will inspire you with a noble ambition to occupy distinguished positions, and the ability to fill them creditably to yourself and your friends.

You are all blessed with good constitutions. You can safely submit to the confinement and labor that will be required of you. You all have the requisite natural capacity. Nothing is necessary to complete success at the Academy but indomitable energy and perseverance. I do not expect too much of you in the outset. I have told your parents that they must be satisfied with a low report the first month from each of you, but that if you have proper application to study, the firm resolution to please them, and honor yourselves, your monthly reports will grow better and better. Remember that you are now laying the foundations of your whole course. Skip nothing; understand thoroughly all that you go over; and your future studies will become comparatively easy. Remember, my dear boys, that I have a deep interest in you, I desire your welfare. I hope you will each give me further cause to be proud of our noble State of Iowa. May God bless you all who claim Iowa as your home!

Mr. Grimes introduced a bill with reference to letters of marque, and explained his own views upon the subject, July 12th–15th.:

Here is a proposition to call to our aid the militia of the seas, to assist in upholding the constituted authorities. Were I the Secretary of the Navy, or the President of the United States, I would not recommend it. I do not believe abstractly in the doctrine of privateering. I am, however, representing those who desire that this measure should pass. There are at this time some ten or twelve valuable iron steamers lying at Bermuda, Nassau, and at other points in the vicinity of the West Indies, under the British flag, but prepared at any time, whenever they can see a favorable moment, to haul down that flag, and raise the Confederate flag, and become privateers against the commerce of the United States. So large an amount of the American Navy is compelled to watch those vessels, that to some extent the resources of the Navy are crippled. It is solely for the purpose of allowing private citizens to take their risk in capturing these private-armed vessels of the Confederates, that this bill is sought to be passed.

In introducing it, I am not representing myself or my own opinions, but the opinions of the Administration, who desire this privilege, if an emergency should arise; and I am willing to trust them. If I had the power, I would abolish all privateering, and rely upon the armed vessels of my Government. I think one of the greatest political errors ever perpetrated by the Government of the United States was, the rejection of the proposition of the Paris Treaty; but it was rejected: and now when we have proposed to come in, and become a part of it, it is understood that we have been repelled. We therefore have the authority to use privateers.

The bill failed at this session, but a law was passed at the close of the next session authorizing letters of marque. The unfriendly acts of England and France, especially Napoleon's armed intervention in Mexico, had given a threatening aspect to our foreign relations. With some modification of the views previously expressed, Mr. Grimes said, February 17, 1863:

I have a few words to say to the Senate on the bill now under consideration. I shall be brief, and endeavor to speak to the subject in hand.

What real objection can be urged against the policy of granting letters of marque, that may not be urged against the employment of the militia upon land? I can imagine none. Do not vessels carrying letters of marque have our commission? Do they not sail under our flag? Are they not manned by our countrymen? Are they not responsible to our laws? Must not their captures be condemned under our admiralty laws and in our courts?

Doubtless, the nations of Europe who were parties to the Treaty of Paris, in 1855, and who rely wholly upon standing armies for their support, would be pleased to enter into treaty stipulations with us, by which we also would place our entire reliance upon a regular army. Shall we gratify them in this regard also? Shall we abandon our militia, because they do, and impoverish ourselves by the support of immense standing armies? If we will not, if we adhere to our traditionary policy, and rely upon the citizen soldiery as the cheapest and best national protection, why shall we not also adhere to our ancient policy in regard to letters of marque and the "militia of the seas?" Because England and France, compelled as they are to support immense navies, find it convenient to establish a new rule for their future guidance, shall we, at their politic suggestion, subject ourselves to new rules and to additional burdens? They are able to support large navies. They are compelled to support them. Their very proximity to each other constrains them to do so. They can well say to weaker naval powers, and especially to those possessing a large commercial marine, needing protection in time of war, that the practice of issuing letters of marque should be abolished. But can we afford to say so? Can we afford to declare that when war shall exist between us and any foreign nation, our whole merchant marine shall rot at our wharves, and no private vessel be commissioned to go forth as an armed volunteer upon the sea to meet our nation's enemy? Ask the merchants of New England and New York if they can afford it.

The attempt is made to render this well-settled practice of issuing letters of marque by nations in time of war odious, by calling vessels to which they are issued "privateers," "semi-pirates," "marine highwaymen." With what justice can these epithets be applied to them, when they sail under our flag, carry our commission, and are amenable to our laws? It is said that they receive the compensation for their services in the booty they capture. This is true in part, and it is true also of every ship-of-war that floats or that ever floated, belonging to Great Britain or to the United States. By our laws, one-half of the value of all property of an enemy captured on the sea is the lawful prize of the captors. Has that fact caused our naval officers to tarnish their reputation, or that of their profession, by unmanly acts of cupidity or barbarity? If, indeed, it be true that such application of the proceeds of captured property is immoral, and if it be true that the receiver of goods improperly obtained is as guilty as he who obtains them, it would require the nicest casuistry to determine that we ourselves, who receive one-half of the value of the captured goods in the one case, are not morally as guilty as the privateer who receives the whole value in the other. The immorality of the act would hardly be lessened by a division of the spoils. The truth is, there is no moral principle involved in this matter. What difference does it make whether my vessel is captured by a seventy-four-gun ship, with an admiral in command, or by a fishing-smack, armed with a blunderbuss, provided both are governed by the same laws, and are responsible to the same authority for the exercise of the power which capture gives to them? How does the division of the proceeds of the capture among the captors affect me, or the legality or the morality of the capture itself?

We are told that this proposition is against the public sentiment of the age; that it will encourage uncivilized warfare. All warlike acts are uncivil. War, in its best conditions, is only organized, legal barbarism. Still, war is necessary. Does it make any difference to me, whether I meet in hostile array a recent volunteer, or an antagonist all his life trained to martial deeds, provided each fights under the same banner, carries a commission issued by the same authority, and is bound by the same laws of war? In what manner can civilization or Christianity be affected, one way or the other?

Private-armed vessels carrying letters of marque are in effect national vessels. They are not let loose against merely unarmed commerce for its destruction. They are to be the pickets of the great naval armada of the nation. They are to procure information, convey intelligence, annoy the enemy, cripple his resources, attack his small armed ships, assist in maintaining blockades, and in this way materially aid to enforce peace. In the Revolutionary War, as well as in the War of 1812–'15, American privateers attacked and destroyed armed vessels of the British Navy. Will we say that it may never be done again?

It is said [1] that we can readily secure all the advantages that might be derived from the passage of this bill, by authorizing the Secretary of the Navy to purchase all the vessels he chooses, and receive them into the regular Navy. The proposition is wholly impracticable. In the first place, it would put in the hands of the Secretary of the Navy the power to determine the policy of the Government, and the means of carrying that policy into execution. In the next place, the Secretary of the Navy does not possess, and we cannot bestow upon him, the means to purchase, fit out, man, officer, repair, and control such a number of vessels as might be desirable, and probably would be required for this service. It will hardly be necessary to attempt to demonstrate this. The pay of the agents alone who would be required to conduct a business of such magnitude would soon bankrupt the Treasury. Not more impracticable is the proposition to authorize the Secretary of the Navy to *hire* vessels, to be used as war-ships for a limited time. To the suggestion that a bounty or reward for the capture of an enemy's vessel should be offered, it is a sufficient answer that such a proceeding would be against the law of nations, unless the vessel making the capture bore a commission from the nation to which she belonged; and, if she did bear a commission, she would be neither more nor less than a letter of marque.

[1] "An enactment, authorizing the Naval Department to employ all the mercantile marine of the country in the national service, under the national flag, as a part of the Navy, would be practicable and reasonable. Such a marine will, in a just sense, be the militia of the sea. Such a militia I am in favor of. Let the Secretary of the Navy hire private ships."—(MR. SUMNER, *February 14th and 17th.*)

For myself, I am not prepared to abandon our well-settled national policy on this subject. I stand by the traditions and the policy of our fathers. I am unwilling to impose, upon the people I represent, the burden of supporting in time of peace such a naval establishment as will be adequate to protect our commerce in time of war, and at the same time to inflict such chastisement upon the enemy as will insure a speedy and honorable peace. I regard the present a proper time to reaffirm our national doctrine on the subject of maritime rights.

I am aware that this bill confers extraordinary powers upon the President. It grants no power, however, that I am not anxious to bestow upon him. I wish to confer upon him ample means to restore the Union, and to defend the national honor abroad, and I will hold him and his immediate constitutional advisers responsible for the manner in which that power shall be exercised. If he shall wield it feebly, if he neglects his best opportunities, if he dallies with treason, if he crouches before the insolence of a foreign power, no part of the responsibility or the disgrace shall be traced to me. Before I leave here on the 4th of March next, I intend, so far as my vote will do it, to deposit in the hands of the President every means and appliance for overcoming the rebellion that I can give him, and in the name of the people demand of him *success*. I believe that *success* can be achieved, and the country, history, will hold him and his cabinet responsible for a failure.

It is said by the opponents of this bill, that the so-called Confederate States have no commerce, and hence there is no necessity for the passage of this act. To this I answer that they have already on the ocean a large number of fast steamers, and are now building in England a fleet of vessels designed to break our blockade of their coast. The vessels owned by them, and by parties in Europe in complicity with them, can already be counted by the score. But I frankly own that my purpose is to declare a principle, which shall have a general as well as a special application. I wish to say to the world that, however much other nations have changed or may change their policy on this subject, we will adhere to ours. If the President shall find himself environed with new difficulties, involved in new complications, I wish him to have the power to "let slip the dogs of war" against any new enemy that may declare against us.

In voting as I shall, I am satisfied that I shall reflect the sentiment of the people of Iowa and of the entire Northwest. No matter what others may tell you, Senators, be assured that the people of the upper valley of the Mississippi River are loyal to this Government. That loyalty is confined to no party. Since I have held a seat in this body, I have never, so far as I can recollect, even alluded to a party organization of any kind. I only allude to it now for the purpose of absolving, so far as I may be able, the Democratic party of that section from the charge of disloyalty to the Government. It embraces dissatisfied, revolutionary, and disloyal members, who have in some instances secured control of the party organization, but the great mass of that party are patriotic, law-abiding men. Misled, I think, many of them are, as they think I am; but treason has never found a lodgment in their hearts. They scorn the idea that they would consent to a dissolution of the Union; and when the issue shall be fairly presented to them, disconnected from the idea that this war has not been prosecuted with sufficient vigor by the party in power, they will cause the wave of political oblivion to sweep over those who are attempting to dupe them into concession and compromise with treason. This much is due from me to the mass of the Democratic party in Iowa, who have no representative in Congress, and among whom I count many of my oldest and most cherished personal friends. The promise of a new confederacy has no charms for the people of Iowa of any political persuasion. They abide by the Union in its integrity. They will not follow false prophets into disunion and anarchy. Presumptuous political leaders may for a time beguile the unwary, and engender local discontent, but a loyal public sentiment will soon rectify all such evils. The great mass of the people of that State, irrespective of party ties or affinities, have ventured their all in behalf of the unity of this Government. They have given freely of their blood in its support. They will never consent to its dismemberment. They ask me to place in the hands of the President all the necessary means to maintain it intact. I obey their voice when I give my vote for the passage of this bill.

Mr. Grimes was chairman of a select committee, appointed December 22 and 23, 1862, to investigate the facts in regard to the employment of transport-vessels for the Banks Expedition, and the employment of transports generally by quartermasters and agents of the War Department. In performance of this duty the committee examined persons at New York, Philadelphia, and Washington, and made two detailed reports, Jan. 15 and Feb. 9, 1863, showing acts of fraud and negligence by ship-owners, brokers, and officers and agents of the War Department. The exposure was very thorough, and was sustained by the testimony of fifty witnesses, many of whom were persons implicated. A resolution of censure upon several parties was submitted by Mr. Hale.

Mr. Grimes remarked, January 29, 30, 1863:

It seems to me that there are some very important lessons to be drawn from this investigation, which ought to govern Congress and the executive officers of the Government in future. I desire to occupy a few minutes in calling the attention of this body and of the country to some defects in getting up this expedition.

The first great error was in not fairly and openly advertising for vessels, specifying the character of the vessels required. There was no earthly reason why this should not have been done. There was no greater secrecy attained by the method adopted than would have been observed if advertisements had been published in the newspapers. That has been the method pursued by the Government until the commencement of this war, and it has always worked well. The select committee, when in New York, took the testimony of some of the most prominent ship-owners in that city on the subject, and they all testified that that was what the ship-owners and ship-masters desired, and that the Government interests had hitherto been promoted and protected by doing so, and that there was no reason why that system should not have been continued.

The next error was in not following the law of Congress, approved February 12, 1862, which was passed at the instance of the War Department, and which authorized the President to detail three competent naval officers for the service of the War Department in the inspection of transport-vessels. Why was this not done? Why did not the Secretary of War comply with that law, and have three competent naval officers—a sea-officer, an engineer, and a naval constructor—detailed for this specific duty, men who were experts in the particular branches to which they were to be assigned? That was not done, at the instance of the very gentleman whom the Senator from New Hampshire proposes to strike out of his resolution, Commodore Vanderbilt. The Secretary of War sent for him to come here from New York, to have a conference with him in regard to getting up this expedition. Mr. Stanton proposed that a commission be appointed to inspect vessels. Commodore Vanderbilt said: "That is of no use. Congress has passed a law that every vessel that clears from a custom-house must have her inspector's papers, and these papers have to be renewed every twelve months. Is not that enough for this expedition?" Mr. Stanton said: "I would like to make this doubly sure. There will be no harm in having them doubly inspected." One inspector was appointed, Commodore Van Brunt. He was directed to report immediately to General Banks; and what was he authorized to do? To inspect vessels? No; but merely to supervise the outfit. He said to General Banks that he was incompetent to the discharge of that particular kind of duty, so far as it related to steamships. General Banks replied that they had discussed this subject of appointing a man to assist him, so far as steamships were concerned, and that person was Mr. Charles H. Haswell.

A third error of Commodore Vanderbilt, for which I think he was in a great degree censurable, was chartering the steamboat Niagara without seeing her, without knowing her. She was an old boat that had been built for the trade on Lake Ontario nearly a score of years ago. She had been bought for something like ten thousand dollars, and brought around, and some repairs put upon her, and some four hundred and fifty men and officers of the Fiftieth Massachusetts regiment were forced to go upon her at New York, destined for New Orleans. In smooth water, with a calm sea, the planks were ripped out of her, and exhibited to the gaze of the indignant soldiers on board, showing that her timbers were rotten. The committee have in their committee-room a large sample of one of the beams of this vessel, to show that it has not the slightest capacity to hold a nail. The testimony is from Commodore Vanderbilt, that he had never seen the Niagara, that he knew nothing about her character, or capacity, or seaworthiness. I think that for the chartering of that vessel he was censurable.

Another great defect was the concealment from the inspectors of the destination of the expedition. It was attempted to keep it entirely secret from everybody, except Mr. Stanton, General Banks, and Commodore Vanderbilt; and what was the result? Mr. Haswell and Mr. Van Brunt would have a vessel pointed out to them by Commodore Vanderbilt. Now, there is one class of steamers adapted for what are called outside passages, capable of navigating the ocean anywhere; while there is another class, many of which were employed in this expedition, that are only capable of navigating inland waters. Mr. Haswell and Commodore Van Brunt both testified that, if they had known that the expedition was going beyond the capes of the Chesapeake, they would have protested against several of those vessels being chartered; and yet it is proposed to strike out the name of the man who did know where the expedition was going, and censure those who did not know anything about it.

Another difficulty, against which we should guard in future expeditions, was the crowding of too great a number of persons on board these ships. Some of the vessels, which under your emigration act would only be permitted to carry three hundred and fifty passengers, carried nine hundred and fifty soldiers. The most intelligent ship-owners who were before us testified that, in their opinion, soldiers could be crowded together conveniently and humanely more than immigrants coming across the Atlantic. They estimated that possibly six hundred soldiers might have been accommodated, whereas nine hundred and fifty were placed on board. When the question was asked of Commodore Vanderbilt and of other gentlemen connected with the expedition, why this was, and why they did not take navigators, and see that there were instruments and charts on board, the answer was, the insurance companies and owners of the vessels took that risk, as though the Government had no risk in the lives of its valiant men, whom it has enlisted under its banner, and sent out on an expedition of this kind. The man who embarks his merchandise on board a ship has the option of putting it on this vessel or on that; and I, exercising my volition as a passenger, can go or not go; I can go upon one ship or upon another; but you order your soldiers to go on board of a vessel, and they have no power to determine whether that vessel is susceptible of carrying them safely, or whether they are to be humanely or inhumanely packed when they get on board.

I do not desire to say much in regard to the manner in which these charter-parties were effected. It shows a chapter of fraud from beginning to end. Men making the most open professions of loyalty, patriotism, and perfect disinterestedness, coming before the committee, and swearing that they acted from such motives solely, were yet compelled to admit—or one or two were—that in some instances they had received as high as six and a quarter per cent. Since then—for the committee desired to expedite the business and make a report as speedily as possible to the Senate—the committee have satisfied their own minds that the per cent. was greater than was in testimony before them. Now, Mr. Vanderbilt did not exercise reasonable judgment and sagacity to prevent frauds upon the Government in chartering these vessels. What are the facts? It was generally understood in New York that no vessel could be chartered except through Southard, and only after the owner, or the representative of the owner, had paid tribute to him. It is true that Commodore Vanderbilt testifies that he did not know this, and we are to presume that he did not. Was it not his business to know it? When this report was circulated throughout Broad and South Streets, and was in the mouths of shipping-men in New York, how happens it that Commodore Vanderbilt was profoundly ignorant of it? Not from any corrupt motive, I am prepared to say and believe; but I cannot say that he did exercise that reasonable diligence, foresight, and sagacity which a man occupying the position he occupied was bound to exercise, when so momentous a trust was committed to his hands. I am not going to pass judgment upon that gentleman by anything that he has or has not done formerly. The question is, not whether he has been generous to the Government by making a present to us of a fine steamship, but whether, in connection with this single transaction which is now under consideration, he did his whole duty. I cannot lay my hand upon my heart and say, as a Senator, that I believe he did.

A few facts from the report of the committee, submitted by Mr. Grimes, February 9th, will show something of other acts of fraud and extortion that were revealed by the investigation:

Charles Coblens, of Baltimore, appeared before the committee as an extensive ship-owner, in possession, in whole or in part, of ten steamers, three barges, and eighty acres of valuable land in the vicinity of Baltimore, though but a few months before comparatively a poor man. A Prussian by birth, an Israelite by descent, a peddler and a horse-jockey by profession, in his business relations with the Government, fraud, bribery, and perjury, struggle for the most prominent place. His transactions in the chartering of transports for the War Department show that he was receiving from the Government at the rate of $345,655 per annum on a capital of $65,283, which is equal to 529½ per cent. per annum on his investment!

Amasa C. Hall, of Baltimore, has played a very conspicuous part in connection with the chartering of transport-vessels at that port. Hardly any vessel has been chartered there during the past eighteen months that has not been secured through his agency, and of whose earnings from five to twelve per cent. has not found its way to his pocket. He bought an old boat, the Patapsco, that had been thrown away as useless by the commissioners for deepening the harbor at Baltimore, for $1,200, and put her in Coblens's name, and chartered her to the Government at eighty dollars per day. Her running expenses were not more than twelve dollars per day; and she yielded a clear profit to her owner at the rate of $26,645 per annum. The barge Delaware, whose running expenses were not more than seven dollars per day, was chartered to the Government at seventy dollars a day by Mr. John Tucker, through Mr. Hall, Captain Hodges signing the charter-party, and her net receipts were at the rate of $22,995 per annum. That this chapter of fraud may want no odious and shameless feature, Mr. Hall affirms that Captain Hodges and Mr. Tucker thought she was the cheapest thing they chartered.

The committee have failed to discover any satisfactory reason why Hall was permitted to enjoy this monopoly of chartering vessels. There was nothing in his antecedents or character to justify it. He was a poor man eighteen months ago, with a character not wholly above reproach; he is now rich, and fast growing richer by the receipt of a large daily revenue from commissions upon the earnings of vessels still in the Government employ. The bestowal of this large patronage almost exclusively upon him cannot be reconciled with any theory of strict integrity on the part of Government officers. Although the testimony may not warrant the conclusion that any officer actually shared with him the profits derived from his business, yet the fact that these officers, who knew all the circumstances, acquiesced in the continuance of this monopoly, should subject them to severe reprehension; and it is not easy to suppose that motives of charity alone impelled them to throw such vast sums of money into his pocket.

The committee find Captain Richard F. Loper, of Philadelphia, to be in receipt of enormous revenues from the chartering of transports, derived partly from commissions received on vessels, where he acted at the same time as agent of the Government and agent of the owners; partly from the charters of vessels belonging to transportation companies, of which he is a large stockholder; partly from vessels owned by himself, and chartered by himself, as Government agent, to the Government; and partly from his "influence." Mr. Hall testifies that he paid Loper $13,000 at one time for "getting the business for him," the chartering of certain transports for the McClellan Expedition. Being president, treasurer, business-manager, and stockholder of the Philadelphia Steam Propeller Company, and "assistant agent of the War Department," Captain Loper had extraordinary facilities for making the charters to suit himself. It rarely happens, in the ordinary avocations of life, that a person enjoys the privilege of buying his own property for another person, and fixing his own price upon it, or of buying other people's property for a third person, and regulating his compensation by the amount of money he squanders; yet such seems to have been the manner in which the Government has been served, not only in Captain Loper's agency, but in nearly all the business connected with the transportation, by water, of troops, supplies, and munitions of war.

Facts and testimony force the committee to the conclusion that Mr. John Tucker, late Assistant Secretary of War, had more or less connection with these gigantic and shameless frauds on the Government.

The committee are overwhelmed with astonishment and sorrow by the revelations which have been made; but they believe that nothing which so intimately concerns a free people should be concealed from them, and they hope that this investigation may lead to a more honest and economical administration of this department of the public service. The War Department can only restore confidence in connection with army transportation, by inflexibly adhering to the rule that contracts shall only be made with the owners of vessels, or their legitimate agents, and that every officer who shall be shown to be influenced in the slightest degree in awarding a charter by fear, favor, affection, or the hope of reward, or who shall give reasonable ground for suspicion of the honesty of his conduct, shall be summarily punished, if guilty.

Mr. Grimes opposed increase of pay to any civil officer while soldiers in the field were unpaid. He said, January 31st:

I am not conscious of having voted for the creation of any civil office at this session of Congress, and I do not intend to do so, especially while a portion at least of the soldiers from my State have not, or had not at the last I heard from them, received one dollar of pay since November, 1861. With that fact staring me in the face, I do not see how I can consistently vote money out of the Treasury to support civil officers here in the city of Washington, who will draw their pay regularly every month, which ought to go to support the families of the soldiers in my State who have gone to the battle-field.

Mr. Grimes was among the first to discern that the new naval warfare had made obsolete the old system of fortifications for harbor defenses. He said with reference to appropriating more than six million dollars for fortifications, February 18th:

I think it has been pretty well demonstrated during the last twelve months that these fortifications, in the present condition of maritime warfare, are of very little value. New Orleans has sufficiently demonstrated that, and several other actions have confirmed this belief of mine. Hence I am under the impression, as at present advised, that the continuance of these old fortifications upon the plans originally projected will be virtually throwing money away. Entertaining that opinion, I am constrained to vote against the bill, not for the reason that I am not willing and anxious to defend every harbor on the Atlantic coast—as a Representative of the United States from the State of Iowa, I am compelled to do so—but I do not believe that the methods adopted are best calculated to promote that end.

Mr. Grimes voted for the Pacific Railroad bill, June 20, 1862, and for establishing the gauge of the road from the Missouri River to the Pacific Ocean at four feet eight and a half inches (February 18, 1863). Upon the latter measure he said:

One of the great reasons that induced me to vote for the bill was to enable the country to defend herself in case of war with any foreign power. Suppose war should exist, and your road was completed, and you wanted to transport troops over it, how would you do it? That road would never be able to transport with its own furniture an army of twenty-five thousand men. Cars have been brought from Iowa and Illinois to assist in the transportation of the army between here and Baltimore, and for other purposes. The moment we allow this gauge to be fixed at five feet, we deprive ourselves of all opportunity to furnish furniture to that road to transport an army whenever any exigency of that kind shall arise. That is to me a conclusive argument.

I believe it would be the interest of the country that it should be a uniform gauge from the Atlantic to the Pacific. If parties have been injured by our action, it would be better to appropriate money out of the Treasury to indemnify them for any loss they may have sustained than have a break in the gauge. So far as the State I have the honor in part to represent is concerned, if I were controlled by any local interests, I should be in favor of the break of the gauge, because where there is a break there is always a large amount of business to be done, and a town springs up; but I trust that I look at this question in a national point of view; and in that view, it seems to me, we ought to make the gauge uniform.

In reply to objections against the incorporation of an institution for the education of colored youth in the District of Columbia, he said, February 27, 1863:

The very crude notions entertained and expressed by the Senator from Virginia (Mr. Carlile) in regard to education, sufficiently account to me for a great many things that have hitherto been wholly inexplicable. It may be true that in that section of the country where that Senator is most acquainted the whole idea of education proceeds from the fact that a person is to be educated merely because he is to exercise the elective franchise; but I thank God that I was raised in a section of the country where there are nobler and loftier sentiments entertained in regard to education. We entertain the opinion that all human beings are accountable beings. We believe that every man should be taught, so that he may be able to read the law by which he is to be governed, and under which he may be punished. We believe that every accountable being should be able to read the word of God, by which he shall guide his steps in this life, and be judged in the life to come. We believe that education is necessary in order to elevate the human race. We believe that it is necessary in order to keep our jails and penitentiaries and almshouses free from inmates. In my section of the country we do not educate any race upon such low and groveling ideas as seem to be entertained by the Senator from Virginia.

A few words will set this matter right in the mind of every right-thinking man. Some humane persons a few years ago raised a sum of money with which they purchased a lot in this city, now estimated to be of the value of ten or twelve thousand dollars, the proceeds of which were to be appropriated exclusively to the education of girls of the colored race. The purpose is to allow the trust to be fulfilled, that these colored girls may be educated, and to allow this corporation to receive any other gifts or bequests that any humane people in the country may see fit to bestow.

Asked by Mr. Powell, of Kentucky, March 2d, if he would be willing to have the President's proclamation withdrawn, the confiscation laws repealed, and the Crittenden compromise with the Powell amendments adopted, Mr. Grimes replied:

I have no hesitation in saying that I would not. No power on earth could induce me to consent to any State, or any set of States, or any people in any portion of the United States, dictating with arms in their hands the terms upon which I would make peace with them, and a change of the Constitution. I do not look to separation. I look to a restoration of the Union, and I look to it by force, if necessary.

U. S. Ship Ironsides.

§ 3.—*In the Thirty-eighth Congress.*—1863–1865.

The following letters refer to the naval attack upon Charleston, to Mr. Grimes being a candidate for reëlection to the Senate, and to his labors before the people of Iowa in a political canvass of the State:

81.—*To Admiral Du Pont.*

BURLINGTON, *March* 27, 1863.

I feel the difficult and responsible position in which you are placed, and the great questions that are to be settled by the issue. The country feels them. There are inconsiderate and senseless men who complain that an attack has not been earlier made; but they know nothing of the true posture of affairs, and their opinions would be worthless if they did. Every one is satisfied that you will attack at the time your judgment shall decide to be the *best* time, and everybody whose opinion is worth anything is satisfied that your opinion as to when that *best* time arrives will be correct. In a word, it gratifies me to be able to assure you that the people of the whole country have entire confidence in your capacity and your patriotism, and those who have watched your career do not suffer themselves for one moment to doubt your complete success. It may be that the conflict may be over before this reaches you. I trust it may, and that this may be accepted as my congratulations upon the result. If otherwise, if it reaches you on the eve of battle, then in God's name, in the name of the country, in behalf of your friends, in the name of a good government and of our common humanity, I bid you "*good cheer.*" May God in his wisdom and mercy protect, defend, and give you success! No grander spectacle can be presented to the human vision than a patriotic, Christian man going forth to battle in defense of a wise, paternal, and humane government.

I regret as much as you can the failure of Congress to provide means to assist the States of Missouri, Maryland, and Delaware, to secure emancipation. I do not doubt that freedom will soon be universal in those States. Just such bills would have been a sort of culmination and rounding off of the acts of the late Congress that would have reflected glory upon it and upon the country. The Thirty-seventh Congress, much maligned as all assemblies of a legislative character have been in revolutionary times, composed to a very great extent of men who had not been trained to statesmanship—elected in a time of profound peace upon a multitude of issues, but no one of them in anticipation of a war—that Congress, in my conviction, has immortalized itself, and stands second only to the first Continental Congress. Still it might, it ought to have done more.

My policy at the last session in regard to naval legislation was "hands off." All sorts of attempts were made to overturn the legislation of the preceding session, but we in some manner or other defeated all such efforts.

82.—*To the Editor of the Linn County Register.*[1]

BURLINGTON, *May* 2, 1863.

I have no very great desire to be reëlected to the Senate. On the contrary, I am rather averse to the idea of continuing in public life beyond my present term. Our friends have insisted that I shall serve another term, and I have consented to do so, if, after having surveyed the whole field, they are satisfied that the interest of the country and our party require it, or that they are unable to secure the services of a better man. I have no great love for the place, and can leave it without a single regret, whenever a better man can be sent to Washington who can more faithfully represent our State. I did not seek nor did I anticipate the nomination for Governor, in 1854. When nominated without any agency of mine, as the representative of certain principles, I did my best to be elected. I never asked a man to vote for me to the Senate six years ago, though I was very grateful for the support I got. I have not asked and shall not ask any man to vote for me now. I cannot improve my condition in any respect by reëlection. Every one knows my standing there; and, if satisfied with it, I shall receive their support; if dissatisfied with it, I ought not to receive it.

83.—*To Admiral Du Pont.*

BURLINGTON, *May* 26, 1863.

Absence from home, and very numerous duties in the State, crowded into the comparatively short period of the recess, have caused me to be neglectful of the fact that I have not written you

[1] In answer to an inquiry whether he was a candidate for reëlection to the Senate.

since you attacked Charleston, though I recollect writing very near that time. The result was not such as we all hoped, and as I confess I anticipated, though I will at the same time honestly confess that I could never give a reason for the faith that was in me. I always supposed that there was to be some coöperative land-force; I was mistaken in this, it appears. I have carefully read all the reports of the engagement. They have been read by every one. You may rely upon it that the public fully justifies you in withdrawing from the contest when you did. It would have been extreme folly to continue it longer. It is evident to every one that the article in the *Baltimore American* was prompted by some sinister motive, and in receiving that attack you only experience what all our commanders upon land or water have been or will be subject to, no matter how successful they may have been, or may be. It must be a gratification to you to feel that the same amount of confidence is reposed in you that was placed in you both by the Department and the nation before the battle.

We are now rejoicing over a *supposed* victory at Vicksburg. Our people are as truly loyal, devoted, and determined as ever. I see not the slightest abatement among the people of this region of their firm resolution to crush out the rebellion, and to have indeed a "*Nation*."

July 30th.—I duly received your favor of the 20th inst., and on the same day the gun captured on the Atlanta, sent by express. Accept my thanks for the present. I have fired it to-day, and find it to be a very wicked implement. It seems that Charleston is destined to be "a hard nut to crack," in the hands of Gillmore and Dahlgren, as well as in the hands of their predecessor.

Mr. Grimes participated in a festival given to the ministers and delegates of the churches of the Congregational order in Iowa, assembled at Burlington, June 5th, and made an address in response to the sentiment:

The Senate of the United States—Honor and renown to the Senators from Iowa for unswerving fidelity to humanity and justice, and for a country redeemed and disenthralled by the genius of universal emancipation.

He complimented the clergy for their devotion to liberty and the national cause, acknowledged his indebtedness to their services, and, turning to the Rev. Asa Turner, said: "You call him Father Turner; and I look to him as my political godfather." On the following day he addressed the Association in the course of a discussion upon the state of the country, and "made an able and eloquent speech, embodying in it many sound political and moral truths, which it was refreshing to hear in such a meeting from one in his position," as reported in the *Boston Recorder* by Rev. Lewis Sabin, D. D., who was present as a delegate from the General Association of Massachusetts.

84.—*To Mrs. Grimes.*

GRINNELL, *September* 9, 1863.

I am thus far on my tortuous way. We have very large meetings, never so large in the State before, and, so far as I can learn, the very best of feeling prevails among our friends. I cannot doubt our success in the State. The Democrats were never working so hard before, but we shall beat them.

INDEPENDENCE, *September 20th.*

I have spoken every day since I was at Des Moines, in the open air, to large crowds, and generally in a strong gale of wind. Still I got along very well until yesterday, when I made pretty much of a break-down. I caught a very bad cold, and my strength is nearly exhausted. I do not believe that I can keep up long. I never had anything to do with a campaign that required half the labor that this does.

WEST UNION, FAYETTE COUNTY, *September 28th.*

My course has finally brought me to this place, and my face is at last turned homeward, though I have many angles to make, and about three hundred miles to travel before I reach there.

Stone will be elected by a very large majority; larger, I think, than was ever given to any candidate for Governor. You may be interested to know that the people seem to be unanimously in favor of my reëlection to the Senate. So far as I can learn, no Senator or Representative will be elected by the Republicans who is not pledged to my election. Of course this makes me proud, for I have not electioneered for it.

DUBUQUE, *October 2d.*

It is a comfort to me to know that one week from to-night my labors will be over. My health is very good, save that I am worn down by speaking every day, and nearly every day in the open air. We shall carry the State by an unprecedentedly large majority, because the people are in earnest to sustain the Government.

85.—*To Admiral Du Pont.*

BURLINGTON, *October* 19, 1863.

Your favor of the 11th ult. reached my home about ten days after I began my political canvass of this State, and I only returned three days ago. Hence it is that it has been so long unanswered. I know so little of the official etiquette of your profession, or of any other, for that matter, that I am the last man in the world to advise you on the matter about which you ask my opinion. I can, however, give you what I believe to be the best advice; to follow the promptings of your own cool, good judgment. If you do, you will not much err, I am convinced.

I wish I could do something for Rodgers, and, if the matter is not disposed of for the year beyond recall, I will attempt it when I go to Washington next month.. There is no man for whom I have a higher regard, and I know no one who would more adorn the position, or who deserves it more. Should I *write*, the letter would probably be thrown aside, and the subject be prejudged without a full hearing.

I think everybody is becoming convinced that your recall from the South Atlantic Fleet was a hasty, ill-advised measure, and that the clamor raised against you, and finding utterance in the *Baltimore American*, was wholly groundless. Such, at any rate, is the sentiment of those with whom I have conversed, and I think it is universal.

I shall go eastward in about four weeks. I do not expect hereafter to have much connection with naval matters, nor do I intend to serve any longer on the Naval Committee of the Senate.

86.—*To Mrs. Grimes.*

PORTLAND, *November* 24, 1863.

I reached Mr. Fessenden's without accident, and am now at his house. I wanted to leave to-day for Boston, but he has restrained me, and I shall not go until to-morrow. I shall be in Boston until Friday, when Mr. Fessenden is to meet me, and we shall go to Washington together. I judge Portland to be one of the very pleasantest cities in the United States. Fessenden has a grand old place; house and everything in it appearing to be not less than fifty years old and upward. He expressed his regret that you were not with me. All of his family, including sons, brothers-in-law, etc., seemed to be pleased to see me, and all inquired kindly for you, as though they knew you. In Fessenden's chamber I found four framed pictures, his wife, Samuel, who is also dead, my wife, and my wife's husband.

BOSTON, *November 26th.*

I have been to church at King's Chapel, and heard a good, patriotic sermon (Thanksgiving-day). Judge Collamer is at Cambridgeport with his whole family on their way to Washington.

Upon the assembling of Congress Mr. Grimes asked the Senate, December 18th, to excuse him from further service on the Naval Committee. It is the practice of the Senate to excuse a member who asks to be excused. Mr. Anthony, of Rhode Island, said: "I hope the Senator will withdraw his request for the present;" "or, if not," said Mr. Harris, of New York, "that the Senate will decline to excuse him." Mr. Foster, of Connecticut, said: "I would excuse him from some other committee rather than lose his services on this." "For one," said Mr. Clark, of New Hampshire, "I shall vote not to excuse him." Mr. Hale, of New Hampshire, said: "There is nobody in the Senate, certainly, in whom the Senate have more confidence on naval matters than they have in the Senator from Iowa." The consideration of the question was indefinitely postponed.

Mr. Grimes labored to stimulate the Government in the employment of colored troops. Inquiring as to the number in the military service, and being told that there were fifty thousand, he said, January 12th:

I am rejoiced at the response. The country will be glad to know that the Administration has established a policy in regard to the recruitment of colored persons. I have heard for twelve months givings out that such was to be, or was the policy of the Administration, but the results have never satisfied me that it was their real, genuine intention; for, if there had been the proper agencies, and the proper degree of practical sagacity exhibited, there might have been, and ought to have been, two hundred thousand colored men in the field at this moment, and, instead of being compelled to appropriate twenty million dollars for bounties, we need not have required a single new white soldier to enter the Army. I trust there will be some effort from this time forward to raise colored regiments in Missouri. It is only a few months since there was an effort to raise a colored regiment in that State, but the officers were thwarted in it by authorities who had control there, so that they were obliged to make the rendezvous of the regiment in my State, in Keokuk. I am gratified, and my constituents will be gratified, and the whole country will be gratified, that from this time forward we are to have an earnest, persistent, energetic effort on the part of the Government to enlist colored men. I have been for that from the commencement of this war. No man has been ahead of me in that particular.

I want them called into service as United States troops, and not as substitutes for white soldiers from any State. I am utterly opposed to the selection of these colored men as representatives of the citizens of any State. I do not care whether it be mine or any other State, that has not filled up its quota. I do not want any State to be permitted to go down and pick up negroes, and claim them as part of her quota. Suppose you let Massachusetts go down, and with her munificent bounties recruit fifteen thousand men in General Banks's department, to be substitutes for Massachusetts men who were drafted, or who ought to go into the service under the draft. In that department there are, perhaps, two or three regiments of Massachusetts soldiers, and at the same time there are twelve or fourteen regiments from my State. My State is too poor to send down agents with large bounties in their pockets to enlist troops. How long do you suppose there would be a good military and moral sentiment existing between the soldiers from Massachusetts and the soldiers from Iowa, if they were permitted to fill out their quota with colored men, and we were required to fill our quota up by the best blood we have in our State?

It is true that my State has but little interest in the present draft. We have exceeded the demands upon us, and probably very nearly come up to filling the second quota that may be called for; but I am contending for a principle that I believe to be abstractly right. It seems to me unjust to permit the agent of a State to go down and recruit negroes out of that common fund which belongs to my State as well as to the State that is in default. Do not Senators see that, if they want to avoid a second draft, they must reserve this body of colored men for United States soldiers, and not to be the soldiers of any particular State? If, after this draft shall be completed, we can only stimulate the War Department to put one hundred thousand colored men in the field, there will then be no necessity for a draft.

Contrary to this remonstrance, a law was passed, approved July 4th, authorizing the Executive of any State to send agents into the rebellious districts to recruit volunteers, who should be credited to the State enlisting them. At the next session of Congress Mr. Grimes opposed this law, February 6, 1865, as manifestly unjust, and it was repealed.

He advocated giving the same pay and bounty to colored soldiers as to white soldiers, with guarantees of freedom to their wives and children. He said, February 13, 1864:

From the very outset, my colleague from Iowa and myself have been in favor of arming negroes. We believed that it was not only the right but the duty of the Government. We have insisted from the beginning that they should be paid and put upon a perfect equality with white men.

On the same day, Mr. Wilson, of Massachusetts, alluding to Mr. Sumner and Mr. Grimes, said:

They have both from the beginning comprehended this rebellion, understood its cause, and advocated the proper remedies. If their opinions had been the opinions of the Senate and House of Representatives, of the President and his cabinet, and had been sustained by the country, I believe this rebellion would have been crushed long ago, and the cause of all this trouble and misery ground to atoms.

Mr. Grimes, however, was willing to act in the spirit of accommodation. He said, February 19th:

We cannot carry out all our humanitarian views here in the Senate, or in legislating for the country. We want to fill up the Army, and as rapidly as possible. We want to prevent any disagreement between the two Houses of Congress. Hence I consented to some provisions which are slightly objectionable to me personally. I am not going to allow my personal predilections in regard to any of these questions to control my vote in such a manner as to prevent the armies being replenished for the spring campaign.

Mr. Powell objecting to the enrollment and drafting of slaves, Mr. Grimes said:

I am willing to acknowledge to the Senator from Kentucky that I vote for this measure, believing it to be a genuine antislavery measure. I am not disposed to go beyond the Constitution and the laws, for the purpose of striking at slavery, but, when I see that there is an opportunity fairly and legitimately to strike at slavery, I believe it is not only my right but my duty to do it, and I am going to vote for this measure on that ground, among others, because I cannot conceive anything that can be devised in a constitutional and legal form that will strike so severe a blow at the institution.

On the 23d of June he gave his vote for the repeal of the fugitive-slave act of 1850, and all acts and parts of acts for the rendition of fugitive slaves.

On the 16th of January Mr. Grimes was chosen United States Senator from Iowa, for six years from March 4, 1865, receiving the votes of all the members of the General Assembly in joint convention but six; one hundred and twenty-eight out of one hundred and thirty-four.

A strict economist, and recalling the historical facts that Washington and Winfield Scott were not elevated to the rank of lieutenant-general until many years after the period of their distinguished services, Mr. Grimes opposed the reviving of that grade in the Army. He said, February 24th:

I am satisfied that a man can perform the duties of commanding an army just as well with the rank of major-general as with the rank of lieutenant-general. The pay of six thousand dollars which General Grant now receives is adequate to the rank and position he holds, and it is not necessary for me to assist in running the hands of Congress into the national Treasury for the purpose of giving him between thirteen and fourteen thousand dollars a year. I have come here this session with the determination to assist in creating no new office, and in increasing the salary of no officer that now exists.

A year later, February 24, 1865, speaking of bills for a superior organization of the Army, he said:

I want to record my vote against these continual attempts to build up grand, stupendous military establishments.

Upon a motion for extra compensation to employés of Congress, he remarked, December 22, 1864:

This question is a very broad one; if we begin in one department, it will have to run through all the employés of the Government. It ought to begin with the men in the field—the soldiers and sailors—not with the men who are here receiving ten times their compensation as employés about the Capitol.

Watchful against extravagance in the public service, Mr. Grimes exposed it in the Government printing, in advertising in the Washington newspapers, and in the multiplication and pay of officers. Opposing subsidies generally, he voted against the appropriation of one hundred and fifty thousand dollars a year for a steam line to Brazil, May 20th, and warned the Senate whither they were drifting, and of the increase of taxation that would be necessary, if the principle was established that the Government should subsidize steamships in order to compete for the commerce of the world.

He remarked with reference to a proposed subsidy for an international telegraph, June 21st:

We are willing to grant the right of way, to give the lands, and that vessels of war should be employed in transporting material, making surveys and soundings, and in laying down the cable. What I object to is the subsidy, which is not given by the Russian or the British Government. I am not to be put in a false position in the matter: I do not intend to have it thrown in my teeth that I am opposed to granting every reasonable facility for making this line of telegraph. I am willing to do what is necessary in order to secure the telegraph; but I know, and I think every man who has conscientiously investigated the subject knows, that this telegraphic line can and will be constructed without any subsidy from us. It is in the hands of one of the richest companies on the face of the earth—the Western Union Telegraph Company.

Advocating investigation as to alleged frauds in the Navy Department, February 1st, Mr. Grimes took the opportunity to present a summary of the work of the Navy in the war:

The Navy Department is peculiarly constructed. It is differently organized from any other. It is almost a specialty in and of itself. It takes a man a year at least before he can understand its organization and details. Even the Committee on Naval Affairs are not thoroughly conversant with the details of the Navy Department. I confess, as one of them, that I am not, though I have endeavored as far as I could to inform myself.

I have no doubt that great frauds have been perpetrated. There are Senators around me who know very well that three years ago, before the commencement of this war, I called the attention of the Senate to the necessity of some change in the laws, as they related to contracts for the naval service. There is an officer known as a navy agent. So far as I am able to learn, there is no law of Congress that authorized the creation of that office. He was originally a mere agent of the Department, appointed by the head of the Department for a temporary purpose; but we have acts of Congress that recognize his existence; and now, at the commencement of every Administration, the President sends down to us nominations for these agencies. There is great opportunity for frauds to be perpetrated by them, and by the contractors under them, and under the Department proper. The Department are conscious of this. They are as anxious to ferret out these frauds as any member of the Senate or any person in the country can be. I wish the Senate to understand that I am not a "thick-and-thin" defender of the Navy Department. I claim no infallibility for that Department, or for any other. I have condemned some of its acts, as I have condemned some of the acts of every department of this Government. They know that I often differ from them. I have frankly told them, when I condemned them. I have always gone before them and told them what my opinions were in regard to any particular measure that I disapproved. Sometimes I have convinced them that they were wrong; sometimes they have convinced me that I was wrong; and sometimes we have both remained of the same opinion as before. I differed from the Navy Department in regard to their treatment of Commodore Du Pont. I told them so, frankly. But I have not allowed my private grief in that connection, or on any other subject, to control my action as a Senator. I believe that that gallant admiral would be one of the first to rebuke and condemn me, if he supposed that I allowed my feelings in his behalf to influence me in the slightest degree in my conduct here. He loves the country and he loves the service, of which he is so distinguished an ornament, too much for that. I disagreed with them in regard to the restoration of certain officers who had resigned several years ago, and had recently come back to the service. I thought that action was unjust to the younger officers who had stood by our flag, and carried it in honor and in triumph over every sea and in every clime. The Navy Department thought differently, and the Senate of the United States finally confirmed its action, and there was the end of it. I do not pretend that the right man is always selected for the right place. What man or what Department does not commit mistakes? The true question is, What is the grand total of results accomplished by the Department?

When this war began, we had but eight vessels that could be of any real value to the Government for the purpose of prosecuting the war. We have to-day between five and six hundred. I stated the other day, in answer to the clamors which had been raised, and which had found an echo here in the Senate, that I was satisfied, from a pretty thorough examination, that it would be discovered that, instead of having the slowest vessels in any existing navy, we really had the fastest naval ships in any service in the world. Immediately after giving utterance to that opinion, I was deluged with letters from engineers, ship-builders, and various amateurs in the naval profession, all of which went to confirm the statement that I had made.

But it is asked why we do not catch the Alabama, if our vessels are so fast? I might ask, why do you not catch Moseby? Moseby for eighteen months, or nearly that time, has been living within the lines of the American Army, and has destroyed three times as much property as the Alabama has. Do you condemn the Army, or the War Department, because he is not caught? Why do you not catch Forrest? It was with a good deal of difficulty that you were even able to catch Morgan in Ohio. Morgan traversed the States of Indiana and Ohio, and would have got away scot-free at last, had it not been for the much-abused Navy. The trouble is not that our vessels have not speed enough to catch the Alabama. The difficulty is in finding where she is. People do not reflect upon the difficulty of finding these corsairs. When found they will be easily caught, unless in the vicinity of a professedly neutral port into which they can dodge.

The real difficulty we have to encounter in the capture of the Alabama is the position assumed by foreign powers, that allows her, the moment that one of our vessels gets near her, to slip into a neutral port, and we are not permitted to follow her in. We are not permitted to lay off abreast the port until she comes out, and, if we do follow her in, our vessels are compelled to remain there twenty-four hours after she escapes, and during those twenty-four hours she will have had such a start that it will have become almost impossible to capture her. When one of our vessels went to the harbor of Nassau, where the rebel vessels had received supplies that they might prey upon our commerce, our vessel was denied the same privilege that had been granted to the rebel cruisers. Captain Baldwin, who has just returned on the Vanderbilt, would have captured the Alabama at Cape Town, had not his letters, giving the information he desired to insure her capture, been retained by the postmaster at that place.

During this war a great many grand and noble things have been done, a great many gallant deeds performed; but, in my conviction, fifty years hence it will be the verdict of mankind that the most wonderful thing has been the stupendous blockade that has been kept up by this nation so successfully and so long. The blockade is recognized by all foreign nations as the most efficient that has ever been maintained. The Navy Department, commencing with only eight steamships that could be used for blockading purposes at the commencement of the war, and they scattered all over the world and beyond its reach for many months, has kept up a blockade along the coast from Cape Henry to the line of Mexico, of thirty-five hundred and forty-nine statute miles. In this line there are one hundred and eighty-nine rivers, bays, harbors, inlets, sounds, or deep openings, of which forty-five are under six feet in depth at mean high water, seventeen are between six and twelve feet, forty-two are between twelve and eighteen feet, and thirty-two are over eighteen feet in depth. Not one man in a thousand has an adequate conception of the difficulties attending the building, equipping, furnishing, and manning the vessels required for such a service, nor the hardships endured by the officers and men to whom the duty is assigned. I say, without hesitation, that the ability of this nation to build and prepare the ships necessary to maintain as effective a blockade as it has been able to maintain during the last three years will hereafter excite the wonder and admiration of the world.

This is not all. While we have been able to do this, we have been able to keep a fleet in the Western waters, traversing the Red River, the Yazoo, the Cumberland, the Mississippi, the Ohio, Arkansas, Tennessee, and all the small streams that empty into the Mississippi south of the Ohio—a service for which we of the Northwest are willing always and at all times to return the Navy Department our most profound thanks. No man can over-estimate the services that the Navy has rendered to us in that quarter; and these services have been rendered after overcoming the greatest obstacles.

A distinguished naval officer wrote to Mr. Grimes, February 5th:

I have read your speech with deep interest and pleasure. I have seen nothing for a long time that has gratified me so much as your noble allusion to our old friend Admiral Du Pont. I thank you fervently for this outspoken expression of confidence and respect from your high place in the Senate, where you are deservedly recognized as the Senator best qualified to speak with authority on naval affairs.

Mr. Grimes's counsel was often sought in matters of great moment, and in cases of peculiar difficulty. A gentleman requesting his interposition for a son wrote:

In sending the inclosed letter, and asking a perusal of it, I should feel that I was asking a strange and indelicate favor, had not my intercourse with you, slight as it has been, given me implicit confidence in your manly, straightforward principles of action. My son's letter, written in the sacred confidence of com munion with his mother, could be intrusted to no eye but that of one who could fully appreciate, as we believe you will, the motives that have actuated us.

Mr. Grimes at once rendered the service solicited, and in a few days received the response:

I can but very poorly express my sense of the great debt of obligation you have laid me under for your sympathetic and prompt action. I know not how I shall ever be able to repay a debt of this kind, but one thing I can do, not forget that I owe it. My wife feels more sensibly than myself your kindness to her boy.

Upon a proposal to raise the grade of the minister to Belgium, Mr. Grimes inquired whether it originated in the fact that the King of Belgium, Leopold, was the father-in-law of Maximilian, and whether it was designed to propitiate the influences that were likely to control him if he became our neighbor in Mexico. He thought the country ought to know whether there was any indication of truckling to a foreign power. "I do not know anything about diplomacy," he said, "but my idea has always been that matters of state should be made public" (March 15th).

On the 17th of March he proposed an amendment to the rules of the Senate, that all Executive nominations should be submitted, considered, and decided in open Senate.

In advocating, April 12th, the return of the Naval Academy to Annapolis in 1865, Mr. Grimes gave the following sketch of the history of that institution:

The idea of establishing a Naval Academy originated with Alexander Hamilton, and was first suggested in his letter to Oliver Wolcott, written on the 5th of June, 1798. In a letter from Hamilton to Mr. McHenry, then the Secretary of War, his ideas on this subject were elaborated. He proposed that an academy should be established to "consist of four schools; one to be called the foundation school, another the school of engineers and artillerists, another the school of cavalry and infantry, and the fourth the school of the Navy." He suggested that naval and military cadets should be instructed in the foundation-school, for two years, in those branches of mathematics and science that are common and fundamental to both professions, and that they should then be instructed two years longer in those branches of scientific and practical knowledge that are peculiar to their respective professions. He even specified the branches of learning that he considered it desirable to be taught to naval cadets; and what is singular is, that they are substantially the branches taught to-day. Hamilton immediately inclosed to General Washington a copy of his letter to Mr. McHenry; and on the 12th of December, 1799, only two days before his death, that great man wrote to Hamilton, and the last letter I believe that he ever wrote on public affairs, approving of his plans, and saying that "the establishment of an institution of this kind upon a respectable and extensive basis has ever been considered by me an object of primary importance to this country." This was before a naval school had been established by any nation, and, so far as I know, before it had anywhere been proposed to establish one.

In 1802 the Military Academy at West Point was established, but no provision was made for the naval school that Hamilton had proposed should be connected with it. In 1808 Mr. Jefferson transmitted to Congress, with his approval, the recommendation of General Williams, the superintendent of the Military Academy, that that institution should be enlarged so as to include naval cadets, who should be instructed in nautical astronomy, navigation, etc., but the proposition failed to meet the approval of Congress. In 1813 the Secretary of the Navy was authorized to appoint a limited number of naval schoolmasters, who were detailed on board of the larger class of vessels-of-war, and required to instruct midshipmen in the rudimental learning of their profession. By the act of 1842, these schoolmasters were dignified with the title of professors of mathematics. Of this system of instruction on shipboard, Mr. Upshur, in his annual report in 1842, said: "Through a long course of years the midshipmen were left to educate themselves and one another. Suitable teachers are now provided, but their schools are kept in the midst of a thousand interruptions and impediments, which render the whole system of little or no value;" and he repeated the recommendation of Secretaries Jones, Thompson, Southard, and Paulding, and of President John Quincy Adams, that a Naval Academy should be established upon a proper basis. I will not repeat the arguments of those eminent men, in which they demonstrated that it was the highest dictate of economy, honor, and duty, to give to our naval officers, who are our representatives abroad, the armed embassadors of the nation, the highest professional education possible.

Finally, in 1845, by a mutual understanding between Mr. Bancroft, the Secretary of the Navy, and Mr. Marcy, the Secretary of War, and with the assent of President Polk, Fort Severn, on the Severn River in Maryland, was transferred to the Navy Department, and the midshipmen then afloat were ordered there for instruction. There has never been any act of Congress positively establishing a Naval Academy, but there have been numerous acts recognizing its existence at the place I have mentioned. The ground upon which Fort Severn was erected was purchased by the Government in 1808, and the fortifications were built under the direction of the present General J. G. Totten—the first labor, I believe, of that eminent officer and faithful public servant. The original site included only seven acres. The grounds have been enlarged to forty-seven and a half acres, furnishing ample parade and exercise grounds. A more favorable position could not be found for a Naval Academy, and more satisfactory accommodations for the students could not be devised, than existed at Annapolis at the breaking out of this rebellion. Its immediate proximity to Chesapeake Bay, the quiet retirement of the city in which it was established, the salubrity of the climate, and the length of the seasons in which out-door military exercise could be indulged, all tended to make Annapolis, in my opinion, a better place for the concentration of youth for nautical combined with general instruction than any place within my knowledge in the whole country. I think I hazard nothing in saying that no institution for professional training was ever conducted with more eminent success. It realized all the expectations of its founders, and furnished to the country the most accomplished naval officers to be found in any navy, the benefit of whose services the nation is now enjoying.

On the 14th of April Mr. Grimes gave the following account of the loss of the gunboat Baron de Kalb, which was commanded by his nephew, Lieutenant-Commander John G. Walker:

It so happens that I know something about the history of that vessel, and know the man who commanded her at the time she was blown up. I shall not speak of him particularly, because he is a townsman and relative of mine. She was the original St. Louis, and was rechristened the Baron de Kalb, comprising a part of Foote's fleet, then of Davis's, and then of Porter's. She was a vessel that lay within sixty yards of the embrasures of Fort Hindman, and if anybody wants to know how she was managed then, when she was under the command of the same officer who commanded her when she was blown up, he can refer to the report of Admiral Porter. She was then sent up the Yazoo River, and on the third expedition up there passed over a torpedo, and was entirely blown up, completely destroyed. There was no allegation of any want of good seamanship, or of proper conduct on the part of any of the officers or men on board. The men lost every thing they had. I believe they recovered nothing, and so of the officers; but it has never been the policy of the Government to allow the officers anything in such cases, whether of the line or of the staff, because they are considered as being responsible for the management, and even if an accident befalls them, as in this case, which was unavoidable, which they could not have foreseen, I know of no case in which an officer has been paid; but to the men, who generally have their all embarked in the little kit they have on board, it has been the practice of the Government to pay the sum of fifty dollars each. I remember that, the first winter I was here, five years ago, my attention was called to it. The Government lost a sloop-of-war in the Pacific, and we made the allowance in that case, and similar allowances have been made to the sailors of the Cumberland, the Congress, the monitor Ericsson, and all the vessels that have gone down.

On the 23d of May Mr. Grimes made a detailed *exposé* of frauds and corruptions connected with contracts for naval supplies, and recommended various remedies: among others, that navy agents and storekeepers should be commissioned officers, with permanency in their tenure of office, and that they should be held under similar responsibility with quartermasters and commissaries in the Army. He said:

A dishonest quartermaster may render abortive the best-matured plan of a military commander, by furnishing defective transportation, clothing, or shoes. May not a navy agent cripple the effects of a whole fleet by furnishing adulterated oils for steam machinery, and has it not been done? In one case, the dishonest or incompetent officer would be brought before a court-martial, tried, convicted, deprived of his commission, and otherwise punished; in the other, he is permitted to go wholly unwhipped of justice, and allowed to proceed in his career of crime. All dishonest transactions, all complicity with fraud, on the part of any of the Government employés at the yards, should be promptly investigated before military tribunals, and summarily punished. It is only by a vigorous administration and swift justice that you can prevent false estimates of the supplies needed, false reports of the amounts on hand, false measurements, false inspections, false reports of weights and quantities. At present you have no means of punishing such offenses. What folly to rely upon removal from office as a restraint upon crime, when the guilty person would realize more money by suffering himself to be a party to one fraud than by two or three years' salary in the employment from which you eject him! Such men only laugh at your stupidity, and mock at your punishment.

The time has arrived when it should be thoroughly understood that our navy-yards are national establishments, to be controlled for the benefit of the nation exclusively, and not for the benefit of the neighborhoods in which they are established, or of the politicians who surround them. They cost us too much money, we have too deep an interest in them, to permit them to be surrendered to local influences. Let me say to gentlemen representing Atlantic States, in which are our navy-yards, that we of the States remote from the seaboard are as much inclined to support and cherish the Navy as you are. We are interested in your commerce and manufactures. We want the flag that floats at the mast-head of your ships protected upon every sea, and recognized as an emblem of the power of a great nation. To do this we know that we must give of our substance, and we will give it cheerfully, if we have the assurance that naval affairs are conducted economically and wisely. We must know that the affairs of this Department are managed by the officers of the *nation*, acting for the common interest, and not by your officers, acting for the interest of a few contractors among you. I beg Senators to remember that the people of the great section of which I am a citizen are very slightly identified with the Navy. There are no navy-yards among them, and not one in a hundred of them ever saw a naval officer or a ship-of-war. Unless they have the assurance of economy and fidelity in its entire administration, therefore, it is the department of the public service that they will be least likely to cheerfully tax themselves to support. Give them that assurance, and the Navy will have the unwavering support of the agricultural people of the West.

With reference to establishing a navy-yard at Cairo, Illinois, Mr. Grimes said, June 27th:

I know Cairo; the levee which keeps the water out is required to be as high as the top of a two-story house; and though it is only at extreme high water, occurring once in from three or four to ten years, that the water breaks over the levee, yet every year in the season of high water it slips through, so as to make from five to ten feet of stagnant water inside. Knowing, as I do, that more money can be expended there than at any other point on the Mississippi or Ohio, with less advantage to the Government, I did feel alarmed when I saw the Senate make the appropriation on a day when gold was 256 in New York, and I did desire that the appropriation should be defeated. I wanted a commission of skillful officers appointed to go and determine where this navy-yard should be established, and not by an act of Congress, without recommendation from anybody, absolutely fix it at Cairo. It is because I love the Navy, and I want to protect it.

In the discussion upon the Pacific Railroad bill, May 19th, Mr. Grimes advocated limiting the amount of stock that could be held by any one person to two hundred thousand dollars, according to the original act of 1862. When that was stricken out, he said:

We have created a perfect monopoly by the bill as it stands now. It has the appearance—I know it was not the intention of the Senator (Mr. Trumbull) or of the Senate—of being the most stupendous monopoly ever devised on this continent. Allow me to ask if the Senator ever knew of a corporation that was to have such beneficent advantages, prerogatives, and privileges, conferred upon it? Why, you are putting your hands into the Treasury, and bestowing upon this corporation most lavishly. The idea of giving to one man or any ten men this great boon—ninety millions, I believe, under the bill as it now stands—does, I confess, strike me as most monstrous. Let it not be understood that I am opposed to the Pacific Railroad. I am in favor of it, and represent a constituency that is probably more interested in it than the constituency of any man here. Had we not better avoid even the appearance of creating a monopoly?[1]

The amended Pacific Railroad act, approved July 2d, made a land-grant to the Burlington & Missouri River Railroad Company, for the purpose of aiding in the extension of its road in Nebraska. Mr. Grimes was a stockholder in that company. He did not vote for the bill, or do anything to promote its passage in the Senate, for the reason that he held some of the stock, and he did not see fit to take any part in connection with the subject while it was under consideration in the Senate.

Mr. Grimes disapproved of allowing the cotton-trade or any commercial intercourse with the rebels, and voted against a bill for that object, June 28, 1864. He held that either there should be an absolute, unqualified, and unconditional exclusion of trade, or else that every man should be permitted to trade who chose to do so. He did not believe in the theory of allowing trade to be carried on under the direction of anybody. He said, March 3, 1865:

I never entertained any doubt as to the propriety of stopping this traffic, and stopping it effectually, sealing it up hermetically, so that neither Army, nor Treasury, nor Navy, nor anybody else, could carry on commerce with the rebels. I never could conceive of the propriety of professing to carry on war with one hand, and trading with the enemy with the other, furnishing supplies to strengthen and support them, and to invigorate the armies with which they propose to take our lives. Is it not the testimony of every military officer, that nothing is more calculated to demoralize the public military service than this system of trading with the enemy? Is it not so in the nature of things? Is there a man of reflection and common-sense who is not satisfied that that must be the result? If we are going to put

[1] "When the honorable member from Iowa speaks of this being a monopoly, which may redound with great wealth to those who may embark in this business, he ventures an opinion that perhaps the result may not realize. It is a great enterprise. It is great certainly in one particular: it is great in the hazards which are run by those who may embark in it."—(MR. REVERDY JOHNSON, *in Senate, May* 19*th.*)

down the rebellion, and close this war, it must be done by fighting, not by trading. Either withdraw your armies, and go to trading, or else cease trading and continue to fight.

The Senator from Massachusetts (Mr. Wilson) says the cotton must be got out of the rebel lines. I will tell him how it can be got out, and that is by fighting it out, never by trading it out. That cotton is ours now. No man was more strenuous in favor of the passage of the confiscation law than the Senator from Massachusetts. Why is he willing to abandon his right, and the right of his constituents, and of the soldiers of my State, to that cotton? Why is he willing to pay for it to the men who have been attempting to take the lives of our soldiers? The whole thing proceeds upon a fallacy. Either let us carry on this war as war, or disband the Army, and let the Treasury undertake to trade us through the war. It is the height of ridiculousness to me for a great nation to be professing to carry on a war, taxing its people, using a conscription law to reënforce its armies, using all its energies, and at the same time trading with the men that you are carrying on the war with, and allowing supplies to go through the lines of your army in order to enable the enemy to continue to carry on that war; for that is the conclusion to which it all comes at last. I stand where I have ever stood, where I stood last year when this bill was passed. Either let there be untrammeled free trade, or else no trade at all, and let this be a war, and not transactions in merchandise. The purpose of the bill is to enable parties to go within the rebel lines, in order to get out cotton; and it is to that, General Canby, in command of the Department of the Mississippi, particularly objects, and says that information will be carried by these Treasury agents and contractors to the rebels, so that an army of fifty thousand additional men will be required in order to support ourselves in his department alone. Let me state a case that is on record here in the Senate. It is not more than four weeks ago that a vessel came out of one of the North Carolina rivers in the sound, loaded with articles contraband of war, cotton, turpentine, and rosin. She went back loaded with provisions and clothing, and the moment she reached the line that divided the two armies, rebel soldiers in rebel uniform were put on board of her, and carried her back whence she had come. There is nothing to prevent anybody coming within our lines, bringing in their cotton, taking back supplies, and taking back what is of more advantage to the rebels and more injury to us—information as to the movements of our troops.

In a discussion with reference to filling up the ranks of the army, Mr. Grimes said, June 29th:

We are at length, in one of the very last days of the session, approaching the consideration of the most momentous subject that can be considered during this session of Congress. We are to determine whether or not the treasure that has thus far been spent and the blood that has been spilled in this controversy are to be wasted and sunk into the ground, or whether they are to accomplish the purpose that the country desires; that is, the restoration of the Union. We are to decide whether or not we are to have an army, or whether we shall suffer the forces that are now in the field to be frittered away, to be devastated by war, and nothing be substituted in the place of the men now standing in the ranks.

I need not say that I have always been opposed to commutation for military service. I have believed that every citizen of the country owed his property, his service, and his life, to the country, if it was necessary, and I have always therefore steadily voted against commutation. We ought to have had a conscription and a draft long ago.

Speaking of citizens of his own State, he said, February 7, 1865:

I have seen men of family and of substance who have been drafted, and who had the capacity and the opportunity to procure substitutes, but who said that they did not believe that it was a manly and generous course for them to pursue, and they shouldered their muskets, leaving their families and their property behind them, and are now under General Sherman.

Mr. Grimes gave careful consideration to a bill for establishing a Bureau of Freedmen's Affairs, to mature and perfect it in harmony with our institutions of government and civilization, and said with reference to certain propositions submitted by Mr. Sumner, June 15-28, 1864:

The purpose which the Senator desires to secure is one that commends itself to my heart. I want to do exactly what he wants to accomplish; but I think most conscientiously that he is not attaining that object by the bill which he seeks to have us pass, and hence I am compelled to vote against the passage of the bill. I think that it is violative of some of the fundamental principles of the institutions of this country ; it would violate my convictions of duty and of right; and therefore I cannot support it.

The Senator says I have proceeded upon a wrong representation, that I seem to entertain the notion that these men are not freemen. It is because I do entertain the opinion that they are freemen, and because I am anxious that they shall forever remain freemen, that I oppose this bill. According to my conviction, the only way to treat these men is as freemen. You have to give them alms, to exercise acts of humanity and friendship to them, for a while. They will be jostled, as we are all being jostled through this life, but in a little while they will settle down into the position that Providence has designed that they shall occupy under the new condition of affairs in this country. It is not by any such processes as are attempted to be enacted into a law that you are going to really alleviate the wants and difficulties under which these people now suffer. The bill puts every colored man who was ever a slave under the "general superintendence" of the commissioner at the head of this bureau. The Senator admits that it is the purpose of the bill to confer this extraordinary power, but says he is going to have it executed beneficially for these colored men. If we pass this bill, that is the way, I trust, these great powers will be exercised; but I am fearful that, if we confer upon officials such extraordinary powers, they may not always and in all cases exercise them for the benefit of these men.

Looking on them as really freemen, I do not very much admire the idea of creating a bureau to take care of them. They are the same class of men upon whom, three or four weeks ago, a portion of the members of the Senate were attempting to bestow the elective franchise. I submit that there was a very great mistake then, or there is a very great mistake now, when we undertake to put under the control of general superintendents all the colored men within their respective departments, and authorize the commissioners to enforce with the military power the alleged contracts which this unfortunate and despised class of people may be said to have entered into. I would rather appoint a bureau to take care of the confiscated and abandoned estates, and let the care of the freedmen, so far as they shall be cared for, be an incident of the establishment of the bureau and of the care that shall be exercised over these estates.

It is proposed by the Senator from Massachusetts that we shall not direct the assistant commissioners to be appointed, as in ordinary cases, by the President, and to be confirmed by the Senate, but that they shall be appointed by the Secretary of the Treasury, and be mere tenants by his will. I am unwilling to confer such power on any Secretary, or upon the President, without the constitutional check upon him of a confirmation by the Senate. What are we here for, but to give our advice and consent to the appointment of such responsible officers as these? We have declared, this session, that every acting master in the Navy, to whom you pay one thousand dollars a year, shall be appointed by the President, and sent here to be confirmed by us, men who are merely required to perform watch duty on the decks of your men-of-war, through whose hands not one dollar of money is to pass, to whom is confided no such trusts as are confided by this bill to your commissioners. And yet it is seriously proposed that these commissioners, who are to have the control of hundreds of thousands of human beings, of whose character for humanity, and discretion, and wisdom, we know nothing, and can know nothing, who are to have the control of hundreds of thousands and doubtless millions of property in the course of a year, are not to be sent to the Senate for us to advise and consent to their nomination!

I confess to the Senator that I have been anxious to vote for his bill. I told him, at the beginning of the consideration of it, that several amendments must be made before I will vote for it, and this is one of them. I have as much respect for the Secretary of the Treasury as any man has, but I never will consent, so long as I occupy a seat in this body, to place in the hands of any Government officer the overwhelming power that is placed in the hands of this public officer by the proposition of the Senator. I want to know the character of these men, the character they have maintained hitherto, whether they are humane men, Christian men, honest men, and will do their duty to the men, women, and children, who are committed to their charge; and, if the Senator's proposition is adopted, I unhesitatingly say that I will vote against the bill.

The consideration of the bill as amended by the Senate was postponed in the House, July 2d, to the next session. Mr.

Grimes said, February 21, 1865, that his purpose was to get a Freedmen's Bureau bill that he could vote for; and in reply to further strictures by Mr. Sumner:

It will not do for the Senator to raise an issue with me on the ground that I am not in favor of the rights of the freedmen, or to insinuate that I am not so much in favor of liberty and freedom as he is. I am just as much in earnest, I am just as much in favor of protecting these freedmen, as he is; I will go just as far and spend as much of my own money, or of the money of my constituents, as he will spend; but I want to be satisfied that it is going to reach the objects of my bounty, and that all their rights will be protected under the law I am to vote for.

87.—*To Mrs. Grimes.*

WASHINGTON, *April* 24, 1864.

Frank Fessenden has been wounded and captured. It is not known how badly he is wounded. His regiment behaved well, and so did he. Everybody curses Banks loud and deep. I have not seen Fessenden since the news came. I send you Foster's speech on Sumner. It is regarded as capital here.

April 29th.—I was never half so comfortable in Washington, without you, as I am now. I am in one of the best, most genteel, quiet, cultivated families I have ever known in Washington; my apartments are two nice, airy, neat, and convenient rooms, and I have the only breakfasts I have ever eaten at any boarding-house in Washington. My colleague Wilson, and Henderson, of Missouri, dine with me. Fessenden will adopt the same mode of life, and begin to dine with us on Monday, and Clark and Morrill are to be admitted to our club during the week. Of course, we have good dinners. So much for my creature comforts.

I have just received a long letter from Dr. Jonathan Blanchard, formerly of Galesburg, the old Orthodox apostle at Galesburg, in which he compliments me in very undeserved terms, and concludes by saying that all of my merits are to be attributed to your instructions and example. I believe that the general impression is, that I am of myself a most perverse mortal, toned and tempered down by you into a reasonably civilized piece of humanity.

We have no news here. Every one is incensed against Banks,

and demands his supersedure. Our disaster in Louisiana was much greater than was reported. There will be no battle here for some weeks, probably; in the mean time a vast force is being concentrated. Last Monday more than forty thousand men marched through town, six thousand negroes, on their way southward. The universal opinion was that the negroes made much the best appearance, and there seemed to be the best of feeling between them and the white soldiers.

88.—*To Mrs. Grimes.*

United States Senate-Chamber,
Washington, *May* 10, 1864.

We have an intense anxiety here about the recent battles, though the people have not been so demonstrative as on many former occasions. The battle on Friday was fiercely contested all day, was almost entirely a musketry-fight, and was a success to us, inasmuch as the enemy did not accomplish his purpose, which was to whip us. We had two men to their one in action. Grant had one hundred and forty thousand men, and all engaged, save one brigade of colored troops, say six thousand men. Grant and Meade estimate Lee's army at seventy thousand, which I suspect is about the truth. On Saturday, Lee slowly and sullenly moved off in the direction of Orange Court-House, expecting, doubtless, that Grant would follow him, and that he would be able to resume the fight where he would have great advantages in the topography of the country. But Grant failed to be caught in that trap, and moved on the direct road to Richmond, *via* Spottsylvania Court-House. We have all sorts of rumors about battles since that of Friday, but there is nothing whatever reliable. Nearly all of our army was some time or other in the day soundly thrashed, but generally rallied very well. There were very few stragglers, less than were ever known before. The enemy's tactics consisted of the most frantic, impetuous and gigantic efforts to break our line by attacking it with large masses. Their troops are far better at this than ours are. At times they drove our whole line back, and took our positions, but we recovered them. We lost one entire brigade at one time, most of a brigade at another, and a regiment at another, by capture. We lost more prisoners than they did. Had the rebels not gone away from the battle-field, it would not have been claimed as a victory by us, for they lost no guns, comparatively no prisoners, no baggage, and carried away their wounded. They are probably far more exhausted by the battle than we are, and we hope that this is the beginning of the end. The rebels fight, though, like very devils incarnate. It is useless to attempt to disguise it, there is an *abandon* about their attacks that is not imitated even by most of our men.

May 12*th.*—Fighting of the most terrific character still goes on only a few miles from us. On our side are not less than forty thousand men *hors de combat.* This includes killed, wounded, and missing. Still the cry is for more blood, and more is to be shed. Our troops are in good condition, hopeful, and anticipate success. Reënforcements of fresh men are being sent to Grant—a relief which it is understood cannot be sent by Lee's pretended government to him. The excitement occasioned by the continuous battles in the neighborhood has been so great, and has so unsettled everybody's mind, that the Senate to-day adjourned to Monday. I think that Grant will in the end destroy Lee's army, but his own will be also destroyed. It will be a sort of Kilkenny cat-fight; they, you know, fought until nothing was left of either but the tail; but Grant's tail is the longest. We have no other news here. We think of nothing else, inquire about nothing else, dream about nothing else.

May 18*th.*—I wish I could satisfy your fears about the Army of the Potomac. Thus far we have won *no victory.* We have suffered a terrible loss of killed and wounded (nearly fifty thousand), and Lee is in an impregnable position. J. Grimes commanded the Seventeenth Regiment of Infantry, until he was finally knocked over by a broken shell. He is not much hurt, only bruised, and will return to the army, and try his chances again next Saturday.

I have just returned to my room from dining at Mr. Eames's with Mrs. Julia Ward Howe—for company, Admiral Davis, Foster, of Connecticut, Gurowski, and your husband—a pleasant time, of course. Mrs. Howe gave what she calls a reading, last night. I did not go, but, as she insists upon my going on Friday, I suppose I must comply.

The news from different directions is not at all pleasant to me. I confess that just at this present writing I feel pretty blue.

May 24*th.*—As you learn by the papers, I made a speech yesterday, but I did not, as they say I did, talk two hours. I think I made a good speech, and such seems to be the general impression, but you will see it in a few days, and can judge for yourself. At least there was no clap-trap and humbug about it.

89.—*To Admiral Du Pont.*

WASHINGTON, *June* 15, 1864.

I would be delighted to visit you near Wilmington, and I know Mrs. Grimes would be, but she went North about the 20th of April, where she remained a few weeks, and then returned to our home in Iowa, where she now is. As you can easily suppose, I am most anxious to leave here that I may join her, and shall not be inclined to tarry by the wayside on my journey westward. I intend some time, with my wife, to make you a visit, and I intend to do it at the first opportunity I have; and in this I am most heartily joined by Mrs. Grimes, for I need not tell you that she is a stanch adherent of yours.

90.—*To Mrs. Grimes.*

WASHINGTON, *June* 19, 1864.

I hope to be at home by the 4th of July. It is possible I may not, however, because I am compelled to stop a day in Chicago, and I do not wish to be there on the 4th, which is the day the convention of the Democratic party assembles there. Rather than be incommoded by that concern in going west, or be mixed up in it, I will remain on the way a day or two. We have no news here. Grant's campaign is regarded by military critics as being thus far a failure. He has lost a vast number of men, and is compelled to abandon his attempt to capture Richmond on the north side, and cross the James River. The question is asked significantly, Why did he not take his army south of the James at once, and thus save seventy-five thousand men?

Smith, Bros. & Co., of whom I made mention in my remarks in the Senate, found themselves in Fort Warren day before yesterday, and will be tried before a court-martial, and will, I doubt not, be convicted.

91.—*To Hon. W. P. Fessenden, Secretary of the Treasury, Washington.*

PHILADELPHIA, *July* 3, 1864.

I left Washington yesterday morning, as I told you I should. I have experienced twenty-six moody and melancholy hours. You have at no time been separated from my thoughts since I left you.

I have tried to picture to myself what would be the effect of your change of position upon the country, upon yourself, and upon our relations to each other.

I need not tell you that for six years I have been drawn toward you by an invisible power, magnetic it may be, that I could never resist, even had I desired to resist it. During the time I have been in the Senate you have exercised an influence over my wayward nature such as was never exercised by any human being except my wife. At times I have been irritated with you, but I can truly say that I never suffered the sun to go down upon my anger. If at any such moment of my weakness I ever gave you a pang of painful feeling, I now most sincerely crave your pardon, begging you to remember that the recollection of any and every intemperate declaration of mine gives me more sorrow than it can possibly give to you.

Now, our relations are to be changed. I had hoped that so long as I remained in the Senate we were to be associated together. It is ordered otherwise, and I trust for the good of the country. You are to have new surroundings, new associations, and doubtless our old friendship will be in a measure forgotten; I trust not destroyed. It fills me with grief to think that this must in the very nature of things be so.

You know what I thought of your going into the cabinet. If you would not deem it offensive to say so, I would say that I really pitied you when I saw you last. I saw at a glance your true situation. I knew that you had feeble health, that the Treasury is in a terrible condition, and that the result of your acceptance of office might be your death. At the same time I believed that no name would give one-half so much confidence to the country as yours, and I knew that your declination by every enemy of the country would be ascribed not to its true cause, your poor health, but to the fact that you knew too well the condition of the Treasury Department to accept the portfolio. In this condition of things, I did not feel like urging you to either accept or decline, but contented myself with recommending you to make such terms as would prevent you from being slandered and back-bitten out of the cabinet in a few weeks by your associates. What is to be the issue in that regard I do not know. You are, or were, when I left, master of the situation, and in my opinion would fix your own terms.

Now let me give you one word of parting advice, and I will never assume to do it again.

Get rid of Mr. Chase's agents as soon as possible. I believe many of them are corrupt, but whether they be so or not they are thought to be, and that is a sufficient reason for supplanting them with new men. One or two men who enjoy your confidence now, I believe to be tricksters, but you will find them out soon enough. Do not send abroad to negotiate a loan, but throw yourself upon the people of this country. Read the *Evening Post* of yesterday, and see what was the demand for United States securities in New York. In the present flush of confidence you can put your loan upon the American market, and do as you wish.

And now, my dear Fessenden, I start for my rustic home on the bank of the Mississippi. If there be an angel on earth, there is one there who prays as devoutly night and morning for your success and welfare as she does for mine. I dare not trust myself to read this letter for fear I would destroy it. I do not expect you to spare the time to answer it. May God give you health and happiness, and to the country peace and safety!

Extract of Letter from Mr. Fessenden to Mr. Grimes.

WASHINGTON, *July* 24, 1864.

Your kind letter has neither been overlooked nor forgotten, for I have wished many times for a moment to acknowledge its receipt, and to tell you how highly I appreciate its assurances of friendly regard. You can well imagine, however, that I have been intensely occupied, and must be aware that I am overwhelmed with perplexities, and surrounded by dangers. Had I known but two weeks beforehand what was to happen, I think that with the aid of Congress I might have placed myself in a somewhat easier condition. But things must be taken as I find them, and they are quite bad enough to appall any but a man desperate as I am. I cannot commit to paper all I would say. If my bodily condition was better, perhaps I might work with more heart and energy; but I am run down with fatigue, retiring exhausted, and rising little refreshed—a poor state for such work as I have to do. But it must be done, and I *will* do it somehow.

I wish to assure you, my dear friend, that there are few people in this world for whom I have so high a regard as for yourself.

There was no man in the Senate with whom I was on such close terms of intimacy, or who knew so much of me as you did. If at any time there was a moment's irritation, it always passed away with the moment, and left no trace behind. May it remain thus between us while we both live! Our country must be served honestly and faithfully, and we must do our duty, even if others fail in theirs. I want your aid and counsel more than ever, and trust you will not withhold either.

Give my love to your wife, and tell her to think as well of me as she can, whatever may be my errors.

In the course of debate, December 19th, upon a bill to appropriate ten million dollars for the defense of the Northern frontier, Mr. Grimes said:

The true mode to defend ourselves on the Northern frontier and on the lakes is to have arsenals and armories there. On the lakes we have ten tons of shipping where the British have one; we own nearly all the steamboats that ply there, and we shall continue to own them so long as we maintain our present navigation laws. All you want, whenever difficulties shall occur between us and Great Britain, is to have armaments which you can immediately throw on board these vessels. Take possession of the mouth of the Welland Canal, and what power will the British have? Where the necessity, therefore, of deciding in advance that we must build fortifications at the mouth of every river, or near every harbor, on the whole upper lakes?

The true way is to repeal the reciprocity treaty. Great Britain is not going to fight for Canada. Canada was an apple ready to drop into our hands when the reciprocity treaty was agreed to. It was consummated through the instrumentality of the men who are now in rebellion against this Government, with a little aid that was furnished to them by the people of the North. Repeal the reciprocity treaty, and you will find that in less than twenty-four months the people of the Canadas, and of the British provinces generally, will be clamorous to come back to us. The newspapers tell us that there is a panic in Canada. I have no doubt of it. It does not proceed from any fear that they have of war; it proceeds from the fear that they have of their pockets. The moment you repeal the reciprocity treaty, the stock of every railroad in Canada will become worthless; every man of wealth and means will become bankrupt. It is caused by the fear they have of the repeal of that treaty, which gives them the carrying trade of the produce from the West, and the power to compete with us in the Eastern markets, which is very much to our injury.

Upon a resolution of inquiry with reference to the military arrest of two citizens of Kentucky, December 20th, Mr. Grimes said:

The Senator from Kentucky (Mr. Powell) says that two eminent men of that State have been arrested, he knows not by whom, he knows not for what; that they have been spirited away, he knows not whither; and as a representative of that State he asks the Senate to institute an inquiry, that it may be learned what disposition has been made of them. I say that it is the right and the duty of this Senate to give to the Senator the answer that he demands. Is it not our duty to make some inquiry in regard to a question of that kind? Are we going to be entirely indifferent to the liberties of the people of this country? I am not sent here for the purpose of sitting with my arms folded in silence and in quiet, and giving no vote in favor of an inquiry of this kind. I have no doubt that when the inquiry shall be pursued properly, there will be a perfect vindication of the officers of the Government; but if it be otherwise, if these men have been improperly arrested, it is the duty of the Senate to say so, and to put its seal of reprobation upon those who have improperly arrested them. I trust that this Senate is not going to sit quietly by, when charges are made by a Senator of arbitrary conduct on the part of any officers of this Government, and refuse to make an inquiry, because it is claimed that to do so would be a proceeding of a *quasi* judicial character. It is one of the prerogatives of this body to protect the liberties of the people of the States, and the rights and interests of the States themselves.

On the 12th of January the Senate was honored with the presence of Vice-Admiral Farragut, the first person holding that position in the American service. Mr. Grimes asked permission to interrupt the regular order of business, and on his motion a recess of ten minutes was taken, to afford Senators an opportunity to pay their respects to that eminent citizen.

THE MANAGEMENT OF THE NAVY.

On the 17th of February, pending a discussion of the Naval Appropriation bill, upon a motion of Mr. Wade to create a Board of Admiralty for the management of the Navy, Mr. Grimes said:

I shall not follow gentlemen in the wandering debate that has characterized this occasion. I have no encomiums to pronounce upon and no denunciations to utter against the old Democratic and Whig parties, for I am content that the dead should bury their dead.

I do not stand here as the defender or advocate of any man, but to maintain what I believe to be the public interest in connection with the Navy Department. It is the public service we are to promote, not the interests of any men or set of men. I shall not seek to defend or palliate any wrong, no matter by whom committed. I believe that this Department, as all other Departments, has made some mistakes ; but the true remedy is not the one set forth by the Senator from Ohio, and, entertaining the opinions I do, there is no alternative for me but to oppose as strenuously as I may be able the amendment he proposes.

I have no fault to find with the Senator for proposing this amendment. It is true that we have a Naval Committee, of which I happen to be a member, and that it is the business of that committee to examine into all the laws in connection with naval affairs, to inform themselves of the operations of the naval organization, to understand not only its written but its unwritten laws, to know what vessels are built, the character of their armament, the character of the machinery by which they are to be propelled, their efficiency and speed, and the contracts under which they are built. I I think I can say that the committee have endeavored, as far as their capacity and time would allow, to inform themselves on all these points. It is their duty also to inform themselves, and I think they have attempted to do it, in regard to the naval organization of the different nations of the earth, and if in their opinion there be any advantages over ours in any of these organizations to suggest them to the Senate for adoption into our own. I think they have informed themselves in regard to each of the many descriptions of vessels—some twenty-five or thirty—that now constitute parts of our Navy.

Nor am I going to find fault with the Senator because as a member of the Committee on the Conduct of the War he examined only one particular type of vessels that had been built, and found some objections to that class. But I submit to the Senate that it would hardly be wise, because there happened to be in the estimation of that committee some objections to that kind of vessels, to overturn the entire Navy organization, when the Naval Committee, who have examined into *all* the various descriptions of vessels, have not deemed it advisable to propose any such change. Informed as we are in regard to the general operations of the Navy, knowing what has been accomplished during the last four years under its present administration, we have unhesitatingly come to the conclusion, as the organ of this body in connection with naval affairs, that this change ought not to be made, and would prove most disastrous if made.

The whole argument upon which this amendment is based proceeds upon one assumption, that there have been mistakes in the construction of the light-draught iron-clads. Admit it. Is that a reason for overturning the Navy Department? Is this the first mistake that has been made? If the Committee on the Conduct of the War had inquired of the Naval Committee, we could have told them that a similar mistake was made in regard to the second class of monitors, that same class which have been doing efficient service at Fort Fisher, and of which Admiral Porter speaks in such eulogistic terms. At least one-half of all the old sailing-vessels that have been built since the establishment of the Navy have been modified and changed. Within five years the Pensacola was changed under our eyes at the navy-yard in Washington, and forty feet added to her length. Was that a reason for overturning the Department?

Nearly all of the British iron-clad vessels, such as the Warrior and Black Prince, are now pronounced failures, and the Warrior is being dismantled, being considered unfit to go to sea. Did the Senator ever know that a peer of the realm or any member of the House of Commons rose in his place in the British Parliament, and proposed to overturn the whole admiralty system of that empire, upon a supply-bill, because mistakes had been made in the construction of iron-clad vessels that have cost millions of pounds sterling?

Admit the mistake to be as great as is charged. Is this the only mistake that has been made? Has no other Department blundered? Have there been no mistakes in the Treasury, and will you put that in commission also? Has the War Department been entirely free from blunders during the last four years, and will you overturn that Department, upon an amendment to the Army appropriation bill?

In regard to the light-draught iron-clads, the facts are very simple. We had a board, in 1861, composed of three superior officers in the Navy, to determine the character of the vessels that should be built with the million and a half of dollars appropriated in July of that year. They reported in favor of three different classes of vessels: the Ironsides, which is an excellent vessel; the Galena, which has turned out to be a failure; and they said to Mr. Ericsson, who proposed to build the original monitor, that he might build that vessel for a given sum of money, a small price, and run his own risk upon her: if she turned out to be a success the Government would take her, and if otherwise it would not. That monitor, at the time she fought the Merrimac, and relieved us of the great weight that rested upon every man here in Washington after the destruction of the Congress and Cumberland, was not the property of the United States, but belonged to John Ericsson and the men who were associated with him in building her.

Now, let us see what is proposed by the Senator from Ohio. Five naval officers are provided for, to hold their offices during the will of the President, and the Secretary of the Navy is to preside over them. It is to be a kind of New England town-meeting. The amendment means to put the Navy Department into commission, to put it into leading-strings, to give the control to these commissioners, or else it means to furnish the Department a subterfuge by which it can at all times avoid responsibility. Do you wish to divide responsibility thus? I surely do not. That will be the effect of this amendment, if adopted. That is the effect of the British Admiralty administration to-day. There is nothing that the members of the naval profession in England are so anxious to get rid of as their admiralty system, after which this amendment is modeled. They saw fit, two hundred years ago, to put their office of lord high admiral into commission, and it is now wielded by such a board as the Senator has proposed to create here; and what is the result? Precisely the result that I predict will follow here. Sir Charles Napier, a great naval authority, says that "no permanent good can be done for the service until the Board of Admiralty is abolished." Sir George Cockburn, having filled the station of confidential or principal sea-lord of the admiralty for more than seventeen years, and feeling that his opinion regarding the constitution of the board might sooner or later be deemed worthy of attention, stated that "he considered the present establishment of that board to be the most unsatisfactory and least efficient for its purpose that could have been devised."

What has been our experience? We had this board once, or something tantamount to it. As a friend said to me yesterday, "When we got rid of the old board, in 1842, we felt as Sinbad the sailor felt when the Old Man of the sea was lifted off his shoulders." It was an incubus on the Navy, and was so regarded by everybody, except some of the old post-captains who were members of the board. It was an inefficient organization, and was so considered by every one whose opinion was worth anything. Every nation that has had it, or anything like it, is attempting to abolish it. The Senator proposes that we now, in a time of war, when of all other times there should not be any division in council, adopt it, and make it part of our system, without consideration, without any report by a committee of this body in favor of it, and upon an appropriation bill.

The Navy Department, it will be remembered by members of this body, made estimates for large iron-clad ships, in obedience to the expressed wishes of the commercial cities on the Atlantic coast, and sent those estimates here. We refused to vote them. I refused my vote because I relied upon that system which is now proved to be the best naval system in the world. Everybody admits that for the purpose for which the monitors were originally constructed, the protection of our harbors, nothing exceeds them. Such is not only the judgment of naval men in this country, but of the commercial marine, and of foreign powers, many of whom are at this moment engaged in constructing them. I am not much of a believer in them as sea-going vessels; I would not recommend them as cruisers, but for harbor defense they are unapproached by anything yet invented by the ingenuity of man. Then we have the fastest sea-going naval vessels in the world. It is utter folly for us to undertake to build a navy with which we can compete with France and England in immense naval battles. That is not our policy. Our true policy is to protect ourselves at home, and then to sweep the commerce of our enemy from the sea; and the system that has been pursued by the Navy Department during the last four years, in building up the Navy we now have, is calculated to accomplish that purpose in a higher degree than any other plan that could possibly be devised.

92.—*To Mrs. Grimes.*

BURLINGTON, *April* 10, 1865.

I send you a copy of "Naval Warfare Ashore and Afloat," a pamphlet composed of the speeches made in the Senate and House of Representatives against Davis's and Wade's amendments. I do not know who got it up, but several copies have been sent to me. My speech is given the post of honor, though not entitled to it; for the other speeches were prepared, and mine was impromptu, and addressed entirely to the subject in hand. Some of the other speeches were orations, while mine, if anything, was a simple argument of the question directly in issue, and only received the corrections that you and I gave it one Sunday afternoon. Read Mr. Pike's speech, if you have not; for I think it a speech of great power and merit, and about as symmetrical and perfect in all its parts as any congressional speech that you have read for many a day. My remarks were the last made on the subject in the Senate, and should properly have been published last, as the other Senators alluded to me by name as being about to follow and close the debate; but I suppose you will discern this. I would have liked also to have the fact appear that after the protracted debate of two days there was but a single vote in favor of Wade's proposition, and forty-odd against it.

93.—*To Admiral Du Pont.*

WASHINGTON, *January* 2, 1865.

The prize law[1] of last winter was drawn up by Judge Sprague and R. H. Dana, Jr., of Boston, and passed the House of Repre-

[1] Approved, June 30, 1864.

sentatives as drafted by them with slight modifications. When it came to the Senate, believing that it would be suffered to sleep the sleep of death in the Naval Committee, I got it referred to the Judiciary Committee, and there intrusted to the guardianship of my friend Mr. Foster, of Connecticut, who soon reported it back with the recommendation that the House amendments be disagreed with, and that the bill be passed precisely as it came from Messrs. Sprague and Dana. This was done, the House concurred, and thus the bill became a law.

With reference to a bill to enlarge the boundaries of the State of Nevada, Mr. Grimes said, February 8th:

There are very grave questions connected with the subject of taking territory from Territories already in existence, and adding it to States whence we cannot hereafter reclaim it. If we take this territory from Utah and add it to Nevada, it cannot be taken from Nevada again. It may become important to erect a new Territory between Nevada and Utah. It is not for the interest of the States of the Northwest that the States to the west of us should be made as large as we are in the habit of making them, because it deprives us of our proper representation in this branch of Congress. This is a matter in which we are all interested, especially the cluster of States of which mine happens to be one, and which are destined to be intimately connected with all the States to the west of us. I want to see prosperous States built up there, and as many of them as possible. I want that section of the country to have its due proportion of influence and power in this branch of Congress, as well as in the other.

STONE FORTIFICATIONS.

In his speech of March 13, 1862, Mr. Grimes had expressed the opinion that the strongest stone fortifications could afford no obstruction to the entrance of iron-clad vessels-of-war into any of our harbors. In 1863 he voted against appropriations for such fortifications. Mr. Grimes said, February 24, 1865:

I rejoice that the Committee on Finance have come to the conclusion which I reached four years ago, and have recommended that the Senate shall not proceed with the costly business of continuing to make large forts. I am willing to admit of the distinguished gentleman at the head of the engineer corps that he is a very scientific, practical, and able man. I am willing to admit also that that corps is the *élite* of the Army; but it should be remembered that it is their profession to make forts, and that when you take away from them the appropriations, and the power to continue the exercise of that profession, their vocation is gone. I trust that the engineer corps are not like the Bourbons, who never forget and never learn anything.

Has not this war taught us something? Has not our experience at New Orleans taught us something? When the expedition against New Orleans was gotten up, there was but one man in the entire engineer corps who did not say that it was utterly impracticable for New Orleans to be taken. There was one single exception. It was General Barnard. Did not your wooden ships pass right by those fortifications, that were deemed by everybody almost, and especially by your engineer corps, as incapable of being passed by any kind of vessels, much less by wooden vessels?[1] Were we not told that Fort Morgan was the strongest fort on this continent? And what was the result when Farragut attacked it? How long was it able to resist wooden ships? What has been our experience with Fort Pulaski, also one of the strongest forts, it was said at the beginning of the war, that we had on this continent? How long was it able to resist the attack of members of this same engineer corps? I apprehend there is not a single fort now in the possession of the United States that is not capable of being reduced by our own vessels; partly growing out of the nature of the constructions, and partly out of the inability thus far to make projectiles and guns which are capable of attacking and destroying iron vessels.

It is not inappropriate for me to read in this connection a letter, published in the London *Post*, written by Mr. Blakeley, the inventor and maker of guns in England, and one of the most distinguished artisans of that country. It will be remembered that, after the taking of Fort Fisher, Admiral Porter made some remarks in

[1] The admirals of the French and British navies at the Balize told Farragut that they had been up to New Orleans, and that it was impossible for him to go, that it was one wall of fire; he replied simply that he was ordered up, that was all.—Mr. James W. Nye, *of Nevada, in the Senate, April* 7, 1868.

his report in regard to the value of the iron-clad monitors, which, he said, had been under the guns of Fort Fisher for five days at a distance of eight hundred yards, and had come out entirely, or almost entirely, uninjured; and he said that with the Monadnock and vessels of her class he would be willing to undertake to cross the ocean, or something tantamount to that, and reduce the towns on the coast of Great Britain. Captain Blakeley says:

"Now that Fort Fisher has fallen, there can be no indiscretion in my giving some information about its armament. The fact most instructive to us is that the fort contained not one gun powerful enough to sink an iron-clad ship. Most of the guns were more powerful than any gun mounted on any fort in England, or on any English ship, except one; yet they failed to injure the Federal fleet. It follows that that fleet could attack Portsmouth or Plymouth with more impunity than Fort Fisher, so far as artillery-fire is concerned."

Mr. Blakeley might further have said that two of the Armstrong guns, which bore the mark of the English arsenal upon them, the best pattern of Armstrong guns, were also in the armament of Fort Fisher.

We have the highest British authority for saying that those iron-clad vessels, if they crossed the Atlantic, were capable of attacking the fortifications of Portsmouth and Plymouth, that were designed to protect the largest navy-yards on the globe, navy-yards which contain more supplies by double than any navy-yard on the globe.

Now, what is the necessity for our going on and proceeding to build more of these forts?

What we want to successfully resist an iron-clad when it attempts to enter our harbor, is a gun mounted on a vessel that can come nearly in contact with the vessel that is attempting to make an encroachment upon us, and not on a fort a mile or a mile and a half away from the channel, as many of these forts are located. I do not think the old forts that have been built will ever be of any material service. It would be a wise expenditure to change them, so that we can use the proper kind of artillery in them; but I am unwilling to vote for prosecuting the construction of forts that were undertaken before the commencement of this war, and before the lessons that have been taught us by Fort Hindman and Fort

Morgan, and St. Philip and Jackson, and Macon and Sumter, had been learned by the nation. I thought there was one thing that was learned from the Crimean War by all nations; I thought Todleben had been a great instructor of people; and that the old necessity of fortifications was an exploded idea, and that, wherever earth could be obtained, earth was the proper material with which to make fortifications. I do not know whether we are prepared to abandon this old and effete system, that has been fastened on us for the last fifty years, but the time is not far distant. The first foreign war that this nation has will demonstrate that the old fortifications are valueless, as this war has demonstrated that our artillery was of no value; as the Mexican War demonstrated that the artillery with which our ships were mounted in 1812, by the side of the artillery we had in 1846, was of no comparative value.

§ 4.—*In the Thirty-ninth Congress.*—1865–1867.

94.—*To Asa D. Smith, D. D., President of Dartmouth College.*

WASHINGTON, *March* 10, 1865.

It has been my fortune to live the last twenty-nine years in a new country, where schools, colleges, charitable institutions, and internal improvements of all kinds, were unknown when I went there, and which I did my share to project, and now feel under obligations to sustain and expand. This, in a country where there is hardly any concentration of capital, is a heavy burden upon the comparatively few men on whom it falls. I say this, not because I wish to avail myself of it as an excuse for withholding any benefaction to Dartmouth College, but as a reason why I cannot give so much as my inclination prompts me to give.

95.—*To Mrs. Grimes.*

BURLINGTON, *April* 13, 1865.

Our place is more beautiful this spring than ever before; indeed, I know no more lovely spot anywhere, and my only want now is that you were here to enjoy it with me. We are having fine weather, with a prospect of an abundant supply of fruit. Cherries and pears are remarkably promising at present, and two or three vine-dressers, who have been here, say my grapes look better than anybody's about here.

Among other strange things that I have done, I gave this week six hundred and forty acres of land, worth I suppose about four to five thousand dollars, to the Congregational College at Grinnell. I thought I would administer thus far on my own estate. The college is overrun with students, and I fancied that as good use would be made of it in this as in any other way.

The whole amount realized from this spontaneous and unsolicited donation was six thousand and forty dollars. It constitutes the Grimes Foundation, and is "to be applied to the establishment and maintenance, in Iowa College, forever, of four scholarships, to be awarded by the trustees, on the recommendation of the Faculty, to the best scholars, and the most promising, in any department, who may need and seek such aid, and without any regard to the religious tenets, or opinions, entertained by any person seeking either of said scholarships." These terms were imposed by Mr. Grimes, and assumed, July 20, 1865, by the trustees. President Magoun says:

This foundation is the largest charity fund belonging to Iowa College. It has been, and it is to be, of great service to deserving young persons of both sexes. The first expression of special interest in the college made to me by Mr. Grimes was on the occasion of its removal from Davenport to Grinnell, in 1858. He said that a rural village is a far better place for such an institution than a business town. In 1864 the trustees made me a committee to secure an address from him at commencement. He replied to my solicitation that discoursing on education was entirely out of his range. Being further urged, and assured that he would be heard with interest on public questions, he said that senatorial duties so absorbed his time and strength as to render preparation for a commencement address impossible; he added, "but I can do something else of more service to the college than to make a harangue at commencement."

96.—*To Mrs. Grimes.*

Burlington, *April* 16, 1865.

Day before yesterday was a day of rejoicing and gladness in Burlington. The country people were in town in large numbers, and there were processions, torchlights, fireworks, illuminations, and every one seemed happy at the thought of a speedy and honorable peace.

That day of jubilee has been succeeded by two very sorrowful ones. About nine o'clock on Saturday, the intelligence reached us of the assassination of Mr. Lincoln, and the attempt upon Mr. Seward's life. Immediately the people began to assemble about the *Hawkeye* office, and soon Third Street became packed with people. And such expressions of horror, indignation, sorrow, and wonder, were never heard before. Shortly, some one began to decorate his house with the habiliments of mourning, and soon all the business part of the town, even the vilest liquor-dens, were shrouded with the outward signs of sorrow. All business was at once suspended, and not resumed during the day, but every one waited for further intelligence from Washington.

This day has been remarkably pleasant, and every one went to church. I went early, and found our church packed full, so that it was with difficulty I found a seat. Many were there whom I never suspected of ever going to church before, among them many German Turners; and many were turned away.

I was kept busy last night trying to prevent the destruction of a foolish woman's store, who, it was said, expressed her joy at Mr. Lincoln's murder. Had she been a man, so much was the old Adam aroused in me, I would not have uttered a word to save her.

I am full of forebodings about Johnson. He is loyal enough, but he is a man of low instincts, vindictive, violent, and of bad habits. His course will depend much upon the hands he falls into at the outset. I hope he will be equal to the occasion, and prove to be a good President. The performance of the fourth of last month was not a very flattering augury of the future.

Mr. Lincoln is to be hereafter regarded as a saint. All his foibles, and faults, and shortcomings, will be forgotten, and he will be looked upon as the Moses who led the nation through a four years' bloody war, and died in sight of peace. Never did men make a greater mistake than did his assassins, if they desired lenity and favorable terms, when they slew him, and attempted to slay Seward; for they had more to expect from them than from any men, indeed, from all men connected with the public councils in the North. Mr. Lincoln was the most amiable, kind-hearted man I ever knew, and would not, if he could avoid it, punish his most malignant enemy.

If I am not greatly deceived, they have got a "Tartar" in his stead.

April 19*th.*—We have four days of universal and heartfelt sorrow and mourning; business has been nearly suspended. There was a meeting in Union Hall on Monday evening, and, although very rainy, the hall was full. I presided, and spoke a few minutes, and was followed by Mr. Salter, Father Donelan, and Mr. Darwin. At twelve o'clock to-day there were religious services in all the churches, and I hear that all were crowded; Mr. Salter's certainly was. In the afternoon there was an immense procession through the streets, ending its march at the hall, where as many entered as could, leaving a large part out-of-doors. I again presided, and opened and closed with a few remarks. There was not a business-house, or a drinking-house even, open during the day, nor an inebriated man to be seen in the town. No Sunday was ever so universally kept sacred in Burlington. The real grief does not seem to be confined to any party or sect. Everybody seems ready to canonize Mr. Lincoln's memory. If there ever was a man who was happy in his death, that man was Mr. Lincoln. He is for all time to enjoy the reputation of carrying the country successfully through a four years' terrible civil war, and is to have none of the odium and hate that are sure to be engendered by the rival schemes and rival parties for the adjustment of our troubles.

97.—*To Mrs. Grimes.*

BURLINGTON, *May* 15, 1865.

We have had a cold and backward spring, but the weather is now intensely hot. Tell M—— that I have the best crop of onions on her garden-plat that I ever raised, and beets ditto. Tell her also that we have had a genuine mocking-bird in the garden, and the noisiest fellow I ever listened to. He is quite tame, and sits on the ground and on the grape-stakes to sing, as well as on the trees. I have a nest of turtle-doves in a fir-tree, with two young doves in it, besides any amount of thrushes and robins. So she will see that we do not suffer for the want of music. I suppose V—— told you that *Moses* was christened yesterday. We are about done with the house repairing and cleaning, and I am heartily glad of it, I assure you.

98.—*To Hon. W. P. Fessenden, Portland, Maine.*

BURLINGTON, *July* 19, 1865.

Your letter leads me to think that you may possibly be inclined to come West, though I am quite skeptical on the subject. I do hope you will come; I think you ought to come, not for your own pleasure, or the pleasure of your friends alone, but as a leading public man you ought to see this country for yourself. I am only a few hours' ride from Chicago, but in a far more quiet, respectable, moral, healthy, comfortable place. I cannot promise you the luxuries of a commercial metropolis on the seacoast, but I will feed you on grapes if you are here in September, and intoxicate you with their pure juice. I have between seven hundred and eight hundred vines loaded down with most promising grapes, though we have much wet weather, which is not propitious.

Of course, I always give a hearty support to the Administration, as in duty bound, but we will reserve our quarrel about the Navy Department, the Administration, and Charles Sumner, until you come here. I prefer to fight you in my own barn-yard. Mrs. Grimes says she shall never forgive you, if you do not come to see us, and spend at least two weeks with us.

99.—*To E. H. Stiles, Ottumwa.*

BURLINGTON, *September* 14, 1865.

I am astonished to learn, as I do by your letter of the 12th inst., that any one has asserted or believed for one moment that I do not fully, freely, and as enthusiastically as I am capable of doing it, support the entire Republican ticket in the pending canvass. You say the report is that I am indifferent to the result "on account of the uncalled-for and unwise action of the Union convention on the suffrage question." I certainly did regard that action as uncalled for and impolitic, and had I been a member of the convention I would have opposed the introduction into the platform of any new issue upon any subject, however just I might believe the principle to be. I would have opposed it because I believe that there has been no time during the last four years when it was more necessary that the Union party of the nation should present an unbroken front and stand as a unit, than at the present moment, and I would have done nothing, consented to nothing, that would have a tendency to repel a single voter from a support of the Union party, which is the support of the Union itself. I believe every vote withdrawn at this time from the support of the Union ticket withdraws just that much moral support from the Administration, and that that support is just as necessary to the Government in the present crisis as it was necessary to support our armies when in the field.

The very fact that in my view the convention erred by introducing a local issue into the canvass when the minds of the people are very properly engrossed by the transcendently great national issues pressing upon them, so far from begetting "indifference," would give me much greater anxiety as to the result of the election, and would call forth a corresponding exertion, did not I know that the people of Iowa thoroughly understand the questions before them, and cannot be diverted from their support of the Government by any side-issue like this of negro suffrage in this State.

There is not an intelligent man in the State who does not fully comprehend all the subjects legitimately embraced in this canvass.

The Union party seek simply to fulfill in good faith their obligations assumed during the war, and to secure to the country as the fruits of four years' struggle permanent unity, peace, and prosperity.

We all know that the Democratic party desire and intend to coalesce with the returned rebels from the South. By that means, if they can succeed in distracting the supporters of the Government and secure a few Northern States, they hope to obtain control of the Government, and then will follow the assumption of the rebel debt, the restoration of slavery under a less odious name, and the return of the leaders of the rebellion to power. It was to this end that the farce was enacted a few weeks ago at Des Moines of nominating a Soldiers' ticket BY THE DEMOCRATIC PARTY.

But of this folly it is hardly worth while to speak. I have neither seen nor heard of a man who is likely to be deceived by it. It is only calculated to make the actors in it ridiculous, and its only final result will be to add one disappointed man to the Democratic party.

No, my dear sir, there never was a time in the history of the Government when it was more incumbent upon every good citizen to support the Union ticket, whatever may be his intentions on the subject of universal suffrage, than now; and if I believed that there was the slightest doubt about the result, though I am admonished by my physician that I can no longer safely speak out-of-doors, as I should generally be compelled to do, I would at once enter personally into the canvass, and use what strength I have to urge upon the people the importance of the contest. But there is no need of it. The people will not be deceived or misled on this subject. The jugglery at Des Moines, when Colonel Benton received the nomination of the men who, during the last four years, have thrown every possible impediment in the way of the Union cause, was too transparent to deceive any one.

Mr. Grimes received the honorary degree of Doctor of Laws this year from Dartmouth College, and also from Iowa College. President Smith wrote to him:

The honor is no great matter to you, honored as you have been by the people and by your associates in the councils of the nation, save as it serves to brighten the links which bind you to your *Alma Mater*. As showing her appreciation of your course, you will value it.

Appointed upon the Joint Committee of Fifteen on Reconstruction, December 21st, and upon the sub-committee to inquire into the condition of Tennessee, he gave anxious and assiduous attention for months to those matters, and aided in developing the clear and conclusive views of the subject, which Mr. Fessenden presented in the final report of the committee, June 8, 1866.

Upon a proposition to grant one million acres of public lands for the benefit of public schools in the District of Columbia, Mr. Grimes gave his views on the expediency of land-grants for such purposes, February 7th:

If this bill shall pass, there will not be a great many schools supported by the funds that will be created by it. This land will not net ten cents an acre to the District. That has been the experience of all to whom grants of this kind have been made.

The Senator from Massachusetts (Mr. Wilson) bases this grant, first, on the poverty of the city of Washington. In regard to that, the Senator is mistaken. According to the assessment returns, this is one of the wealthiest cities in the United States. The poor people of whom he speaks, who have been brought here as mechanics from the North and West, have really the control of the city government. Why do they not levy a tax on the valuable property that is located here? The truth is, not that the people are poor, but that they are not willing to tax the property that is subject to taxation, for the purpose of educating their children; and no grant of land, and no scrip that the Senator can get us to authorize to be issued, is going to improve the people of the District in that regard. Let him turn out as a missionary, and lecture the people in their various wards on the necessity of education, and when he has brought them up to the standard that will justify us in putting money into their hands for this object, let him ask for an appropriation of money out of the Treasury. That we can grant; but the indirect way proposed, while it may be a slight advantage to the District, is destined to be a great disadvantage to the new States.

The Senator says that we have been in the habit of making grants of land to the Western States for education; but they have been granted upon a different principle. The Government had vast tracts of land, subdivided into townships and sections. You wanted to sell those lands. You said to the citizens of the North and East, "If you will go West and buy those lands, we will set apart every sixteenth section in each township for the purpose of educating your children." But here you propose to grant to the city of Washington lands or scrip, which is the same thing, for the purpose of establishing schools in this District. You might with equal propriety issue scrip to support the schools in the city of Boston.

This scrip will, in a short time, find its way at a low rate into the pockets of the wealthy capitalists, and be located on a township or several townships, and that land will remain for ten, twenty, or twenty-five years without a single occupant. That is the danger and damage to the States where this land will be located. I am not speaking of my State—her public lands are exhausted—but for the other States and Territories. We have been through this experience. We have in some portions of our State almost whole counties taken up under the land-warrant system in this way by non-residents, preventing the settlement and development of the State. I am arguing for the purpose of preventing other States and Territories from having the same experience. I do not want to see them put through the same process.

The Senator from Maine (Mr. Morrill) says that he has been appalled at the number of propositions to grant lands for wagon-roads, railroads, etc. I think he will bear me witness that I have voted against as many of them, and have been as urgent against them, as any one in this body. I have opposed nearly all of them, and I think it exceedingly bad policy for the Government to grant so large a portion of them. I want these lands saved for the purpose of enabling his constituents and mine to go upon them and occupy them as *bona-fide* settlers. That is what the Government ought to use them for. Nearly all the grants of land to railroads and wagon-roads find their way into the hands of rich capitalists, and, in eighteen months or two years after this grant is made, the scrip will be held by the wealthy men of the country, and the tendency will be to exclude settlers.

The Senator says that this principle is sustained by innumerable precedents. He quotes one, the Agricultural College bill, and none other, so far as I know, except the grant of one township in Florida over forty years ago to the State of Kentucky, for a deaf and dumb asylum. The precedent in the case of the Agricultural College bill I do not think worthy of being followed; and one of the first subjects that I heard under discussion when I came to Washington was a bill, introduced at the instance of the State of Florida, to compel the State of Kentucky to sell that land. The argument was, that here was an entire township in one of their best counties, that was owned by the State of Kentucky, but with not a single *bona-fide* settler upon it. It retarded the settlement and prevented the development of the country.

AGAINST THE ADMISSION OF COLORADO AS A STATE.

With reference to the admission of Colorado into the Union, Mr. Grimes said, March 13th:

There is probably no State more deeply interested in having a strong and prosperous State in Colorado than Iowa. She is destined to be one of our neighbors. I presume that a larger portion of the population of Colorado emigrated from Iowa than from any other State; and I apprehend we are more intimately connected with her, and the people of Iowa are more thoroughly acquainted with the history and condition of Colorado, than the people of any other State. Hence nothing would afford me greater pleasure, if I thought I could do so in justice to other States and in justice to myself, than to vote for her admission. But entertaining the opinions I do, believing that such a vote is calculated to lead to disastrous consequences in the future, I am constrained, notwithstanding the interest my constituents, I am aware, feel in the admission of Colorado, to vote in opposition to this bill.

The simple objection that I have is that Colorado has not population enough, and that nothing could be more injurious to the people themselves than to permit her to erect herself into a State, with a population of only from fifteen to twenty-five thousand.

I have had about as much experience in Territorial life as almost any one else. It has so happened to me that I have lived in three different Territories, under three different Territorial governments, although I have resided in the same town all the time. Iowa came into the Union upon the old theory, which it was supposed we were always going to adhere to, that no State should be admitted until she had the population required to send a representative to Congress. We had been in a Territorial condition for twelve or fourteen years, and had a vast amount of real estate subject to taxation for supporting the government; yet the first thing that the people of the State of Iowa were compelled to do was to go into the money market of New York and borrow money at the enormous rate of ten per cent., in those days, for defraying the necessary expenses of the government. Gentlemen who have not lived in a new State cannot conceive of the constant drain that is made upon everybody who emigrates to one of these States. Dwellings, schoolhouses, churches, roads, charitable institutions, must be provided, as well as the ordinary State, county, and township taxes paid; and the result is, that the people of a new State, with the population there is in Colorado, and with comparatively no real estate to tax, nothing but personal property, will be oppressed with taxation. If I were a citizen of Colorado I would remonstrate and protest against the admission of the State under all circumstances, until there were at least one hundred thousand people to support the State government. I cannot conceive of anything more injurious to the people of that Territory than to allow her with her small population to come into the Union, and be compelled to pay her own expenses from this time forward.

In 1864 the vote of Colorado on the adoption of the constitution was 6,192: for, 1,520; against, 4,672. There was another election, September 5, 1865, and the total vote was 5,895, less than in 1864, and the majority in favor of the adoption of the State constitution was only 155. Now it is seriously proposed here that we shall admit a State into this Union which, in an exciting election, when all the office-seekers, who expect to be senators and representatives and judges and governors, are arrayed on one side, and are using their influence to bring men to the polls, and when the tax-payers, who are conscious that they are to be oppressed with the burdens of taxation, if they come into the Union, are arrayed on the other, can only poll 5,895 votes ; and that a mining State, where there is a vast preponderance of males over females. I confess that it strikes me as the sublimity of impudence for the State to come here and ask to be admitted into the Union, and be entitled to the same power and influence in this body as the State of Ohio or New York or Pennsylvania.

If I vote to admit Colorado to-day, is there any reason why I shall not vote to admit Nebraska to-morrow, with twenty-six thousand people? If I agree to admit these two Territories, is there any reason why I shall not the day after admit another Territory, Montana? Let me ask Senators if they are prepared to let all the political power and influence of this country be carried up to these mountains, to be wielded by a few miners and men of the most transitory description of population. I am not prepared to do it. I do not believe that it is the part of wisdom and statesmanship, notwithstanding the local interests of my own State might possibly be advanced by admitting this Territory and the adjacent Territory of Nebraska.

I did not vote for the enabling act for Colorado. The chairman of the Committee on Territories (Mr Wade) will bear me witness that I have opposed all these enabling acts. I have always told him, and everybody around me, that I thought nothing could be more deleterious to the interests of these Territories, and nothing more jeopardize the interests of the country, than to hold out the idea that they could be admitted into this Union, having the power of the largest States in this body, with a population of twenty or thirty thousand. The sum and substance of it is, whether or not the Senate is prepared by its solemn vote to create a kind of rotten-borough State in the Rocky Mountains; I mean, a State that a powerful, rich, and influential man can carry in his pocket, or which he can control by that which he does carry in his pocket.

April 19th.—Nor am I willing to indorse this constitution of Colorado to-day, with a perpetual exclusion of the colored people of that State from voting, and then to-morrow undertake to confer the elective franchise upon colored people in the seceded States. I do not consider myself bound by any past action of Congress to give so inconsistent a vote as that; and never, so long as I occupy a seat on this floor, will I consent to do it.

This bill was rejected, March 13th, yeas 14, nays 21; reconsidered and passed, April 25th; vetoed by President Johnson, May 15th.

Supporting a bill to prohibit a register as an American vessel to any ship that had been transferred during the rebellion to a foreign flag, except by act of Congress in each particular case, Mr. Grimes said, February 7, 1866:

We ought to impose a penalty upon ship-owners who have transferred their vessels to a neutral flag. If you do not, when you have another war, the first day that war is declared, all the shipping of the United States will be transferred; and how are you going to reënforce your navy, or secure vessels to keep up a blockade, such as you kept up during the recent war? There ought to be a penalty imposed on these men, who have shirked the payment of the extra insurance which the honest and patriotic ship-owners have paid, and who, having enjoyed the advantages of foreign vessels in the carrying-trade, and filled their pockets with British gold, now come and ask to be put upon the same foundation with the loyal ship-owners, who have been paying this insurance during the last five years. It is due to the shipping interests of the country and to the patriotism of the country that a bill of this kind should pass.

THE SEARCH FOR MISSING SOLDIERS.

Mr. Grimes interested himself in the search for missing soldiers that was undertaken at the close of the war by Miss Clara Barton, and, after personal examination of her work, commended it in the Senate as most valuable to the cause of humanity and the country, and advocated an appropriation to reimburse her for what she had expended, and to aid her further search. He said, February 5th, and March 5th:

The Government owes it no less to the brave men who lie in unknown graves than to the anxious and longing friends in whom hope is not yet wholly dead, to see that no stone is left unturned to complete the personal record of all its preservers. With suitable facilities, some trace may be gained of four-fifths of all who have disappeared amid the quicksands of war. The work must be vigorously prosecuted, as the sources of information are rapidly wasting away by disease and premature decay. Miss Barton was connected with the Sanitary Commission, and was stationed at Annapolis. A great many persons came there in grief and trouble in search of their friends, expecting them on the ships that brought our returned prisoners from Belle Isle and Andersonville. A few were successful in finding their friends, but a large portion were not. They were unable to ascertain whether they were dead, or whether they might expect them on any other transport-ship, and there was no system by which the facts in regard to those missing soldiers could be obtained. Miss Barton devised a scheme herself, and undertook to perform that labor. Whenever the missing soldier's name was handed to her, she obtained the number of his regiment and company, and all the facts in connection with him. She then published lists of missing soldiers, first beginning in a small way, as she was able to write them herself, or procure assistance, and posting them upon barrack-doors and conspicuous places about Annapolis, so as to attract the attention of our returned prisoners. The work greatly enlarged until it was impossible to post them all in this way. It was soon learned that she was in search of those missing soldiers, and letters began to pour in upon her from all sections of the country. I am told (I judge the statement true from what I saw) that she has at this time unanswered nearly six thousand letters from the parents, wives, and relatives in one degree or another of missing soldiers. Her means are exhausted, and the question arose among the people who were interested in the prosecution of this work, What is the best way to carry it forward? When consulted by the chairman of the Committee on Military Affairs (Mr. Wilson, of Massachusetts) as to my opinion, I thought it would be better to enlarge this appropriation a few thousand dollars, and let Miss Barton go on in her own way precisely as she has been doing. She deserves well of Congress, and has accomplished a most humane and excellent work.

AGAINST AN INCREASE OF THE ARMY.

The House of Representatives have killed their army bill, and I congratulate the House and the country. If they will now only kill the army bill we sent them, they will have accomplished an object equally as great and good, for we now have a large army, fifty thousand men, one-half more than we can keep full, and I know of no necessity for increasing the army.—*May 4th.*

Upon a resolution to publish a roll of all volunteer officers in the Army during the rebellion, Mr. Grimes remarked, May 7th:

I would not give a straw for a mere roster of the officers. That indicates nothing. It was not the officers that fought our battles and won our victories. I would like to see the gradations by which those men went up from privates to become officers, which is exhibited by the Adjutant-General's report of my State, showing that a very large proportion of the men who went into the army as officers ceased very soon to be such, and that the men who went in the humblest positions very soon became the commanders, not only of their companies, but of regiments and brigades. We have a report in my State that embraces officers, privates, musicians, everybody connected with the service, showing when he entered, when he went out, what offices he filled during the time he was in service, what has become of him since, where he was born, and in what place he enlisted.

Mr. Grimes regarded it as one of the great sources of corruption in the management of Indian affairs that the Indian agents were usually partners with the Indian traders. He knew a trader to pay an agent twelve thousand dollars for the purpose of being selected as an Indian trader. He proposed to do away with this, and allow the Indians to trade with any loyal citizen, of good moral character, who should comply with the regulations prescribed for intercourse with the Indians.

Explaining his course with reference to some private claims against the Government, Mr. Grimes said, April 11th:

Ever since I have been a member of this body I have had only one rule on these matters; that is, never to vote for putting private bills upon appropriation bills, or agree to make any kind of an omnibus bill, by which a bad claim shall be carried through Congress on the back of a good one.

100.—*To Mrs. Grimes.*

WASHINGTON, *April* 6, 1866.

To-day has been devoted to eulogies on Mr. Foot. Some of them were very good—one, that of Mr. Fessenden, the best I ever heard, and there have now been nine Senators buried since I have been here. Fessenden spoke with much feeling, and his remarks made a very deep impression on all. There was a marked contrast in this respect between his effort and that of Mr. Sumner. The latter gentleman pleased no one. His eulogy was considered as a strained effort to appear learned, and he introduced topics that might as well have been avoided on such an occasion. Fessenden was dissatisfied with his last paragraph—the apostrophe to Mr. Foot—and submitted the question to me whether or not he should omit it. I decided for its retention, and it was delivered, and will be published. I was invited by Judge Poland to say something, but declined, believing that there were enough to speak.

This is the paragraph: "Admirable Senator! patriotic citizen! dear and cherished friend! this scene of your many labors will know you no more, but long will your memory dwell in these halls. This marble pile, bearing the impress of your watchful care, is one of your monuments. Its massive pillars will stand erect, giving their testimony to our country's grandeur, long after we and generations yet to come shall have passed like shadows upon the water; yet he, who like yourself shall have performed his duty in life, and died with a Christian's hope, will survive when all these columns shall be lost to sight in the accumulated dust of ages."

The chaplain of the Senate, Byron Sunderland, D. D., in a funeral discourse over the bier of Mr. Foot, mentioned the following among other incidents of his last hours:

At this time Senator Fessenden approached him, to whom he eagerly stretched out his hand and said: "My dear friend Fessenden, the man by whose side I have sat so long, whom I have regarded as the model of a statesman and parliamentary leader, on whom I have leaned, and to whom I have looked more than to any other living man for guidance and direction in public affairs, the strong tie which has so long bound us together must now be severed. But, my dear Fessenden, if there is memory after death, that memory will be active, and I shall call to mind the whole of our intercourse on earth." The Senator thus addressed, too much affected to reply in words, stooped over and kissed the brow of his dying friend, and turned away in silence.

Afterward Senator Grimes approached him, to whom he said: "Ah, my dear friend Grimes, have you come to see me? I have been through a terrible ordeal the last six weeks." Then noticing that all were deeply affected, he added: "Do not cease to talk; these things cannot alarm me." Then taking the Senator by the hand, he said: "Yes, I know the man, a man about whom there is no deceit; with whom neither in private nor in public was there a deceitful thought or a deceitful word." Then recurring to scenes of the past, in which he had mingled with his friend, as if soliloquizing, he added, "He was one of the first and last and best of my associates, and there was no mistake about him."

101.—*To Mrs. Grimes.*

WASHINGTON, *April* 16, 1866.

To-morrow is the anniversary of freedom in this District, and is to be celebrated by the colored people by processions, displays, etc. The President has invited, I hear, the procession to give him a call, and they will do so. The indications are that the President has become satisfied that he has gone too fast and too far, and is now inclined to cultivate the friendship of the radicals. I am inclined to think that there is something in this report.

Allison and I went to hear Mr. Hale preach. He had a full house, and preached a good sermon, as he usually does, I guess.

The "Central Directory"[1] meet to-morrow, and we hope soon to agree and report upon a plan of reconstruction. I regret that I am one of the committee, but I do not know that I ought to shrink from my share of the very grave responsibility imposed on us.

[1] "An irresponsible, central Directory."—*Speech of President Johnson, February 22d.*

April 30th.—We have at last agreed upon a plan of reconstruction, which will be reported to-morrow, and which, so far as I can learn, is quite acceptable to our friends. It is not exactly what any of us wanted; but we were each compelled to surrender some of our individual preferences in order to secure anything, and by doing so became unexpectedly harmonious. You will observe that the proposition I offered was adopted as the second section, embracing the whole question of representation, negroes, etc., etc.

Mr. Fessenden is able to be out again, and was with the Committee of Fifteen yesterday. I heard Dr. Bellows preach a good sermon this morning, and intended to go to hear him this evening, but was prevented by company.

May 8th.—It is the usual wrangle and jangle in Congress. Thaddeus Stevens attacked Sumner to-day, because of his opposition to the first proposed constitutional amendment, which Sumner was instrumental in defeating. I did not hear him, but of course he was severe, as he always is.

NON-INTERFERENCE WITH MATTERS BELONGING TO THE STATES.

Upon a resolution to cause a rigid quarantine against the Asiatic cholera, Mr. Grimes said, May 8th:

I do not recognize the obligation on the part of Congress, that because certain physicians in the city of New York believe it necessary that there should be a cordon established in order to keep the cholera away from this country, therefore we shall be justified in abandoning all the powers of Congress into the hands of a commission, and in conferring upon the Secretary of the Treasury, the Secretary of War, and the Secretary of the Navy, all control over the military arm of the Government and over the Treasury. The bill does not require that the Government shall adopt the quarantine officers of the State of New York. They are to be new appointees. We are to have another batch of office-holders, innumerable in number, if extended uniformly over the country.

I have not any such fear of the cholera as to induce me to vote for a bill like this. I believe that it will be attended with worse consequences to the country than the most malignant type of cholera that ever prevailed upon this continent. As my friend near me says, one thing would certainly result—it would give the cholera to the Treasury of the United States. It may perhaps be owing to the fact that I have no very great fears of the cholera, having lived in a town with it three years, that I am not willing to break down all the barriers around the Treasury, which some gentlemen seem disposed to do. In my locality we are familiar with this disease. We know that it has no such terrors as it seems to have to gentlemen who are not familiar with it, and we do not want to have our liberty restrained, nor our privilege of locomotion, nor the Treasury afflicted, by any such bill. I trust that the time has gone by when we are going to be called on to legislate in the manner this bill proposes. During the war we drew to ourselves here, as the Federal Government, authority which had been considered doubtful by all, and denied by many of the statesmen of this country. That time, it seems to me, has ceased, and ought to cease. Let us go back to the original condition of things, and allow the States to take care of themselves, as they have been in the habit of taking care of themselves.

THE NAVAL ACADEMY.

Continuing to cherish a generous care for the Naval Academy, Mr. Grimes advocated Annapolis as its proper location, against proposals for removing it to Newport, Rhode Island, or to the vicinity of Newport News, James River, and secured appropriations for enlarging the grounds, for introducing water from the Annapolis water-works, for establishing a foundery and machine-shop, to afford instruction and practice in naval engineering, for a new chapel, and for tablets upon its walls, in memory of persons belonging to the naval service who have fallen in the defense of the country. He said, March 20th :

The Secretary of the Navy has proposed to take the Academy down to the waters of James River; to which I have told him that I was unalterably opposed. He has assigned various reasons why it ought not to be continued at the present place. I believe that nearly every one of those reasons is fallacious. I do not think that he has exhibited his usual good judgment in proposing to take the Academy from Annapolis, and carry it down to a country where there is nobody, remote from all civilization, where there is not a village within thirty miles, I believe; and although I am in the habit, as a general thing, of concurring with him, for I think that his judgment on most things is correct, yet upon this subject I am convinced that he is decidedly in error. I have no sort of partiality for Annapolis. I think I am capable of looking at this question of the location of the Academy with great disinterestedness. I believe that it is now located where it ought to be; in the proper climate, in the right location, central to our country, and near the seat of Government. The grounds are not quite so capacious as they ought to be, but we have made provision to enlarge them. We have expended there more than nine hundred thousand dollars. I do not think it is the dictate of economy to throw away the money, and appoint a roving commission to travel over the country to see if they cannot find a place where they can expend a similar sum for the same purpose.

Mr. Grimes held that seventeen was the proper limit of age for boys to be admitted to the Academy, and said, May 24th:

There happened to be a likely boy who was a little over the age of seventeen, and could not be admitted. I believe it was purely through the influence exerted by the friends of that young man that we changed the period to eighteen years. He was admitted, went to the Academy, was there three months, and was unable to make any progress in his studies, had not any adaptation to the profession, and was dismissed; and we have now upon the statute-book a limit of eighteen in place of seventeen years, when every naval officer concurs in the opinion that the shorter number of years is the proper age for boys to go into the naval service.

THE MONITORS.

Of the progress of improvement in the construction of monitors, Mr. Grimes gave the following explanation, April 17, 1866:

Iron vessels have been built before, but no such vessels as we have built; and almost all of the attachments have been compelled to be of a different character from what was known before. In the first place, it required a good deal of time and ingenuity, and many experiments, to determine the best character of a rudder to apply to these monitors. Then there were constant changes made, in order to obviate the defects which were found to exist in the original monitor, so as to prevent the great overhanging, which was doubtless the cause of the sinking of the original monitor. Then it was exceedingly difficult to arrange the compass; and many experiments were made, and considerable delay occasioned in consequence of the variation caused by the action of the iron on the deck of the vessel upon the compass. They finally devised a way of raising the compass on a high staff, and having a card on which it could be read down in front.

If the Senator (Mr. Guthrie) will go with me to the navy-yard, I will show him two monitors, one built in 1862, and another one built recently, the Tonawanda; and he would hardly suppose that the original monitor was the prototype and original of the perfect vessel that is now lying at the wharf. These changes have been going on gradually. Every battle that has been fought, every storm that they have encountered, every experienced and capable man who has commanded one of them, has made some suggestive changes; and when these changes have met the approval of the proper advisory officers of the Navy Department, although a vessel might be upon the stocks, availing themselves of the clause in the contracts which authorized them to change the specifications, they have done so. Manifestly it was the interest and the duty of the Government to make such changes. I am happy in being able to say, what is my own honest conviction, that we have to-day the most perfect iron vessels in the world; and they have all sprung out of a defective original vessel, and been perfected through those changes which have been gradually going on in the various ship-yards, either private ship-yards or our own.

I rose not for the purpose of entering into a discussion, but simply not to let it be inferred that I believed there had been any improper blundering in regard to these iron-clads. I know that the Navy Department have made mistakes, egregious mistakes in regard to one class of vessels. I am not here to defend those mistakes, but I am here to defend every improvement and change that has been made toward making a perfect ship-of-war, which I think we have done.

Mr. Grimes made the following remarks with reference to the Assistant Secretary of the Navy, Hon. G. V. Fox, May 15th:

When the resolution congratulating the Emperor of Russia upon his escape from assassination was adopted by Congress, it was suggested by the Secretary of State, and by some other persons connected with the Administration, that Mr. Fox should be deputed to carry the congratulatory resolution to Russia; it was also suggested to him that he should withdraw his resignation as Assistant Secretary of the Navy, for the reason that it would be more acceptable to the Russian Government if he went in his official capacity as second in authority in the Navy Department than if he went as a private individual. Mr. Fox proposes to start in the Miantonomoh, an iron-clad ship, a class of improved impregnable vessels, for which this country is indebted to him more than to any other person, except Mr. Ericsson; the best iron-clad ship, I believe, in the world, and which we hope, and he believes, will safely cross the Atlantic. I believe the appearance of that ship in European waters would have a greater tendency to promote peace between the nations of Europe and this country than all the diplomats we shall be likely to send to Europe during the next thirty years.

In explaining a bill to regulate the appointment of officers in the Navy, Mr. Grimes said, June 14th:

Heretofore, since the time of Decatur, who was promoted over the heads of other officers for his distinguished merit, all promotions, with the exception of six, I believe, have been made by regular gradation. Captain Worden, Commodore Rodgers, Lieutenant Cushing, Commodore Rowan, Admiral Porter, perhaps one or two more, were promoted over the heads of persons who stood before them, for distinguished merit. This bill proposes to authorize a few persons to be promoted over the heads of those who have not distinguished themselves. The purpose is to recognize the valuable services of officers who during four years have been engaged, some of them, almost in constant battle, and to enable them to be promoted, even at the expense of others who have not seen any service during that time.

Section seven provides that the annual compensation of the admiral shall be ten thousand dollars a year. I need not say that that provision was intended for Admiral Farragut, to give him a corresponding rank to that which is contemplated to be bestowed upon General Grant. These ranks are relative. A bill has been passed by the House of Representatives, making General Grant a full general; and then it was proposed that Admiral Farragut should be made a full admiral. He is now on leave, and gets five thousand dollars a year. The officer in the Army of corresponding rank gets between seventeen and eighteen thousand dollars. It is proposed by this bill to make an admiral, and give him all the time a salary of ten thousand dollars. I think the country will say that if there be any man who is really entitled to ten thousand dollars a year salary it is Admiral Farragut.

102.—*To Mrs. Grimes.*

WASHINGTON, *May* 11, 1866.

The House has passed the constitutional amendment by an unprecedented majority. We take the matter up in the Senate next week, will have a long debate, possibly make an amendment, and I think finally pass the measure by the constitutional majority of two-thirds. Debate rages in the Senate on the same old subjects, rehashed to us by the same orators.

May 23d.—Mr. Fox and wife left the city this morning. He expects to sail for Europe in a few days in the Miantonomoh. The selection of him, by a unanimous vote of the Senate, and by a large majority in the House of Representatives, to carry the congratulatory resolutions of Congress to the Emperor of Russia, was a fine culmination of his public services, and ought to be regarded by him as very complimentary.

LETTER OF HON. G. V. FOX, ASSISTANT SECRETARY OF THE NAVY, TO MRS. GRIMES.

BOSTON, MASS., *May* 27, 1866.

I have left Washington forever as a residence, and only await the cessation of a storm to cross the Atlantic in a monitor. There is no tie severed which causes me more regret than that which has existed between Mr. Grimes and myself. Besides the esteem which every one has for him, I have felt confidence and courage, leaning upon him, and not only have defied the public enemies, but by his aid have triumphed over them. He has known, better than any other person, my thoughts, feelings, and actions, and his good opinion and yours are the result of such knowledge. It is to be esteemed by such friends, that I find more solace than any reward

Government could bestow. Wishing you both every happiness, I bid you farewell.

103.—*To Mrs. Grimes.*

WASHINGTON, *May* 26, 1866.

Day before yesterday, I went to Annapolis with Governor Morrill, of Maine, and came back last night. The examination is going on there, and among the examiners is Mr. Scammon, of Chicago, who was appointed at my instance. Two years ago he was an examiner at West Point, and I wanted a comparison between the two schools, drawn by some one in whose judgment I had confidence. I am happy to be able to say that he gives the preference most decidedly to the Naval Academy. His opinion is that, while the instruction is quite as thorough and critical as at West Point, there is as much again of common-sense here. It is quite evident that a very great improvement has been made in the school within the last year, and Porter turns out to be, what I believed he would not be, an excellent superintendent. He has secured the confidence and affection of the young men, and they have made unprecedented progress since they were placed under his charge. I need not say that I was highly pleased with all that I saw and heard of the school, and do not regret anything that I have done for it in the past, and that has been a good deal, as you know.

We shall, I think, get through the reconstruction measures this week without any difficulty.

104.—*To Mrs. Grimes.*

WASHINGTON, *June* 6, 1866.

I twice made the attempt yesterday to write, but was so sleepy and exhausted by my trip to West Point and back that I was actually unable to do it. I was away three days and nights, and had sleep only one of the three nights. I made with friends two trips through the Central Park, when in New York, and was delighted with what I saw. It is certainly the most beautiful place I have ever seen, and I judge it is destined to be, when the trees are grown, and the work completed, the most beautiful place in the world.

I am satisfied from what I saw and heard at West Point that the Naval Academy is the superior institution of the two. The truth is, I came away rather disgusted with the Military Academy people, though Iowa has four very bright, accomplished young fellows there, who stand very high in their classes; young Griffith is in point of scholarship the third in his class, and young Hoxie the first in his class.

June 11*th.*—You learned long ago of the passage of the reconstruction measures. I am happy to be able to say that they meet with general approval, and we feel much more confident, and stronger, since their passage than before. The final report of the committee, which was drawn by Mr. Fessenden, is regarded by everybody here, I think, as a very able paper; the ablest, in my opinion, submitted to Congress as a report, or in the form of a speech, since I have been in the Senate.

June 18*th.*—Fessenden is very poorly, and it seems to me as though his prediction that he will be the next to go is likely to be true. I have made the Navy officers all glad by passing a bill for their benefit, but I fear it may meet with trouble in the House of Representatives.

Mr. Grimes's views of Napoleon III., of his interference in Mexico, and of the Paris Universal Exposition, to be held in 1867, were given June 13th:

It seems to me that the whole question is in a nutshell. Every gentleman who has visited France since this exposition has been projected, has returned entertaining the opinion that it was gotten up more for the purpose of glorifying the present Imperial Government of France than for any other purpose; and that for that reason the infant Napoleon has been made president of the exposition. Now, I am not disposed to be in any way instrumental in accomplishing the object of the Imperial Government in this particular at any time, and especially not so long as their troops shall remain within the territorial jurisdiction of the republic of Mexico, which would not have been sent there, as everybody knows, but for the difficulties that were occurring in this country at that time. They were sent out to take advantage of the unfortunate posture of public affairs in this country. I do not want to assist in elevating in public estimation in any part of the world the present dynasty in France, so long as it shall stand really, morally, and militarily, in an antagonistic position to this Government; and France does stand in that position, so long as her troops remain in Mexico.

I am utterly opposed to the principle of the bill (making appropriations for the exposition). There is no authority from the Constitution to make any such grant of money from the Treasury; and I believe the whole scheme is antagonistic to the spirit of republican liberty, which should be propagated by the Congress of the United States.

In favor of authorizing the construction of a bridge over the Mississippi River at Burlington, by the Chicago, Burlington & Quincy Railroad Company, Mr. Grimes said, April 30th and July 18th:

I suppose if there is anybody here who is peculiarly interested in the navigation of the Mississippi River, I am as much interested as any one else. I have for thirty years lived immediately upon its banks, and am familiar with the condition of the commerce of the country connected with that river. A portion of the people of the town in which I live, fancying that the construction of a bridge will not be to their own individual benefit, would not favor the passing of this law; while those who take the most comprehensive and correct view would favor it.

But, whatever may be the opinions of my fellow-citizens of that town, there cannot be any question that the commerce and the interests of the State at large demand that there should be facilities for crossing the river without breaking the bulk of the freights that are to go over. The Chicago, Burlington & Quincy Railroad Company are about to build a bridge at that place. They have the authority to do it from the State of Illinois and the State of Iowa. They will not put in as wide a draw as is required by this statute, unless this statute is passed. We are entirely satisfied that the construction of a bridge with a draw one hundred and sixty feet wide, forty feet wider than the two bridges now built across the Mississippi River, will be ample. If found to be otherwise we will cause them to be removed, as can be done under the provisions of this bill.

We are deeply interested in the navigation of the river, which has been the building up of my town. We want for the present time, and we want for all future ages, to have uninterrupted navigation of the stream; but we want at the same time, if it can be done, and we are satisfied that it can be done, opportunities to get eastward, as well as southward and northward. We want to be able to transport our produce and ourselves with as little inconvenience as possible to the Eastern markets; and that is the reason why we insist that these railroad companies shall have opportunity to bridge the Mississippi River, provided they do so without interfering in any degree with the navigation of the stream.

I think I represent the agricultural interests of my State, when I vote not for the benefit of a particular railroad corporation, but for the benefit of the universal commerce of the Northwest, that there shall be bridges across the Mississippi River, not constructed in such a way that they can by any possibility obstruct navigation, but so as to promote the interests of commerce crossing the river. I live in a wheat-country. That is one of the staple productions of the region. However valuable and rich in a commercial point of view St. Louis may be, yet Chicago, the great wheat-market of the continent, is the point to which we desire to send our wheat. It is the estimate of everybody in the town where I live, that there is a loss of seven bushels upon every car-load that is transferred across the river according to the present plan, which, at the present price of wheat in the neighborhood of two dollars a bushel, is fourteen dollars on a car-load, that is sustained by the agricultural interest. That interest, also the interest of the consumer in the East, demands that such a loss may be obviated.

Early in the course of this year, upon the urgent solicitation of Mr. Oakes Ames, a gentleman for whose integrity, capacity, and public spirit he had high respect, Mr. Grimes became interested in the construction of the Union Pacific Railroad, and took stock in the company that completed it. He saw no impropriety in a member of Congress being connected with a railroad company, as he remarked in the Senate. He had been an advocate of railroads, and of a railroad to the Pacific, all his life, and a stockholder and director in several companies. Those who first undertook to build the road had faltered; public confidence had been shaken; capitalists generally were suspicious of the hazards and risks. In this juncture, he had confidence in Mr. Ames, and, with his energy and resources devoted to it, in the success of the enterprise ultimately.

Upon a bill to incorporate the Niagara Ship-Canal Company Mr. Grimes said, June 28th and July 12th:

I entertain very great doubts whether we have the power to create a corporation, and endow them with authority for commercial purposes to go within the jurisdiction of the State of New York and construct a canal; but whether we have that power or not, believing that we can do the work ourselves, and control it, I am wholly unwilling to agree that Congress shall devolve this power on a private corporation, to enjoy the benefits of the immense water-power that will be created, and establish such tolls upon the transportation of our agricultural products as they may see fit. This is one of the grandest privileges and will result in being one of the most tremendous monopolies ever devised on this continent. I am not disposed to put the agricultural interests of my section of the country into the keeping of any such corporation.

No man is more anxious to have proper channels of communication between the Northwest and the Atlantic and the Gulf of Mexico. I have no doubt as to the constitutional power of Congress to make those channels of communication. I am as anxious as anybody is that Congress shall do it, although not so anxious as some gentlemen seem to be for the purpose merely of making the West an agricultural country, continuing us merely as an agricultural population, as the producers of heavy articles for export. If the Committee on Commerce will report a bill providing that appropriations shall be made and expended under our engineer corps, who are created and maintained for just such purposes, to construct a line of communication between Lake Erie and Lake Ontario, I will vote for it. I will go farther, and vote for a bill continuing the construction of a ship-canal beyond Lake Ontario. But I do not want to put the public Treasury into the hands of a private corporation for building any such channel, and allowing that corporation to fix such tolls as they please. My sole purpose is to make it truly a national work. I never will consent to the Government of the United States making it in any other light than as a national work. It may cost the Government more than if this company undertakes to build it; but we can afford to pay a great deal more. When we have made it, we are not to be oppressed with tolls in the future; we shall have the control of that subject. All that will be necessary will be to keep it in repair, and furnish the gate-keepers and the agents. They can be paid through a small toll to be levied, or directly from the Treasury of the United States.

At the next session he again pledged his hearty support to such a measure, February 26, 1867.

Upon a bill for the leasing of saline lands, Mr. Grimes said, June 29th:

I suppose members of the Senate are aware that by the passage of this bill we are to inaugurate a new system in this country, and that is, the leasing of the public lands for manufacturing purposes. The result will be that these salt-lands will never be half developed under such a system. We shall have agents, appointed by the central power here, who will have control of these salt-springs, and I cannot apprehend that any advantage will result to the Government. The right way is to sell these lands, let them be owned by citizens of the country, and let them develop them. The Government ought never to become the landlord of a portion of the people of this country. That is not the relation that is encouraged by the laws of our States to any considerable extent, and it ought not to be encouraged by the Government of the United States. The true principle in a republican government is, that so far as possible every man shall be the owner of his own soil, and of his own tools, labor, and machinery. So long as you undertake to maintain the relation of landlord to the persons who are going to carry on these salt-works, the country will never realize a tenth part of the advantages that we would realize if they were conducted by private enterprise. That is the experience of this Government, and has been from its foundation. It is the experience of every government on the face of the earth. I feel a great deal of interest in this subject. I do not know of any salt-springs of value on the public domain except those in Kansas and Nebraska, immediately west of the State in which I live. We hope that the time is not far distant when we shall be able to secure our supply of salt from that region. We do not want to be compelled to become tributary to any such parties as may happen to be able to secure a long lease under the provisions of this bill. Why not apply the principle to your iron on Lake Superior and in Missouri? Why not apply it to your gold and silver? Why is it that this necessity of life, without which we cannot exist at all, is selected and put into the keeping of a few men, who manage to secure a lease from the Government?

Opposing a resolution to release the Pacific Mail Company's steamships, engaged to carry the mails between the United States and China, from the obligation to touch at Honolulu, Mr. Grimes said, July 2d:

It has so happened, in the last three or four years, that I have every day almost been brought in contact with persons who have been stationed more or less of their time at the Sandwich Islands, mostly officers of the naval profession. A large proportion of the property there is owned by citizens of the United States, and, until the last eight or ten years, American interests have been vastly in the preponderance. A few years ago the present king overturned the constitution, and established a new government, and this new government has been in the interest of Great Britain. The question is, whether at this juncture we ought to relax any of our efforts to keep up a close and immediate communication between this continent and the Sandwich Islands. There are political interests of the highest consideration that should restrain us at all hazards, no matter what it may cost, from allowing a single tie to be severed that can possibly bind us to the Sandwich Islands. About the only thing in the bill, when it passed originally, that gave me any sort of consideration for it, was that these steamships would be compelled to touch at Honolulu, and, by bringing us in connection with our friends there, serve to maintain them in their position, and in some measure overthrow the British interest that is so much antagonized to us.

THE TARIFF.

Upon a motion for a tax of three per cent. *ad valorem* upon agricultural implements, Mr. Grimes said, June 21st:

If necessary that everything in the hands of the farmer be taxed, I am content that tax shall be levied, provided it be levied upon everything in commerce and manufactures, as well as in agriculture. My objection is, that there are exceptions in favor of manufactures and commerce to a considerable extent in the free list, while there are not corresponding exemptions to the agriculturists and the manufacture of implements used in agriculture. I trust we shall not have this burden thrown upon us, if the free list at any rate is to remain as it now is.

A tariff bill that had passed the House of Representatives was, on his motion, July 12th, postponed to the next session. He said:

We are now in the eighth month of a very long and arduous session. This tariff bill, which affects the prosperity of the country, and the personal and business interests of every man in it, reaches us at this late period; and I undertake to say that the members of this body are not prepared to enter upon a consideration of such a subject at this time. A bill making such radical changes as this proposes, should be laid a sufficient length of time before the people of the country, that there may be some response from them as to what their judgment is of the merits of the proposition.

I think it will be some time before we shall be able to bring the people of the Northwest to the belief that it is to their advantage to increase the duty on salt, an essential to their existence and prosperity, thirty-three per cent. I do not believe that you can convince the people of my State that it will be to their advantage to put a duty upon lumber, without which they cannot fence their farms and make them productive of a single cent, of three dollars a thousand; or to increase the duty on iron variously from ten to fifty dollars a ton; or the duty on low grades of cutlery, such as go into every farmer's house, six hundred per cent.

I stand here as the representative of the laboring-man, quite as much as the Senator from Ohio (Mr. Wade), and it is not to be thrown in my teeth that I am not as willing as he, or anybody else, to protect the laboring-man. I do not stand here as the representative of a class, of the wool-growers alone, who among my constituents are not more than one in a thousand. I come here to represent the mass of the people of my State, who wear the woolen fabric when it is made up into goods; and they do not tell me to vote for any such provision as this, to oppress the mass of the people for the sake of securing an advantage to a select few.

I was raised as a tariff protection Whig, and still entertain the same notions in regard to tariffs as those in which I was early educated. But I am not in favor of this tariff, nor of any tariff except the one upon our statute-books, until we can see what may be the operation of our internal revenue law that we have already passed. This question is vital to the interests of the State that I have the honor in part to represent. The passage of this bill, in anything like the shape in which it is now lying upon your table, will be ruinous to the prosperity of Iowa.

THE AGRICULTURAL BUREAU.

This is altogether too great a thing to be run by a central government here at Washington, and we shall discover that after a while. We must have these organizations in each State. The idea of one man here at Washington undertaking to tell the people of this country, extending as it does through so many parallels of latitude and longitude, what may be the particular fruits or cereals adapted to a particular kind of soil or climate, is a great humbug. It is too big a business. So long as the Federal Government arrogates to itself the power of concentrating all information here, so long the States will neglect to obtain that kind of information; but the moment we decline to do it, your agricultural colleges in the various States will undertake this service, and you will get such information as will be of value to the people of the respective States (July 25th).

Mr. Grimes advocated a provision of law that in the city of Washington all public money should be deposited in the Treasury of the United States, and, in cities where there is a sub-Treasury, with the sub-treasurer. He said, July 19th:

The result of depositing in the banks is to cause that very inflation which the Secretary of the Treasury says he is attempting to check. I do not profess to be a financier; it may be that all knowledge on questions of this kind is confined to a few men in this body or out of it; but this is a question that has been before this body for the last six months. I introduced a resolution months ago, calling on the Committee on Finance to investigate this whole subject. According to the last report I read, there were forty-seven millions of the public money deposited in the different banks, the bulk of it in the large cities. It is used there as the basis upon which the banks make discounts; and the purpose with which the banks seek to hold these deposits is to inflate the currency, the very thing which I understand it is the purpose of the Government to avoid, so far as practicable. I should think we had had a warning by the occurrences of the last few months in this city in this regard. I should think, when a bank right under the eyes of the Treasury Department explodes, in the manner in which the National Merchants' Bank of Washington did, holding some half a million of the public money, from which, I understand the Government will not realize one farthing, that should be a sufficient warning to us in regard to the proper methods in which we should dispose of the public deposits.

It is said that it would be some inconvenience to men to procure greenbacks with which to pay their taxes. I do not believe it. If it be, then I am in favor of withdrawing more of your national currency, and issuing more of your greenbacks, if they are better than your national currency. That is the way to obviate that. I voted against your national banking system. I voted against every amendment to it. I believed that the true system was to issue your greenbacks. I did not believe there could be any better security. But now after you have created your national banks, when we propose to render the Treasury perfectly secure and safe, by providing that the public money shall not be deposited with the national banks, but with the sub-Treasuries, the argument is presented that we ought not to allow this national currency to be received in the discharge of public dues, and nothing except the national Treasury notes. I had not anything to do with bringing about that condition of affairs. It having been brought about, it seems to me that the safest and wisest way now is to begin to remedy the evils in which we find ourselves involved, by restoring the old sub-Treasury system, so far as we can. If the sub-Treasury and the Treasury of the United States are to be administered in the interest of banks, of course the provision of the law which compels the collector to receive national-bank notes in discharge of the national taxes, but does not allow him to pay that kind of currency over to the sub-Treasury, will be permitted to remain upon the statute-book; and that will always furnish an admirable argument for never authorizing deposits of any other description, and anywhere else except in the vaults of these pet banks. The Secretary of the Treasury cannot foresee the evils that will result, when he succeeds in what he says he is attempting to do, to curtail the currency and bring us back to specie payments. Then will come the time when these deposit banks will not be able to respond to the demands that will be made upon them; and I am disposed to have the record appear in such a shape, that I shall not be put in the category of those who voted in favor of allowing the public treasure to remain in their hands. Why is it that we authorize the collector to receive national-bank notes, and yet refuse to receive them from him at the sub-Treasury? Is it not because we are administering the Government in the interest of the banks?

His motion was non-concurred in: yeas 13, nays 22.

Mr. Grimes voted against the resolution to increase the pay of members of Congress to five thousand dollars per annum, July 25th.

105.—*To Mrs. Grimes.*

WASHINGTON, *December* 5, 1866.

I went to *see* Ristori last night. She is a large, tall woman, with a long, prominent Roman nose, and is ease and grace personified. Such tall women are not unfrequently awkward, but every step, gesture, and movement, was so artistic and perfect as to be most pleasing; and although I did not understand a word that was uttered, yet I could not take my eyes away from her; and I imagined, at least, that I was following and comprehending her by her pantomime. She is not pretty, nor are any of the Italian women in the company; the men are better looking. It is an excellent company, and the only one I ever saw in which there was no one who ranted in the play.

We are getting along quietly thus far, and the indications are that we shall have an easy-going session. Still, no one can say what may be done. I think that the policy I started out with of letting the President severely alone will finally be the policy of Congress.

NEBRASKA.

Upon the question of the admission of Nebraska into the Union, Mr. Grimes held it the duty of Congress to provide that there should be no denial of the elective franchise in that State by reason of race or color, and that a majority of the voters of the Territory should assent to this condition, in order to place it beyond the possibility of an adverse decision by any tribunal. He said, January 8th:

If that shall be adopted, although I have many doubts as to whether there be a sufficient number of people in the Territory to entitle her to a representation in Congress, yet I shall forego those doubts, and vote for the passage of the bill. If that be not adopted, I shall not vote for the bill. Are we willing, upon a mere matter of expediency, to abandon that principle which our constituents hold so dear, when it is in doubt whether or not the people of Nebraska will ratify this condition? There is no doubt as to our power to legislate in regard to the District of Columbia, and we have exercised that power. There is no doubt as to our power to control the constitution of the State of Nebraska, and determine the form in which it shall be presented to us. There is some doubt in the minds of many as to our power to control the subject in some of the States lately in rebellion; and are we going to foreclose ourselves to-day, by saying that we will not undertake to control this question in a State where confessedly we have the power? For my part, having as a matter of principle voted the other day for free suffrage in the District of Columbia, and having voted for it again over the presidential veto yesterday, I am not to-day to be hurried by a consideration of expediency to ignore and turn my back upon that vote, and to say that I was wrong then. We have the power to fix this question now, beyond cavil and doubt, and I want to have it thus fixed before it goes out of our hands.

The proposition to submit the matter to a vote of the people of Nebraska failing, Mr. Grimes voted against the bill. Subsequently, an amendment being adopted, requiring the Legislature of Nebraska to assent to the proposed condition, and to declare that it shall be held as a part of the organic law of the State, he voted for the bill, over the President's veto. He also voted for free suffrage in Colorado, while he continued to oppose the admission of Colorado as a State, for the reasons assigned in his speech of March 13, 1866.

TENURE OF OFFICE.

Upon a bill regulating the tenure of office, Mr. Grimes said, January 16, 1867:

I have abandoned nearly all the political theories of the party into which I was born; but that sentiment is yet remaining in my breast, which was the war-cry of that party when I first became a voter, the curtailment of executive power and patronage. That sentiment I have always entertained, and entertain as strongly to-day as at any period of my life. I propose to record my vote in favor of the amendment, that every officer of the United States who receives a salary exceeding one thousand dollars shall be sent to the Senate for confirmation. We now have that law applying to postmasters. Why should it not apply to other officers? It is said that they are too numerous, that we cannot attend to it. I know it will throw great burdens upon your committees. That is no reason why we should not pass the law. Make new committees; organize them in a different manner, and you will be able to transact the business. The very fact that you have the right to pass upon the nominations will exercise a restraining influence on the appointing power. Confirm them in groups, if you please; but leave any Senator, who knows about bad men being appointed, to select those whom he knows to be unworthy. Do you suppose that, if the power of confirmation or rejection had been lodged in the Senate in regard to inspectors, a man would have been appointed from my State as an inspector who only last year was guilty of smuggling cigars, and who condoned his offense by the payment of several thousand dollars? I want the opportunity to put my seal of condemnation upon such men; and if there be only one man rejected in a State, or in the whole United States, for having violated your laws, that will have a moral influence and a political influence upon the President, and upon others who make appointments.

Mr. Grimes voted for the bill to regulate the tenure of certain civil offices, over the President's veto, March 2d.

THE TARIFF.

Mr. Grimes called attention in the Senate, January 18th, to a libelous attack in *The Iron Age*, the organ of the manufacturers of iron and cutlery in the United States, with reference to his motion for the postponement of the tariff bill, July 12, 1866, representing that he had "used his influence as a member of the Senate to promote his own private ends." Mr. Reverdy Johnson remarked:

The honorable member from Iowa, wherever he is known, and he is known well to all of us, needed not for his vindication anything to be said by himself in contradiction of the charge. I cannot say all that I think in his presence; but I may, without violating any good taste, I hope, say that every Senator upon this floor must be convinced that there is no member of the body who is more incapable of acting from improper or interested motives. His appearance in this Chamber is not of a day only; he has been with us for years, he was reëlected by an almost unanimous vote of his Legislature, and has resolved, wisely I suppose for himself, long before his term expired, to do nothing more than serve out that term, and then retire to private life, where I am sure he will be respected, as much as he has been respected, and, by those who know him, beloved, by the members of this body. The public, however, may not know the character of the honorable member, and I think it is due—a debt which we owe each to the other at all times and under all circumstances—when we find a brother member assailed, to denounce it, if we believe it to be false, as a groundless slander. Such, I am sure, is the case in this instance.

Mr. Fessenden remarked:

I am informed that the article makes an allusion to the Committee on Finance, and to the influence that was probably exerted by the honorable Senator from Iowa upon that committee. I can answer only for one of them, and I will say very frankly that, if there is a man in or out of this Senate who possesses influence with me, it is the honorable Senator from Iowa. No man possesses more. I have great respect for his opinions, and for the uniform integrity of his character, as we all have. But I must say in justification of the Senator, and of the committee, or of the chairman of it in this particular instance, that the honorable Senator never spoke to me, that I know of, upon the subject referred to, or alluded to it in any way whatever. All I ever heard him say on the subject was said here, on the floor of the Senate.

Upon the tariff bill Mr. Grimes said, January 24th:

The man who opposes the passage of this bill must expect to be slandered. The "protectionists," as they choose to call themselves, have opened the vials of their wrath upon those whose opposition they anticipated. Threats of political extinction are hurled against every man who, in the exercise of an independent judgment, is not prepared to impose upon his constituents the burdens which the various manufacturing combinations demand. That portion of the public press suborned to their interest is rife with charges that "the capital is thronged with free-traders, and that British gold is operating to secure American legislation for British interests." Every man is condemned in advance, who would inquire before he would vote.

We know what this means; that two or three large manufacturing interests, not satisfied with enormous profits during the last six years, are determined at whatever hazard to put more money in their pockets, and to this end have persuaded some and coerced other manufacturing interests to unite with them in a great combination demand for what they call protection to American labor, but what some others call robbery of the American laborer and agriculturist. It seems that the men specially interested in the passage of this bill are bent upon taking the legislation of the country into their own hands, are unwilling that there should be impartial, free inquiry into the subject; that, conscious of the interested motives from which their own action springs, they cannot conceive it possible that those who disagree with them can be inspired by any other than selfish considerations.

This mad-dog cry of "free trade and British gold" passes by me like the idle wind. Nor am I alarmed at the scheme of sending free of charge to every prominent man in Iowa, and elsewhere in the Northwest, a weekly copy of a "protectionist" journal of New York, for the double purpose of building up a sentiment there in favor of high duties, and of politically destroying such members of Congress as may not vote in favor of them. The people have not asked for this bill; so far as we know, they are satisfied with the present tariff laws. The members of this Congress were not elected upon any issue of this kind. This enactment is solely demanded by the manufacturers of iron, and a few wool agriculturists and speculators, who call themselves the wool-growers of the country. They have organized associations, contributed large sums of money to mould public sentiment through the press, and formed combinations with other interests to control legislation. The result is before us, and we are to determine whether we will permit these clubs and associations of interested parties to govern us in our action, as the clubs and associations of revolutionary France governed the constituent assembly of that country.

It is the fashion to denounce every man who does not favor a prohibitory tariff as a free-trader. The charge is made that free-trade agents are at work to influence Congress. Who has seen these free-trade agents? I have yet to see the first man who is in favor of free-trade, nor have I seen any man who was opposed to a revenue tariff which should incidentally protect such branches of American industry as needed the fostering care of the Government. It is on questions of detail that we differ, as to how much shall be taken from the pocket of Peter to support and enrich his brother Paul.

We are told that for some centuries England maintained a protective system almost amounting to prohibition, and grew rich and powerful under it; and that example is presented to us as worthy of imitation, as though the world had made no progress in arts and sciences, in productive resources and machinery, in the science of political economy, and the application of its principles to practical life. God forbid that we should go back to the early days of the British Empire, or to her more modern days, for laws or policies upon which to model our systems, national, social, or economic! Besides, the prosperity, wealth, and renown of England are due in a far greater degree to her commerce than to her manufactures. It is commerce that is the great civilizer and elevator. It is commerce that has poured the wealth of the world into the lap of England.

The measure before us purports to be a bill "to provide increased revenue from imports, and for other purposes." If this bill, when passed into a law, would "provide increased revenue from imports," no man could support it more cheerfully than I would. That is precisely what my constituents desire, and believe the interests of the country demand. They would be glad to see that kind of legislation adopted which would secure such an "increased revenue from imports" as would be sufficient to pay the annual governmental expenses and the interest on the public debt, without resort to internal taxes. True relief is only to be found in the abolition of the manufacturers' tax. But the friends of this bill do not support it upon any such theory as that. They do not pretend that it will "provide increased revenue from imports." If they thought it would, they would utterly repudiate it. It is for precisely the reverse reason assumed in the title of the bill—it is because it will not "provide increased revenue from imports;" it is because they believe that under its provisions foreign products, coming in competition with American products, will be so excluded from our ports that no duty at all can be collected on them, that they require its passage. The title is a misnomer. Let it be amended so as to read, "An act to prevent the collection of duties from imports, and defray the expenses of Government by direct taxation."

This bill is said to contain a provision for the benefit of the wool-growers of the Western States, and on that account my aid is invoked to secure its passage. No one could be more gratified to render to that class of our people any legislative assistance in my power, provided I could do so without detriment to the common interests of the whole country; and not otherwise. The Wool-Growers' Association, and the Wool-Manufacturers' Association, co-operating with them to secure the adoption of this bill, demand that for every cent of duty imposed on wool there shall be four cents per pound imposed on imported woolens, and thirty-five per cent. *ad valorem* added, to cover the cost of chemicals, dye-stuffs, transportation, etc. What will be the effect? Granted, for the argument, that it will increase the price of both domestic and foreign wools, to the temporary advantage of the home producer; but at whose cost? Of course, every man knows that the profits of both the wool-grower and wool-manufacturer must be derived from the consumer. I would not advise the people of my State, under the stimulus of a high duty, to rush into attempts to produce wool on a large scale, which cannot be of advantage to the State, and must be disastrous to them. From the time of the Shepherd Kings down to the present moment, no nation, people, or community, that devoted their energies principally to the husbandry of flocks, ever became rich or powerful.

I admit that the agriculturist who diversifies his labor, the farmer with fifteen horses, forty cattle, fifty swine, and one hundred head of sheep, is a benefactor, and should be encouraged. Let us see how this bill encourages him. His one hundred head of sheep will furnish two hundred and fifty pounds of wool, which will be increased in value by the passage of this bill, if it does what its most ardent friends claim, fifteen cents a pound. But, in order to secure this, he must consent to be taxed six cents a bushel on the salt that he feeds to his sheep, and with which he cures his meat and seasons his food; he must agree to an additional tax upon the ploughs, harrows, shovels, hoes, and reapers, with which he cultivates his crops, and the engine that drags his products to market; upon his clothing, the household utensils used in preparing his food, and the table cutlery with which he eats it. I would be pleased to know where the net profit on the one hundred head of sheep would be found in this transaction; and, if that would be small, where would the equally deserving farmer, who was not the owner of sheep, find a compensation for the additional taxation put upon him by this bill? And let it be remembered that those who raise wool are only as one in a thousand, by the side of those who consume it. But the truth is, this bill will not cause any permanent and reliable advance in the price of wool. There may be a sort of spasmodic rise brought about, for the benefit of speculators holding large quantities, but it cannot last. This bill will only benefit the manufacturer by placing the consumer completely in his power. Never was the innocent sheep more completely shorn than the wool-growers have been in the combination they entered into with the manufacturers to increase the price of wearing-apparel and blankets on the consumer.

The iron-makers insist that they are in distress and must be relieved. I do not profess to be as well informed upon the subject of iron-manufacture as some others, or perhaps as I ought to be; but, so far as my observation and inquiries have extended, I am convinced that every iron establishment in the country, properly located and economically conducted, is yielding reasonable profits to its owners, and some of them yield enormous profits. The average varieties of iron used by blacksmiths, machinists and ship-builders, now protected to the extent of fifty-five per cent., are advanced by this bill fifteen per cent. Nail-plate, hoop-iron, and small bar-iron, now protected by sixty per cent. duty, are advanced from fifteen to seventy-five per cent., and some of them over one hundred per cent. But the iron-manufacturers are not satisfied with the monstrous duties apparent upon the face of the bill. By adroitly changing the classification of iron, several descriptions have been carried from lower to higher classes, thus making an additional increase, not apparent to a casual observer. The rates of duty average somewhat over one hundred per cent. on the cost, on shipboard, at the port of shipment.

Is it possible that we are prepared to place such a tax upon iron, which is the raw material of all our industries, and which it has been the policy of all civilized nations to afford to their people cheap? Can I justify myself to my constituents, for voting to double the cost of iron, by pleading that in their behalf we secured the blessed boon of compelling them to pay double for all the clothing they wear?

The steel-manufacturers tell us that in 1859, under an *ad valorem* duty of twelve per cent., the manufacture of steel became an assured success; that the duty fixed by the act of 1861 was agreed on between the importers and manufacturers, and was well adapted to the then existing state of the manufacture in this country. Now, they demand an increase of from forty-six to sixty-seven per cent. on the existing tariff. Upon Bessemer steel rails is fixed a duty of forty-five dollars per ton, intended to be prohibitory, for the benefit of the rich monopolists who are the assignees of the patented process by which it is manufactured.

Now, what is to be the effect of this great increase in the price of iron and steel? Need any one be told that iron and steel are the bases of all production, and that the enhancement of their value will increase the cost of every variety of manufacture? Can any one name a single fabric the cost of which will not be augmented by this increased duty? The manufacturers of every variety of hardware and cutlery asked, with great justice, that we should give to them an increased protection, because of the anticipated increase in the value of what is to them the raw material, iron and steel. There is not a single industry that does not demand and need greater protection, because of the increase you will give to these articles. The manufacturers of machinery require, they tell us, that the duty on machinery be raised from thirty-five per cent. to sixty-five per cent. *ad valorem*. They insist that a machine for spinning cotton-yarn, costing in gold ten thousand dollars, shall have added to it a duty of six thousand five hundred dollars, and all other machinery employed in the manufacture of cotton and wool must be enhanced in a corresponding degree. Mills already built will become monopolies.

Do the advocates of this measure insist that this is the way to build up manufactures and make cheap goods? Is this the way to spread prosperity through the land, and make glad the hearts of the poor? Is any one so blind as not to see that the effect of the bill will be to increase the colossal fortunes of iron and steel masters, and of owners of woolen and cotton mills, at the expense of consumers of their products? Is this the way to pay the interest on the public debt? Will an increase of price of every necessary of life and of every consumable fabric enable the people to more easily pay their internal taxes, or make them more willing to do it? These are questions that it would do well for us to ponder. Yet we are expected to vote for all this, because we are permitted to have an increased duty on wool! We were reminded that the farmers' interests were to be specially protected under this bill, and so it contains a provision by which the duty on salt is increased one hundred and sixty per cent. above its cost. We in the West produce beef and pork, which are packed and sent to foreign countries, where they come in competition with that which is packed elsewhere with salt that pays no tribute, free salt. Yet the farmers' interests are protected!

Another effect of this bill will be to destroy the commerce of this country. I am not interested either in manufactures or commerce. I speak from the knowledge of historic facts I have gathered in the course of my life. I hold that no nation can be great and powerful, and occupy a prominent and respectable position in the family of nations, without commerce. When I said this to one of the gentlemen outside of the Senate, who were advocating the passage of this bill, he denied my proposition, and referred me to Austria, as a great nation without commerce—priest-ridden, bankrupt, despotic, disintegrating Austria—as an example to the country! You have already by hostile legislation nearly destroyed your commerce. You have destroyed your business with Mexico and with Central America; your carrying-trade is to a great extent done in foreign bottoms. I am told by those upon whom I rely that where ten years ago there were ten vessels of this country in the South American ports, there is not one now. This change has not been wrought by the Alabamas and Floridas, but by us. This bill will effectually destroy your trade with the countries of Northern Europe.

The true relief for the manufacturer and the people alike should be sought in a reduction of the internal tax on manufactures. But the passage of this bill will preclude us from making such a reduction; for its practical effect would be to increase the duty for the benefit of the manufacturer, and throw so much greater burden upon the other sources of internal revenue. This measure will derange the business of the country, and afford relief to no considerable portion of the people. Its inequalities and partialities and onesidedness will receive the condemnation of the people, whenever they shall have an opportunity to pass upon it.

With reference to the plea that a high tariff protects American labor, Mr. Grimes said, January 28th:

We have other laborers than those employed in manufactures; the labor of the country is done upon the farms; and the basis of our products and of all our manufactures and commerce is dug out of the earth by the farmers. But it is proposed to increase the cost and expense of the products of the American farmer, by an additional imposition even upon the grindstones with which he sharpens his tools. That tax upon the importation of grindstones will be an excuse for the owners of quarries in Ohio and Michigan to increase the price, in the proportion that Congress increases the duty.

A Senator having represented Mr. Grimes as denying the whole principle of protection to American industry, he replied, January 30th:

The gentleman is entirely misinformed. I have never declared myself a free-trader, but am in favor of a revenue tariff with incidental protection to such branches of American industry as need the fostering care of the Government. The question at issue is as to what these branches are, and how the duties can be properly laid.

He added:

I do not know but that this constant iteration and reiteration of the charge of free-trader against me will finally lead me to believe myself that I am actually one; but I did not come here with that conviction on my mind, and up to this time I have never avowed myself to be such.

LEAGUE ISLAND.

Mr. Grimes continued to advocate earnestly the removal of the navy-yard at Philadelphia to League Island. The matter had been upon his hands for more than four years, and he was anxious to have it disposed of. He said, February 12th:

The country does not want another navy-yard. The great trouble with us is that we have too many, and those we have are too small. A simple proposition comes from the Navy Department, asking that the present yard at Philadelphia be enlarged; and the question was, whether we should enlarge that yard by acquiring the adjacent property, taking it out of the business property of the city that is necessary for commercial uses, or whether we should move it to another locality. We decided that it was best for the Government to move to another locality, and then the question was, whether we should move it a mile and a half off to League Island, or farther down the river to Red Bank or Chester.

We have been enlarging our yards ever since the foundation of the Government. In 1798 the Navy Department was established. An act of Congress was passed authorizing the construction of six frigates. At that time Benjamin Stoddart was the Secretary of the Navy. There was never any authority of Congress to establish the six navy-yards that we had in this country; but Mr. Stoddart, under the latitudinarian notions that prevailed in John Adams's Administration (as his enemies said), thought that the authority to construct the six frigates carried with it the power to purchase the land upon which they should be built; and therefore that Secretary of the Navy, the first one we had, bought small pieces of ground at different points, upon which the ships were built, and from that day to this we have been continually enlarging these yards. Since I have been a member of this body, we have made two purchases to add to the Philadelphia Navy-Yard; and it is in that way that all our navy-yards have sprung up. We have never succeeded in getting a yard as an entirety, except that noble one which we possess on Mare Island, on the Pacific coast. Now, there is an opportunity to secure a yard as an entirety, to lay it off as it ought to be, to make such a yard as is demanded by the commercial and naval interests of the country, and worthy of a great maritime power.

I did not commit myself in favor of League Island until I had made personal inspection of it. I examined it before I reported in favor of it. I have been there three times. It is a common, low, interval land, like the land you find along the streams where there is tidal water in any of the Northern States. The soil is firm, and admits of as good constructions being raised upon it as the ground of any navy-yard we have, unless it be at Kittery and Mare Island, where we have stone; and for some purposes, as the construction of works for the fabrication of arms, and working with trip-hammers, it is better.

It will be to our advantage that the ground is low. What are the necessities of navy-yards at this time? Let me read an extract showing what Great Britain is doing, and what we shall be compelled to do, if we intend to occupy a first-class position as a naval power:

"The designs for the enlargement of the Chatham yard will necessitate the taking in of three hundred and eighty acres adjoining the present establishment, by which the entire area will be enlarged to nearly five hundred acres. Of this, seventy-four acres will be deep-water space, consisting of three basins; the fitting-out basin of thirty-three acres, the repairing-basin of twenty-one acres, and the factory-basin of twenty acres."—(CHATHAM, *January* 17, 1867. *London News.*)

The time will come when we shall have to make preparations for establishing as extensive navy-yards as they have in Great Britain. Need I undertake to illustrate and prove before the members of the Senate that it is to our advantage that the ground is low? The earth which will be taken from the excavations for the basins will be sufficient to elevate the adjacent ground to the necessary height; and the nearer your dumping-ground to the place you are excavating, the greater is the saving in expense; whereas, when you take your navy-yard to some other place, where you have a granite or a hard-pan formation, the expense for preparing the grounds for basins will be immense.

THE DES MOINES RAPIDS.

Advocating the improvement of the navigation of the Des Moines Rapids of the Mississippi River as of great importance to the people of the Northwest, and to the commerce of the whole country, Mr. Grimes remarked, February 25th:

The first survey of the rapids by authority of law was made in 1836 or 1837, by Lieutenant Robert E. Lee, the late general of the rebel army. He reported that it was feasible to blow out the "chains" across the river which make the rapids; and appropriations of a small amount have from time to time been made for the purpose of carrying out his views. Another survey, but not a minute one, I think, was subsequently made by General Warren, who decided that, although such a process as that might not make the most perfect navigation, yet it would very much—I think he used the expression—ameliorate the condition of the stream. Last year an appropriation was made for the same purpose, and General Wilson was sent to make a survey. He reports in favor of a canal, instead of the course that was recommended by Lieutenant Lee. On the strength of this recommendation, it is proposed that we appropriate one million dollars for the purpose of improving navigation "on the Mississippi River," and I suppose the word "on" is used in that phrase to convey the idea, and is to be regarded as authority by the War Department, to make a canal, instead of improving the navigation itself. I am not prepared to say that a canal is the right way to improve these rapids. I do not think it is. I am unwilling, unless there shall be something more done than the mere survey of General Wilson, that the commerce of the country shall be liable to the interruption which, I think, a canal will impose upon it. But I am willing that the Secretary of War, calling to his aid a board of competent officers, and taking the report of General Wilson, in connection with that of Lieutenant Lee, and that of General Warren, shall decide the question; and I am willing to abide the result.

On his motion, the proviso was incorporated into the law, that any canal constructed around the rapids shall be and forever remain free to navigation and commerce, and no tolls shall ever be collected thereon.

106.—*To Mrs. Grimes.*

WASHINGTON, *January* 25, 1867.

I made a speech yesterday, which is regarded as a pretty good one, but for which I shall be roundly abused by those who call themselves protectionists, but who are more properly prohibitionists.

February 1st.—I send the inclosed from the *New York Tribune*,[1] to show you what a fool your husband is. Horace thinks that when one becomes a man, he ought not, like St. Paul, to put away childish things.

February 9th.—I attended the performance of Händel's "Messiah" last evening; it was worth a thousand operas. The leading female voice was the celebrated Miss Houston, of Boston. There were about one hundred voices in the chorus, and it was grand, according to my judgment.

I notice that the papers are still discussing me and the tariff. The tariff is dead; perhaps it may be the death of me also.

107.—*To Mrs. Grimes.*

WASHINGTON, *February* 18, 1867.

I postponed writing until yesterday, Sunday, expecting to have leisure; but, when yesterday came, I was hardly able to wield a pen. On Friday we were in session until half-past three o'clock, Saturday morning; Saturday, in committee at 10 A. M., and in session from 12 M. to half-past six o'clock, Sunday morning. Our bill was the new reconstruction measure, which the House are now trying to defeat.

My health has been excellent this winter, but that session put a great strain upon me, and I have not entirely got over it. I have about made up my mind not to sit up through another session in the night.

I found Mary's abstract of her history very pleasant, and do not doubt that it will greatly improve her, if she makes a similar synopsis of each chapter, as she reads, and then a full and general one of each volume. It will improve her style, and teach her to think. Advise her to keep it up, therefore.

I am still of the opinion that we shall get away by the middle of March. I shall go at any rate.

[1] An article, entitled "A mirror for Grimes," concluding thus: "The outcry against protection, as favoring Pennsylvania and New England, at the cost of the West, is a false, delusive clamor, which old Clay Whigs, like Mr. Grimes, ought to be ashamed of."

§ 5.—*In the Fortieth Congress.*—1867–1869.

The impeachment of President Johnson was first bruited in the House of Representatives, January 7, 1867. It was regarded by Mr. Grimes, at the time, as an impolitic measure, and without sufficient warrant. In the course of this year affairs assumed a gloomy aspect. Mr. Grimes had serious apprehensions of anarchy for a time. The excesses of the President provoked extreme measures in opposition. New constructions were given to the Constitution. The powers of the respective departments of the Government were disturbed. As Mr. Grimes predicted, the Republicans lost ground in the fall elections. The first session of the Fortieth Congress was held in March, July, and November.

108.—*To Mrs. Grimes.*

WASHINGTON, *March* 12, 1867.

The impeachment project is subsiding; it being the almost universal opinion that, while the President has been guilty of many great follies and wickednesses, he has not been guilty of those overt, flagrant, corrupt acts that constitute "high crimes and misdemeanors," and make an impeachable offense; and that it is not worth while to establish an example which might result in making ours a sort of South American republic, where the ruler is deposed the moment the popular sentiment sets against him. We have very successfully and thoroughly tied his hands, and, if we had not, we had better submit to two years of misrule, which is a very short space in the lifetime of a nation, than subject the country, its institutions, and its credit, to the shock of an impeachment. I have always thought so, and everybody is now apparently coming to my conclusion.

AGAINST CLASS LEGISLATION.

Upon a proposition to place in the care of the Freedmen's Bureau moneys due colored soldiers, to be deposited in the Freedmen's Savings and Trust Company, Mr. Grimes remarked, March 13th:

I do not know that any very great degree of consistency is expected of public men nowadays. Certainly I do not think we exhibit any very great degree of it. During the session that has just closed, we solemnly declared by act of Congress that all the colored men of this country have intelligence enough, and position enough, and consequence enough in the country, to entitle them to the elective franchise. We have made them citizens. We have said nobody shall exercise guardianship over them. And now comes a resolution which declares that the Freedmen's Bureau shall take possession of the property of these men; that the bureau, or its agents, shall be authorized to receive the drafts issued to them from the Treasury Department for their bounty, pay, or pensions; and that under certain circumstances the money shall be deposited to the credit of the commissioner, not in a sub-Treasury of the United States, not in a national bank, but in the Freedmen's Savings and Trust Company; which, so far as I know, the Senator from Massachusetts knows no more about the solvency of than I do; which has made no exhibit of the condition of its affairs to the Senate, or to Congress, or to the Military Committee; and which may be no more solvent than the bank in the neighborhood of the Senator, at Newtonville, which, I suppose, he would have been willing to indorse two weeks ago, in as emphatic terms as he has indorsed this savings-bank to-day.[1]

The men belonging to the party to which the Senator from Massachusetts and I belong have always claimed that this class legislation was a great error, that it was wrong, that it was wicked; that we should not single out one class, and say that the nation should take the guardianship of that class, to the exclusion of another class, and confer upon them a consequence which we would not confer upon another class. I had thought and hoped that that time had gone by; that we were successful; that we had triumphed in this regard; and that we were to see and hear no more of class

[1] In 1873, a national-bank examiner, under instructions from the Controller of the Currency, examined the books of the Freedmen's Bank, and reported its affairs to be unsatisfactory, and pointed out a number of irregularities, which might well have been characterized first as last as so many robberies. In 1874, another examination was held, and the concern was pronounced insolvent. And in little less than a year from the time that the insolvency of the bank became known—such was the involved and atrocious condition of its affairs—none of its wronged and needy depositors has received a cent.—(*The Nation*, *April* 15, 1875.)

legislation. But what is this proposition but placing, by an act of Congress, the business affairs of all the colored men who have been in the Army and Navy and marine corps, under the guardianship of the Government and of the Freedmen's Savings and Trust Company? I have no doubt that wrong has been perpetrated on colored men in the collection of this money. So it has on white men, and there is no reason why we should pass such a law applicable to colored people, and not apply it to the white people.

With reference to tendering the thanks of Congress to several generals for their civil administration in the South, Mr. Grimes said, July 8th:

I think it would be exceedingly immature and improper for the Congress of the United States, upon the little testimony they have before them on the subject, to adopt these resolutions. Until within the last two or three years, a vote of thanks of Congress was regarded as the highest benefaction that could be bestowed upon an American citizen. We have already greatly lowered it in the estimation of the public by conferring it upon civilians [1] for no distinguished merit; and now it has been proposed, not, as heretofore, in regard to Army and Navy officers, for distinguished services in the field where they have periled their lives, but for, it is supposed, civil administration. I do not know enough about the administration of these men to be able to pronounce such a judgment as I ought to be able to pronounce, when I cast a vote for such a proposition. So far as General Sheridan is concerned, we have thanked him for his services in the field. What do we know about his administration at New Orleans, except such information as we get through the newspapers?

THE COTTON-TAX AND THE PROSPERITY OF THE SOUTHERN STATES.

I considered this cotton-tax at the time it was imposed, two years ago, as a temporary tax. All the taxes imposed at that time were, in fact, experiments. We all so regarded them, and spoke of them. We have been taking them off from some articles, and putting them on others, and changing them every session since we began this system of internal direct taxation. The question is,

[1] Cornelius Vanderbilt, George Peabody.

What has experience taught on this subject? Is it wise to continue the tax? Does the condition of our finances require it? Will it improve the industries of the country? Can its continuance be longer justified? I have always voted for taxes on cotton, not because they are based upon the slightest principle in the world, except the same principle that will justify a forced loan.

I should like to call the attention of the Senate to the chapter that we are now making in American history, as it is to be read in the future. There were eleven States of the Union that undertook to destroy our Government, for the sake, as they insisted, of preserving their property in men. They levied war and appealed to arms. In those eleven States, slaves had been held as property for many generations. In six of those States, slaves were employed almost exclusively in the production of cotton for nearly a century. That was the means by which they supported and accumulated wealth for their masters, and procured their own daily bread. They are accustomed to no other kind of labor. The rebellion against the Government was crushed. We have been the victors. As the victors, we have imposed terms upon the rebels. One of those terms is, that the slaves shall be free men from this time forward. We have done that as an act of precaution, and as an act of justice. We have felt it to be our duty to elevate, to educate, and to make free men, in every sense, of these colored people, and have bestowed upon them the elective franchise. And now, while attempting to elevate and ennoble that class of men, we propose to strike at the industry to which they have been accustomed—the only instrumentality which it is in the power of those men to use, in order to educate and support their families—by selecting the article of cotton, the only agricultural product reared upon American soil that is taxed, and impose upon it a tax of twenty-three per cent. And you do this, when you protect free labor in the North, by imposing an average duty of sixty-five per cent. upon all articles which come in competition with Northern labor from abroad. Do you say that this is not striking at free labor in the South? We all know that it is. If it be not, what becomes of the argument of forty years' standing, that the free labor of the country needed protection, and that your tariff had a tendency to foster, protect, ennoble, and dignify American labor? Yet here you take from the very poorest, the most dependent agricultural laborer in the country, twenty-five per cent. of the value of his product, while you protect the skilled laborer of the country to the average extent of sixty-five per cent., knowing at the same time that this burden which you impose upon the needy American producer of cotton operates as a forty per cent. bonus to the grower of cotton in India and Egypt, to enable the latter to drive your own producer out of the markets of the world. This is the chapter of history we are making.

We are deeply interested in this subject. We are not anxious, as some gentlemen avow that they are anxious, that the production of cotton in the South shall be broken up, and the people of that section only produce corn and the cereals in the place of cotton. We want labor in the South to be rehabilitated and reorganized. We want the old productions resumed, and labor there to have its proper reward. We want the Southern States to furnish in the future, as they once did, a reliable market for the agricultural products of the Northwest. Is there anything improper in this? What is the argument that our New England friends urge here in favor of their sixty-five per cent. upon all the imports of the country? That by the aid of that duty they build up a market where our agricultural products are consumed. Are they unwilling that we should have two markets? Is it not as proper for us to be interested in having a market at the South, and to that end allow the Southern people to raise such products as they please, as that we should vote to enforce sixty-five per cent. of duties on such imported articles as we consume, and then attempt to justify ourselves on the ground that we thereby make a market for agricultural products in the Eastern States?

I am willing that the tax should be suspended for one year, until we can see what may be the effect of that suspension upon the industry and finances of the country; otherwise, I shall vote for its entire repeal (December 20th).

In the fall of 1867, before leaving home for Washington, Mr. Grimes expressed to a few friends his desire to aid in founding a public library in Burlington. An association was organized for that purpose, February 22, 1868. His original donation was five thousand two hundred and four dollars and twenty-five cents, which he expended in the purchase of twenty-one hundred and four volumes, many of them large and costly books.

Subsequently, he sent from Europe two hundred and fifty-six volumes in the German language. He also contributed six hundred volumes of public documents, covering the period of his service in Congress.

109.—*To Henry W. Starr, Esq., Burlington.*

WASHINGTON, *January* 20, 1868.

If the citizens of Burlington will organize a library association, by whatever name and in whatever manner they choose, so that it shall be virtually a free library, and give ample assurance of being always preserved and maintained as such, I will place in the hands of a gentleman, competent to the task, the sum of five thousand dollars, with which to purchase such books as shall form the nucleus of a permanent library.

I do not wish to designate the names of the trustees. I only hope that they will be worthy men, who will take some interest in the subject; but I do not intend to become in the most remote degree responsible for the management of the library. I have read the constitution of the Keokuk Association. I am not much of a believer in lectures or lecturers. They are, as a class, rather shallow, and their productions as shallow as the authors. Still I do not object to lectures being established as a part of the plan.

You can make use of this letter, so you do not permit it to get into the newspapers. I think there is no one who dislikes to see his name in a newspaper as much as I do, and especially in connection with a charity, or with such an object as this. If the library succeeds, I shall probably do something further for it, but I do not think it wise to place myself under any obligation to that effect, and therefore shall not pledge myself to anything of the sort. Money must be raised from other sources to furnish the necessary appurtenances of a library, such as furniture, carpets, shelves, light, fuel, and to keep the property owned by the association forever insured.

Advocating a resolution authorizing the President to appoint naval officers on the retired list, not below the rank of commander, to vacant consulates, Mr. Grimes remarked, January 16th:

A naval officer is a man taken when a youth and educated for the service of his country, who has been instructed at the Naval School in international law. During a service of twenty or twenty-five years he has mingled among gentlemen, both in our own country and abroad; it is his business to understand the commercial laws, for that is a part of the profession of a naval officer, and he is sent abroad for the purpose of enforcing them; and we think that competent men may be selected from that branch of the service to perform consular duty. We think that is a very good school in which to prepare them for these consulates. The Government will save a considerable amount of money by allowing naval officers, who are receiving half-pay, to be appointed consuls. In doing so we follow the practice of every commercial nation. One-half of the consulates of Great Britain throughout the world are held by half-pay officers, both of the army and navy. It is the same with the other governments of the world. The question as to whether a particular man was competent to fill one of these offices would be determined by the President when he appointed him, and by the Senate when they came to act upon his confirmation. We have a surplus of officers. Some are unqualified for sea-duty, but they all have the capacity for doing shore-duty, such as pertains to a consular agency.

THE NAVAL PENSION FUND.

When the Navy was established, at the beginning of this century, there was a law passed that in all future time the proceeds of prizes captured upon the high-seas by vessels of the United States, and brought into ports of the United States and condemned, should be distributed, one half to the captors, in the proportion specified by the law, and the other half should go into the naval pension fund, from which the widows and orphans of naval officers and seamen should be guaranteed the payment of their pensions. That is the way in which this fund was created; by the earnings, in effect, of the sailors and men belonging to the Navy. Whether it be true that the Government technically pledged its faith to preserve the fund intact or not, it is true that they are regarded by the seamen of the country as having made that pledge, and it has stood good for about seventy years.

Whenever a sailor who has been employed in the service of the United States presents his claim for prize-money, and he finds that it is not as great as he had anticipated, he is immediately told, "It is true your distributive share is not as great as you think you are entitled to, but you must remember that one-half of the whole proceeds of the prizes, in the capture of which you took part, has gone into the Treasury, and is part of a fund in Washington, which is dedicated to your benefit and the benefit of your children, and which the Government of the United States is under a moral obligation, at any rate, if not a legal obligation, never to interfere with." Now, the question is, whether it is advisable to change the course of the Government during the last seventy years, and say that an act shall be done, which will be considered by these seamen, whether correctly or not, as a violation of the public faith.

I am free to say that I am in favor of letting the matter stand as it is. If ever there was a fund equitably and justly administered, this has been; and the only difficulty is, that it has been so well administered that these sailors and officers have gathered together so large a fund that it is proposed by certain gentlemen to put their hands into the Treasury and grab it, because it has become so large. But it is said that we ought to abolish the naval pension fund for the purpose of simplifying the accounts. How far would that simplify the accounts? Three or four years ago we passed a bill directing the Secretary of the Treasury to invest all this money in registered securities of the United States; but we all know that it is really no indebtedness of the United States, that it is simply keeping the money; and the proposition is to take this money out of one pocket and virtually put it into another.

Am I, then, asked why I object to the proposition? It is because it bears upon its face, in the estimation of a large class of our fellow-citizens, the idea that it is diverting a fund which has been dedicated for their benefit. This fund is composed of the earnings of men in our employment. We pledged ourselves that, when they attacked the enemy's vessels and captured them, if they would bring them into our ports, where they could be condemned by our courts, this fund should be dedicated for all time to come for a specific purpose. I am free to confess that the subject of this fund has given me a good deal of thought. I am willing to admit that it has been accumulating too rapidly; not that we have gathered too many prizes, but that the fund is getting larger, probably, than it ought to be. My effort has been to find some way in which we could dispose of this matter without violating what is understood to be the public faith of the country. I have been waiting for some proposition, not like this, to sweep the whole fund away, but such as that of the Senator from Maine (Mr. Fessenden), to pay the surplus of interest into the Treasury of the United States. I would be content to vote for a proposition that would reduce the rate of interest on the certificates which are held by the Secretary of the Navy in trust, as a trustee, for this fund, say to three per cent., or to such other rates as shall pay the ordinary pensions of the officers and men of the Navy. What I want to preserve is the principal of the fund, and the faith of the nation pledged to these men, as they understand it (March 7th).

THE PENSION SYSTEM.

It is not a gratuity, to reward men for what they have done; but we say to the citizens of this country in advance: "We have established a pension system; if you choose to volunteer, or are drafted for the service of the United States, and are killed or wounded, you shall be provided for, in the one case during the balance of your life, or your family in the other." That has been the policy of the Government from its foundation. We have proceeded upon that idea, and it is a part of the national system; if you choose to call it so, to encourage patriotism. It says to the poor man, "If you choose to leave your family and risk your life, in the defense of the country, and in holding up its flag when it is attacked, your family shall be provided for, and your wants supplied in the future." It was never intended to meet a charitable case, if you please, but is part of a system.

Now, the question is, whether or not we had better establish a precedent, by which we shall pay all the deputy provost-marshals. But the principle extends beyond a deputy provost-marshal. Why shall we not extend it to a deputy-marshal, who in the execution of the process of a United States court is shot down? A Senator says we ought to do so. That may be his idea. His idea of the Government may be that of a great system of pensioned citizens. That is not my idea, and that, I apprehend, was not the idea of the men who founded the Government (March 12th).

THE NAVY.

Mr. Grimes advocated its reduction to eight thousand five hundred men, as before the war. In this he stood alone, among those who were regarded as friends of the Navy. No other member of the Senate Committee on Naval Affairs, nor the Navy Department, approved such a reduction. The proposition was attributed to an extraordinary fit of economy. Of the Marine Corps, he said:

I know no reason why there should be a greater number of men or officers in it now than before the war; and I give notice to those gentlemen who are electioneering about the Senate in behalf of the Marine Corps, that, if I can reduce them to where they were before the war, I shall use my utmost effort to do it.

In reply to some criticisms upon his views, he remarked:

I have never arrogated to myself any particular knowledge upon naval affairs. It has so happened that during my past life I have been brought into rather intimate connection with the subject, and during the term of my service in the Senate I have been on the Naval Committee. I have done the best that was in my power to inform myself upon the subjects that came before the committee, and have honestly attempted to convey the information I have obtained to the body of which I was a member.

He said, March 2, 1869:

The proper way to conduct the Department, if a civilian is to be at the head of it, is for the Secretary of the Navy to detail a naval officer to act for the time being as Assistant Secretary.

Explaining the system of naval apprentices, Mr. Grimes said, April 6th:

That is a system which has grown up during the war. It was discovered, both in the commercial and in the naval marine, that the number of sailors was gradually diminishing, and that it was almost impossible to secure the service of men who were fit to perform duty as man-of-wars-men. It was, therefore, thought advisable to establish what is known in our service as the apprentice system, picking up boys along the coast, and putting them upon old sailing-vessels, under the charge of naval officers, where they are instructed in the rudimentary branches of education, enlisting them until they are twenty-one years of age, preparing them for the performance of the duties of petty officers on board ship; and, in order to encourage this class of young men to enter the service, we have said that ten of them shall every year be taken from on board these practice-ships, and be sent to the Naval Academy, to be educated as officers. The opinion of naval officers is, that this system has worked admirably. They do not desire that it should be disturbed. The purpose I had in view was to save this system, to encourage the education of this class of boys for the naval and the commercial marine in the future.

ADMIRAL FARRAGUT.

The Franklin is the only large ship we have now afloat. She is in the European waters, and bears the pennant of the only admiral this country ever saw. Festivities have been enjoyed by that gentleman, whose father was a native of one of the islands in the Mediterranean, such as have never been enjoyed by any one else in this country; and greater honors have been bestowed upon him. Let me relieve any who may have apprehensions on this subject, by saying that not a dollar is spent by Admiral Farragut in any of the festivities in which he participates, or that he gives, which does not come out of his own pocket, and that ours is the only nation on the globe, that has a fleet, that does not furnish money to its admirals, situated as he is, to entertain distinguished people where they cruise (April 7th).

THE TARIFF.

Proposing a reduction of duties upon all importations, to the extent of ten per cent., Mr. Grimes said, March 18th:

I offer this proposition for several reasons:

1. To redeem the faith of the Government, that, if not technically, is virtually pledged to a proportionate reduction of the duties on imports, as the taxes on domestic manufactures shall be removed. We passed a war tariff in 1861, by which we greatly increased the duties imposed by the tariff of 1857. The argument urged by the advocates of the tariffs of 1862 and 1864 was, that it was necessary to pass those acts in order to adjust the tariff to the existing internal taxes. In fact, the internal tax law was the only pretext for imposing the high rates of duties under the tariff acts of those years.

2. Because it is but fair that while we relieve the manufacturers of the country, and enable them to make money, we should at the

same time relieve the consumers of the country, and enable them to save a little money; for, however we may arrange our tariff and tax laws, or however we may reason about them, we cannot escape from the conclusion that the revenues of the Government, through whatever channels paid into the Treasury, are wholly drawn from the consumers. Without the amendment I propose, the advantage will be exclusively to the manufacturers and not to the consumers. Every dollar that we prevent going into the Treasury for the benefit of these manufacturers, only serves to so much increase the tariff upon the consumers.

3. Because it is fair and important that all branches of industry should understand what is to be the whole policy of the Government. The manufacturers are a comparatively small class in this country. While it is important to them to know whether their products are hereafter to be taxed, it is of equal importance that the mercantile, the commercial, and the agricultural interests should know whether or not we are to be content to improve the condition of the manufacturers, and ignore the claims of all other classes of people and all other descriptions of industry.

4. Because a reduction of the tariff will greatly increase the revenue from imports, and for two reasons: first, as we increase the cost of an article, we diminish the number of those who will be able to consume it; and, second, because you will thereby lessen the amount of frauds upon the revenue. Your tariff laws now furnish an incitement to smuggling, and the passage of the act as reported will stimulate that description of enterprise still further. I can enumerate many imported articles now openly sold in the market of New York at one-half the import duty. Why? Because your high duty has encouraged smuggling.

I do not know that it makes much difference to the Senate or the country what may be my opinions, or whether or not I have changed my opinions; whether or not I was once in favor of protection, and am now in favor of free trade. But it is not true that I ever was a protectionist, if by a protectionist you mean what I understand to be meant by the high-tariff men of this body, a prohibitionist, or a restrictionist, and there is not any difference. The word "protection," as applied to this subject, is a misnomer. It never should be used in connection with it, for there cannot be a protection unless to the extent that the article is protected; to that extent it is prohibited. There are certain impediments thrown in the way of carrying on commerce or trade, so as to protect the man who manufactures the article at home against the man who manufactures it abroad; and, so far as it is a protection, it is a hinderance, a restriction, a prohibition upon trade. I never was a protectionist of that description. I never voted, as I have been charged in the *New York Tribune* and other places, for Mr. Clay. I never had an opportunity to do it. The first presidential vote I ever gave was in 1848. As I am charged here with being a free-trader, I will say that if it be a free-trader to try to obtain just as much money as possible for the benefit of the United States from imports, I am a free-trader. I am in favor of a revenue tariff. That is legitimate and proper; but the moment the Government undertakes to go beyond that, and take money from my pocket, or take the profit of my labor, for the purpose of building up a particular manufacture for the benefit of the Senator from Vermont, that moment the Government transcends its obligation and its duty. That is the kind of a free-trader I am. I am in favor of getting just as much money as possible, and I would, if I could, pay the entire expenses of this Government from the duties received from imported articles. There is not any trouble about building up manufactures. They will be created just as fast as the capital of the country shall become concentrated, and can be used in that way more profitably than in any other business. Some specific articles of domestic production might be taxed. I speak in general terms with regard to the tariff. In my conviction a man has a right to his limbs, and he has as much right to the product of his limbs, to the productions of his industry, as he has to his person; and when you undertake to say that I shall not be permitted to send the product of my industry, in the shape of wheat, to Montevideo, to Brazil, or to Buenos Ayres, to obtain with twenty bushels of my product a thousand pounds of wool with which to clothe my family, but, on the other hand, I shall buy only a hundred pounds of wool from a farmer of Vermont, it is incumbent upon the Government to show a good reason why I should thus be restrained. And the only reason they can assign is, that it is necessary in order to procure the means with which the Government can be conducted. To that extent it has a right to restrain me, and no further.

110.—*To H. W. Starr, Esq., Burlington.*

WASHINGTON, *March* 6, 1868.

Mr. Spofford, the Librarian of Congress, and a noted bibliopolist, is making out for me a catalogue of books to cost five thousand dollars. He is very familiar with the subject, and will try to secure the very best editions. If money can be raised to put Marion Hall in complete order, and heat it with steam, the only proper method of heating a library, I would be in favor of buying it.

The Senate is now organized as a court, and we have a six months' job upon us in the trial of the President. About a dozen men are determined to convict, about the same number are determined to acquit, and the balance intend to hear the evidence and weigh the law before they pronounce judgment. The President, as you observe, is to be defended by the most eminent lawyers in the country, and the House managers are no match for them. It will be the greatest trial in history, but I wish to Heaven that I had nothing to do with it, for it is sure to be to a great extent partisan, and, in so far as it may be, it will in the future be discreditable to all concerned in it. I am over the ague, etc., and pretty well.

The Burlington & Missouri River Railroad will be completed at once. I do not see why the prospects for Burlington's prosperity are not bright at present.

March 15*th.*—With the proper action, Burlington will become the most important city in Iowa.

We are in a tumult here. I advise you to believe nothing you see or hear from Washington, until you see the proof; especially believe no telegraphic reports. They are generally lies, and sent from here by the most worthless and irresponsible creatures on the face of the earth.

A resolution for the impeachment of President Johnson was adopted in the House of Representatives, February 24th, and on the following day a committee of the House appeared before the Senate, and impeached him of high crimes and misdemeanors in office.

In the discussions preliminary to the trial, Mr. Grimes held that it was not proper to establish rules of procedure and practice beforehand, as to the admission or exclusion of testimony, the number of counsel that should be heard, or limitations of time upon arguments, but that these matters should be determined after the Senate was resolved into a court, and when presided over by the Chief-Justice. Different views prevailed, and the Senate, March 2d, adopted rules of proceeding. The court was formed March 5th, and on that day Mr. Grimes took the prescribed oath, administered upon the Bible by Judge Chase, in the following words:

I do solemnly swear that in all things pertaining to the trial of the impeachment of Andrew Johnson, President of the United States, I will do impartial justice, according to the Constitution and the laws: so help me God.

The following day, the rules of procedure adopted by the Senate, at the suggestion of the Chief-Justice, were adopted by the body sitting as a court. Mr. Grimes gave close attention to the conduct of the trial through all its weary stages, and having heard the testimony, and having weighed the whole matter thoroughly, on the 11th of May delivered his

OPINION.

The President of the United States stands at the bar of the Senate charged with the commission of high crimes and misdemeanors. The principal offense charged against him is embodied in various forms in the first eight articles of impeachment. This offense is alleged to consist in a violation of the provisions of the first section of an act of Congress entitled "An act regulating the tenure of certain civil offices," approved March 2, 1867, in this, that on the 21st day of February, 1868, the President removed, or attempted to remove, Edwin M. Stanton from the office of Secretary for the Department of War, and issued a letter of authority to General Lorenzo Thomas as Secretary for the Department of War, *ad interim.*

The House of Representatives charge in their first three articles that the President attempted to remove Mr. Stanton, and that he issued his letter of authority to General Thomas with an intent to violate the law of Congress, and with the further "intent to violate the Constitution of the United States." The President, by his answer, admits that he sought to substitute General Thomas for Mr. Stanton at the head of the Department of War; but insists that he had the right to make such substitution under the laws then and now in force, and denies that, in anything that he has done or attempted to do, he intended to violate the laws or the Constitution of the United States.

To this answer there is a general traverse by the House of Representatives, and thereon issue is joined; of that issue we are the triers, and have sworn that in that capacity we will do "impartial justice according to the Constitution and the laws."

It will be perceived that there is nothing involved in the first eight articles of impeachment but pure questions of law growing out of the construction of statutes. Mr. Johnson's guilt or innocence upon those articles depends wholly on the fact whether or not he had the power, after the passage of the tenure-of-office act of March 2, 1867, to remove Mr. Stanton and issue the letter of appointment to General Thomas; and upon the further fact, whether, having no such legal authority, he nevertheless attempted to exercise it "with intent to violate the Constitution of the United States."

Mr. Stanton was appointed Secretary for the Department of War by Mr. Lincoln on the 15th day of January, 1862, and has not since been reappointed or recommissioned. His commission was issued to continue "for and during the pleasure of the President." His appointment was made under the act of August 7, 1789, the first two sections of which read as follows:

"There shall be an executive Department to be denominated the Department of War; and there shall be a principal officer therein, to be called the Secretary for the Department of War, who shall perform and execute such duties as shall from time to time be enjoined on or intrusted to him by the President of the United States, and the said principal officer shall conduct the business of the said Department in such manner as the President of the United States shall from time to time order and instruct.

"There shall be in the said Department an inferior officer, to be appointed by said principal officer, to be employed therein as he shall deem proper, and to be called the chief clerk of the Department of War; *and whenever the said principal officer shall be removed from office by the President of the United States*, and in any other case of vacancy, shall, during the same, have charge of the records, books," etc.

At the same session of Congress was passed the act of July 27,

1789, creating the Department of Foreign Affairs. The two first sections of the two acts are precisely similar except in the designations of the two Departments. Upon the passage of this last act occurred one of the most memorable and one of the ablest debates that ever took place in Congress. The subject under discussion was the tenure of public officers, and especially the tenure by which the Secretaries of the Executive Departments should hold their offices. Without going into the particulars of that great debate, it is sufficient to say that the reasons assigned by Mr. Madison and his associates in favor of a "tenure during the pleasure of the President" were adopted as the true constitutional theory on this subject. That great man, with almost a prophetic anticipation of this case, declared, on the 16th of June, 1789, in his speech in the House of Representatives, of which he was a member from Virginia, that—

"It is evidently the intention of the Constitution that the First Magistrate should be responsible for the Executive Department. So far, therefore, as we do not make the officers who are to aid him in the duties of that department responsible to him he is not responsible to the country. Again, is there no danger that an officer, when he is appointed by the concurrence of the Senate and his friends in that body, may choose rather to risk his establishment on the favor of that branch than rest it upon the discharge of his duties to the satisfaction of the executive branch, which is constitutionally authorized to inspect and control his conduct? And if it should happen that the officers connect themselves with the Senate, they may mutually support each other, and for want of efficacy reduce the power of the President to a mere vapor, in which case his responsibility would be annihilated, and the expectation of it unjust. The high executive officers joined in cabal with the Senate would lay the foundation of discord, and end in an assumption of the executive power, only to be removed by a revolution of the Government."

It will be observed that it is here contended that it is the Constitution that establishes the tenure of office. And, in order to put this question beyond future cavil, Chief-Justice Marshall, in his "Life of Washington," volume ii., page 162, says:

"After an ardent discussion, which consumed several days, the committee divided, and the amendment was negatived by a majority of thirty-four to twenty. The opinion thus expressed by the House of Representatives did not explicitly convey their sense of the Constitution. Indeed, the express grant of the power to the President rather implied a right in the Legislature to give or withhold it at their discretion. To obviate any misunderstanding of the principle on which the question had been decided, Mr. Benson moved in the House, when the report of the Committee of the Whole was taken up, to amend the second clause in the bill so as clearly to imply the power of removal to be solely in the President. He gave notice that if he should succeed in this he would move to strike out the words which had been the subject of debate. If those words continued, he said, the power of removal by the President might hereafter appear to be exercised by virtue of a legislative grant only, and consequently be subjected to legislative instability, when he was well satisfied in his own mind that it was by fair construction fixed in the Constitution. The motion was seconded by Mr. Madison, and both amendments were adopted."

And Judge Marshall adds:

"As the bill passed into a law it has ever been considered as a full expression of the sense of the Legislature on this important part of the American Constitution."

And Chancellor Kent says, when speaking of the action of this Congress, many of the members of which had been members of the convention that framed the Constitution, the chiefest among them, perhaps, being Madison, who has been called the father of that instrument:

"This amounted to a legislative construction of the Constitution, and it has ever since been acquiesced in and acted upon as of decisive authority in the case. It applies equally to every other officer of the Government appointed by the President and Senate whose term of duration is not specially declared. It is supported by the weighty reason that the subordinate officers in the Executive Department ought to hold at the pleasure of the head of that department, because he is invested generally with the executive authority, and every participation in that authority by the Senate was an exception to a general principle, and ought to be taken strictly. The President is the great responsible officer for the faithful execution of the law, and the power of removal was incidental to that duty, and might often be requisite to fulfill it."—1 *Kent's Commentaries*, 310.

Thus the Constitution and the law stood, as expounded by the courts, as construed by commentators and publicists, as acted on by all the Presidents, and acquiesced in by all of the Congresses from 1789 until the 2d of March, 1867, when the tenure-of-office act was passed. The first section of this act reads as follows:

"That every person holding any civil office, to which he has been appointed by and with the advice and consent of the Senate, and every person who shall hereafter be appointed to any such office, and shall become duly qualified to act therein, is and shall be entitled to hold such office until a successor shall have been in a like manner appointed and duly qualified, except as herein otherwise provided."

Then comes what is "otherwise provided:"

"*Provided*, That the Secretaries of State, of the Treasury, of War, of the Navy, and of the Interior, the Postmaster-General, and the Attorney-General, shall hold their offices respectively for and during the term of the President by whom they may have been appointed, and for one month thereafter, subject to removal by and with the advice and consent of the Senate."

The controversy in this case grows out of the construction of this section. How does it affect the act of 1789, and does it change the tenure of office of the Secretary for the Department of War as established by that act? To this inquiry I propose to address myself. I shall not deny the constitutional validity of the act of March 2, 1867. That question is not necessarily in this case.

The first question presented is, Is Mr. Stanton's case within the provisions of the tenure-of-office act of March 2, 1867?

Certainly it is not within the body of the first section. The tenure which that provides for is not the tenure of *any* Secretary. *All* Secretaries whose tenure is regulated by this law at all are to go out of office at the end of the term of the President by whom they shall be appointed, and one month thereafter, unless sooner removed by the President, by and with the advice and consent of the Senate, while all other civil officers are to hold until a successor shall be appointed and duly qualified. The office of Secretary has attached to it one tenure; other civil officers another and different tenure; and no one who holds the office of Secretary can, *by force of this law*, hold by any other tenure than the one which the law specially assigns to that office. The plain intent of the proviso to the first section is to prescribe a tenure for the office of Secretary different from the tenure fixed for other civil officers. This is known to have been done on account of the marked difference between the heads of Departments and all other officers, which made it desirable and necessary for the public service that the heads of Departments should go out of office with the President by whom they were appointed. It would, indeed, be a strange result of the law if those Secretaries appointed by Mr. Lincoln should hold by the tenure fixed by the act for ordinary civil officers, while all the other Secretaries should hold by a different tenure; that those appointed by the present and all future Presidents should hold only during the term of the President by whom they may have been appointed, while those not appointed by him should hold indefinitely; and this under a law which undertakes to define the tenure of all the Secretaries who are to hold their offices under the law. I cannot come to that conclusion. My opinion is that, if Mr. Stanton's tenure of office is prescribed by this law at all, it is prescribed to him as Secretary of War, under and by force of the proviso to the first section; and if his case is not included in that proviso it is not included in the law at all.

It is clear to my mind that the *proviso* does not include, and was not intended to include, Mr. Stanton's case. It is not possible to apply to his case the language of the proviso unless we suppose it to have been intended to legislate him out of office; a conclusion, I consider, wholly inadmissible. He was appointed by President Lincoln during his first term of office. He cannot hereafter go out of office at the end of the term of the President by whom he was appointed. That term was ended before the law was passed. The proviso, therefore, cannot have been intended to make a rule for his case; and it is shown that it was not intended. This was plainly declared in debate by the conference committee, both in the Senate and in the House of Representatives, when the proviso was introduced, and its effect explained. The meaning and effect of the proviso were then explained and understood to be that the only tenure of the Secretaries provided for by this law was a tenure to end with the term of service of the President by whom they were appointed, and, as this new tenure could not include Mr. Stanton's case, it was here explicitly declared that it did not include it. When this subject was under consideration in the House of Representatives on the report of the conference committee on the disagreeing vote of the two Houses, Mr. Schenck, of Ohio, chairman of the conference committee on the part of the House, said:

It will be remembered that by the bill as it passed the Senate it was provided that the concurrence of the Senate should be required in all removals from office, except in the case of the heads of Departments. The House amended the bill of the Senate so as to extend this requirement to the heads of Departments as well as to their officers.

The committee of conference have agreed that the Senate shall accept the amendment of the House. *But, inasmuch as this would compel the President to keep around him heads of Departments until the end of his term who would hold over to another term, a compromise was made by which a further amendment is added to this portion of the bill, so that the term of office of the heads of Departments shall expire with the term of the President who appointed them,* allowing these heads of Departments one month longer.

When the bill came to the Senate and was considered on the disagreeing vote of the two Houses, and Mr. Doolittle, of Wisconsin, charged that, although the purpose of the measure was, in his opinion, to force the President against his will to retain the Secretaries appointed by Mr. Lincoln, yet that the phraseology was such that the bill, if passed, would not accomplish that object, Mr. Sherman, of Ohio, who was a member of the conference committee, and assisted to frame the proviso, said:

I do not understand the logic of the Senator from Wisconsin. He first attributes a purpose to the committee of conference which I say is not true. I say that the Senate have not legislated with a view to any persons or any President, and therefore he commences by asserting what is not true. We do not legislate in order to keep in the Secretary of War, the Secretary of the Navy, or the Secretary of State.

Then a conversation arose between the Senator from Ohio and another Senator, and the Senator from Ohio continued thus:

That the Senate had no such purpose is shown by its vote twice to make this exception. That this provision does not apply to the present case is shown by the fact that its language is so framed as not to apply to the present President. The Senator shows that himself, and argues truly that it would not prevent the present President from removing the Secretary of War, the Secretary of the Navy, and the Secretary of State. And, if I supposed that either of these gentlemen was so wanting in manhood, in honor, as to hold his place after the politest intimation by the President of the United States that his services were no longer needed, I certainly, as a Senator, would consent to his removal at any time, and so would we all.

Did any one here doubt the correctness of Mr. Sherman's interpretation of the act when he declared that it "*would not prevent the present President from removing the Secretary of War, the Secretary of the Navy, and the Secretary of State?*" Was there any dissent from his position? Was there not entire acquiescence in it?

Again, said Mr. Sherman:

In this case the committee of conference—I agreed to it, I confess, with some reluctance—came to the conclusion to qualify to some extent the power of removal over a cabinet minister. We provide that a cabinet minister shall hold his office not for a fixed term, not until the Senate shall consent to his removal, *but as long as the power that appoints him holds office.*

But, whatever may have been the character of the debates at the time of the passage of the law, or whatever may have been the contemporaneous exposition of it, I am clearly convinced that the three Secretaries holding over from Mr. Lincoln's Administration do not fall within its provisions under any fair judicial interpretation of the act; that Mr. Stanton held his office under the act of 1789, and under his only commission, issued in 1862, which was at the pleasure of the President; and I am, consequently, constrained to decide that the order for his removal was a lawful order. Any other construction would involve us in the absurdity of ostensibly attempting to limit the tenure of all cabinet officers to the term of the officer having the power to appoint them, yet giving to three of the present cabinet ministers an unlimited tenure; for, if the construction contended for by the managers be the correct one, while four of the present cabinet officers will go out of office absolutely, and without any action by the Senate, on the 4th of March next, they having been appointed by Mr. Johnson, the three cabinet officers appointed by Mr. Lincoln will hold by another and different tenure, and cannot be removed until the incoming President and the Senate shall mutually agree to their removal.

If I have not erred thus far in my judgment, then it follows that the order for the removal of Mr. Stanton was not a violation of the Constitution of the United States by reason of its having been issued during the session of the Senate. If Mr. Stanton held his office at the pleasure of the President alone under the act of 1789, as I think he did, it necessarily follows that the President alone could remove him. The Senate had no power in reference to his continuation in office. I am wholly unable to perceive, therefore, that the power of the President to remove him was affected or qualified by the fact that the Senate was in session.

It has sometimes been put forward, as it was by Mr. Webster in the debate of 1835, that the usual mode of removal from office by the President during a session of the Senate had been by the nomination of a successor in place of A B, removed. This would naturally be so in all cases except the few in which the officer could not be allowed, consistently with the public safety, to continue in office until his successor should be appointed and qualified, and also should refuse to resign. Such cases cannot often have occurred. But, when they have occurred, I believe the President has exercised that power which was understood to belong to him alone, and which in the statute tenure of most offices is recognized by the acts of Congress creating them to be the pleasure of the President of the United States. A number of cases of this kind have been put in evidence. I do not find, either in the debates which have been had on the power of removal, or in the legislation of Congress on the tenure of offices, any trace of a distinction between the power of the President to remove in recess and his power to remove during a session of the Senate an officer who held solely by his pleasure; and I do not see how such a distinction could exist without some positive and distinct provision of law to make and define it. I know of no such provision. If that was the tenure by which Mr. Stanton held the office of Secretary for the Department of War, and I think it was, then I am also of the opinion that it was not a violation of the Constitution to remove him during a session of the Senate.

If Mr. Stanton held under the act of 1789, no permission of the President to continue in office, no adoption of him as Secretary for the Department of War, could change the legal tenure of his office as fixed by law, or deprive the President of the power to remove him.

My opinion on the matter of the *first* article is not affected by the facts contained in it, that the President suspended Mr. Stanton and sent notice of the suspension to the Senate, and the Senate refused to concur in that suspension. In my opinion that action of the President could not and did not change the tenure of Mr. Stanton's office, as it subsisted by law at the pleasure of the President, or deprive the President of that authority to remove him, which necessarily arose from that tenure of office.

If the order of the President to Mr. Stanton was a lawful order, as I have already said I thought it was, the first question under the *second* article is whether the President did anything unlawful in giving the order to General Thomas to perform the duties of Secretary for the Department of War *ad interim.*

This was not an appointment to office. It was a temporary designation of a person to discharge the duties of an office until the office could be filled. The distinction between such a designation and an appointment to office is in itself clear enough, and has been recognized certainly since the act of February 13, 1795. Many cases have occurred in which this authority has been exercised. The necessity of some such provision of law, in cases of vacancy in offices which the Executive cannot instantly fill, must be apparent to every one acquainted with the workings of our Government, and I do not suppose that a reasonable question can be made of the constitutional validity of a law providing for such cases.

The law of 1795 did provide for such cases ; and the President, in his answer, says he was advised that this was a subsisting law not repealed. It may be a question whether it has been repealed; but, from the best examination I have been able to bestow upon the subject, I am satisfied it has not been repealed.

I do not propose to enter into the technical rules as to implied repeals. It is a subject of great difficulty, and I do not profess to be able to apply those rules; I take only this practical view of the subject: When the act of February 20, 1863, was passed, which it is supposed may have repealed the act of 1795, it is beyond all dispute that vacancies in office might be created by the President; and there might be the same necessity for making temporary provision for discharging the duties of such vacant offices as was provided for by the act of 1795. The act of 1863 is wholly silent on this subject. Why should I say that a public necessity, provided for in 1795 and not negatived in 1863, was not then recognized; or why should I say that if recognized it was intended by the act of 1863 that it should not thereafter have any provision made for it? Comparing the act of 1863 and the cases it provided for, I see no sufficient reason to say that it was the intention of Congress in 1863 to deprive the President of the power given by the act of 1795 to supply the temporary necessities of the public service in case of vacancy caused by removal.

But if I thought otherwise I should be unable to convict the President of a crime because he had acted under the law of 1795. Many cases of *ad interim* appointments have been brought before us in evidence. It appears to have been a constant and frequent practice of the Government, in all cases when the President was not prepared to fill an office at the moment when the vacancy occurred, to make an *ad interim* appointment. There were one hundred and seventy-nine such appointments specified in the schedule annexed to the message of President Buchanan, found on page 584 of the printed record, as having occurred in little more than the space of thirty years. I have not minutely examined the evidence to follow the practice further, because it seems to me that if, as I think, the President had the power to remove Mr. Stanton, he might well conclude, and that it cannot be attributed to him as a high crime and misdemeanor that he did conclude, that he might designate some proper officer to take charge of the War Department until he could send a nomination of a suitable person to be Secretary; and, when I add that on the next day after this designation the President did nominate for that office an eminent citizen in whose loyalty to our country and in whose fitness for any duties he might be willing to undertake the people would be willing to confide, I can find no sufficient reason to doubt that the President acted in good faith and believed that he was acting within the laws of the United States. Surely the mere signing of that letter of appointment, neither attended nor followed by the possession of the office named in it, or by any act of force, of violence, of fraud, of corruption, of injury, or of evil, will not justify us in depriving the President of his office.

I have omitted to notice one fact stated in the second article. It is that the designation of General Thomas to act *ad interim* as Secretary of War was made during a session of the Senate. This requires but few words. The acts of Congress, and the nature of the cases to which they apply, admit of no distinction between *ad interim* appointments in the sessions or the recess of the Senate. A designation is to be made when necessary, and the necessity may occur either in session or in recess.

I do not deem it necessary to state any additional views concerning the *third* article, for I find in it no allegations upon which I have not already sufficiently indicated my opinion.

The *fourth*, *fifth*, *sixth*, and *seventh* articles charge a conspiracy. I deem it sufficient to say that, in my judgment, the evidence adduced by the House of Representatives not only fails to prove a conspiracy between the President and General Thomas to remove Mr. Stanton from office by force or threats, but it fails to prove any conspiracy in any sense I can attach to that word.

The President, by a written order committed to General Thomas, required Mr. Stanton to cease to act as Secretary for the Department of War, and informed him that he had empowered General Thomas to act as Secretary *ad interim*. The order to General Thomas empowered him to enter on the duties of the office and receive from Mr. Stanton the public property in his charge. There is no evidence that the President contemplated the use of force, threats, or intimidation; still less that he authorized General Thomas to use any. I do not regard the declarations of General Thomas, as explained by himself, as having any *tendency* even to fix on the President any purpose beyond what the orders on their face import.

Believing, as I do, that the orders of the President for the removal of Mr. Stanton, and the designation of General Thomas to act *ad interim*, were legal orders, it is manifestly impossible for me to attach to them any idea of criminal conspiracy. If those orders had not been, in my judgment, lawful, I should not have come to the conclusion, upon the evidence, that any actual intent to do an unlawful act was proved.

The *eighth* article does not require any particular notice after what I have said of the first, second, and third articles, because the only additional matter contained in it is the allegation of an intent to unlawfully control the appropriations made by Congress for the military service by unlawfully removing Mr. Stanton from the office of Secretary for the Department of War.

In my opinion, no evidence whatever, tending to prove this intent, has been given. The managers offered some evidence which they supposed might have some tendency to prove this allegation, but it appeared to the Senate that the supposed means could not, under any circumstances, be adequate to the supposed end, and the evidence was rejected. Holding that the order for the removal of Mr. Stanton was not an infraction of the law, of course this article is, in my opinion, wholly unsupported.

I find no evidence sufficient to support the *ninth* article.

The President, as Commander-in-Chief of the Army, had a right to be informed of any details of the military service concerning which he thought proper to inquire. His attention was called by one of his Secretaries to some unusual orders. He sent to General Emory to make inquiry concerning them. In the course of the conversation General Emory himself introduced the subject which is the gist of the ninth article, and I find in what the President said to him nothing which he might not naturally say in response to General Emory's inquiries and remarks without the criminal intent charged in this ninth article.

I come now to the question of intent. Admitting that the President had no power under the law to issue the order to remove Mr. Stanton and appoint General Thomas Secretary for the Department of War *ad interim*, did he issue those orders with a manifest *intent* to violate the laws and "the Constitution of the United States," as charged in the articles, or did he issue them, as he says he did, with a view to have the constitutionality of the tenure-of-office act judicially decided?

It is apparent to my mind that the President thoroughly believed the tenure-of-office act to be unconstitutional and void. He was so advised by every member of his cabinet when the bill was presented to him for his approval in February, 1867. The managers on the part of the House of Representatives have put before us and made legal evidence in this case the message of the President to the Senate, dated December 12, 1867. In that message the President declared:

"That tenure-of-office law did not pass without notice. Like other acts it was sent to the President for approval. As is my custom, I submitted its consideration to my cabinet for their advice upon the question, whether I should approve it or not. It was a grave question of constitutional law, in which I would of course rely most upon the opinion of the Attorney-General and of Mr. Stanton, who had once been Attorney-General. Every member of my cabinet advised me that the proposed law was unconstitutional. All spoke without doubt or reservation, but Mr. Stanton's condemnation of the law was the most elaborate and emphatic. He referred to the constitutional provisions, the debates in Congress—especially to the speech of Mr. Buchanan when a Senator—to the decisions of the Supreme Court, and to the usage from the beginning of the Government through every successive Administration, all concurring to establish the right of removal as vested by the Constitution in the President. To all these he added the weight of his own deliberate judgment, and advised me that it was my duty to defend the power of the President from usurpation, and to veto the law."

The counsel for the respondent not only offered to prove the truth of this statement of the President by members of the cabinet, but they tendered in addition thereto the proof "that the duty of preparing a message, setting forth the objections to the constitutionality of the bill, was devolved on Mr. Seward and Mr. Stanton." They also offered to prove—

"That at the meetings of the cabinet, at which Mr. Stanton was present, held while the tenure-of-office bill was before the President for approval, the advice of the cabinet in regard to the same was asked by the President and given by the cabinet; and thereupon the question whether Mr. Stanton and the other Secretaries who had received their appointment from Mr. Lincoln were within the restrictions upon the President's power of removal from office created by said act was considered, and the opinion expressed that the Secretaries appointed by Mr. Lincoln were not within such restrictions.

And—

"That at the cabinet meetings between the passage of the tenure-of-civil-office bill and the order of the 21st of February, 1868, for the removal of Mr. Stanton, upon occasions when the condition of the public service as affected by the operation of that bill came up for the consideration and advice of the cabinet, it was considered by the President and cabinet that a proper regard to the public service made it desirable that upon some proper case a judicial determination on the constitutionality of the law should be obtained."

This evidence was, in my opinion, clearly admissible as cumulative of, or to explain or disprove, the message of the President, which narrates substantially the same facts, and which the managers have introduced and made a part of their case; but it was rejected as incompetent testimony by a vote of the Senate. I believe that decision was erroneous; and inasmuch as there is no tribunal to revise the errors of this, and it is impossible to order a new trial of this case, I deem it proper to regard these offers to prove as equivalent to proof.

We have in addition to this testimony as to the intent of the President the evidence of General Sherman. The President desired to appoint General Sherman Secretary *ad interim* for the Department of War, and tendered to him the office. The complications in which the office was then involved were talked over between them. General Sherman says that the subject of using force to eject Mr. Stanton from the office was only mentioned by the President to repel the idea. When General Sherman asked him why the lawyers could not make up a case and have the conflicting questions decided by the courts, his reply was "that it was found impossible, or a case could not be made up; but," said he, "if we can bring the case to the courts it would not stand half an hour."

Here, then, we have the President advised by all of the members of his cabinet, including the Attorney-General, whose duty it is made by law to give legal advice to him, including the Secretary for the Department of War, also an eminent lawyer and an Attorney-General of the United States under a former Administration, that the act of March 2, 1867, was unconstitutional and void, that the three members of the cabinet holding over from Mr. Lincoln's Administration were not included within its provisions, and that it was desirable that upon some proper case a judicial determination on the constitutionality of the law should be obtained.

Now, when it is remembered that, according to Chief-Justice Marshall, the act of 1789, creating the Department of War, was intentionally framed "so as to clearly imply the power of removal to be solely in the President," and that, "as the bill passed into a law, it has ever been considered as a full expression of the sense of the Legislature on this important part of the American Constitution;" when it is remembered that this construction has been acquiesced in and acted on by every President from Washington to Johnson, by the Supreme Court, by every Congress of the United States from the first that ever assembled under the Constitution down to the Thirty-ninth; and when it is remembered that all of the President's cabinet and the most eminent counselors within his reach advised him that the preceding Congresses, the past Presidents and statesmen, and Story, and Kent, and Thompson, and Marshall, were right in their construction of the Constitution, and the Thirty-ninth Congress wrong, is it strange that he should doubt or dispute the constitutionality of the tenure-of-office act?

But all this is aside from the question whether Mr. Stanton's case is included in the provisions of that act. If it was not, as I think it clearly was not, then the question of intent is not in issue, for he did no unlawful act. If it was included, then I ask whether, in view of those facts, the President's *guilty intent* to do an unlawful act "shines with such a clear and certain light" as to justify, to require us to pronounce him guilty of a high constitutional crime or misdemeanor? The manager, Mr. Boutwell, admits that—

"If a law passed by Congress be equivocal or ambiguous in its terms, the Executive, being called upon to administer it, may apply his own best judgment to the difficulties before him, or he may seek counsel of his advisers or other persons; and acting thereupon without evil intent or purpose, he would be fully justified, and upon no principle of right could he be held to answer as for a misdemeanor in office."

Does not this admission cover this case? Is there not doubt about the legal construction of the tenure-of-office act? Shall we condemn the President for following the counsel of his advisers and for putting precisely the same construction upon the first section of the act that we put upon it when we enacted it into a law?

It is not necessary for me to refer to another statement made by a manager in order to sustain my view of this case; but I allude to it only to put on record my reprobation of the doctrine announced. It was said that—

"The Senate, for the purpose of deciding whether the respondent is innocent or guilty, can enter into no inquiry as to the constitutionality of the act, which it was the President's duty to execute, and which, upon his own answer, and by repeated official confessions and admissions, he intentionally, willfully, deliberately set aside and violated."

I cannot believe it to be our duty to convict the President of an infraction of a law, when in our consciences we believe the law itself to be invalid, and therefore having no binding effect. If the law is unconstitutional it is null and void, and the President has committed no offense and done no act deserving of impeachment.

Again, the manager said:

"The constitutional duty of the President is to obey and execute the laws. He has no authority under the Constitution, or by any law, to enter into any schemes or plans for the purpose of testing the validity of the laws of the country, either judicially or otherwise. Every law of Congress may be tested in the courts, but it is not made the duty of any person to so test the laws."

Is this so? It is not denied, I think, that the constitutional validity of this law could not be tested before the courts unless a case was made and presented to them. No such case could be made unless the President made a removal. That act of his would necessarily be the basis on which the case would rest. He is sworn to "preserve, protect, and defend the Constitution of the United States." He must *defend* it against all encroachments from whatever quarter. A question arose between the legislative and executive departments as to their relative powers in the matter of removals from and appointments to office. That question was, Does the Constitution confer on the President the power which the tenure-of-office act seeks to take away? It was a question manifestly of construction and interpretation. The Constitution has provided a common arbiter in such cases of controversy—the Supreme Court of the United States. Before that tribunal can take jurisdiction a removal must be made. The President attempted to give the court jurisdiction in that way. For doing so he is impeached, and for the reason, as the managers say, that—

> "He has no authority under the Constitution, or by any law, to enter into any schemes or plans for the purpose of testing the validity of the laws of the country, either judicially or otherwise."

If this be true, then if the two Houses of Congress should pass by a two-thirds vote over the President's veto an act depriving the President of the right to exercise the pardoning power, and he should exercise that power nevertheless, or if he should exercise it only in a single case for the purpose of testing the constitutionality of the law, he would be guilty of a high crime and misdemeanor and impeachable accordingly. The manager's theory establishes at once the complete supremacy of Congress over the other branches of Government. I can give my assent to no such doctrine.

This was a *punitive* statute. It was directed against the President alone. It interfered with the prerogatives of his Department as recognized from the foundation of the Government. It wrested from him powers which, according to the legislative and judicial construction of eighty years, had been bestowed upon him by the Constitution itself. In my opinion it was not only proper, but it was his duty, to cause the disputed question to be determined in the manner and by the tribunal established for such purposes. This Government can only be preserved and the liberty of the people maintained by preserving intact the coördinate branches of it—legislative, executive, judicial—alike. I am no convert to any doctrine of the omnipotence of Congress.

But it is said that in our legislative capacity we have several times decided this question, and that our judgments on this trial are therefore foreclosed. As for myself, I have done no act, given no vote, uttered no word, inconsistent with my present position. I never believed Mr. Stanton came within the provisions of the tenure-of-office act, and I never did any act, or gave any vote, indicating such a belief. If I had done so, I should not consider myself precluded from revising any judgment then expressed, for I am now acting in another capacity, under the sanction of a new oath, after a full examination of the facts, and with the aid of a thorough discussion of the law as applicable to them. The hasty and inconsiderate action of the Senate on the 21st of February may have been, and probably was, a sufficient justification for the action of the House of Representatives, as the grand inquest of the nation, in presenting their articles of impeachment, but it furnishes no reason or apology to us for acting otherwise than under the responsibilities of our judicial oath, since assumed.

The *tenth* article charges that, in order to

" bring into disgrace, ridicule, hatred, contempt, and reproach, the Congress of the United States, and the several branches thereof, to impair and destroy the regard and respect of all the good people of the United States for the Congress and legislative power thereof (which all officers of the Government ought inviolably to preserve and maintain), and to excite the odium and resentment of all the good people of the United States against Congress, and the laws by it duly and constitutionally enacted; and in pursuance of his said design and intent, openly and publicly, and before divers assemblages of the citizens of the United States, convened in divers parts thereof, to meet and receive said Andrew Johnson as the Chief Magistrate of the United States, did, on the 18th day of August, in the year of our Lord 1866, and on divers other days and times, as well before as afterward, make and deliver with a loud voice certain intemperate, inflammatory, and scandalous harangues, and did therein utter loud threats and bitter menaces."

These speeches were made in 1866. They were addressed to promiscuous popular assemblies, and were unattended by any official act. They were made by the President in his character of a citizen. They were uttered against the Thirty-ninth Congress, which ceased to exist more than a year ago. That body deemed them to be unworthy of their attention, and the present House of Representatives decided by an overwhelming majority that they, too, did not consider them worthy to be made the ground of impeachment. The first amendment to the Constitution of the United States declares that "Congress shall make no law abridging the freedom of speech." Congress, therefore, could pass no law to punish the utterance of those speeches before their delivery; but, according to the theory of this prosecution, we, sitting as a court *after* their delivery, can make a law, each for himself, to govern this case and to punish the President.

I have no apology to make for the President's speeches. Grant that they were indiscreet, indecorous, improper, vulgar, shall we not, by his conviction on this article, violate the spirit of the Constitution which guarantees to him the freedom of speech? And would we not also violate the spirit of that other clause of the Constitution which forbids the passage of *ex post facto* laws? We are sworn to render impartial justice in this case according to the Constitution and the laws. According to what laws? Is it to be, in the absence of any written law on the subject, according to the law of each Senator's judgment, enacted in his own bosom, after the alleged commission of the offense? To what absurd violations of the rights of the citizen would this theory lead us? For my own part I cannot consent to go beyond the worst British Parliaments in the time of the Plantagenets in efforts to repress the freedom of speech.

The *eleventh* article contains no matter not already included in one or more of the preceding articles, except the allegation of an intent to prevent the execution of the act of March 2, 1867, for the more efficient government of the rebel States. Concerning this, a telegraphic dispatch from General Parsons, of Alabama, and the reply of the President thereto, each dated in January preceding the passage of the law, appear to be the only evidence adduced. These dispatches are as follows:

"MONTGOMERY, ALABAMA, *January* 17, 1867.

"Legislature in session. Efforts making to reconsider vote on constitutional amendment. Report from Washington says it is probable an enabling act will pass. We do not know what to believe. I find nothing here. LEWIS E. PARSONS,
"*Exchange Hotel.*

"His Excellency ANDREW JOHNSON, *President.*"

The response is:

"UNITED STATES MILITARY TELEGRAPH EXECUTIVE OFFICE,
WASHINGTON, D. C., *January* 17, 1867.

"What possible good can be obtained by reconsidering the constitutional amendment? I know of none in the present posture of affairs; and I do not believe the people of the whole country will sustain any set of individuals in attempts to change the whole character of our Government by enabling acts or otherwise. I believe, on the contrary, that they will eventually uphold all who have patriotism and courage to stand by the Constitution, and who place their confidence in the people. There should be no faltering on the part of those who are honest in their determination to sustain the several coördinate departments of the Government in accordance with its original design. ANDREW JOHNSON.

"Hon. LEWIS E. PARSONS, *Montgomery*, *Alabama*."

I am wholly unable, from these dispatches, to deduce any criminal intent. They manifest a diversity of political views between the President and Congress. The case contains ample evidence outside of these dispatches of that diversity of opinion. I do not perceive that these dispatches change the nature of that well-known and, in my opinion, much-to-be-deplored diversity.

I have thus, as briefly as possible, stated my views of this case. I have expressed no views upon any of the questions upon which the President has been arraigned at the bar of public opinion, outside of the charges. I have no right to travel out of the record.

Mr. Johnson's character as a statesman, his relations to political parties, his conduct as a citizen, his efforts at reconstruction, the exercise of his pardoning power, the character of his appointments, and the influences under which they were made, are not before us on any charges, and are not impugned by any testimony.

Nor can I suffer my judgment of the law governing this case to be influenced by political considerations. I cannot agree to destroy the harmonious working of the Constitution for the sake of getting rid of an unacceptable President. Whatever may be my opinion of the incumbent, I cannot consent to trifle with the high office he holds. I can do nothing which, by implication, may be construed into an approval of impeachments as a part of future political machinery.

However widely, therefore, I may and do differ with the President respecting his political views and measures, and however deeply I have regretted, and do regret, the differences between himself and the Congress of the United States, I am not able to record my vote that he is guilty of high crimes and misdemeanors by reason of those differences. I am acting in a judicial capacity, under conditions whose binding obligation can hardly be exceeded, and I must act according to the best of my ability and judgment, and as they require. If, according to their dictates, the President is guilty, I *must* say so; if, according to their dictates, the President is not guilty, I *must* say so.

In my opinion the President has not been guilty of an impeachable offense, by reason of anything alleged in either of the articles preferred against him at the bar of the Senate by the House of Representatives.

Two days after delivering this opinion, Mr. Grimes was attacked with paralysis in the Senate-Chamber, and suffered extreme prostration. On the 16th of May, though continuing to be very feeble, he went to the Senate, determined that no risk should deter him from his public duty. Much apprehension was felt by friends as to the consequences. On that day a vote was taken on the eleventh article of impeachment. When his name was called, Judge Chase said he might remain seated. With the assistance of friends, however, he rose. The Chief-Justice said: "Mr. Senator Grimes, how say you? Is the respondent, Andrew Johnson, guilty or not guilty of a high misdemeanor, as charged in this article?" Mr. Grimes answered, "Not guilty." Thirty-five Senators voted "Guilty;" nineteen voted "Not guilty." The Chief-Justice, announcing the vote, said: "Two-thirds not having pronounced guilty, the President is, therefore, acquitted upon this article." The vote was taken on the second and third articles, May 26th, with the same result, when the Senate, sitting as a court of impeachment, adjourned without day.

Mr. Grimes's vote brought upon him foul abuse and detraction. The country was in a blaze of excitement. Honest opinion was divided. Many able and true men had felt assured of guilt and evil designs on the part of the President. In expectation of his removal from office, arrangements had been presumed upon with reference to the high offices of the Government, and many persons were dazzled by visions of place and power. Mr. Grimes kept aloof from partisan considerations. He remarked to an old friend: "Perhaps I did wrong not to commit perjury by order of a party; but I cannot see it in that way." He was upon his oath. He heard the whole case, and, under a sense of responsibility to the Supreme Judge and to the country, gave his verdict.

In the storm of calumny and vituperation that fell upon him, Chief-Justice Chase called, and, sitting by his bed with friendly anxiety and sympathy, said to him: "I would rather be in your place, Mr. Grimes, than to receive any honor in the gift of our people." In a few years, time and reflection altered many men's judgments, and the integrity of Mr. Grimes, and the political wisdom and sagacity of his general views upon the subject, were approved to the country. In facing clamor and prejudice and passion with firm resolution and an heroic spirit, he gave a fine example of unshaken and unterrified faith, loyalty, and zeal, in a crisis of the nation.[1]

111.—*To Henry W. Starr, Esq., Burlington, Iowa.*

WASHINGTON, *May* 17, 1868.

Am writing my first letter after paralysis. Am getting better, but doctors say I must leave here, and shall go as soon as I can travel. Am covered with blisters. This attack admonishes me that my political career is nearly over, that it is quite probable the last vote I shall ever give I gave yesterday; and I can say before God that I never gave one more conscientiously, nor one I am better satisfied with.

The following card is a sufficient reference to the calumnies of the period:

[1] "On the trial of Marshal Ney for treason (1815), the Duke de Broglie was the only peer who voted "Not guilty." The man, the place, and the hour all considered, the violence of political passions outside, the fear of fresh convulsions within—this was certainly one of the most heroic actions recorded in parliamentary history. It was a vote worthy of the son-in-law of Madame de Staël; and, whatever may be thought of the weakness and guilt of Ney, many a courtier, a soldier, and a peer, lived to regret that he did not vote as Victor de Broglie voted on that memorable day."—*Edinburgh Review, April,* 1872.

A Card to the Chicago Tribune.

WASHINGTON, *May* 26, 1868.

It is not true that I have now, or ever had, any hostility to Mr. Wade. I never had the slightest misunderstanding with him in my life.

It is not true that I ever sought to be, or ever desired to be, a candidate for Vice-President or President *pro tempore* of the Senate.

It is not true that Chief-Justice Chase sought to influence my judgment in the impeachment trial. I never had a word of conversation with the Chief-Justice on that subject, nor on the subject of a new party or of any political party; nor did he ever mention the subject of the presidency to me. I have not been in the house of the Chief-Justice for more than two years.

It is not true that I have ever been dissatisfied with the reconstruction plan of Congress. So far from it, I was one of the seven Senators who were members of the Joint Committee on Reconstruction, and signed the report. I was chairman of the sub-committee on the State of Tennessee, and it was upon my recommendation that that State was so early restored to the Union.

It is not true that I am now or ever was, either directly or indirectly, interested in the Chicago *Tribune* newspaper. I do not know nor ever have known how the *Tribune* corps is organized, what is its capital, who are its stockholders, or the value of its stock. Nor have I ever sought to influence the course of that paper on any measure, public or private. I am sorry to be compelled to add that the story, so circumstantially related and published, that the wife of the editor of that paper is my daughter, is not true.

It is not true that I ever had the slightest sympathy with the general policy of Mr. Johnson's Administration. I have had no personal intercourse with Mr. Johnson for two years; never asked him for a favor, and never received one from him.

It is true that, when I took an oath that "in all things appertaining to the trial of the impeachment of Andrew Johnson I would render impartial justice according to the Constitution and the laws" I ceased to act in a representative capacity. I became a judge, acting on my own responsibility and accountable only to my own conscience and my Maker; and no power could force me to decide in such a case, contrary to my convictions, to suit the requirements of a party, whether that party were composed of my friends or my enemies. JAMES W. GRIMES.

112.—*To Hon. William P. Fessenden, Washington.*

YONKERS, N. Y., *June* 10, 1868.

I am doing well; have recovered the use of my arm, though I cannot wield a pen with ease, and hence use a pencil. My leg is improving, but is weak, and I suppose will be for some time.

You must accept the Boston dinner. A great deal depends on it. If you do, it will hurt Sumner; especially if you and Trumbull call up and press his resolutions [1] lately introduced about impeachment, or at any rate make speeches about them. Those resolutions are "the last straw," are odious, and will be fatal to him, if you press him on them. Even this little use of my arm weakens it, and I must stop.

June 16*th*.—I am an egotist, as you know, and therefore will begin by saying that I am improving, am gaining flesh and strength, though I fear that my increase of strength is not equal to the increase of weight. This is partly owing to the fact that I now eschew tobacco in all its forms.

I hope you can attend the Boston dinner, and make a prepared speech. If you do not, you must write a long letter. I would carefully avoid the slightest allusion to Sumner personally, but you ought to state in the strongest terms your convictions of the revolutionary tendencies of the demands of the impeachmentites, and insist, as is the fact, that we saved the country.

[1] June 3d, Mr. Sumner submitted resolutions declaring the constitutional responsibility of Senators for their votes on impeachment:

1. That even assuming that the Senate is a court in the exercise of judicial power, Senators cannot claim that their votes are exempt from the judgment of the people, etc.

2. That the Senate is not at any time a court, invested with judicial power, but always a Senate with specific functions; that the proceeding by impeachment is from beginning to end political, and that the vote of a Senator on impeachment, though different in form, is not different in responsibility from his vote on any other political question, etc

3. That the simple requirement of the Constitution, which says, "Senators when sitting to try impeachment shall be on oath or affirmation," was never intended to change the character of the Senate as a political body, and cannot have any such operation, etc.

You are right in supposing that I am not surprised at the course of Mr. Stanton. You need never expect forgiveness from him. Governor Fish inquired for you to-day, and so does almost every one I meet. I see no one who does not sustain you in your course. I am satisfied that, with a few well-directed blows now that we have the anarchists down, their reign will forever end.

BATH, ME., *July* 7, 1868.

I see that Butler has made a report, but fails to report the testimony. From the extracts I have seen, I judge that it is the most discreditable public paper ever issued in this country. I have not heard of a man here who disapproved of your course on impeachment, after he came to understand it. Nor did I in Boston. I discovered that Hooper telegraphed and went to Boston, while the matter was pending, to get up a public meeting, petitions, etc., in favor of conviction, and it was to head off that movement that R. H. Dana, Jr., introduced his resolutions into the House, which came so near passing that body.

BATH, ME., *August* 1, 1868.

I have been watching the Portland press to notice the announcement of your return home, and not seeing it I judge that you have not yet reached that to me very desirable place. Had you done so, I should have been tempted to make a descent upon you, though I am in a very poor condition to make a visit to anybody. I leave on Monday for Rye Beach. I want to see you very much, but my physician orders surf-bathing, and I must obey. Notwithstanding his order, however, I think I should lay over a day in Portland, were I sure you were there.

I am happy to say that my original trouble is over, so far as I can see, but, having been compelled to cease smoking, I have grown quite fleshy, and am troubled with weakness and neuralgic pains in my hips and thighs. Added to this, my head is in a constant whirl. So you see I would not be a very agreeable visitor were I to go to see you.

113.—*To Mr. N. C. Deering.*

WASHINGTON, *January* 29, 1869.

I thank you for your letter of the 19th instant. I had no doubt, when I gave my vote on the question of impeachment, that the storm would beat upon me, and that many good men whose opinions I esteemed would always believe that I was influenced by improper motives; still there was only one course open to me, and that was to obey my oath, to "do impartial justice according to the Constitution, the laws, and the evidence," and submit to the consequences, let them be what they might. Neither the honors nor the wealth of the world could have induced me to act otherwise, and I have never for a moment regretted that I voted as I did. I shall always thank God that he gave me courage to stand firm in the midst of the clamor, and by my vote not only to save the Republican party, but prevent such a precedent being established as would in the end have converted ours into a sort of South American republic, in which there would be a revolution whenever there happened to be an adverse majority in Congress to the President for the time being.

In January Mr. Grimes made a donation of five thousand dollars to Dartmouth College: to found two scholarships of one thousand dollars each; a prize fund of one thousand dollars, the income to be given annually in two prizes to members of the senior class for excellence in English composition; a fund of one thousand dollars, the income to be annually awarded to that member of the senior class who, in the judgment of the Faculty, has made the most satisfactory progress during his college course, taking into consideration his preparation when he entered; and one thousand dollars to the "Social Friends," a literary society, of which he was a member when in college.

President Smith, acknowledging the donation, said, February 3d:

Allow me to thank you in the name of the Faculty, the trustees, and, I will add, of the young men, who, in all future time, will be benefited by your bounty. For you have given such direction to your gift that, in one way or another, it will affect every member of the institution. I note what you say about giving "unnecessary publicity" to your benefaction, and I appreciate your wish to escape newspaper notoriety. But the thing cannot be kept in a corner. The students must know it, and they will be delighted with it; and gladness, you know, has always a tongue. Besides, your name is an honored one in New Hampshire, and I almost think the good people have a right to know that you have thus remembered the one college of your native State.

INCREASE OF DUTY UPON COPPER.

I am glad to know upon what theory this bill proceeds. We learn from the Senator from Vermont (Mr. Morrill) that it is a charitable measure, that it originated in a pure spirit of humanity. It seems that there is a class of people somewhere in the State of Michigan who are in a starving condition, and, because they are in a starving condition, the Senator has been willing to acknowledge here that he is content to destroy all the commerce of this country that is used in connection with this copper interest, and increase the value of every spike and nail, and the sheathing and yellow metal with which vessels are covered, to the extent of a very large per cent. If that is the spirit in which this bill originated, it seems to me it would be better to organize a branch of the Freedmen's Bureau, to take charge of those famishing and suffering people, than to increase the duty on every article of household economy that is made of copper. This increase comes off of every laboring-man, artisan, and mechanic. It comes off of every man who is compelled to buy a cooking-stove. Instead of taking money out of the wealth of the country for feeding these famishing people in Michigan, you make every man in my State and in Illinois poorer to the extent that the Senator has succeeded in inducing this body to increase the duty from thirty-five to forty-five per cent.

There is another question I should like to have solved. I should like to know how much copper there is on hand. They protected us in my country, two years ago, by putting a high duty on wool, by which they succeeded in lowering the value of wool in my State from forty-five or fifty-five cents down to no market at all; but there were parties who were protected, and they were the people who had large quantities of wool on hand. The immediate effect was that everybody in the Western country attempted to increase the production of wool, and doubled his flocks, or increased his flocks to the largest extent possible. While doing that, you put a high duty on the imported wool, which was necessary to be used in order to manufacture the articles that each one wears here to-day, and the result was, there was not any market for our wool. But there were parties that were benefited, who had, in anticipation of the passage of that law, imported large quantities of foreign wool, which they were able to sell, realizing the advance we put upon the tariff. The price rose in anticipation of the law, just as copper has risen to-day in anticipation of the passage of this bill. I am told there is a vast quantity on hand, and the passage of this bill will put immense sums in the pockets of the men owning it. That is the advantage of passing tariff bills in this way. I need not indicate, I think, that I shall vote against this bill, and against all other tariff bills that are not levied strictly for revenue purposes (January 19th)

Congratulating Mr. Cameron, of Pennsylvania, upon his liberal ideas in favor of free banking, Mr. Grimes said, February 22d;

I trust in a few months he will be able still more to liberalize his conceptions of public affairs, and that he will then be in favor of more liberal laws and rules in regard to commerce and trade, and that it will be but a little while before I shall be able to welcome him into my party of free trade.

Upon a resolution to admit books, maps, regalia, apparatus, art collections, etc., for certain purposes, free of duty, he said:

While in favor of throwing as few obstacles as possible upon the importation of such articles, I am not prepared to vote to put three hundred per cent. duty upon copper, that is used in all sorts of domestic purposes, and, at the same time, entirely exempt such articles from duty (February 24th).

In favor of paying three thousand dollars to the widow of Samuel T. Hartt, naval constructor, Mr. Grimes said, February 11th:

This man, while in the performance of his duties at the Norfolk Navy-Yard, conceived the idea of a new kind of elevator, such as had never been used in our own or any other navy, by which to elevate and depress the breech of a gun. Up to that time it had always been elevated by inartificial and awkward blocks, if I may be permitted to use an unprofessional phrase here. The sloop-of-war Portsmouth was about being fitted out at the Norfolk Navy-Yard, and was going to the Asiatic squadron in the Chinese seas, under the command of the late lamented Rear-Admiral Foote. He thought favorably of this plan, and, at his instance, the Secretary of the Navy allowed the guns of that vessel to be fitted out in this particular way. She sailed for China, and engaged in a conflict with the Canton Barrier forts, where the guns had a fair opportunity of being tested with this experiment, and with very great success. Shortly after, Mr. Hartt died, leaving a widow and four helpless children. She took out no letters-patent, nor did Hartt in his lifetime. Finding that it was a success, and that this screw absolutely became necessary, we have been introducing it into our ships, and using it with all our guns. Now the widow comes to us and says that she is entitled to some compensation for the use of her husband's method for elevating and depressing guns, and the Naval Committee have agreed with her in that. I agree with the Senator from Pennsylvania (Mr. Cameron) as to the general principle that an officer in the employ of the Government ought to bestow upon the Government his undivided services; but I think that this bill does not come within that rule, and this is the first case where I have ever consented to report such a bill to the Senate favorably.

Advocating the publication by Congress of the medical and surgical history of the war, Mr. Grimes said, February 13th:

I think it is but due to poor humanity, that we should let it know what has been accomplished by medical science during our war to save human life, for the benefit of the world in the future. The war drew to it the most eminent medical ability in this country, and the result is that medical science in the United States to-day stands higher than it does in any country in Europe. There may be individual physicians and surgeons in Europe, who have devoted their time to particular specialties, who have a higher reputation than any surgeons in this country; but, as a mass, in consequence of the developments of this war, I am assured, not by men who are interested in the publication of this work, but by men outside of the army-surgeons, and by men connected with the profession in other countries, that American medical science has a higher reputation than that of any country in Europe; and it grows out of the experience of this war. I think it is due to the country, it is due to humanity, that we should let the world know what these developments have been, in the most authentic way possible.

§ 6.—*In the Forty-first Congress. — First Session — March, April,* 1869.

The country still groaning under the burden of taxation, Mr. Grimes continued to urge economy in all public expenditure. He introduced a bill, March 6th, to reorganize the Navy, mainly for the purpose of reducing its expenses, so that the number of officers should be a little less than at the beginning of the war; and advocated similar economy with reference to the Army and the Indian Department. Upon a motion to appropriate five thousand dollars for medallions of the President, to be distributed to Indian tribes, he remarked:

I am satisfied this is a custom more honored in the breach than in the observance. At an early day I lived in the neighborhood of Indians, and I have seen a dozen of these medallions hung up in corner groceries, where they had been bartered off by the Indians for whiskey. Once in a while an old fellow may carry one for some years, but generally they soon are lost, or fall into the hands of the whiskey-sellers.

Upon the introduction of a bill to authorize the prepayment of interest on the public debt, a letter from the Secretary of the Treasury being read in favor of the measure, Mr. Grimes asked why the Secretary preferred to do this, rather than to comply with the law in regard to a sinking-fund. Mr. Sherman said, "Many persons are opposed to a sinking-fund." Mr. Grimes replied:

Many people may be opposed to it, but Congress is not. When we authorized the debt to be created, we declared that there should be a sinking-fund. That fund exists only upon the statute. The law authorizes the Secretary of the Treasury to buy the bonds of the United States. Where should we save any money by paying the interest in advance, over buying up the bonds of the United States, and putting them into the sinking-fund? (March 23d).

Mr. Grimes advocated the repeal of the tenure-of-office act, of March 2, 1867. That act was passed to tie the hands of President Johnson. It trammeled alike those of the new President. To repeal it, however, seemed to many Senators, as Mr. Morrill, of Vermont, remarked, like eating their own words, when they voted Andrew Johnson guilty of violating the Constitution, as well as the act in question. Mr. Grimes had no occasion for such scruples. He held that the Government could be properly administered only by enforcing a speedy and strict accountability of all officers to the Executive. He did not wish to have a hand in perpetuating such troubles and conflicts between the Executive and Congress as had existed to the injury of the public service under Mr. Johnson.

114.—*To Henry W. Starr, Esq., Burlington.*

WASHINGTON, *March* 18, 1869.

I shall go to Europe next month. Am glad to hear that the library is so successful, and trust that an effort will be made to keep it up.

The impeachment *furor* has entirely subsided here, and those who voted for it are now on the defensive, rather than those who voted against it. Between us, I am satisfied that I am stronger in the Senate in every respect, where I am so well known, than I ever was before I was tried in the furnace of impeachment. The only evil-resulting to me from that attempt to act according to my convictions, has been the injury to my health. I am slowly overcoming that, however, and I hope that I shall some time be nearly, if not quite, restored.

CHAPTER V.

TRAVELS IN EUROPE.—RETURN HOME.—DEATH.—CHARACTER.

1869–1872.

Mr. Grimes sailed for Europe, April 14, 1869, and remained abroad until the summer of 1871. He was in London early in May, and found there a state of great excitement, growing out of a recent speech of Mr. Sumner's on the Johnson-Clarendon treaty. In interviews with a number of English gentlemen, who occupied places of authority and influence, and by a letter to the *Times*, which one of those gentlemen assured him would be of great service at that moment, he assisted to correct and quiet the public mind. "It is gratifying," said the *Times*, "to receive so emphatic a disclaimer of Mr. Sumner's extravagant propositions."

115.—*To the Editor of the London Times.*

Will you permit an American, who has read all the articles published in your columns within the last two weeks on American affairs, and who thinks he has a tolerably correct judgment of the public sentiment of his country, to assure you—

1. That there never has been a time within the last fifty years when there was in the United States less of a disposition to go to war with any country, least of all with Great Britain, than there is at the present moment.

2. That the Senate of the United States, by their vote on what is called "the Alabama Treaty," simply agreed to the conclusion

at which Mr. Sumner arrived in his speech in the executive session of that body, and not to the processes by which he reached that conclusion, or the arguments by which he supported it.

3. That Mr. Sumner delivered an elaborate speech on this subject, which he had been four weeks preparing, and from which he desired the injunction of secrecy to be removed,[1] a request that is always granted by the Senate. All other remarks made on the occasion were informal and conversational, and the speakers neither felt nor expressed any similar desire for publicity.

4. That there were various causes not generally known, and which it is needless to allude to, that conspired to secure the rejection of the treaty, not the least of which were the unwise declarations of members of the British legation in Washington, which, coupled with the manner of constituting the commission, as agreed upon in the treaty, gave an appearance, at least, of probable unfairness in the arbitration.

5. That England's offense in the eyes of Americans is not "that she conceded belligerent rights to the Confederacy, at a time when the Southern States had apparently established themselves as an independent power," or that she recognized their belligerent rights at any time, nor that we did not enjoy the full sympathy of her citizens during the rebellion. Their real grievance is that the Alabama, built and fitted out in an English port, never ran into a Confederate port so as to acquire the legal character of a Confederate belligerent, technically or otherwise; that she was in truth an English vessel, sailing from a British port, under the British flag, manned by British sailors, was everywhere cordially received, supplied and coaled at British stations, while such hospitality was denied to American cruisers; that she never had any other home than the port of Liverpool, from which she originally departed, and remained in law and conscience a British vessel until she sank beneath the waves. This is our grievance. All else is the embellishment of the advocate and orator.

6. That while it is not to be denied that there is a desire in the Northwestern States of the Union to see the British provinces added to their Government, for the purpose of securing control of the navigation of the St. Lawrence River, which drains a large portion

[1] "The removal of the injunction of secrecy was not made at my request. It was the spontaneous act of the Senate."—(MR. SUMNER *to* MR. GRIMES, *May 28th.*)

of their territory, it is also true that many of the Atlantic States are opposed to their acquisition, because they fear that if acquired the West will have uninterrupted water communication with Europe, without passing through and being tributary to them. The intelligent people of the West are patiently biding their time, in the full faith that when the British Government concludes, as it sooner or later will conclude, that the provinces are an element of expensive weakness to it, and that it will no longer support them, they will be quite as anxious to join the United States as their public men, who almost exclusively enjoy the bounty bestowed by the home Government, now profess to be unwilling to do so. There is not a respectable minority of any party in any State in the Union that would for a moment justify an attempt to wrest the Canadas, by force, from the British crown.

7. I am not prepared to say what may be the specific instructions with which Mr. Motley may come to England; but I am prepared to say that they will not be other than of the most pacific character. It should be borne in mind that under our Government the Senate is a part of the treaty-making power; that the rejection or amendment of a treaty by that body is of frequent occurrence, and that such a rejection furnishes no reason to the American mind why efforts at negotiation should not be renewed again and again. Possibly Mr. Motley may not be instructed to take the initiative in a new treaty, but that should not be the cause of uneasiness on the part of any one, and certainly cannot be the cause of war.

AN AMERICAN CITIZEN.

1 CHARGES STREET, *May* 10, 1869.

116.—*To Hon. W. P. Fessenden.*

LONDON, *May* 10, 1869.

You have no idea of the tumult that has been created here by Sumner's speech. Our friends during the war are much grieved about it, for it has had the effect to place them in a false position entirely. Mr. Bright told me to-day that Johnson brought to him a letter of introduction from Sumner, indorsing him and what he might do, in the strongest possible manner, that Mr. Seward furnished substantially the terms of the treaty, and he offered to show me a letter from Sumner to him, received about three weeks ago, in which he said that if the treaty had been submitted to the Senate twelve months ago, it would have passed that body with no dissentients. He denounced Sumner quite vigorously, for a quaker, and wound up by saying that he was either a fool himself, or else thought the English public and their public men to be fools. He sent for me to call on him, and I had a long talk with him. He is undoubtedly a true friend of our country. It cannot be comprehended how the Senate could remove the injunction of secrecy from Sumner's speech, so full as it is of vituperation, and not remove it from the supposed other senatorial speeches, unless the whole body is in full sympathy with his sentiments. I have explained all that in the *Times.* Our bonds here have fallen five per cent., and the English people are really anticipating war with us, in which they expect to be aided by France. I have laughed and continue to laugh at the panic, but it is really becoming serious.

The truth is, that Sumner has greatly injured our cause by presenting so many perfectly absurd arguments, and urging them with so much bitterness. The true way is to present our real grievance in the Alabama case, which is a grievance patent to all. But he covers up that confessedly evil act in so much rhetorical verbiage about the sympathies of the English people, which this Government could not control, and their declaration of belligerent rights, which *we* recognized first, that he fritters away the strength of his strong point. I suppose this will all blow over in time, but it has really been looking blue here for a week. There is a talk here among Americans that Mr. Bright may be sent on a special mission to America, to adjust this matter. No one here denies their liability on account of the Alabama depredations, and they are anxious to settle it. They do not want war, but they are ready for it. They can borrow money at three per cent., while we would be unable to borrow it at all, and while they would sweep our commerce from the seas, they would also ravage our coasts with their vastly superior navy, and blockade all our ports.

We have been in England two weeks, and in London one; have been seeing and shall continue to see the sights for a week yet, and then go to Paris and then to the Aix-la-Chapelle baths, whither I have been ordered by the doctor.

When Mr. Grimes had been about three weeks in Paris, he suffered a second attack of paralysis. He then believed that he should never be able to resume his place in the Senate, and soon afterward sent in his resignation of the office of Senator to the Governor of Iowa.

117.—*To the Hon. W. P. Fessenden.*

PARIS, *July* 9, 1869.

Your welcome letter came duly to hand. You have perhaps heard that I have had the misfortune to be attacked a second time by my terrible enemy, the paralysis. This time the attack was of the left side. It occurred about five weeks ago in this city, just as we were about to leave it, and the very day I had pronounced myself to my wife as well as I was before my first attack. I am slowly recovering, and hope to be nearly if not quite well in time. My head has been a good deal affected, and this is the first time I have attempted to write, read, or think, without giddiness and suffering in that important organ. This attack closes up my political career. I shall never, I am sorry to say, sit by your side as a member of the Senate again. I shall not return to America this year, but shall resign my place as Senator before Congress meets. So much of a personal character, for which you must pardon me; but I thought you might wish to know my condition and plans.

I received a letter from Sumner about two weeks ago, grieving over my letter to the *Times*. I had a mind to answer it publicly, but have concluded to let him go. I could *scare* him terribly. I hear it from undoubted authority that he has written to Motley, complaining of his Liverpool speech as not being sufficiently belligerent. I have not seen an American in Europe who is not ashamed of Sumner's speech, and but feels humiliated that such a speech should be regarded as the highest attainment of senatorial eloquence on a great international question.

There is one thing we lack in America, more than anything else, to make up an accurate history of our country, and that is, memoirs of public men. I am greatly struck with that fact here, where they have ever been so abundant. What kind of a history can any man coming after us make up of the last ten years from the newspapers? None at all. Now, you have lived in the most eventful period of our country's history. You have had a leading part in public affairs for twenty-five years; you have a cool head, a retentive memory, and a facile pen. I insist that you ought, in justice to the future, in behalf of your own memory, and for the common good, to spend a few leisure hours every day in preparing your memoirs. You need not necessarily take up subjects *seriatim;* begin with any one of the many interesting topics, and after one is completed you will be more in the humor to begin another. If you do not choose to publish them in your own time, leave them to be published in some future time, in vindication of your memory, and to promote the cause of truth.

118.—*To Henry W. Starr, Esq., Burlington.*

PARIS, *July* 23, 1869.

I had about six weeks ago another stroke of the paralysis, this time affecting my left side, from the crown of my head to the sole of my foot. I had thought I was entirely recovered from the first attack, which you remember was of the right side, and began to be imprudent in my diet, labor, etc. This attack came on in the night. The day before, which was a warm Sunday, I did not go out of the house, and said to my wife, when going up-stairs after dinner, that I believed I was now entirely well again. The next morning I was prostrated. This attack was much more violent than the first one, affecting my head much more. I have not written a letter until within three days without the very little mental exertion causing a pressure upon the brain, and a sense of giddiness or lightness, so that I would be compelled to rest every minute. I feel this sensation to some extent now, but I am rapidly gaining on it. I have had three of the most eminent physicians in Paris. They are certainly very intelligent men, and appear to understand the subject. Their course is exactly opposite to that advised by the American physicians: in America I was dosed with strychnine, and in Paris with arsenic. I am gaining slowly, am keeping house, have been compelled to remain in Paris, am advised to ride and be in the open air, and therefore keep a span of horses and a driver, and have seen the outside of everything in and around Paris, and Mrs. Grimes and Mary have seen nearly everything inside. We have been here now three months. We are told that we can go to Homburg, in Germany, next week, but we shall remain here a week after that, in order to see John Walker, who is on his way hither, in command of the frigate Sabine, with the class of graduating midshipmen, George Remey, young Bridgman, etc.

I was shocked to hear of the death of Mr. Carpenter.[1] There seem to be very few, if any, of our early contemporaries left about Burlington.

I wrote the Alabama letter when in London, and published it at the instance of John Bright, who had been all through the war our friend, is such now, and always will be, but who at the time was terribly disturbed by the taunts of Roebuck, Laird, and the rest of our enemies. It was known all through London who wrote it, and it was said to have produced a good effect. Such men as Robert Chambers, of Edinburgh, called on me to thank me for it, etc. You can have no conception of the effect of Sumner's speech. Our bonds fell five per cent. in London in one day, and would have fallen twenty, but for the German buyers, who stepped in and held up the market, and made themselves rich by it. Would you believe it possible that John Bright could have a letter from Sumner, written as late as January last, in which he said that, had the Alabama treaty been presented to the Senate one year ago, it would have been confirmed without a dissenting voice? Yet it is true, for I have seen the letter; and yet Sumner made that speech.

I must from this time forward cease to attend to business of any kind. It is rather hard that just at this time, when I feel myself in the full vigor of my mental powers, I should be compelled to surrender all the ambitions of a lifetime. I have the consolation of feeling that, however much I may have erred, my error was one of judgment, and, sweetest of all, I have the consolation of knowing that on the subject about which I really made shipwreck of my health, I have daily, hourly evidences that the intelligent sentiment of the country applauds the course I took, and that that sentiment will increase more and more from year to year.

119.—*To Mr. Lyman Cook, Burlington.*

AIX-LES-BAINS, SAVOY, *August* 27, 1869.

Your long and very agreeable letter of the 8th of August has just reached me here, for which I am greatly obliged to you. I assure you that your letters have the effect to dissipate for some time the feeling of homesickness and the blues, with which I am a great deal of the time much oppressed.

I flatter myself that you want to hear about myself and my con-

[1] Anthony W. Carpenter, mayor of the city, 1868.

dition and future movements. Ten days ago we came to this place, which is a village of four thousand people, on the bank of Lake Bourget, and entirely surrounded by high mountains, making it for about six hours in the day the hottest place in the world. It is six and a half miles from Chambéry, the ancient capital of Savoy, a few miles from the Mont Cenis Tunnel, three and a half hours by rail from Geneva, and about fifty miles from Mont Blanc. There is a celebrated hot sulphur spring here, known to the Romans, who erected baths, a temple to Diana, etc., the remains of which are still conspicuous, and a splendid gateway to the baths is standing, which was erected in the fourth century. The water is about 120° Fahr., and for the most part administered by douches, and with friction. There are about three thousand visitors here at present, and the number is about ten thousand during the year. I fancy that I have been helped by the baths. The immediate effect of them is to greatly bleach, and reduce the strength of the patient. Such to some extent has been my experience. I am not as strong as when I came here, and I am as white as a ghost; still I hope and believe that I am better. The physician advises me to leave here after bathing a few days longer, and go to the alkaline waters at Evian, a small watering place on Lake Geneva. We shall, therefore, leave here on the 4th of September for that place, where we shall remain about three weeks, when we shall go to Nice, *via* Lyons and Marseilles, to meet John Walker and the frigate Sabine, and shall probably go on her to Naples. My great difficulty is with my head, which is full of uncomfortable and sometimes excruciating pains. I fancy that I am destined to overcome them in some measure in the future—at any rate my experience has taught me the necessity of taking care of myself.

These Savoyards are a very quiet, simple people, and inhabit a most interesting country. It was in relation to these people that Milton wrote his grand invocation beginning—

> "Avenge, O Lord, thy slaughtered saints!"

and for whom also Cromwell demanded and obtained religious toleration. Then, they were a part of the dukedom of Savoy, afterward belonged to the kingdom of Sardinia and Italy, and in 1860 were ceded to France, in consideration of the assistance rendered by the latter country to Victor Emmanuel in his war with Austria. It is curious to see the hills cultivated in places to their very tops, to see fig-trees as large as our apple-trees, to see the olive-orchards, and the grapes twined tree to tree, and hanging in festoons between.

You may be interested to know that I have had the honor of importing the American fever and ague to this Alpine country, and that that infernal disease, which I have had for thirty-four years, is the assigned cause for my disease of paralysis. It seems that I shall never be rid of it.

I am, of course, most happy to know that the eclipse was a great success.[1]

You have, doubtless, noticed that I have resigned my place in the United States Senate. It may be that Iowa will secure abler, more brilliant men, to represent her in the Senate, but she will obtain no one more anxious always to promote her best interests. After thirty-one years, off and on, of political experience and office-holding, I have now laid down the *rôle*, never in any event to be resumed. What may be my future course, I know not.

I hope you will come to Europe in the spring, and spend a few months at least. I doubt if you could better dispose of yourself and the small amount of money it will cost. Do not fail to write often, and remember me kindly to all friends, of whom I trust that I have a few yet remaining in Burlington.

120.—*To Hon. W. P. Fessenden.*

Aix-les-Bains, Savoy, *August* 31, 1869.

Your letter of the 8th inst. has just reached me, in the midst of the Savoy Alps, being douched and soaked in hot sulphur-water.

Perhaps you have observed that I have resigned my place in the Senate. The truth is, the place has become irksome to me. There are so many men there with whom I have not and never can have a particle of sympathy, so much corruption in the party with which I would be compelled to act, so much venality and meanness all around, that, aside from my ill-health, I had about made up my mind that the Senate was no longer the place for me. To this is to be added the fact that I am bound, I suppose, to regard myself hereafter as a broken-down man, unfit for active duties anywhere, much less in such a body as the Senate. I regret to leave on your account, and on Trumbull's. I have just counted the Senators over,

[1] An eclipse of the sun, total in Burlington, sky clear, August 7th.

and find that I leave seven men there who were members when I entered the body.

But if you are going to be as virtuous as you say you will be, you will not be reëlected to the Senate.[1] Why, the war has corrupted everybody and everything in the United States. Just look at the senatorial elections of the last winter! They were all corrupt. It is money that achieves success in such affairs nowadays. Thank God, my political career ended with the beginning of this corrupt political era!

We are in a valley, on the bank of Lake Bourget, surrounded on all sides by mountains five thousand feet high, which makes it the hottest place in the world. The water comes gushing right out of the mountain, hot enough to boil potatoes. The village has about four thousand patients and three thousand inhabitants. I am quite well satisfied that I have improved here, and that my trial of the waters was a wise act on my part. The American congressional delegation in Europe is quite numerous, and very eminent. The truth is, that a quiet gentleman, like myself, does not feel highly honored by coming in contact with a large majority of his countrymen whom he meets in Europe. They are, to a very considerable extent, of the shoddy species.

I need not say that we shall not return to America this year. We have it in contemplation to spend the winter in Italy, a considerable part of it in Rome, and I shall take the liberty to kiss the pope's great-toe on your account, and in your behalf. Read Milton's invocation beginning—

"Avenge, O Lord, thy slaughtered saints!"

and then fancy that we are right among the descendants of the "saints."

121.—*To Mr. Lyman Cook, Burlington.*

VEVAY, SWITZERLAND, *October* 10, 1869.

You don't know how much good yours of the 19th of last month did me, which reached me day before yesterday. I do not know

[1] "I shall be a candidate; for duty to myself and the State requires it of me. If money is to be used, be it so. It will not be used by or for me. I will have no hand in corrupting legislative morals. If elected at all, it must be on my merits, and because the people so decree. For corrupt and corrupting honors, I have no desire. My hands are clean thus far, and I mean to keep them so. Any but an honest and high-minded people I have no desire to serve."—(MR. FESSENDEN *to* MR. GRIMES, *Portland, August* 8, 1869.)

that I shall be able to answer it, for I must tell you that I am afflicted with some sort of nervous trouble of the head, which becomes immediately aggravated by the slightest mental exertion. I can read without difficulty, but continuous thought for five minutes plays the deuce with me. I may therefore be compelled to stop in writing this at any minute. . . .

As I feared might be the case, I was obliged to cease writing last night, and resume my letter to-day.

I have never been so afflicted by the death of any one as by the sudden decease of Mr. Fessenden.[1] He was my most intimate, sincere, and attached friend, and the sentiment was most cordially reciprocated. I knew him as no other man knew him, for he always made me his confidant; I admired as only those admired him who knew him intimately, and I loved him as I never loved a brother. He was the highest-toned, truest, noblest man I ever knew. I never knew or expect to know a man who can approach him in the qualities that go to make a grand man and a noble statesman. The man does not live who can take his place in the Senate. To tell you the truth, his death has been a severe blow to me. I suppose it is to be in some measure attributed to my disordered and weak state; but sure it is that the news nearly upset me. I have not been able to think of much else since I heard it. Only four days before the news came, I received a long, cheerful, and characteristic letter from him. But I must stop for the day.

October 12th.—We leave here for Nice the 14th. I won't worry myself by attempting to describe this beautiful place, which is on Lake Leman, surrounded by mountains, some of them, as Byron says, with a thousand years of snow on them. We have been here just four weeks. We shall probably be as long at Nice; so you see we become pretty well acquainted wherever we go. I must stop, for the suffering from my head is too great to endure.

122.—*To Mr. Jacob Rich, Dubuque.*

GLION, SWITZERLAND, *January* 9, 1870.

It is a happy circumstance that you renew your professional calling so full of hope and faith. As you know, I do not share either your hope or faith. I do not pretend that the Democratic party is

[1] September 8, 1869.

pure. Where it has unlimited sway, as in New York, it is unquestionably corrupt; but not a whit more corrupt than the Republican party in Philadelphia and Washington. It is the possession of uncontrolled power that makes every party corrupt, and almost every man. I notice that in your paper you cite, as evidences of corruption in New York City, that some men received pay as office-holders who never rendered any duty. Why, I know a dozen men who received pay as clerks in the departments, who never entered them but on the last day of each month to receive their pay. No, no; power makes all parties corrupt, and there is nothing more essential than a change; especially is a change for the good of the country needed now. . . .

Was there ever such an outrage as the attempt to foist upon the country, in the interests of the corruptionists, the annexation of San Domingo? This purchase was on the carpet when I was in New York last month two years ago, and I was advised with about it. A friend asked my advice as to investing money in the public debt, in buying up Baez, etc.; and I dissuaded him from it. I could not imagine that there was a man in America who had the slightest quantum of brains, or an aspiration toward statesmanship, who would ever think of the annexation of San Domingo.

The Iowa members-elect are not thinking men enough to study and comprehend the whole subject of revenue reform. They will say that we want one hundred and sixty-one millions, and must not take off anything; when, if they would take off one-half, they would probably get twice one hundred and sixty-one millions. I am a revenue reformer, and I am for raising all revenue from imports. I therefore insist upon the highest rate that an article can stand, so as not to prevent its introduction. They say it protects people at home by preventing importations from abroad. It is enough to make the de'il laugh with glee, to see the farmers of Iowa voting to support a high tariff, which doubles the cost of railroad-iron, spikes, chairs, locomotives, tenders, cars, etc., the effect of which is to double the cost of transportation of all that they produce, and all that they consume, and then hear them growl about the high rates of passage and freight; not for a moment reflecting that they by their votes impose these high rates of freight on themselves.

The country needs a terrible shaking up and shaking down, financially, politically, and morally. The war and the easy way of making money have demoralized everybody in America, and we need a discipline as much as the French did at the beginning of their war, and we shall get it sooner or later.

From a letter of Hon. H. B. Anthony, Senator from Rhode Island, to Mr. Grimes:

WASHINGTON, *February* 14, 1870.

MY DEAR ADMIRAL—for admiral you still are, although Cragin has been promoted to that grade, *vice* Grimes, placed on the retired list, at his own request—we miss you much in the Senate, and especially in the Naval Committee, where your name is often on our lips, and when we are discussing naval questions with too little information, I put down the other side with, "That is what Grimes said."

123.—*To Mr. Lyman Cook, Burlington.*

BERLIN, *May* 14, 1870.

You will never be able to imagine how thankfully any news from home is received, until you shall yourself be in a foreign country a year or two.

Since I last wrote, I have spent two days at the world-famous Leipsic Fair, where were assembled people from all over the world, and with the products of all the world exposed for sale in thousands of tents and booths. It was a wonderful sight, and worth crossing the Atlantic to see. Of course when at Leipsic we rode over the ground where, in 1813, four hundred and fifty thousand men fought for four days, commanded by the greatest generals of the world, with a loss of one hundred and ten thousand human beings.

Berlin is one of the very finest cities in Europe, with a population of about seven hundred and fifty thousand. Last evening I saw the King of Prussia and the Emperor of Russia. I do not know that the latter potentate came down expressly to meet me, but fortunately we met here, and our intercourse thus far has not been unpleasant.

I am filled with admiration of the German people. Such industry, such order, such sobriety, such neatness, such cultivation of everything that is beautiful and æsthetic, such schools, such freedom from poverty and misery, is to be found nowhere else in the world.

I am having some German books selected for the library. I

shall buy three or four hundred volumes, including, I am told, almost all of the standard authors in German literature. I do this for the benefit of the Germans in Burlington, and of their children, who, unless they have access to books, will have a very superficial knowledge of the German language and literature; and of such people of American lineage as choose to cultivate the German. I hope the effect will be, and I think it will be, to stimulate the Germans in Burlington to take an interest in the library, which they do not probably at present feel.

After spending a week here we go to Hanover, thence to Cologne, and then up the Rhine to Frankfort, and then for a while into Switzerland. We hope to be at home in October, but I have not the slightest idea that I can endure the climate of Iowa next winter. It is wonderful how the climate affects me. The wind blowing from the south makes me nervous, sleepless, and rheumatic, and I am experiencing these sensations at the present moment, because the weather is warm and cloudy with a southerly wind.

124.—*To Mr. Lyman Cook, Burlington.*

GLION, SWITZERLAND, *December* 11, 1870.

I always knew you to be a philosopher, and the imperturbable manner in which you speak of the city taxes of six per cent., and of our city government for the last few years, always in fact except when you were mayor, goes to show that I had a true appreciation of you. I, too, am trying to be a philosopher in my afflictions, and especially just at this time, for I am confined to my room by lumbago. With the aid of sweats, cathartics, liniments, etc., I am much better, but it is so painful to move that I am compelled to sit in one position. This will in part account for my elegant handwriting, for I am propped up at the table, with the use of no part of my body but one hand.

It is about half-past four o'clock of a beautiful Sunday afternoon. I sit and muse, looking at the lake, the mountains, and the skies, thinking of my distant home and friends, and try to think as little of myself as possible. And yet I cannot help thinking of myself, much as I know it injures me to do so.

Almost every American newspaper I see brings the news of the death of some old friend and associate, and I cannot help feeling that in the course of Nature my time will soon come, and when I ask myself, "What have I done to make the world better for having lived in it?" I cannot help pronouncing the judgment that my life has been a failure. I do not mean to say that it has been a failure in what I have done for my State and for mankind, in comparison with what has been done by other men, but in comparison with what I might and ought to have done. And, strange as it may seem to you, who have not thought much of the matter, sitting here calmly, and reviewing my whole course, I have no hesitation in saying that I regard that act for which I have been most condemned, my vote on the impeachment trial, as the most worthy, the proudest act of my life. I shall ever thank God that in that terrible hour of trial, when many privately confessed that they sacrificed their judgments and their consciences at the behests of party newspapers and party hate, I had the courage to be true to my oath and my conscience, and refused, when I had sworn to "do a man impartial justice according to the Constitution and the laws," to do execution upon him according to the dictation of the chairman of the Republican congressional committee, or the howlings of a partisan mob. I would not to-day exchange the recollection of that grasp of the hand and that glorified smile given me by that purest and ablest of men I ever knew, Mr. Fessenden, when I was borne into the Senate-Chamber on the arms of four men to cast my vote, for the highest distinction of life. Yet we had no desire to save Johnson as Johnson; I wanted to save my own self-respect, and my oath, and I wanted to save the country from the wild, revolutionary career upon which the party was entering. But enough of this. It is growing dark, and I must quit.

125.—*To Hon. F. A. Pike, Calais, Maine.*

GLION, SWITZERLAND, *January* 10, 1871.

I write in the hope that this may find you in the land of the living, though it is so long since I have heard from you that you may well have been translated and glorified before this time. We spent the spring and summer in Germany; the war drove us away in the end of July. We have been six months in Switzerland, four months of that time in Glion, near the upper end of Lake Leman, not far from Vevay.

What is being done in America? Was there ever anything so absurd, so wicked, indeed, as the attempt to force the country to accept San Domingo against its will? I have no great admiration for Sumner, but I glory in his pluck, and I wish I were able to be in Washington to fight by his side. Is Maine always to adhere to the protective system, by which she is proportionally growing poorer and poorer every day?

I am near the war. I watch it with intense interest. The Germans are the greatest soldiers in the world.

126.—*To Mr. J. W. Cadwallader, Burlington.*

GLION, SWITZERLAND, *January* 24, 1871.

Since I left America, two years ago, I have received no letter that gratified me more than your very kind one of the 1st of this month. It is a great comfort for me to know that there are people who care for me, and who think kindly of me in my absence.

Within the last two years I have been over a great part of Europe, but unfortunately I have been compelled to travel as an invalid. Perhaps you know that in Paris, shortly after arriving, I was suddenly stricken with a paralysis, against which I have ever since been struggling. It seems the culmination of a complaint of which I had had premonitions for years; the first one, I think, was the last time I undertook to address an assembly of people in my hall some four or five years ago. I am happy to be able to say that I am now nearly well, but I am required to use a great deal of care as to my diet, exercise, etc. I still have a little trouble with one arm and side, and at times a good deal with my head, which is the seat of my disease, but I think I am slowly improving, though I have given up all idea of ever being entirely well again. For several months I could not write a sentence without the most intense pain. I can now write without the slightest trouble.

We are spending the winter on the side of a mountain in Switzerland, looking down upon the beautiful Lake Leman, and across it to mountains twelve thousand feet high, or twice as high as the White Mountains in New Hampshire. There is some snow here, no wind, and the air is mild, bracing, and comfortable. We leave here in March for a watering-place in Germany, where we were last year, and then to England, and shall embark for the United States in June or July next. Our journey has been full of interest; still we shall all be glad to be at home again.

I am glad to know that Burlington is improving. It ought to

be a good town, and I think it will become such in a little time. I am happy to know that Ella is in the high-school. I remember she was a very fine scholar for her age, and I presume to say she continues to be such. Mrs. Grimes and Mary wish to be kindly remembered to you, your wife and daughter, and I beg you to accept the thanks of all of us for your very kind and acceptable letter.

127.—*To Mr. Lyman Cook, Burlington.*

GLION, SWITZERLAND, *February* 6, 1871.

As you see, we are at our old quarters, enjoying ourselves as usual. I am eating my meals regularly, reading the newspapers, and thinking of the past and the absent. It is becoming pretty lonesome and tedious, but I must endure it until the latter part of next month, when we start on our travel again. I have all my life thought of the happy time coming when I should be entirely free from all business and care and anxiety, and when nothing and nobody could in any way control or influence my conduct and movements. Well, I have reached that period in my existence, and I do not find what I expected. One cannot sever himself from the world; he cannot be free from care, and he must become perplexed about his own affairs and about the affairs of others. One's thoughts must be occupied, or else the discomfort following from mental laziness will soon kill him.

I have employed myself ever since it began with studying the war. I thank the Lord that the Germans are not on our side of the Atlantic. Brave and patriotic as our people are, the Prussians would sweep over our whole country in three months. *They* have generals, and the only ones now in the world so far as is known. I wish you could see a Prussian brigade or division; you would then see what an army is. The North German is a larger man, better educated, has more *vim*, and is a better warrior than the South German. I see that all sorts of war news are published in America, but the truth is, that the Germans have not lost a battle from the beginning, and the French were never in the neighborhood of gaining one. A French army of eighty-four thousand men has just taken refuge over here, and we are now overrun.

128.—*To Hon. Charles Mason, Burlington.*

[Written in reply to a letter inquiring whether his health and inclination would permit him again to engage in public life.]

GLION, SWITZERLAND, *February* 27, 1871.

Yours of the 9th is at hand. I have irrevocably resolved to have nothing more to do with public life. I am impelled to this resolution both by necessity and inclination. My physicians with one voice warn me against it, and predict that I would not survive the attempt to mingle in political excitement but a very short time. The truth is, I am a terribly shattered man. I look well enough, quite as well as ever, if not better. My appetite is good, though nearly everything I eat disagrees with me, and my locomotion is perfect, without the aid of a cane or other help, but my left arm and side lack animation, or rather have too much of it. My head constantly afflicts me, and at least half of my nights are sleepless. This is my true condition. I am far better than I have been, but I am not sanguine enough to believe for a moment that a man at my age, blasted as I have been, will ever entirely recover.

So much as to the necessity of abstention from politics. I am happy to be able to say that I have used so much philosophy as to be able to completely reconcile myself with the necessities of my position. I rejoice that I have ceased to have any active part in politics, and I assure you that no man could be more happy to get into the Senate than I was to get out of it, after the inroad of the carpet-bag knights of the South.

129.—*To Mr. Henry K. Edson, Principal of the Academy at Denmark, Lee County, Iowa.*

HEIDELBERG, GERMANY, *April* 9, 1871.

In the two years we have been in Europe we have traveled slowly, and seen much of France, Germany, Austria and Bohemia, Italy, and Switzerland. We have yet to visit Holland and Belgium. I am not one of those Americans who see nothing to admire on this side of the Atlantic. The Prussians (I by no means include all Germans—only about one-half) are in all respects the greatest people on the face of the earth ; the best educated in the mass, the most learned in the professions, the most industrious, the most warlike when war comes, the most peaceful in their instincts, with fewer pauper and abject poor than any country in Europe, less, indeed, than in the old States in America, and with less crime than in any country in Europe, or in the world. Nowhere are life and property so safe, and, I suppose, contrary to what you have believed, nowhere does such a deep religious sentiment pervade the masses of the people.

Mr. Grimes reached home, September 22d, apparently in improved health and in good spirits. He was gratified to find a change in many minds as to his course upon the trial of the President. Men who three years before looked askance at him, because he acted as a judge rather than as a partisan, now thanked him for what he did. He was invited to public receptions at Burlington and other places in the State, without distinction of sect or party, but invariably and firmly declined. He insisted upon entire repose. He felt that his safety depended upon it.

The following extracts from letters which he received expressed the sentiments of many old friends. Hon. Eliphalet Price, one of the early settlers at the "Dubuque Mines," in 1834, and a Representative in the third General Assembly, 1850–'51, wrote:

GUTTENBERG, CLAYTON COUNTY, *October* 18, 1871.

I have learned with pleasing emotions of your safe return to Iowa, in the historic volume of which your name will pass on to other generations with an honorable record. Your vote on the impeachment trial, I am frank to admit, awakened in me, at the time, emotions of sorrow and regret. My mind was keyed to the highest pitch of excitement. The scenes of the war alone lived in my remembrance. But time has carried me forward to a belief that your vote was correct, and those who have long known you personally, as well as the future historian, will not hesitate to admit that your action as an impeachment juror was prompted by a far-seeing wisdom, which few persons would have had the courage to carry out at that time.

STATE OF IOWA, EXECUTIVE DEPARTMENT,
DES MOINES, *October* 23, 1871.

I write to congratulate you upon your safe return to Iowa, and especially on the restoration of your health. Iowa is proud of you, and rejoices to see you once more walking her soil. Long and well have you, in an eminent manner, served your State. Much of our greatness, present and prospective, is largely due to your early efforts. May God bless you with a long life, and at its close an honored grave upon our soil!

With sentiments of high respect,

SAMUEL MERRILL, *Governor.*

On the twenty-fifth anniversary of Mr. Grimes's marriage, November 9th, a few friends came to his silver wedding, bringing their congratulations upon the felicity, serenity, and sweet content of his domestic life.

The closing months were spent in the bosom of home, in the society of friends, with books, amid alternations of health and disease. On some days he was in fine spirits, and felt about as well as ever. He read during the winter the histories of Gibbon and Motley, a history of Switzerland, and was reading Tacitus at the last.

He went to the polls at a city election, February 5th, and cast his vote in favor of water-works, without voting for city officers. On the evening of February 7th, sitting in his parlor, in conversation with his old friend, Mr. Lyman Cook, he was attacked with sharp and severe pains in the region of the heart; but having had two similar attacks a few days before, no serious apprehensions were excited. On feeling relieved, conversation was resumed. In half an hour another attack came on, when Mr. Cook insisted on going for a physician; but Mr. Grimes, becoming easier, said it was unnecessary, as the doctor would call in the morning. Soon after, Mr. Cook having gone for the physician, a more violent attack supervened, and, with paroxysms of intense suffering, death came quickly. A *post-mortem* examination revealed organic disease of the heart. His father, twenty years previously, died suddenly of heart-disease.

Funeral services were held at the Congregational church, Sunday afternoon, February 11th, and were attended by an immense concourse of citizens. There were present, as representatives of the State, the Governor, Hon. C. C. Carpenter, the Secretary of State, Hon. Edward Wright, the Treasurer of State, Hon. Samuel E. Rankin, and ex-Governors Hon. R. P. Lowe and Hon. Samuel Merrill. The following gentlemen acted as pall-bearers: Hon. A. C. Dodge, Messrs. W. H. Postlewaite,

Thomas Hedge, John H. Gear, John Patterson, George C. Lauman, E. D. Rand, John G. Foote, James Morton, J. S. Schramm, C. E. Perkins, and J. C. Peasley. The remains were deposited in Aspen Grove Cemetery.

The City Council, the Old Settlers' Association, the bar of the county, and the trustees of the Public Library, adopted resolutions of profound regret at his death, expressing their sense of his ability, integrity, public spirit, and eminent services, and their respect for his character as "one who fearlessly performed whatever he deemed his duty, uninfluenced by party bias, popular prejudice, or personal interest." The public press presented many tributes to his honor and fame. The General Assembly of Iowa, by a resolution approved April 23, 1872, ordered his portrait to be procured and placed in the Capitol.

Hon. G. V. Fox wrote to Mrs. Grimes:

I mourn with you at the loss of one who stood very close to my heart. Our mutual feelings intertwined during great events, when I learned to respect, to admire, and to love him.

The widow of a gallant officer, who laid down his life in the war, wrote:

I hope you will let me express to you my sympathy for you, and my respect and admiration for Senator Grimes. Besides my own feeling for you, I have always associated you both with my husband, and I like to think that I am sending you his sympathy with my own. I wish the whole country could feel, as I do, that Senator Grimes has given his life for the nation, as truly as those did who died in the war, and how deep a debt we owe him for his steadfast clinging to what he knew was right, when the struggle was so hard a one. What a blessing it must be to you to feel that through all his public life you have helped and upheld him!

A companion of the later portion of his public life said:

I feel more indebted to Mr. Grimes than any one for the little success I have achieved. His early friendly recognition of me at Washington gave me a position and companionship that would otherwise have required years of patient labor. To enjoy his friendship was to secure the confidence of the truest and best men

THE TOMB IN ASPEN-GROVE CEMETERY. p. 388

of the country. The inducements to temptation and folly are so great at Washington that, but for his friendly counsel and guidance, I might have yielded to them. In his death the State and the country have suffered a great loss, and the young men who enjoyed his confidence, and looked to him for guidance in the future, will look in vain to find one suited to take his place.

Hon. H. B. Anthony, of Rhode Island, who sat next to him in the Senate, and was with him upon the Committee on Naval Affairs, says:

Mr. Grimes's ability, sterling common-sense, capacity for business, and unquestioned and straightforward integrity, gave him great influence in the Senate. He was not a frequent speaker, never a dull one. He spoke only when he had something to say, and always with a knowledge of the subject; always for effect in the Senate, never for Buncombe. I have seldom seen a man who had such thorough contempt for humbug. In this, as in many other respects, he resembled his intimate friend Mr. Fessenden, whom he shortly followed to the "undiscovered country." He had the greatest knowledge of naval affairs of all the men that I ever knew. We used on the committee to call him "The Admiral." His acquaintance with the *personnel* of the Navy was equal to his acquaintance with its history, its condition, and its need. It may never be fully known how much the Navy owes to him for the glorious successes of the war. He was of immense value in reorganizing it, and in the legislation that was required. Touching his course on the impeachment, of his entire honesty in that, as in all his public life, I never heard a doubt expressed; I have reason to suppose that it gave him great pain to differ from so many of his friends, but no consideration could swerve him from the line of duty that his judgment and conscience had marked out.

Hon. Joseph S. Fowler, of Nashville, Tennessee, wrote:

It was not my fortune to know him so long and so well as many of his more intimate friends, but I knew him during one of the most eventful trials that any public servant was ever called upon to undergo. How often have I recalled the agony of that great, earnest, tender heart! How well I remember that divine sense of justice and right, that braved calumny and threats, and the fears of misguided friends! Never shall I cease to remember the devoted purpose that looked far into the future for approval. During that trying ordeal it was my fortune to meet him alone. It was then I learned the deep recesses of his heart, and its pure fountains of life. His warm friend and elder brother, and great companion, preceded him a few years. In many respects they were alike, in many different. Both were earnest, brave, faithful, and commanding Senators. They lived above mean and debasing purposes, and were among the most illustrious men that have adorned our annals.

Mr. Grimes was five feet eleven inches in height, with a well-proportioned frame, and a commanding presence. Careless of appearance, and somewhat rough and ungainly in early life, he grew with years into suavity, and grace, and dignity of bearing. He had the canny qualities of the stock from which he came. Plain in dress, and frugal in his habits, he was unassuming in every situation; simplicity, straightforwardness, and independence characterized both his manners and his mind. He abhorred pretension and indirection. Having great power of secretiveness and reserve, he seemed cold and repellent to many, and could chill with indifference those whom he distrusted or disliked. If thrown in the way of such persons, he would turn aside quietly, or pass on. To those who enjoyed his confidence, he was frank and hearty, and open as summer. Exposed in the political agitations of his career to animosity and abuse, he kept himself scrupulously from personality and recrimination. The popularity which he enjoyed at different periods was never won by any arts, or by seeking it. His candor was proverbial; friends sometimes objected that, in political discussion, as was said of his practice at law, he conceded too much to opponents. His speeches and letters reveal, without reserve, his principles, sentiments, and habits. His words and deeds afford a better indication of his character than can be given by another hand.

His mind was not imaginative or fanciful, but critical and

exact, with a superior power of analysis and comprehension. His perceptions were quick and clear; his memory ready and retentive. Of strong common-sense, he was cautious and deliberate in judgment. Forming his opinions from thorough information, he was positive and tenacious in conviction. It was hard to move him, when he had made up his mind. He had a remarkable insight into men, and estimated character and capacity with surprising accuracy. He seemed to discern virtue and merit, or detect artifice and pretension, at a glance. It was not easy to cheat him, or to win his favor for visionary or unworthy schemes. Corrupt men, who sought his aid for intrigue or to obtain office, did not call upon him the second time.

He had a genius for public affairs, and evinced superior tact and practical wisdom in the Legislative Assembly of an infant Territory and State, in the Executive chair of a growing Commonwealth, and in the Senate of the nation. He loved deliberative assemblies and the cares of state. The prosperity of great communities and the well-being of future times were objects of his ambition. In office, he disclaimed considerations of party, and declared that he would not allow his conduct to be influenced by appeals upon that ground. In the Senate he maintained the dignity of the Chamber, and vindicated its ancient boast of unlimited debate, discussion, and deliberation. He felt the full responsibility of the place, and regarded no other position as affording a better opportunity to conserve and promote good government. Thoroughly imbued with American principles, jealous for constitutional and representative government, and familiar with the history and legislation of the country, he sought to preserve the balance of power between the different departments of the Federal Government, and between the respective States and the United States, and, maintaining the prerogatives of each, resisted alike encroachments from either side. In the changes from peace to war, and from war to peace, he knew the seasons, and was prompt to take occasion by the hand, and conform his political action to new and altered conditions. He held those who had been enemies in war, as in peace, friends. In war, no bugle blew a bolder blast; in peace, no one bade heartier farewell to all pride, pomp, and circumstance of war, or sought more sincerely the things that make for peace.

In the matter of appointments to office he exercised his influence with a conscientious regard to the public service, delicately, without patronizing airs, imposing no obligation upon appointees, and, following the ancient tradition that offices should seek men, oftentimes without personal solicitation.

A leader more than a follower of opinion, his guiding hand was upon the institutions and laws of a new era in the State of Iowa, and in the nation. He was foremost in the organization of the Republican party, in 1855, and gave early and efficient help in bringing up the country, and President Lincoln and his cabinet, to the great measure of emancipation. The naval victories of the war were organized with his counsel, and under his eye. No Senator was more successful in carrying measures which he believed to be right. Never obtruding himself, but with apparent unconsciousness, and keeping out of public sight, he came to be recognized by common consent as one of the triumvirate, with his particular friends Fessenden and Trumbull, whose opinions ruled the Senate in the era of the nation's transformation. Foremost in discerning the peril that threatened the land in the impeachment trial of President Johnson, the nation owes its escape and safety at that crisis to him more than to any other one man.

The foundation of his character was in a strong sense of justice, truth, and moral obligation. Among religious teachers he preferred Channing and those of his school. Distrustful of dogmas, and fully assured only of the ethical, the practical, and the humane parts of Christianity, he gave unqualified assent to no particular creed. He held that men should judge in themselves what is right, and that the preparation necessary for another world is to do our duty in this. The writings of Channing gave a powerful impulse to his hatred of slavery and to his interest in humane institutions. At home he was a regular attendant at the Congregational Church.

Richly blest and supremely happy in his home, no other place was so dear to him, he cherished no other influences so constantly and warmly, and none were more helpful to his character and life. With the children and youth who were members of his family he was upon easy familiarity, entering into their interests, guiding their studies, and counseling them in their preparation for life. One who lived several years under his roof says:

> My recollections of him are almost as of a father, always lenient, and ready to help, and to forget my faults. I have heard him called stern and severe; for with his firm and decided views on honesty in politics and business he was apt to be impatient with men who did not walk in his own straight paths; but there was nothing of this at home. No one could be gentler with all about his household.

He was a lover of good men, and in every situation won the respect and confidence of the wisest and the best. His friendship with Mr. Fessenden, who was of a different temperament, and ten years his senior in age, was one of the beautiful incidents of his life, and presents a rare case of pure and unalloyed affection among eminent men, called to stand side by side, and to act each a prominent part in great events, and amid severe conflicts of opinion.

The cares, anxieties, and disquietudes of the years Mr. Grimes served in Congress proved too great a strain upon many of the public men of the period. Not a few have wasted away with premature decay. Not alone on the battle-field, and in ships-of-war, were the costly sacrifices made that saved the nation. This volume is a record of a valiant man worn out, his health impaired, and nervous power paralyzed, by the watchings and debates and discussions through which the life and integrity of the republic were assured to future times.

INDEX.

THE END.

RECENT PUBLICATIONS.

THE AËRIAL WORLD: A Popular Account of the Phenomena and Life of the Atmosphere. By G. HARTWIG, M. and P. D. 1 vol., 8vo. With 8 Chromolithographic Plates and Woodcuts. Price, $6.00.

"The plan which I proposed to myself, in writing this book, was not to enter into minute details or learned disquisitions, such as would be required in a Hand-book of Meteorology. My less ambitious aim was merely to give a general view of the phenomena of the atmosphere, to point out the manifold relations between the aërial ocean and man, and to describe the life of which it is the ever-busy scene."—*Extract from Preface.*

THE GREVILLE MEMOIRS. Complete in two volumes. Price, $4.00.

"'The Greville Memoirs' has produced a profound sensation in London, and has elicited the indignation of the Queen, whose uncles and mother are portrayed therein in colors the reverse of flattering."—*Boston Post.*

"Of Greville's revelations it can be said they are not vulgar, though probably a correct *exposé* of the worst side of English court-life in his day."—*Troy Times.*

"These two volumes have been awaited with much interest, and their appearance will gratify the curiosity of thousands of intelligent readers on both sides of the Atlantic."—*New York Observer.*

MARTIN'S LIFE OF THE PRINCE CONSORT. Vol. I., with Portraits and Views. Price, $2.00.

"Purporting to tell the life of the Prince Consort, it includes a scarcely less minute biography—which may be regarded as almost an autobiography—of the Queen herself."—*Athenæum.*

"Mr. Martin has accomplished his task with a success which could scarcely have been anticipated. His biography of Prince Albert would be valuable and instructive even if it were addressed to remote and indifferent readers who had no special interest in the English court or in the royal family."—*Saturday Review.*

NATURE AND LIFE. Facts and Doctrines relating to the Constitution of Matter, the New Dynamics, and the Philosophy of Nature. By FERNAND PAPILLON. Translated from the second French edition by A. R. Macdonough.

"This volume consists of a series of essays mainly devoted to the discussion of the relations of life to the natural forces, light, heat, electricity, etc. They contain much information of a scientific character, and, to physiologists and physicians, will be of special interest."—*N. Y. Observer.*

"These excellent papers have been collected, revised, and added to, so as to present a methodical and uniform whole, combining exactness in details with generality of doctrines, and distinctly tracing the precise aspect of each group of phenomena in the picture of the close and universal relations that bind the whole together. In this way an exposition is presented under an elementary form, in language freed from technical dress, of the most essential truths established of late by physics, chemistry, and biology, regarding the mechanism of natural forces and the arrangement and combination of the fundamental springs of being in the world, especially in the living world."—*Cleveland Herald.*

D. APPLETON & CO., PUBLISHERS, 549 & 551 BROADWAY, N. Y.

ALICE BRAND. A Romance of the Capital. By A. G. RIDDLE. 12mo. Cloth. Price, $1.75.

"Mr. Riddle may congratulate himself upon having written a good, if not a great novel. Its prime merit is its truthfulness as a representation of life. It is written with vigor rather than elegance, and in places is marked by extraordinary dramatic power."—*Boston Literary World.*

HEREDITY: A Psychological Study of its Phenomena, Laws, Causes, and Consequences. By THÉODORE RIBOT, author of "Contemporary English Psychology." 12mo. Cloth. Price, $1.75.

"We wish that our space would allow us to give in some detail the serried masses of facts with which the author illustrates each general assertion. We can only commend the book as a simple and valuable contribution to the most important of modern problems."—*Philadelphia Times.*

"M. Ribot has treated the tremendous question of Heredity in the work before us with great amplitude and minuteness."—*Chicago Tribune.*

"Eminently philosophical in its method and arrangement, and pleasing in its style: beyond the large mass of scientific works, the book deserves, and will undoubtedly have, a wide circle of thoughtful readers."—*Detroit Free Press.*

THE NATIVE RACES OF THE PACIFIC STATES OF NORTH AMERICA. By HUBERT H. BANCROFT. Complete in 5 vols., 8vo, with Maps and Illustrations. Price, per vol., bound in Extra English Cloth, $5.50; Sheep, library style, $6.50; Half Calf, gilt, $8.00; Half Russia, $8.00; Full Russia, $10.00.

Vol. I. Wild Tribes; their Manners and Customs.
Vol. II. Civilized Nations of Mexico and Central America.
Vol. III. Mythology and Languages of both Savage and Civilized Nations.
Vol. IV. Antiquities and Architectural Remains.
Vol. V. Aboriginal History and Migrations: Index to the Entire Work.

These five volumes form a magnificent panorama of the multitude of nations inhabiting this vast domain at the time of its conquest, and before the people were demoralized by foreign civilization. Now they are gone, and all that is known of them is here collected where it may be forever preserved. Here is pictured their condition; here their customs and characteristics are described; here their story is told. All their strange ways and doings; their inner life and outer forms; their weird beliefs, and Babel tongues, and mighty monuments; their wanderings to and fro and the history of their past are here related with vividness and correctness unexampled in the early history of mankind.

"A storehouse of facts, gathered with admirable industry and care, and arranged with skill and judgment."—*North American Review.*

"An undertaking, we suspect, without a parallel in literature."—*Harper's Magazine.*

"Mr. Bancroft is the historian for whom we have all been looking, and we may count ourselves fortunate in finding him so worthy of his task."—*The Galaxy.*

"He has been an antiquarian society, an archæological society, and an historical and genealogical society, all in one."—*Boston Journal.*

"I am amazed at the extent and minuteness of your researches."—*William Cullen Bryant.*

"It is a production of almost incredible labor, of excellent management, and admirable execution, everywhere betraying the union of quiet enthusiasm and sound judgment."—*N. Y. Tribune.*

SCIENTIFIC LONDON. By BERNARD H. BECKER. 1 vol., 12mo. Cloth. Price, $1.75.

"On becoming a frequent visitor at the meetings of learned societies, I was astonished to find the written records of their deeds were few and far between. According to my lights, I have striven, in unambitious fashion, to supply this gap in the literature of Science, and, in the little book now offered to the public, have attempted to describe in a compact form the rise, progress, and present condition of these great Scientific Institutions of which London—and for that matter, England—is justly proud."—*Extract from Preface.*

D. APPLETON & CO., PUBLISHERS, 549 & 551 BROADWAY, N. Y

www.ingramcontent.com/pod-product-compliance
Lightning Source LLC
LaVergne TN
LVHW011156110826
845150LV00006B/1231

* 9 7 8 1 4 2 5 5 4 6 3 2 8 *